THE
GREATER MEN AND WOMEN
OF THE BIBLE

THE GREATER
MEN AND WOMEN
OF THE BIBLE

EDITED BY THE REV.

JAMES HASTINGS, D.D.

EDITOR OF "THE EXPOSITORY TIMES" "THE DICTIONARY OF THE BIBLE"
"THE DICTIONARY OF CHRIST AND THE GOSPELS" AND
"THE ENCYCLOPÆDIA OF RELIGION AND ETHICS"

MARY—SIMON

Edinburgh: T. & T. CLARK, 38 George Street

PRINTED IN GREAT BRITAIN BY
MORRISON AND GIBB LIMITED
FOR
T. & T. CLARK, EDINBURGH

FIRST IMPRESSION . . . . November 1915
SECOND IMPRESSION . . . May   1920
THIRD IMPRESSION. . . . November 1923
FOURTH IMPRESSION . . . January 1938

INDEX TO CONTENTS.

NAMES AND SUBJECTS.

v

TEXTS.

MARY THE VIRGIN.

I.

THE EVENTS IN MARY'S LIFE.

LITERATURE.

Adeney, W. F., *Women of the New Testament* (1899), 1, 14.
Bushnell, H., *Sermons on Living Subjects* (1872), 9.
Dawson, W. J., *The Reproach of Christ* (1903), 139.
Gibbon, J. M., *The Veil and the Vision* (1914), 46.
Hancock, B., *Free Bondmen* (1913), 1.
M'Intyre, D. M., *The Upper Room Company* (1906), 123.
Newman, J. H., *Parochial and Plain Sermons*, ii. (1868) 127.
Orchard, W. E., *Advent Sermons* (1914), 53.
Palmer, A. S., *The Motherhood of God* (1903), 104.
Plummer, A., *The Humanity of Christ*, 132.
Ramsay, W. M., *Pauline and Other Studies* (1906), 125.
Robertson, F. W., *Sermons*, ii. (1875) 220.
Sanday, W., in *Critical Questions* (1903), 123.
Smith, D., *The Days of His Flesh* (1905).
Spurr, F. C., *The Holy Family*, 13.
Vaughan, C. J., *Doncaster Sermons* (1891), 364.
Watson, J., *The Life of the Master* (1902), 53.
Whyte, A., *Bible Characters* : Joseph and Mary to James (1900), 1.
Christian World Pulpit, lxiii. (1903) 65 (W. Sanday).
Congregationalist, i. (1872) 474.
Dictionary of the Bible, iii. (1900) 286 (J. B. Mayor).
Dictionary of Christ and the Gospels, ii. (1908) 140 (J. M. Harden).
Encyclopædia of Religion and Ethics, viii. (1915) 474 (J. Cooper).

THE EVENTS IN MARY'S LIFE.

Blessed art thou among women.—Luke i. 42.

WHERETO shall we liken this Blessed Mary Virgin,
Fruitful shoot from Jesse's root graciously emerging?
Lily we might call her, but Christ alone is white;
Rose delicious, but that Jesus is the one Delight;
Flower of women, but her Firstborn is mankind's one flower:
He the Sun lights up all moons thro' their radiant hour.
"Blessed among women, highly favoured," thus
Glorious Gabriel hailed her, teaching words to us:
Whom devoutly copying we too cry "All hail!"
Echoing on the music of glorious Gabriel.[1]

1. Many qualities go to the making of that image of the Perfect
Woman which every man carries in his heart and first associates
with his mother, which he protects from the stain of every evil
thought, and which is daily alluring him to holiness.   Beauty is
here in the nature of things, for one does not think of form and
colour, but of the soul, which makes heaven of the face; and it is
not merely the unbroken tradition of the Church, or the fame of
the women of Nazareth, but a sense of fitness as we read her life,
that represents the Virgin with a face of meek and holy loveliness, as becomes "the handmaid of the Lord."   The face of the
Madonna was the first thing of earth the Infant saw when He
opened His eyes in the manger, and through His boyhood its
spiritual grace would be as a bit of that heaven from which He
came.

Whether a mother be brilliant or clever is of little account,
but it is of great price that her mind be noble and sensitive to the
highest—that she be visited by those profound thoughts which
have their home in the unseen, and be inspired by unworldly
enthusiasms.   Mary was only a village maiden, but the Spirit of

[1] Christina G. Rossetti, *Poetical Works*, 173.

3

God "bloweth where it listeth," and to her we owe one of the most majestic hymns of the Church Catholic. It mattered nothing that she was not learned after the fashion of the scribes; she had seen the angel who stands in the presence of God; it was less than nothing that she lived in a house of two rooms, since it opened into Eternity. For her Divine motherhood Mary was prepared twice—once because she had so little of the world which is seen, once because she had so much of the world which is not seen.

¶ Mighty is the force of motherhood! says the great tragic poet to us across the ages, finding, as usual, the simplest words for the sublimest fact—δεινὸν τὸ τίκτειν ἐστίν. It transforms all things by its vital heat; it turns timidity into fierce courage, and dreadless defiance into tremulous submission; it turns thoughtlessness into foresight, and yet stills all anxiety into calm content; it makes selfishness become self-denial, and gives even to hard vanity the glance of admiring love.[1]

¶ Mary of Nazareth, the mother of our Lord, was the only mother in the world that ever found it an impossibility to make an idol of her child. There were many virgins in Israel in the days of Herod the Great, but only to Mary was the lofty privilege given to bear on her maternal breast the Bright and Morning Star, as the blue heavens bear up the star of day—the noon-day sun. So old pious masters had been used to represent the mother robed in blue—in blue raiment—with the sunlight beating upon her breast. She had the lofty privilege to be the mother of our Lord—a lofty privilege of which all mothers of the race might well have been ambitious, down from that Eve, the mother of us all, who said, "I have got a man," or rather *the* man, thinking she had got the promised Lord. Poor Eve! like many of her daughters after her. Well might the angel Gabriel salute Mary with "Blessed of the Lord art thou among women"; and her cousin repeat the salutation—"Blessed art thou"; and that she herself should sing—"My soul doth magnify the Lord; my spirit hath rejoiced in God my Saviour, for he hath regarded the low estate of his handmaiden."[2]

2. When we escape from the weary labyrinth of legend that the fancy of centuries has woven round the name of Mary, and resolutely confine our attention to those traits of her character

[1] George Eliot, *Scenes of Clerical Life* ("Janet's Repentance").
[2] W. B. Robertson, in *Life*, by A. Guthrie, 326.

which are indicated in the gospel records, we may suffer some disappointment on discovering how few and faint they are. Compared with the picture of Jesus that comes to us down the ages, still vivid in its convincing realism, the New Testament portrait of the Virgin is but a dim shadow, flitting across the page for a moment here and there, and then fading away into total obscurity. So marked is this contrast that we are almost tempted to suspect a deliberate design on the part of the Evangelists to reduce the mother to relative insignificance in the presence of her Divine Son. And yet the narratives are too artless to admit of any such subtlety. The simpler explanation is that this slightness of texture is itself a note of genuine portraiture; for the reason that Mary was of a retiring nature, unobtrusive, reticent, perhaps even shrinking from observation, so that the impress of her personality was confined to the sweet sanctities of the home circle.

It is noticeable that among the Evangelists St. Luke alone gives a full and intimate account of the Mother of our Lord. St. Matthew commences his Gospel with the briefest possible memoir of Mary, passing at once to the scenes in Bethlehem, and the visit of the wise men; St. Mark commences with the public ministry of Christ; St. John, who is the interpreter of ideas rather than the biographer, is entirely silent on these matters. It is to St. Luke that we owe the story of the journey to Bethlehem, the story of the shepherds in the fields by night who hear a wind-borne heavenly music, and all the earlier stories of the visit of Mary to Elisabeth, the scenes at the circumcision of Christ, the blessing of Simeon and the prophecies of Anna. The last time that Mary is mentioned in the New Testament is in the opening chapter of the Acts of the Apostles, which is also the work of St. Luke; and he alone records the deeply interesting fact of her association with the infant Church.

I.

Mary first meets us at a time when she can scarcely have crossed the threshold of womanhood. Marriage is early in the East; and a Jewish maiden still only betrothed and looking forward to her wedding as an event of the future must be very young, a girl hardly full grown. To this child, brought up in a peasant's home, accustomed to the little round of daily duties that is the lot of the daughters of the poor, wholly ignorant of the great world and its ways, there comes the most startling and overwhelming revelation. She is to be the mother of the promised Redeemer of her people! Her first thoughts could not but be full of bewilderment and dismay. The hope and the terror of expectant motherhood are upon her!

Wonder and alarm are Mary's most natural feelings at the moment when the amazing truth dawns upon her. But as she gathers assurance she bows in quiet submission. This is the Evangelist's conclusion. Mary is the handmaid of the Lord; let it be to her as His messenger has said. As yet there is no word of joy, no note of exultation, no sign of triumph. The trembling girl simply accepts the tremendous fact as the will of her Lord.

¶ Painters of various schools have given us their several interpretations of the Annunciation, but perhaps none have seized upon the purely human aspect of the scene so evidently as Rossetti. It may be said that the nineteenth-century pre-Raffaelite artist cannot emancipate himself from the age in which he lives, and in spite of his archaic sympathies is still essentially modern in thought, so that the expression of his Madonna is also distinctly modern. And yet it is only modern in the sense that it is frankly human. Rossetti tells what the old painters with a fine reticence concealed. To them the Divine glory of Gabriel's message extinguished all earthly considerations in its ineffable splendour. To us the study of the Nazareth maiden in this crisis when she suddenly passes from girlhood to womanhood in its most profound significance cannot but be of primary interest. We want to know how it affected her girlish consciousness; and Rossetti, who, if not exactly a theologian, is a poetic interpreter of human life, clearly answers that question. Mary shrinks from the splendid angel, almost cowers at his feet; but not because she is dazzled by the coming into her presence of one of his lofty estate, for she fixes her eyes upon him in a steadfast gaze. Those dark eyes have in them the terror of the hunted deer. It is not Gabriel, it is his overwhelming message, that smites her with alarm. Her maiden modesty is troubled. There is nothing of the joyous gratitude of the *Magnificat* in the picture. And yet is not this just such an attitude as would be natural to the startled innocence of a peasant girl?[1]

[1] W. F. Adeney, *Women of the New Testament*, 4.

This is that blessed Mary, pre-elect
God's Virgin. Gone is a great while, and she
Dwelt young in Nazareth of Galilee.
Unto God's will she brought devout respect,
Profound simplicity of intellect,
          And supreme patience. From her mother's knee
Faithful and hopeful; wise in charity;
Strong in grave peace; in pity circumspect.

So held she through her girlhood; as it were
An angel-watered lily, that near God
          Grows and is quiet. Till, one dawn at home
She woke in her white bed, and had no fear
At all,—yet wept till sunshine, and felt awed:
Because the fulness of the time was come.[1]

II.

"Mary arose these days, and went into the hill country with haste, into a city of Judah," where she found refuge in the house of Zacharias and Elisabeth. She arose in haste; for her journey was both an expulsion and a flight. Fear of shame and unkindness made her an exile; and this was the first act in the long and sorrowful drama of her life.

¶ She is a happy maiden who has a mother or a motherly friend much experienced in the ways of the human heart to whom she can tell all her anxieties; a wise, tender, much-experienced counsellor, such as Naomi was to Ruth, and Elisabeth to Mary. Was the Virgin an orphan, or was Mary's mother such a woman that Mary could have opened her heart to any stranger rather than to her? Be that as it may, Mary found a true mother in Elisabeth of Hebron. Many a holy hour the two women spent together sitting under the terebinths that overhung the dumb Zacharias's secluded house. And, if at any time their faith wavered and the thing seemed impossible, was not Zacharias beside them with his sealed lips and his writing-table, a living witness to the goodness and severity of God? How Mary and Elisabeth would stagger and reason and rebuke and comfort one another, now laughing like Sarah, now singing like Hannah, let loving and confiding and pious women tell.[2]

[1] D. G. Rossetti, *Collected Works*, i. 353.
[2] A. Whyte.

III.

Months passed, and a new cause of pain arose in the census of Cæsar Augustus. Whatever was the nature of the imperial edict, it became necessary for Joseph and Mary to visit Bethlehem; and for Mary the journey was full of peril and alarm. On that starry night, then, long ago, behold these two fugitives from Nazareth drawing near to Bethlehem, full of fear and hope, and conscious, too, of a force of destiny which holds their feet in a pre-appointed way. It is the smallest of the towns of Judah they approach; a cluster of grey houses on a limestone cliff. At the base of the hill stands Rachel's tomb, that pathetic memorial of a man's love, and of a woman's travail and untimely death. How significant would it appear to this woman whose hour had come! With what a sidelong glance of fear and apprehension, perhaps of natural presentiment, would she regard it! But there was more than fear in Mary's heart that night; surely faith shone like a torch upon her path. It was perhaps not of Rachel she thought so much as of Ruth—Ruth the Moabitess, her own far-off kins-woman, driven into Bethlehem by calamity and misfortune, to find herself the unexpected mother of a race of kings. Nor would she forget the ancient prophecy of Micah, that little as Bethlehem was among the thousands of Judah, yet out of it should come One who should be the "ruler of Israel, whose goings forth have been from of old, from everlasting." There were strange portents in the sky that night, but Mary saw them not. Faith alone was her star as she climbed the weary hill. In the crowded market-place she stands, lonely, confused, insignificant, unrecognized. No door is opened to the suffering woman, not because the fine traditional hospitality of the Jew has failed, but because already every house is thronged with exiles like herself. There is no place of refuge for her but a rough chamber, hewn in the limestone cliff, and used as a stable. How great the contrast between that Divine dream which stirred her heart with rapture and this grim reality of pain and poverty! Was it thus that kings were born? Was it in such a rude abode that the mother of the Christ should taste the joy and pain of motherhood? Even so was it ordained; for it was God's will that in all things Mary should prove her faith, and live by faith, not by sight. She pondered in her heart the things the angel had told her; and never were they sweeter than in this hour when her first-born Son lay upon her bosom. If God denied to her what He gave to shepherds on the plain, and to Magians far off in the mysterious East, this at least He gave her, the light of faith in that rude stable; and her blessedness was that, not having seen, she had believed.

A month later, in obedience to the Law, Mary, accompanied by Joseph, took her Child from Bethlehem to Jerusalem, at once to make the offering for her own purification and to pay the five shekels which were the ransom for the life of her first-born Son. The offering of purification was properly a lamb, but in case of poverty "a pair of turtledoves, or two young pigeons" sufficed; and this "offering of the poor," as it was called, was all that Mary could afford. There was in Jerusalem in those days an aged saint named Simeon, one of those who in that dark and calamitous time were expecting the Dayspring from on high and the consolation of Israel. "It had been revealed to him that he should not see death, before he had seen the Lord's Christ"; and, like an imprisoned exile, he was yearning for his release. He was in the sacred court, engaged in the offices of devotion, when the Holy Family entered; and, recognizing the Child, he took Him in his arms and blessed God with a glad heart: "Lord, now lettest thou thy servant depart in peace, according to thy word; for mine eyes have seen thy salvation." Not in vain had Simeon mused on the Messianic Scriptures. While his contemporaries were dreaming of a victorious King, he had laid to heart the prophecies of a suffering Redeemer; and he forewarned Mary what would be: "Behold, this child is set for the fall and rising again of many in Israel, and for a sign which shall be spoken against (yea, a sword shall pierce through thine own soul also), that the thoughts of many hearts may be revealed."

While Simeon was speaking, another saint appeared on the scene—an aged prophetess named Anna, who, since she had been a widow for eighty-four years, must have been over a hundred years of age. She haunted the Temple, giving herself night and day to fasting and prayer. Entering the sacred court while Simeon was still speaking, she took up the refrain of praise, and afterwards spoke of the Holy Child to such as, like herself, "expected Jerusalem's redemption," quickening their hope and

preparing a welcome for Him when He should be manifested unto
Israel.

IV.

So far had the education of Jesus been carried, when He was
but twelve years old, that He was already entered into the great
questions of the doctors, and was so profoundly taken by their
high discussions overheard in the Temple that He must needs
have a part in them Himself, asking questions of His own. All
this He did with so little appearance of pertness, and such
wonderful beauty of manner, as well as in a tone so nearly Divine,
that they could only be "astonished at his understanding and
answers." And there next day He was found by Joseph and
Mary, when He should have been a whole day's journey on His
way back with them to Galilee. They remonstrated with Him
only in the gentlest and most nearly reverent manner, and
had nothing more to say when He answered: "How is it
that ye sought me? wist ye not that I must be in my Father's
house?"

Her Son's striking answer must have conveyed to Mary a
rebuke. We cannot suppose that Jesus intended anything of the
kind. He was far too dutiful a son to be found taking upon Him
the part of mentor to His mother. We should do a great wrong
to our idea of the Divine Child if we credited Him with conduct
which in any other boy of twelve years would be justly designated
priggish. Most assuredly He spoke in absolute simplicity—"Did
you not know that I must be in my Father's house?" He had
not imagined that they would search the whole city before looking
for Him in the Temple. He had assumed that if they had wanted
Him this was the first place where they would have looked for
Him, because it was the most natural thing in the world that He
should be there. What more likely place is there in which to find
a child than his father's house? What more appropriate duty
than his father's business? But at that innocent saying of His,
spoken in the simplicity of childhood, Mary felt the first chill
approach of the terrible sword which was to pierce her to the
heart in later years. Here was something for her to ponder
over; and at this point St. Luke repeats his significant statement, that Mary "kept all these sayings in her heart." Yet he

is careful to tell us that Jesus still remained "subject unto" His parents.

¶ There is working to-day in England a man, of whom most of you have heard, but whom I hesitate to name, who is serving in a high position, but serving as simply and humbly as though he passed his days in a cottage; he might be obscure, so childlike is he, and so simple in his way of facing life. He is the son, too, of a great man, and this is what he tells me was an experience of his in relation to that father. He said the greatest crisis of his life, the most overwhelming sorrow he ever passed through, was when God called that father home. "But," he said, "I made him my model and my inspiration—not that I have ever reached to the height to which he towered. In one of my darkest hours, when trouble had made me ill, and I lay, as it seemed, between life and death, I dreamed that I was a child again, and when I woke and opened my eyes for the moment it seemed as if it could not be a dream. I remember turning to look up in my father's face, and I felt round me my father's arms. Is it too much to suppose that I dreamed what was true?" I do not answer his question here, save to give it a larger meaning. He dreamed what was true; he lost his father, as it seemed to his earthly consciousness, for the time being; but he lived in his memory, in his atmosphere, and then there came the one moment of insight when he felt as if the father was not gone, but the loving arms were around him still. If it was true of the earthly father, a thousandfold more is it true of the Heavenly Father.[1]

V.

Jesus is now a man thirty years old. The report arrives of John's preaching down by the Jordan. Hastening down at once to hear him, and approaching to be baptized, He is saluted by him strangely, on sight, in the crowd—"Behold, the Lamb of God, which taketh away the sin of the world!" The consecrating Dove descends upon Him, and He is sealed for His call by a word of sanction from above—"This is my beloved Son, in whom I am well pleased." He is verily come now into His Father's business. Yes, He is to be Messiah! and the discovery breaks upon His mind like a storm upon the sea. By this Spirit-storm He is hurried off into the wilderness, to consider and to get His bosom throes quieted and His thoughts in train for the great strange future

[1] R. J. Campbell, *The Song of Ages*, 233.

before Him.   And when this is ended, when His mind has become composed and adjusted, He goes back to Nazareth.   He finds Mary not at home, but away at the little village of Cana, back among the hills, where she is gone to attend the festivities of a wedding, at the house of a relative.   Receiving an invitation that was left for Him, He goes up to the wedding Himself. And there we are let into a new chapter, at the very hinge of His public life, and the new relation He is to have to His mother. The general impression is that He breaks off from her in a sense, at this earliest moment, reprimanding her, with a good deal of severity, for what He considers to be her forwardness and officious meddling.

The wine of the feast gave out, as it would seem; whereupon the mother tells Him, "they have no wine," as if expecting of Him just the miracle He is going to perform.   Whereupon Jesus turns upon her sharply, saying, "Woman, what have I to do with thee? my hour is not yet come."   She pays, we notice, no attention to His rebuke, as she certainly would if she had felt the severity we do in it, but goes aside to the servants, telling them to wait His orders and do whatever He bids them.   She has no idea what that will be; but she evidently hopes that He will somehow make up the deficiency and permit them to go on with the distribution.

"His mother saith unto the servants, Whatsoever he saith unto you, do it."   These are the last recorded words of the Virgin Mother.   We hear of her on one or two subsequent occasions in the gospel history, and with regard to one of these we are told something as to her wishes; but this is the last occasion on which the words which she uttered have been preserved for us.   It is worth while remarking that most of what we know respecting her words and acts is told us of the time before, or just after, her Divine Son was born.   The sum-total of what is told us in Scripture respecting her does not amount to very much, but by far the larger portion of what is recorded refers to the time before, or immediately after, the birth at Bethlehem.

¶ Life breaks down first of all on the side of its exhilarations. "*They have no wine!*" said Mary at the feast in Cana of Galilee. And she might say it still.   It is life's first point of collapse. Health holds out. Money increases. Friends multiply.   We have abundance to eat, plenty to drink, and warm beds to sleep in. But the wine fails. Life somehow loses its sparkle and its sprightliness. The gaiety and the elasticity depart. An eminent art critic stood before a picture. "Yes," he said, "it is very good; but it lacks *that*"—expressively snapping his fingers. Every man discovers sooner or later that he lacks "*that*." [1]

¶ *We* have our troubles and perplexities, and there are times when they seem to be overwhelming. But in all such seasons of trial there are some commands of Christ about which there can be no doubt, some duties which beyond all question we ought to do. Let us pay more than ordinary attention to them, and do what we are quite sure about with increased care. Trouble too often makes us slack about plain duties. But the loyal discharge of plain duties is often a refuge from trouble and sometimes a remedy for it. But, whether we are in trouble or in prosperity, we can have no better guide for our daily life than the last recorded utterance of the Mother of the Lord, "Whatsoever he saith unto you, do it."

And let us also take to ourselves the command which He gave to those servants: "Fill the water-pots with water." All round us the empty water-pots are standing. Like those at Cana, they say nothing; but their very emptiness is mutely eloquent, and the Lord speaks for them. There are dreary homes, empty of Christian peace and Christian affection: ignorant minds, empty of everything that can instruct, and enlighten, and ennoble; desolate, withered hearts, empty of all that can brighten, and quicken, and console. Our great cities, hardly less than the distant regions of our great Empire, swarm with heathen, whose condition is one long spiritual thirst, ever recalling the charge, "Fill the water-pots with water." [2]

VI.

Let us look for a moment now at the connexion between Mary and Jesus in the prosecution of His early ministry. She has, besides Him, four sons, and probably three daughters. It has long been debated whether these are Mary's own children or only cousins taken by adoption, or possibly children of Joseph by a former marriage. We need not undertake the question. "These children," says Bushnell, "ought to be Mary's, to complete the Incarnation itself. For if she must

[1] F. W. Boreham, *Mountains in the Mist*, 87.
[2] A. Plummer, *The Humanity of Christ*, 142.

needs live and die in churchly virginity, lest she bring a taint on her Divine motherhood by maternity in wedlock afterward, her incarnation office even puts dishonour on both wedlock and maternity together. Or if she must save her Son from being own brother to anybody by His Incarnation, what genuine significance is there in the fact?"

Soon so great is the strain on Him—pressed on all sides by an eager, selfish crowd, the sick continually appealing to Him for the help of His healing, His disciples needing careful training, the multitude hanging on His utterances in great assemblies gathered by the seashore, the scribes and Pharisees ever on the watch to catch Him in His words—He has no leisure for retirement, no time for rest, not even an opportunity for taking food during the long, busy day. We can well imagine how an anxious mother must have regarded such a mode of life. It was cruel. The strongest could not stand it. Something must be done to save Him from the people, to save Him too from Himself. He is at the call of all who need Him. He has no thought of Himself. Then His friends must interfere.

They send in word, accordingly, that His mother and family are without, desiring to speak with Him. Perceiving at once the over-tender concern that has brought them hither, instead of going instantly forth at their call He finds opportunity in it to say to the multitude about Him that He is here among men, as in a large and most dear family. And who is My mother, and who are My brethren, but you all here present, who can do the will of God? "For whosoever shall do the will of God, the same is my brother, and sister, and mother"—such and so great is the dear blood affinity with mankind into which He is born. The whole significance and beauty of the appeal is from family affection to the broader affection of God's universal family.

¶ The effect of Jesus' exclamation, "Behold my mother and my brethren! For whosoever shall do the will of my Father which is in heaven, the same is my brother, and sister, and mother," may have been modified by its being pronounced with a smile; and it shows how close and tender He felt the natural relation to be that He compared the new spiritual one to it; yet this was a distinct preference of the relationship formed by discipleship to that due to nature.[1]

[1] J. Stalker, *The Ethic of Jesus*, 345.

"My mother—brothers—who are they?"
  Hearest thou, Mary mild?
This is a sword that well may slay—
  Disowned by thy child!

Ah, no! My brothers, sisters, hear—
  They are our humble lord's!
O mother, did they wound *thy* ear?—
  We thank him for the words.

"Who are my friends?" Oh, hear him say,
  Stretching his hand abroad,
"My mother, sisters, brothers, are they
  That do the will of God!"

My brother! Lord of life and me,
  If life might grow to this!—
Would it not, brother, sister, be
  Enough for all amiss?

Yea, mother, hear him and rejoice:
  Thou art his mother still,
But may'st be more—of thy own choice
  Doing his Father's will.

Ambition for thy son restrain,
  Thy will to God's will bow:
Thy son he shall be yet again,
  And twice his mother thou.

O humble man, O faithful son!
  That woman most forlorn
Who yet thy father's will hath done,
  Thee, son of man, hath born![1]

VII.

Mary's presence at the cross fitly ends her story.

The narrative of St. Luke tells us that during a considerable
portion of the Saviour's Passion "all his acquaintance, and the
women that followed him from Galilee, stood afar off, beholding
these things." Now, after nearly three hours of awful endurance,

[1] George MacDonald, *Poetical Works*, i. 225,

there was a lull in the strong excitement of those who hated Him. It was felt by some of those who were dearest to Him that a possibility of approach was afforded. John and a little group of believing women—Mary the mother of Jesus, and two other Marys, the wife of Cleophas and Mary of Magdala—then for a while stood beside the cross of Jesus.

It is not every woman who would have found it possible to be there. The story of the cross has been handled so much as a topic of cold abstract theology, and any real experience of what it means is so very remote from the world in which we live, that the actual horror of it does not affect us in any degree proportionate to the facts of what must have taken place. A man nailed to the beams, hung up in the blazing sun, dragged, strained, longing to shift his posture in an agony of cramp, yet unable to do so, and his slightest movement sending a fresh thrill of torture through his body ; then a burning thirst, a throbbing head, the weight of which on the weary neck grows intolerable; and all this to continue—since no vital organ has been touched—till the relief of death supervenes only from sheer exhaustion, when long-enduring nature can hold out no longer. We shrink with horror from the contemplation of the ghastly spectacle.

Now, this was witnessed by Mary, if not to the very end, still in the agony of its tortures. And the Sufferer was her Son. Could any sword pierce the soul as hers was pierced now ?

And then came the crowning deed of love. Jesus is taking His farewell of the world—His last legacies have been given— only His mother is left. He will not leave her an orphan and unprovided for. Joseph is dead, and there is none to look after her. Bravely she bore in secret shame and misunderstanding on His account in the early days at Nazareth and Bethlehem, now she shall have an open and public honour. His best loved disciple is at the foot of the cross—so good a son is worthy of such a mother, and to him Jesus offers her. " Woman, behold thy son ! Then saith he to the disciple, Behold thy mother ! And from that hour that disciple took her unto his own home."

¶ That Jesus enjoins on John to care for Mary, although the latter had several sons of her own, is not sufficiently explained by the unbelief of the brothers (John vii. 5), for His speedy triumph over this (Acts i. 14) could not be hidden from Him (John

ii. 24, 25); but it presupposes the certainty in His mind that generally to *no other's* hand could this dear legacy be so well entrusted. Ewald well remarks on such traits of individual significance in the Gospel of John as "from that hour the disciple took her unto his own home": "It was for John at a late period of life a sweet reward to call up reminiscences of all that was most vivid, but for the readers it is also, without his will, a token that only he could have written all this."[1]

She sees her son, her God,
Bow with a load
Of borrow'd sins; and swim
In woes that were not made for Him.
Ah, hard command
Of love! Here must she stand
Charg'd to look on, and with a steadfast eye
See her life die:
Leaving her only so much Breath
As serves to keep alive her death.[2]

VIII.

There is but one more scene. The place is an upper room in Jerusalem, and the time, the interval between the Ascension and Pentecost. About a hundred and twenty persons are gathered together for prayer, and among these we note "Mary, the mother of Jesus" (Acts i. 14). And this is where the Bible takes leave of her.

From this moment the Virgin Mary, though her name is just mentioned among those who formed the assemblies of the early believers, practically disappears from Christian history. Even apocryphal tradition scarcely so much as mentions her. It is not known how long she lived. It is not certain whether she died at Jerusalem or at Ephesus. She is not referred to as a source of information, still less as a fount of authority, though she could have told more than any living being about the birth of the Saviour, and the thirty long years of His humble obscurity. She "kept all these sayings, pondering them in her heart." But though she must ever be cherished in Christian reverence as the chosen handmaid of the Lord, and " blessed among women," it is impossible not to see in these indisputable facts the strongest

---

[1] H. A. W. Meyer, *The Gospel of John*, ii. 351. [2] Richard Crashaw.

possible condemnation of that utterly unauthorized worship of the
Virgin which, centuries afterwards, began to pollute the swelling
stream of Christianity. As though by a Divine prevision of the
dangerous aberrations which were to come, in which Christians by
millions were taught to adore the creature even more than the
Creator who is blessed for evermore, the name of Mary is scarcely
noticed in the whole New Testament after the beginning of
Christ's ministry, and indeed after the one incident of His boyhood. In three of the instances in which it *is* introduced, our
Lord says, " Woman, what have I to do with thee ? "; " Whosoever
shall do the will of my Father which is in heaven, the same is my
brother, and sister, and mother "; and, " Yea rather, blessed are
they that hear the word of God, and keep it." It might, therefore, seem as if *special* care had been taken to discourage and
obviate the corrupted forms of Christianity which have thrust the
Virgin Mary into the place of her Eternal Son, and made her
more an object of rapturous worship than God, to whom alone all
worship is due.

¶ In a letter dealing with women's work among the poor, he
remarks, " I sometimes think ' the woman ' is the representative
in the family of the third person in the Holy Trinity, the
Comforter, the Holy Ghost, who is the fountain of all the
beautiful, the tender, the motherly, the womanly—the human
family being considered the reflex of the Divine, who said, ' Let
us make man in our image after our likeness,' and then we read,
' male and female created He them.' Nothing will destroy the
worship of the Virgin Mother in the Romish Church, where in
their pictures she is blasphemously placed upon the same throne
with the Father and the Son, the Holy Spirit, whom she has
replaced, only hovering as a dove over her head—nothing, I
believe, will dethrone her and destroy her worship but a scriptural
understanding of the doctrine of the Holy Spirit as the tender,
the motherly, the womanly. It was after the Athanasian Creed
was made (and you cannot put love and tenderness into a hard,
dogmatic creed) that the personal love and most melting tenderness of the Holy Spirit was lost sight of, and His throne and
worship profanely given to Mary. But any holy woman is such
as she, a representative on earth of Him." [1]

¶ Far in the apse [of the Church of SS. Mary and Donato] is
seen the sad Madonna standing in her folded robe, lifting her

[1] *Life of William B. Robertson, D.D., Irvine* (by J. Brown), 425,

hands in vanity of blessing.   There is little else to draw away our thoughts from the solitary image. . . . The figure wears a robe of blue, deeply fringed with gold, which seems to be gathered on the head and thrown back on the shoulders, crossing the breast, and falling in many folds to the ground.   The under robe, shown beneath it where it opens at the breast, is of the same colour ; the whole, except the deep gold fringe, being simply the dress of the women of the time.   Round the dome there is a coloured mosaic border ; and on the edge of its arch, legible by the whole congregation, this inscription :

Quos Eva Contrivit, Pia Virgo Maria Redemit ;
Hanc Cuncti Laudent, Qui Cristi Munere Gaudent.

The whole edifice is, therefore, simply a temple to the Virgin : to her is ascribed the fact of Redemption, and to her its praise. . . .

Mariolatry is no special characteristic of the twelfth century ; on the outside of that very tribune of San Donato, in its central recess, is an image of the Virgin which receives the reverence once paid to the blue vision upon the inner dome.   With rouged cheeks and painted brows, the frightful doll stands in wretchedness of rags, blackened with the smoke of the votive lamps at its feet ; and if we would know what has been lost or gained by Italy in the six hundred years that have worn the marbles of Murano, let us consider how far the priests who set up this to worship, the populace who have this to adore, may be nobler than the men who conceived that lonely figure standing on the golden field, or than those to whom it seemed to receive their prayer at evening, far away, where they only saw the blue clouds rising out of the burning sea.[1]

[1] Ruskin, *Stones of Venice*, vol. ii. chap. iii. §§ 39, 40.

MARY THE VIRGIN.

II.

THE ELEMENTS OF MARY'S CHARACTER.

LITERATURE.

Adeney, W. F., *Women of the New Testament* (1899), 29, **43.**
Alexander, W., *Verbum Crucis* (1893), 53.
Brierley, H. E., *The Pierced Heart.*
Bushnell, H., *Sermons on Living Subjects* (1872), 9.
Gibbon, J. M., *The Veil and the Vision* (1914), 46.
Johnson, G. B., *The Beautiful Life of Christ*, 145.
Mackay, W. M., *Bible Types of Modern Women* (1912), 315.
Newman, J. H., *Sermon Notes* (1913), 21, 73, 90, 137.
Orchard, W. E., *Advent Sermons* (1914), 53.
Plummer, A., *The Humanity of Christ*, 132.
Robertson, F. W., *Sermons*, ii. (1875) 220.
Sanday, W., in *Critical Questions* (1903), 123.
Simpson, P. C., in *Women of the Bible* : Rebekah to Priscilla (1904), 139.
Spurr, F. C., *The Holy Family*, 13.
Vaughan, C. J., *Doncaster Sermons* (1891), 364.
Watson, J., *The Life of the Master* (1902), 53.
Whyte, A., *Bible Characters* : Joseph and Mary to James (1900), 1.
Williams, J. H., *The Mother of Jesus* (1906).
Churchman's Pulpit : Circumcision of Christ, iii. **103** (W. Bright).
Commonwealth, xviii. (1913) 326 (A. Gilchrist).
Dictionary of the Bible (Single-volume, 1909), 589 (C. T. P. Grierson).
Dictionary of Christ and the Gospels, ii. (1908) 140 (J. M. Harden).
Encyclopædia of Religion and Ethics, viii. (1915) (J. Cooper).

THE ELEMENTS OF MARY'S CHARACTER.

Mary kept all these sayings, pondering them in her heart.—Luke ii. 19.

THAT the Virgin Mary was a woman without character, feeble and featureless, one of those limp beings who come to be reckoned as cyphers in the world, is not for a moment to be supposed. On the rare occasions when the curtain is lifted we catch glimpses of a character not wanting in energy and power of initiation. Have we not all met with people who make their individuality felt within a very limited circle, while beyond that even their existence is scarcely noticed?

In the First Epistle to the Corinthians, St. Paul speaks of the glory of the woman as of a thing distinct from the glory of the man. They are the two opposite poles of the sphere of humanity. Their provinces are not the same, but different. The qualities which are beautiful as predominant in one are not beautiful when predominant in the other. That which is the glory of the one is not the glory of the other. The glory of her who was highly favoured among women, and whom all Christendom has agreed in contemplating as the type and ideal of her sex, was glory in a different order from that in which her Son exhibited the glory of a perfect manhood. A glory different in *degree*, of course: the one was only human, the other more than human, the Word made flesh; but different in *order* too: the one manifesting forth *her* glory—the grace of womanhood; the other manifesting forth *His* glory—the wisdom and the majesty of manhood, in which God dwelt.

¶ For my own part, I do not know the gift or the grace or the virtue any woman ever had that I could safely deny to Mary. The Divine congruity compels me to believe that all that could be received or attained or exercised by any woman would be granted beforehand, and all but without measure, to her who was so miraculously to bear, and so intimately and influentially to nurture and instruct, the Holy Child. We must give Mary her promised due. We must not allow ourselves to entertain a grudge against the mother of our Lord because some enthusiasts for her have given her more than her due. There is no fear of our thinking too much either of Mary's maidenly virtues, or of her motherly duties and experiences. The Holy Ghost in guiding the researches of Luke, and in superintending the composition of the Third Gospel, especially signalizes the depth and the piety and the peace of Mary's mind. At the angel's salutation she did not swoon nor cry out. She did not rush either into terror on the one hand or into transport on the other. But, like the heavenly-minded maiden she was, she cast in her mind what manner of salutation this should be. And later on, when all who heard it were wondering at the testimony of the shepherds, it is instructively added that Mary kept all these things and pondered them in her heart. And yet again, when another twelve years have passed by, we find the same Evangelist still pointing out the same distinguishing feature of Mary's saintly character, "They understood not the saying which he spake unto them: . . . but his mother kept all these sayings in her heart." [1]

Blest in thy lowly heart to store
    The homage paid at Bethlehem;
But far more blessed evermore
    Thus to have shared the taunts and shame—

Thus with thy pierc'd heart to have stood
    'Mid mocking crowds, and owned Him thine,
True through a world's ingratitude,
    And owned in death by lips Divine. [2]

I.

HER FAITH.

What, then, is the great note of Mary's character? It is faith, manifesting itself in meekness, obedience, and love. If the Incarnation is difficult for us to believe, it was a thousandfold more difficult for Mary; yet she believed it with all the energy of a pious and a simple heart. Faith is the ground of all great-

[1] A. Whyte.   [2] Elizabeth Rundle Charles.

ness in human character, but never was there faith so pure, so firm, or so hardly tried as hers.

If we are to apply this sure principle to Mary's case, "according to your faith be it unto you," then Mary must surely wear the crown as the mother of all who believe on her Son. If Abraham's faith has made him the father of all who believe, surely Mary's faith entitles her to be called their mother. If the converse of our Lord's words holds true, that no mighty work is done where there is unbelief; if we may safely reason that where there has been a mighty work done there must have been a corresponding and a co-operating faith; then I do not think we can easily overestimate the measure of Mary's faith. If this was the greatest work ever wrought by the power and the grace of Almighty God among the children of men, and if Mary's faith entered into it at all, then how great her faith must have been! Elisabeth saw with wonder and with worship how great it was. She saw the unparalleled grace that had come to Mary, and she had humility and magnanimity enough to acknowledge it. "Blessed art thou among women: Blessed is she that believed: for there shall be a performance of those things which were told her from the Lord." "Blessed is she that believed," said Elisabeth, no doubt with some sad thoughts about herself and about her dumb husband sitting beside her. "Blessed is the womb that bare thee," cried on another occasion a nameless but a true woman, as her speech bewrayeth her, "and the paps which thou hast sucked." But our Lord answered her, and said, "Yea rather, blessed are they that hear the word of God, and keep it." And again, "Whosoever shall do the will of my Father which is in heaven, the same is my brother, and sister, and mother."

¶ I remember well one conversation that Dr. Martineau and I had concerning the nature of religious faith. I told my friend the old story of the schoolboy or schoolgirl who defined faith as "the power we have of still believing what we know to be untrue." He laughed very heartily at this unintentionally sarcastic definition; and he declared that the state of mind implied by it is a wholly impossible one. In this opinion he was in full agreement with the view of his old acquaintance, Dr. Thirlwall, Bishop of St. David's, who considered that belief, as regards abstract or purely speculative matters, is entirely involuntary, and therefore looked on the "impious threats"—as he called them—of the

Athanasian Creed as quite meaningless. I think, however, that many people really have a power of believing in some degree what they *suspect* to be untrue. Some men deliberately suppress their doubts, and turn their thoughts exclusively to such considerations as favour their cherished convictions. Professor Huxley seems habitually to have looked on religious faith as a more or less *discreditable* state of mind, as a kind of unwarranted prejudice, as an effect of intellectual indolence. He regarded doubt as a kind of beneficent demon sent to trouble the stagnant waters of stupid conventionalism. *Some* doubt unquestionably is of this sort. St. Augustine thought that none really believe deeply save those who have first doubted profoundly. Yet there is also much truth in the teaching of Coleridge, who declared that there never was a real faith in Christ which did not in some measure expand the intellect, whilst simplifying the desires. In *moral and spiritual* matters Martineau certainly thought that a man's character largely determines his belief, that we must be pure in heart if we would in any degree know God. On this subject he agreed with Pascal that divine truths must to some extent pass through our hearts on their way into our intellects.[1]

II.

HER OBEDIENCE.

It has often been observed that a woman's faith is more simple and intense than a man's. Women seldom know the agony of mental doubt. Scepticism is foreign to their nature. And the reason is that woman is more accustomed to submission than man. The habit of obedience is more easily formed, and obedience is the vital fruit of faith. And it is upon such faith as this that the Kingdom of God is built. To accept the voice of God as real, as Mary did, to obey meekly the Divine will, to be faithful to ideal hopes, to believe and love in spite of all the contradictions of fact and circumstance—this is the kind of faith that is most noble in human creatures, and it is the very faith which Christ Himself praises when He says to Thomas, " Blessed are they that have not seen, and yet have believed."

Obedience is one of the distinctive glories of womanhood. In

[1] A. H. Craufurd, *Recollections of James Martineau*, 37.

the very outset of the Bible, submission is revealed as her peculiar lot and destiny. If you were merely to look at the words as they stand, declaring the results of the Fall, you would be inclined to call that vocation of obedience a curse ; but in the spirit of Christ it is transformed, like labour, into a blessing. There is a way of saying, like the Moslem, "Thy will be done" which hardens the heart : to say it as Mary said it is to find oneself suddenly gifted with wings. But no heart *can* truly say it in Mary's tone, unless it has first learned her secret and given itself entirely to the Divine guidance and the Divine indwelling. People do not give a *carte blanche* to strangers, but only to those whom they intensely love and implicitly trust. Is there any repose of mind equal to that which comes through perfect love? And is not our want of repose due chiefly to this, that we do not heartily say to God, "Be it unto me according to thy word"? O that we might hand life over to the kind management of our Father, for only then shall we be perfectly free !

¶ Mary's vocation as the Christ-bearer ordains motherhood, whether actual or spiritual, to be the true calling of woman, and shows its great and sacred nature. In her entire acceptance of the work demanded she manifested the initial strength of her character. She beheld from the beginning the greatness of a Divine Purpose being fulfilled, and remained faithful in response as it was gradually developed before her. . . . Again, in social life, Mary took the part of service, by active kindness, and by bringing others into obedience to Christ. Thus, strong and brave under the inspiration of love, she followed to the foot of the Cross, there by suffering to learn something of the mystery of the Sacrifice which was being offered by her Son, and to offer also her best. There she receives the Divine commission, "Woman, behold thy Son." All false independence disappears here, and life is ordained to be one of mutual service. . . . At the Cross Mary's beautiful human love had to receive its final touch of ideality, its transformation by a higher sacrificial Love, Divine, universal, as she realized more and more that He was truly the Son of God and the Saviour, with His Redemptive work to do, not only for her, but for all mankind. And so all special individual love is the training and starting-point for the true self-sacrificing love of service for all men.[1]

[1] R. M. Wills, *Personality and Womanhood*, 131.

III.

Her Humility.

Another feature of Mary's character, closely associated with her submissiveness, is her humility. It comes out very strikingly in the Magnificat. The terms in which she speaks of herself are notable—" handmaiden " (a slave), " low estate," " low degree," "hungry." These words differ as the east from the west from the terms of glorification which her idolaters have applied to her. These four words can be summed up in the one word—"humility." There is nothing in herself of which she will or can boast; she applies to herself the lowliest possible term, " handmaiden." The English form of this word is altogether too respectable to convey Mary's meaning; the word she used is the feminine form of that expression which in its masculine form is rendered " bond-servant." She is His slave, bound to Him for ever.

Her humility, however, expresses itself not so much by a self-depreciation as by an utter forgetfulness of self. In this humble woman an incomparably great thing was come, but she never thought of herself in connexion with it for a moment—of herself as either worthy or even unworthy. Her soul was lifted quite away from herself, and was full of the thought of God only. Instead of deprecating, however sincerely, that so great an honour should come to her, she simply praised the Lord. " *My soul doth magnify the Lord.*" This is the very perfect flower of humility. There is often a self-depreciation which is just conceit in disguise; and even where this is not so, still self-depreciation is, and must be, always a thought, even if a lowly thought, of self. Perfect humility does not think about self at all. It simply accepts from God, and looks up to God, and is full of God, and praises God. This was Mary's humility. There are paintings of the Annunciation which represent Mary as utterly overpowered by holy fear at the great call, and as shrinking from it with abasement. These feelings must have been in her mind, but they were swallowed up in the thought of God; and Mary, who was troubled and fearful and struck with shame as she had thought of herself, forgot herself and thought only of God, and then sang with an untroubled joy.

¶ It is as difficult to be humble as it is easy to despair. Despair's a very conceited thing, but I might as well hope to be Michael Angelo as to be humble. The grace of the lowliest is only given to the highest.[1]

¶ What is the meaning of this quality of meekness or humility? Surely the ground of it is a recognition of the greatness and majesty of God. Men who have seen life under the white light of eternity will never deport themselves with the pride that marks the man to whom the world is only a mirror of his own majestic dignity. We all need to know the art of self-measurement, but that is beyond us unless we allow some place in the universe for Him who dominates great and small alike; for only His entrance into our life enables us to compute our worth by standards universally applicable.[2]

Yes, and to her, the beautiful and lowly,
  Mary a maiden, separate from men,
Camest thou nigh and didst possess her wholly,
  Close to thy saints, but thou wast closer then.

Once and for ever didst thou show thy chosen,
  Once and for ever magnify thy choice;—
Scorched in love's fire or with his freezing frozen,
  Lift up your hearts, ye humble, and rejoice!

Not to the rich He came or to the ruling,
  (Men full of meat, whom wholly He abhors,)
Not to the fools grown insolent in fooling
  Most, when the lost are dying at the doors;

Nay but to her who with a sweet thanksgiving
  Took in tranquillity what God might bring,
Blessed Him and waited, and within her living
  Felt the arousal of a Holy Thing.

Ay for her infinite and endless honour
  Found the Almighty in this flesh a tomb,
Pouring with power the Holy Ghost upon her,
  Nothing disdainful of the Virgin's womb.[3]

[1] *Gathered Leaves from the Prose of Mary E. Coleridge*, 274.
[2] A. C. Hill, *The Sword of the Lord*, 168.
[3] F. W. H. Myers, *Saint Paul*,

IV.

HER PURITY.

Observe again how delicately and yet distinctly her purity of soul reveals itself in the Magnificat. It does not express itself in any words about either sin or holiness. There is no confession in Mary's song, and no consecration. How, then, does it exhibit the purity of her heart? Just because it is a song. By this quite unconscious revelation that God's coming thus so wonderfully and even overpoweringly near was to her a joy. Only a pure heart rejoices when God is very near. His nearness fills the bad with fear and even the good with awe. Mary felt the awe, but the joy was even greater—the joy of God near. Only a very pure soul could have felt that joy. It is this holy gladness because God was come very near that Fra Angelico and other great painters have sought to depict in the faces of their Madonnas.

¶ In all Christian ages the especial glory ascribed to the Virgin Mother is purity of heart and life, implied in the term "Virgin." Gradually in the history of the Christian church the recognition of this became idolatry. The works of early Christian art curiously exhibit the progress of this perversion. They show how Mariolatry grew up. The first pictures of the early Christian ages simply represent the Woman. By and by, we find outlines of the Mother and the Child. In an after-age, the Son is seen sitting on a throne, with the Mother crowned, but sitting as yet below Him. In an age still later, the crowned Mother on a level with the Son. Later still, the Mother on a throne *above* the Son. And lastly, a Romish picture represents the Eternal Son in wrath, about to destroy the Earth, and the Virgin Intercessor interposing, pleading by significant attitude her maternal rights, and redeeming the world from His vengeance. Such was, in fact, the progress of Virgin-worship. First the woman reverenced for the Son's sake; then the woman reverenced above the Son, and adored.[1]

¶ Mrs. Jameson showed me some exquisite forms of the Virgin by the elder painters, when feeling was religious—Perugino, Fra Angelico, Raphael. Afterwards the form became coarse, as the religious feeling died off from art. I asked her how it is that the Romish feeling now is developing itself so much in the direction of Mariolatry; and she said that the purer and

[1] F. W. Robertson.

severer conceptions of the Virgin are coming back again, and visibly marking Romish art. Briefly, I will tell you what I said in answer to her inquiries. I think Mariolatry was inevitable. The idea most strongly seized in Christianity of the sanctification of humanity attached itself to Christ as the man; but the idea naturally developed contained something more—the sanctification of womanhood. Until, therefore, the great truth that in Christ is neither male nor female—that His was the double nature, all that was most manly and all that was most womanly—could take hold of men, it was inevitable that Christianity should seem imperfect without an immaculate woman.[1]

> But thou no longer art to-day
>   The sweet maid-mother, fair and pure;
> Vast time-worn reverend temples gray,
>   Throne thee in majesty obscure;
> And long aisles stretch in minsters high,
> 'Twixt thee, fair peasant, and the sky.
>
> They seek to honour thee, who art
>   Beyond all else a mother indeed;
> With hateful vows that blight the heart,
>   With childless lives, and souls that bleed;
> As if their dull hymns' barren strain
> Could fill a mother with aught but pain![2]

V.

HER THOUGHTFULNESS.

Of all the wonderful deeds and wonderful words not one escaped Mary's eye or failed to stir her thought and hope. In the first of these exercises she stands in contrast with others. Mary heard the report of the shepherds about the vision of "the angel of the Lord," and the song of the attendant host announcing the Lord Christ the Saviour. Mary witnessed their wonder. But she did far more: she stored away in her heart all the incidents and sayings for future frequent and abiding consideration. She revolved them again and again; placed them in array, side by side, together; so "casting them about" to ascertain and

[1] *Life and Letters of the Rev. F. W. Robertson,* 304.
[2] Sir Lewis Morris, *Songs of Two Worlds.*

appreciate all their force and worth. To her spirit the birth scenes and ceremonies, the prophecies and testimonies of Simeon and Anna, supplied richest material for reflection while the Babe was growing to the Boy of twelve; while that Boy was passing on "in wisdom and in stature," "in favour with God and man," up to manhood; aye, and while that "man Christ Jesus" was so marvellously fulfilling His sublime service and suffering as the world's Redeemer.

The life of our Lord Jesus Christ is so full and deep, its relations are so varied and vital that it takes much "pondering" to comprehend it. Mary did not grudge that care. Mysterious as were many of its scenes, and many of His words and acts; unutterably distressing as was its soul-piercing close, she never ceased to follow and wait. She shared the first revelations of the resurrection morn; she waited with the holy company in the Upper Room; she received of the first gifts of the Holy Spirit at Pentecost, and then was able to piece together in sweetest harmony and completeness the sayings and doings she had stored from the first. Mystery vanished in light, and the light was ineffable glory. Bethlehem, Jerusalem, Nazareth, Egypt; the manger, the ministry, the cross, the sepulchre; angels and men— all became clear, radiant. There was never a thought in that mother's mind, never an affection in her heart, that failed of blessed satisfaction.

But Mary's thoughtfulness is seen more clearly in the long years of waiting. Think of what it means that all at once the wonderful and abnormal is exchanged for the purely commonplace and normal. We hear no more of angel choirs, of strange stars that kindle hope and expectation, of hostile governors, and miraculous escapes. No one appears to have sought out the Child whose birth had evoked such tumult and such marvels. No pilgrim comes to Nazareth inquiring for Him to whom kings had paid obeisance. All these happenings, on whose significance faith and hope could feed, fade into a myth, a legend, which the world forgets. Silence falls upon the scene, impenetrable silence. The Child grows as other children grow, learns His Shema, or His Hebrew catechism, at His mother's knee; plays with other children, unrecognized as the Christ; grows up to take a part in Joseph's trade; lives a simple life, varied only by visits to His kinsfolk or to Jerusalem; and shows no sign of His Messiahship. Can we comprehend what Mary thought in those days? Can we imagine with what weariness of heart she watched the years pass, the uneventful years, and knew her own life passing with them? Was not hers the hope deferred that makes the heart sick? At times no doubt it was; she would not have been human if it were not. Thirty years—it is a lifetime, and oh to think,

> So many worlds, so much to do,
> So little done, such things to be.

Thirty years, during which the world seems settling into deeper sleep, and the times pass without a sign! But through all those years Mary pondered in her heart the things the angel had spoken, and her life was nourished at the springs of faith. Perhaps at times from that sweet childhood, from that full and gracious manhood, there flashed a light that comforted and startled her. We know it was so concerning that journey to Jerusalem, when she found the Boy of twelve disputing with the doctors in the Temple, for we are told that "his mother kept all these sayings in her heart." How full of homely truth that touch. What mother does not cherish in her heart the sayings of her child, which to her, and perhaps to her alone, seem full of wisdom and significance? And we know by another sign also that her faith had not failed. When the marriage feast was held in Cana of Galilee, it was Mary who said to the wondering servants, "Whatsoever he saith unto you, do it." She had subjugated herself already to her Son, as only mothers can; she had a kind of faith in Him possible only to mothers. But how hard the test! How easy to have thought herself deceived, to have relapsed into quiet sad negation of all that had once seemed so miraculous, to have become immersed in ordinary household cares and duties, to have let the light lighted in that secret shrine go out for want of vigilance! The young Christ passed in and out of that simple house; silent, apparently content, seeking no publicity, giving no sign that He was aware of His own great destiny, and yet of Him the angel said, "He shall be great, and shall be called the Son of the Highest: and the Lord God shall give unto him the throne of his father David: and he shall reign over the house of Jacob for ever; and of his kingdom there shall be no end." What but faith could hold that message

true, and ponder it in the heart, and still believe amid a life so
barren of event, amid the passing of the years that gave no
credibility to her dream, amid the silence of God Himself, who
seemed to have forgotten His beloved Son?

> Ah! knew'st thou of the end, when first
> That Babe was on thy bosom nurs'd?—
> Or when He tottered round thy knee
> Did thy great sorrow dawn on thee?—
> And through His boyhood, year by year
> Eating with Him the Passover,
> Didst thou discern confusedly
> That holier sacrament, when He,
> The bitter cup about to quaff,
> Should break the bread and eat thereof?—
> Or came not yet the knowledge, even
> Till on some day forecast in Heaven
> His feet passed through thy door to press
> Upon His Father's business?—
> Or still was God's high secret kept?

> Nay, but I think the whisper crept
> Like growth through childhood. Work and play,
> Things common to the course of day,
> Awed thee with meanings unfulfill'd;
> And all through girlhood, something still'd
> Thy senses like the birth of light,
> When thou hast trimmed thy lamp at night
> Or washed thy garments in the stream;
> To whose white bed had come the dream
> That He was thine and thou wast His
> Who feeds among the field-lilies.
> O solemn shadow of the end
> In that wise spirit long contain'd!
> O awful end! and those unsaid
> Long years when It was Finished![1]

[1] D. G. Rossetti, *Poetical Works*, 245.

HEROD THE GREAT.

LITERATURE.

Bacon, L. W., *The Simplicity that is in Christ* (1892), 288.

Baldwin, G. C., *Representative Men of the New Testament* (1859), 41.

Burn, A. E., *The Crown of Thorns* (1911), 36.

Buss, S., *Roman Law and History in the New Testament* (1901), 1.

Caldecott, W. S., *Herod's Temple* (1913), 1.

Cameron, A. B., *From the Garden to the Cross* (1896), 157.

Candlish, R. S., *Scripture Characters* (1872), 123.

Ewald, H., *The History of Israel*, v. (1880) 406.

Farrar, F. W., *The Herods* (1898), 62.

Hausrath, A., *The Time of Jesus*, i. (1878) 207 ; ii. (1880) **3**.

Little, W. J. K., *Sunlight and Shadow* (1892), 256.

Mathews, S., *The History of New Testament Times in Palestine* (1899), 108.

Schürer, E., *The Jewish People in the Time of Jesus Christ*, I. i. (1890) 400.

Selwyn, E. C., *The Oracles in the New Testament* (1912), 30.

Stanley, A. P., *Lectures on the History of the Jewish Church*, iii. (1889) 362

Stevenson, J. G., *The Judges of Jesus* (1909), 107.

Williams, T. R., in *Men of the New Testament* : Matthew to Timothy (1905), 57.

Catholic Encyclopædia, vii. (1910) 289 (J. J. Tierney).

Dictionary of Christ and the Gospels, i. (1906) 717 (W. P. Armstrong).

Encyclopædia Biblica, ii. (1901), col. 2025 (W. J. Woodhouse).

Jewish Encyclopedia, vi. (1904) 356 (I. Broydé).

HEROD THE GREAT.

**Jesus was born in Bethlehem of Judæa in the days of Herod the king.
—Matt. ii. 1.**

IN the year 109 B.C., John Hyrcanus, son of Simon Maccabæus, subdued the Edomites (Idumæans) and compelled them to adopt Judaism. This achievement looked like the final victory of Jacob over Esau. It was the fulfilment of the ancient prophecy, "And the one people shall be stronger than the other people; and the elder shall serve the younger." But forcible conversions have never yielded satisfactory results. The admission of the Edomites, still unchanged in heart, into the house of Israel was fraught with consequences which no human eye could have foreseen. A little leaven leavens the whole lump. From the very first there was good reason for every Jewish patriot to say, " Beware of the leaven of Edom," just as Jesus at a later time said, "Beware of the leaven of Herod" (Mark viii. 15). For the Idumæans brought a new spirit into the commonwealth of Israel, and it was not long before the conquered gave laws to their conquerors. Only two generations had passed when the Idumæan Antipater was appointed by Julius Cæsar Procurator of Judæa, Samaria, and Galilee, on account of services rendered in the dictator's struggle with Pompey. And the son of Antipater was Herod the Great, king of the Jews.

I.

HIS GREATNESS.

1. Does Herod deserve to be called "the Great"? In comparison with his feebler descendants—the kings and princes of the house which he founded—he may fairly be so designated, although there is only one passage in the works of Josephus (*Antiq.* XVIII. v. 5) where he receives that proud title. He cannot

with any propriety be admitted into the company of those kings and conquerors whom historians agree to call "great" in the absolute sense. But this much may be said with truth, that if he was only relatively great, he was endowed by nature with all the gifts which, had he used them wisely, might have made him great in the higher sense. As it is, his astonishing success is a fact beyond dispute. While some men are born to greatness, and some have greatness thrust upon them, the first Herod achieved all the greatness with which he is credited. By his own efforts he attained the position of power and glory to which his restless ambition aspired. His energy, his daring, his political ability, his personal beauty and power of fascination won in succession the greatest of the Romans to support his cause. And receiving a kingly crown, founding a royal house, and amassing fabulous wealth, he rivalled Solomon in the extent of his dominions, the splendour of his court, the grandeur of his palaces and temples.

¶ Herod was born to be a ruler. Blessed by nature with a powerful body capable of enduring fatigue, he early inured himself to all manner of hardships. He was a skilful rider, and a bold, daring huntsman. He was feared in pugilistic encounters. His lance was unerring, and his arrow seldom missed its mark. He was practised in the art of war from his youth. Even in his twenty-fifth year he had won renown by his expedition against the robbers of Galilee. And then again, in the later period of his life, when over sixty years of age, he led in person the campaign against the Arabians. Rarely did success forsake him where he himself conducted any warlike undertaking.[1]

¶ Even if we contemplate the personality of Herod apart from his friends and flatterers, we cannot deny that there have rarely been united in any ruler so much tenacious strength of mind, so much almost inexhaustible address and sagacity, and so much inflexible activity, as were combined in him : even the surname of the Great, though only applied to him subsequently by a misunderstanding of a Greek expression, he at any rate merits within the series of his own family and in the circuit of the sovereigns of the century. Loving power and command above everything, he was yet not insensible to the blessings of honourable tranquillity and the arts of peace. After such tedious and desolating struggles, the whole country longed for rest, and accordingly the labours of Herod for the external prosperity and honour of his house and his

[1] E. Schürer, *The Jewish People in the Time of Jesus Christ*, I. i. 417.

people found a most happy response in the similar need of repose which was then so forcibly experienced throughout the whole Roman empire. And yet the end of his reign was destined to be practically the end of the new dynasty established by him with such prodigious effort; and what was much worse, his memory was to be justly cursed by his contemporaries and by posterity, and his whole career upon the throne, with all its outward success and splendour, was to be irremediably disastrous and full of affliction; so that there has scarcely ever been a sovereign whose life, passed in the enjoyment of all possible power and glory, terminated more painfully in itself or more mischievously for the kingdom at large.[1]

2. It was in the year 40 B.C. that Herod, walking between Antony and Octavian (afterwards Augustus), was conducted from the Roman Senate to the Capitol, where, with solemn services to Jupiter Capitolinus, his reign was inaugurated. On the same day he was fêted by Antony. "Thus," says Josephus, "did this man come into his kingdom." He was then in his thirty-seventh year, and for the next thirty-four years he shaped the destinies of the Jewish nation, while he was one of the most brilliant figures of the Augustan age.

¶ During the prosperous period of Herod's reign splendid public works were commenced and new cities were built. He rebuilt the city of Samaria, to which he gave the name of "Sebaste," in honour of the Roman emperor. The small town on the seacoast called the Tower of Strato was transformed into a magnificent city with an artificial harbour, on a scale of the utmost grandeur, and named "Cæsarea." Temples in honour of Augustus were multiplied in all directions. To celebrate the quinquennial games which had been instituted in almost all of the Roman provinces, likewise in honour of Augustus, Herod erected in Jerusalem a theatre, an amphitheatre, and a hippo-drome. Citadels and cities rose in honour of the different members of Herod's family: Antipatris, in honour of his father; Cypros, commemorating his mother; Phasaelis, as a memorial to his brother; and the two strongholds named Herodium in honour of himself. Military colonies were planted at Gaba in Galilee, and at Heshbon; and the fortresses Alexandrium, Hyrcania, Machærus, and Masada were rendered impregnable.

Of all Herod's building operations, however, the most magnificent was the restoration of the Temple at Jerusalem. This work,

[1] H. Ewald, *The History of Israel*, v. 418.

begun in the eighteenth year of his reign, was completed in its essential parts in eight years. Its beauty was proverbial. "He who has not seen Herod's building has never seen anything beautiful," was a common proverb of the day. Moreover, Herod did not content himself with erecting architectural monuments in his own country only; Ashkelon, Acre, Tyre, Sidon, Byblus, Berytus, Tripoli, Damascus, Antioch, Rhodes, Chios, Nicopolis, Athens, and Sparta also received proofs of his generosity in many a monumental structure. He defrayed, too, the cost of the erection at Rhodes of a temple devoted to the Pythian Apollo, and gave a fund for prizes and sacrifices at the Olympian games.

All the worldly pomp and splendour which made Herod popular among the pagans, however, rendered him abhorrent to the Jews, who could not forgive him for insulting their religious feelings by forcing upon them heathen games and combats with wild animals. The annexation to Judæa of the districts of Trachonitis, Batanea, Auranitis, Zenodorus, Ulatha, and Panias, which Herod through his adulations had obtained from Augustus, could not atone for his crimes.[1]

II.

His Tyranny.

1. Such a conqueror and such a ruler ought to have been one of the happiest of men. But the suspicious, crafty, ruthless tyrant who rises before our imagination as we read the opening of the First Gospel was manifestly a stranger to happiness. And when we turn to the vivid pages of Josephus and Tacitus, it is the same unhappy face that meets us, the same gloomy character that we find portrayed. Herod began his reign in the usual Oriental fashion, by putting to death all his former opponents and all his possible rivals. He gave orders that forty-five of the most wealthy and prominent Asmonæans—i.e., of the Maccabean family which the Romans had deprived of the kingship—should be executed, and their estates confiscated to fill his empty treasury. His agents showed themselves so greedy as to shake the dead bodies in order that any gold hidden in their shrouds might be disclosed. His next step was to slay the whole Sanhedrin with the exception of Pollio and Sameas, who had rendered him some

[1] I. Broydé, in the *Jewish Encyclopedia*, vi. 358.

service. And these acts of vengeance and cruelty were but the first of the many dark crimes which stain for ever the records of his reign.

It seemed to be his firm determination that no man should be great and no man honoured in his kingdom except himself. Any popularity but his own was in his eyes a crime. In order to strengthen his position, he married the beautiful Asmonæan princess Mariamne, whom he loved with all the ardour of his passionate nature. He was persuaded by her to set aside the high priest Ananel, and to appoint her brother Aristobulus, a lad in his seventeenth year, to the sacred office. As a scion of the heroic Maccabean family, Aristobulus was received by the Jews with demonstrations of joy. And when he had to perform the religious ceremonies at the Feast of Tabernacles, he did so with perfect grace and decorum, standing before the people in the blue and white and gold-embroidered robes of his office, with the golden plate gleaming on his forehead over his dark and flowing locks, and the jewelled Urim upon his breast. But the acclamations of the assembled multitude were the poor boy's death-doom.

The youthful high priest was invited to his mother's palace among the groves of Jericho—the fashionable watering-place, as it had become, of Palestine. Herod received the boy with his usual sportiveness and gaiety. It was one of the warm autumnal days of Syria, and the heat was yet more overpowering in that tropical valley. In the sultry noon the high priest and his young companions stood cooling themselves beside the large tanks which surrounded the open court of the palace, and watching the gambols and exercises of the guests or slaves, as, one after another, they plunged into these crystal swimming-baths. Among these was the band of Gaulish guards, whom Augustus had transferred from Cleopatra to Herod, and whom Herod employed as his most unscrupulous instruments. Lured on by these perfidious playmates, the princely boy joined in the sport, and then, as at sunset the sudden darkness fell over the gay scene, the wild band dipped and dived with him under the deep water; and in that fatal "baptism" life was extinguished. When the body was laid out in the palace the passionate lamentations of the princesses knew no bounds. The news flew through the town, and every house felt as if it had lost a child. The mother suspected, but dared not reveal her suspicions, and in the agony of self-imposed restraint, and in the compression of her determined will, trembled on the brink of self-destruction. Even Herod, when he looked at the dead face and form, retaining all the bloom of youthful beauty, was moved to tears—so genuine, that they almost served as a veil for his complicity in the murder. And it was not more than was expected from the effusion of his natural grief that the funeral was ordered on so costly and splendid a scale as to give consolation even to the bereaved mother and sister.

2. Great without being good, Herod was little to be envied. There is no happiness without love, and, alike as a king, as a husband, and as a father, he alienated all those whose affection he ought to have won. Under his government Judæa became the greatest of all the Eastern kingdoms allied with Rome, but he made no secret of the fact that he did not love, and never could love, the Jews. He openly announced that he cared less for them than for his heathen subjects. We cannot wonder, therefore, that all the material benefits which he conferred upon them were received with cold admiration and little gratitude. He appeared to think that so long as his loyalty to Rome—a loyalty dictated by nothing higher than selfish prudence—secured for him the patronage of the great ones of the earth, he could dispense with the affection of the people whom he governed. "Let them hate so long as they fear" has been the scornful dictum of tyrants in all ages. But happiness has never been purchased on these terms. Herod's case was not unlike that of the Emperor Tiberius, who, in the midst of all his power and glory, confessed to the Roman Senate his utter misery. "Nor was it unadvisedly," comments the historian Tacitus, "that the wisest of all men (Plato) was wont to affirm that, if the hearts of tyrants were bared to view, wounds and lacerations would be seen in them; for as the body is torn by stripes, so is the heart by cruelty, lusts, and evil purposes."

¶ Herod had up to this time moulded circumstances to his will with an almost superhuman energy and capacity; but henceforth ambition led him into entanglements in which retributive Destiny became too strong for him. He could not escape the adamantine link which indissolubly unites sin to punishment. Poets of every age have felt that

Our acts our angels are, or good or ill,
Our fatal shadows that walk by us still;

that

Our deeds still travel with us from afar,
And what we have been makes us what we are.

No stroke of policy seemed more consummate than that which
united the King in marriage with the lovely Mariamne, whose
grandfather he had ousted and whose father he had helped to
slay; but that consummation of his good fortune contained in it
every germ of his unspeakable retribution. Out of the event
which looked like his most brilliant success, adversity formed
"the iron scourge and torturing hour" of his remorse and ruin.
In the volume of human life, says George Sand, "is found no
more disastrous page than that on which are inscribed the two
words—'gratified desires!'"[1]

III.

HIS DOMESTIC SINS.

1. Many a public man whose life is a constant battle finds a
balm for all his wounds and a refuge from all his cares in the love
which welcomes him the moment he crosses the threshold of his
own home.   But Herod the Great never knew that earthly paradise
which is created by the mutual love of husband and wife, of
parents and children. Like Henry the Eighth, whom he greatly
resembled, he had many wives, and Josephus' story of his domestic
feuds is one of the most sordid records of crime which have come
down from ancient times. His court was full of spies and
slanderers who played upon his worst passions, and in one of his
fits of jealous rage he gave orders for the execution of the beautiful, beloved, and innocent Mariamne, who walked in noble silence
to her lonely death. The result was what might have been
expected.

No sooner was she dead than the furies of remorse "took their
seats upon Herod's midnight pillow." Overcome with anguish,
torn by the pangs of regret for her whom he had so intensely
loved, haunted by her ghost, he caught the pestilence which was
raging among his subjects. Under pretence of desiring to hunt,

[1] F. W. Farrar, *The Herods*, 84.

he retired to Samaria, where his strength was so prostrated, and his reason so entirely unhinged for a time, that many expected his death.

¶ Perhaps the most affecting and convincing testimony to Mariamne's great character was Herod's passionate remorse. In a frenzy of grief he invoked her name, he burst into wild lamentations, and then, as if to distract himself from his own thoughts, he plunged into society; he had recourse to all his favourite pursuits; he gathered intellectual society round him; he drank freely with his friends; he went to the chase. And then, again, he gave orders that his servants should keep up the illusion of addressing her as though she could still hear them; he shut himself up in Samaria, the scene of their first wedded life, and there, for a long time, attacked by a devouring fever, hovered on the verge of life and death. Of the three stately towers which he afterwards added to the walls of Jerusalem, one was named after his friend Hippias, the second after his favourite brother, Phasael, but the third, most costly and most richly worked of all, was the monument of his beloved Mariamne.[1]

> Oh, Mariamne! now for thee
>   The heart for which thou bled'st is bleeding;
> Revenge is lost in agony,
>   And wild remorse to rage succeeding.
> Oh, Mariamne! where art thou?
>   Thou canst not hear my bitter pleading:
> Ah! could'st thou—thou would'st pardon now,
>   Though Heaven were to my prayer unheeding.
>
> And is she dead?—and did they dare
>   Obey my frenzy's jealous raving?
> My wrath but doom'd my own despair:
>   The sword that smote her's o'er me waving.—
> But thou art cold, my murder'd love!
>   And this dark heart is vainly craving
> For her who soars alone above,
>   And leaves my soul unworthy saving.
>
> She's gone, who shared my diadem;
>   She sunk, with her my joys entombing;
> I swept that flower from Judah's stem,
>   Whose leaves for me alone were blooming;

[1] A. P. Stanley, *History of the Jewish Church*, iii. 376.

And mine's the guilt, and mine the hell,
This bosom's desolation dooming;
And I have earn'd those tortures well,
Which unconsumed are still consuming![1]

2. Herod recovered, but only to imbrue his hands again and yet again in innocent blood. Mariamne's two sons, Alexander and Aristobulus, who inherited her beauty and gloried in their Asmonæan descent, naturally grew up without any love for the murderer of their mother, and the gulf between them and their father gradually widened until at last he asked Augustus' leave to put the hapless youths to death. The Emperor gave cold permission to have their case tried at Berytus, where Herod appeared in person as the frantic accuser of his own sons. A reluctant verdict was given against them, and they were strangled at Samaria, where Herod had married their mother, the fair young Mariamne, nearly thirty years before.

¶ Macrobius, who wrote in the beginning of the fifth century, narrates (Saturn. ii. 4) that Augustus, having heard that Herod had ordered his own son to be slain in Syria, remarked: "It is better to be Herod's swine (ὗς) than his son" (υἱός). In the Greek text there is a bon mot and a relationship between the words used that etymologists may recognize even in English. The law among the Jews against eating pork is hinted at, and the anecdote seems to contain extra-biblical elements.[2]

3. From that time forth Herod's mind was haunted by the ghosts of his sons as well as that of their mother. But every crime he committed seemed to be the prelude to yet another. His eldest son Antipater, the evil-minded prince who had poisoned his father's mind against his half-brothers, now regarded his own succession to the throne as assured. But his ill-concealed joy at the prospect of soon wearing a crown was duly reported to the dying tyrant, who, five days before his own miserable end, gave the command that his son should be executed and his body cast into an unhonoured grave. And it is said that in a last fit of madness he left orders—happily never carried out—that all the most distinguished men of the nation should forthwith be summoned to Jericho, shut up in the hippodrome, and massacred

[1] Byron, Hebrew Melodies.
[2] J. J. Tierney, in the Catholic Encyclopædia, vii. 290.

by his soldiers, that so his funeral might be accompanied with genuine lamentations of the whole people, who hated him.

It is inconceivable that anyone should ever love such a man. Sophocles says wisely that "the gifts of enemies are no gifts," and Herod learned the bitter truth of these words. He was one of the greatest "benefactors" of his age, and scores of cities at home and abroad—some of them, such as Sebaste and Cæsarea, founded and built by himself—basked in the sunshine of his princely favour. He made Judæa a first-rate kingdom; he vastly increased its wealth; he put down brigandage with a high hand, making life and property safe; he obtained many edicts in favour of the Jews; in particular, he won for them exemption from military service, and immunities which secured the due performance of their religious rites. But it was all to no purpose. His labour was lost, because it was not love's labour. The nation remained stubbornly unregardful of those magnificent boons, and brooded so fiercely on his infractions of their Law that latterly he did not even care to attempt the impossible task of trying to win their approval. In his own country the king of the Jews lived and moved amid a chaos of hatreds. He may well have exclaimed in the words which are put into the lips of another Jewish king, "All is vanity and vexation of spirit," though it is doubtful if he ever got so far as the disillusioned poet who said:

> Without a sigh would I resign
> This busy scene of splendid woe,
> To make that calm contentment mine
> Which virtue knows, or seems to know.

IV.

HIS RELATION TO THE MESSIAH.

1. It was towards the end of this tyrant's reign, probably in the year 6 B.C.—the common chronology being erroneous—that Jesus was born in Bethlehem. Tertullian makes the strange statement that some of the Jews were of opinion that Herod himself was the Christ—"Christum Herodem esse dixerunt." That is incredible. Herod might more correctly have been

designated the Anti-Christ than the Christ. Bishop Westcott says truly that "the history of the Herodian family presents one side of the last development of the Jewish nation. Side by side with the spiritual Kingdom of God, preached by John the Baptist, and founded by the Lord, a kingdom of the world was established, which in its external splendour recalled the traditional magnificence of Solomon. The simultaneous realizations of the two principles, national and spiritual, which had long variously influenced the Jews, is a fact pregnant with instruction. In the fulness of time a descendant of Esau established a false counterpart of the promised glories of the Messiah."

2. But the star of the true Messiah arose, and shone over Bethlehem, in the dark night of history when Herod's star was near its setting. And the momentary conjunction of the names of two so diverse Kings of the Jews is one of the strangest things in the book of time. Herod's conduct towards the Magi is just what we should have expected. All his morbid jealousy, all his lying craftiness, and all his bloodthirsty cruelty, are revealed in the Evangelical narrative. He who had built a temple to the God of the Jews, and many temples to the gods of the Gentiles, had no religion of his own. His proposal to worship the child at Bethlehem, who was "born king of the Jews," only masked his intention to destroy one more rival. And when he found the Magi had, as he said, "befooled" him, he would doubtless have dealt with them, could he have laid his hands upon them, as he was wont to deal with all who crossed his purposes. It was well for them that they received a warning to return to their own country by another way. But it was ill for the innocent babes of Bethlehem, who were left to bear the brunt of the tyrant's wrath. In the hope of laying his murderous hands on one young life—which, however, was far beyond his reach—he spread a wide net. "He sent forth, and slew all the male children that were in Bethlehem, and in all the borders thereof, from two years old and under." These were the first Christian martyrs. At least theirs was the first innocent blood that was shed for Jesus' sake.

¶ The truth of this story [of the massacre of the innocents] has been questioned. The chief ground is the silence of Josephus on the subject. While he speaks of many cruel deeds of Herod, he passes this one by. But it is plainly quite of a piece with Herod's well-known character, and, indeed, compared with his other deeds of monstrous cruelty, it would easily escape notice. The whole number of victims, probably not more than twenty or thirty, would not make a very great sensation at that time. Besides, the whole of Josephus' statements in regard to the Messianic expectations and doings of his time are to be looked upon with some suspicion, for he seems to have been afraid to make many clear and direct allusions to those matters. The deed illustrates well Herod's general character for bloodthirsty cruelty and short-sighted folly.[1]

3. But at last the wicked cease from troubling. The Evangelist's words, " Herod was dead," are more than a statement of historical fact; they are a sigh of relief heaved by a long-suffering universe. Heaven as well as earth could now breathe more freely. In a dream Joseph heard a sympathetic angel say, " Arise . . . for they are dead that sought the young child's life." The plural number " they " expresses a general idea, a class, though only a single person is meant. Herod and all his kind " have their day, and cease to be." Of course he received a splendid funeral. " There was a bier all of gold . . . the conclusion of the life of Herod " (Josephus, *B.J.* i. xxxiii. 9).

> The boast of heraldry, the pomp of power,
> 　And all that beauty, all that wealth e'er gave,
> Awaits alike the inevitable hour.
> The paths of glory lead but to the grave.

Meanwhile the Child of Bethlehem, born in this tyrant's reign, and providentially saved from the massacre of the innocents, was opening His eyes to all the wonder of the world—the world which He had come to redeem. The Herodians played their part for a little while upon the stage of history, and then sank into oblivion. Their sovereignty had none of the elements of stability. But while Herod Antipas was tetrarch of Galilee, and Herod Philip tetrarch of Ituræa, Jesus the true Christ founded the spiritual Kingdom which is to endure unto all generations; the Kingdom which is righteousness, and peace, and joy in the Holy Spirit; the Kingdom which is to bring to all mankind numberless, priceless, endless blessings. That Kingdom has come, is now

---

[1] D. M. W. Laird, in the *Dictionary of Christ and the Gospels*, i. 829.

coming, and is yet to come. Herod's palaces soon crumbled into dust; of his temple not one stone was left upon another; and all his cities are one with Nineveh and Tyre. The Great Herod is dead, but the Holy Child, whose blood he tried to shed, is alive for evermore. King of kings and Lord of lords, He lives to emancipate the world from all Herodian tyrannies, to enfranchise the whole human family with the glorious liberty of the sons of God.

> So be it, Lord! Thy throne shall never,
> Like earth's proud empires, pass away;
> Thy kingdom stands and grows for ever,
> Till all Thy creatures own Thy sway.

¶ Everybody in this room has been taught to pray daily, "Thy kingdom come." Now, if we hear a man swear in the streets, we think it very wrong, and say he "takes God's name in vain." But there's a twenty times worse way of taking His name in vain than that. It is to *ask God for what we don't want.* He doesn't like that sort of prayer. If you don't want a thing, don't ask for it: such asking is the worst mockery of your King you can insult Him with; the soldiers striking Him on the head with the reed was nothing to that. If you do not wish for His kingdom, don't pray for it. But if you do, you must do more than pray for it; you must work for it. And, to work for it, you must know what it is; we have all prayed for it many a day without thinking. Observe, it is a kingdom that is to come to us; we are not to go to it. Also, it is not to be a kingdom of the dead, but of the living. Also, it is not to come all at once, but quietly; nobody knows how. "The kingdom of God cometh not with observation." Also, it is not to come outside of us, but in our hearts: "the kingdom of God is within you." And, being within us, it is not a thing to be seen, but to be felt; and though it brings all substance of good with it, it does not consist in that: "the kingdom of God is not meat and drink, but righteousness, peace, and joy in the Holy Ghost"; joy, that is to say, in the holy, healthful, and helpful Spirit. Now, if we want to work for this kingdom, and to bring it, and enter into it, there's one curious condition to be first accepted. You must enter it as children, or not at all: "Whosoever will not receive it as a little child shall not enter therein." And again, "Suffer little children to come unto me, and forbid them not, *for of such is the kingdom of heaven.*" [1]

[1] Ruskin, *The Crown of Wild Olive,* § 46 (*Works,* xviii. 427).

JOHN THE BAPTIST.

I.

JOHN AND THE JEWS.

LITERATURE.

Abbey, C. J., *The Divine Love* (1900), 13.

Alford, H., *Quebec Chapel Sermons*, ii. (1855) 263 ; v. (1856) 32.

Andrews, S. J., *The Life of Our Lord* (1892), 12, 146.

Arnold, T., *Sermons Chiefly on the Interpretation of Scripture* (1878), 109

Brooke, S. A., *Sermons Preached in St. James's Chapel*, i. (1873) 148.

Carpenter, W. B., *The Son of Man among the Sons of Men* (1893), 235.

Connell, A., *The Endless Quest* (1914), 213.

Cumming, J. E., *John : The Baptist, Forerunner, and Martyr*.

Davidson, A. B., *The Called of God* (1902), 229.

Dawson, W. J., *The Man Christ Jesus* (1901), 29.

Edersheim, A., *The Life and Times of Jesus the Messiah*, i. (1887) 133.

Farrar, F. W., *The Life of Christ* (1894), 74.

„   „   *The Life of Lives* (1900), 227.

Feather, J., *The Last of the Prophets* (1894).

Ferrier, J. T., *The Master : His Life and Teachings* (1913), 65.

Geikie, C., *The Life and Words of Christ*, i. (1877) 84.

Holtzmann, O., *The Life of Jesus* (1904), 108.

La Farge, J., *The Gospel Story in Art* (1913), 165.

Lange, J. P., *The Life of the Lord Jesus Christ*, i. (1864) 346.

Lee, F. T., *The New Testament Period and its Leaders* (1913), 56.

Matheson, G., *The Representative Men of the New Testament* (1905), 25.

Meyer, F. B., *John the Baptist* (1911).

Neander, A., *The Life of Jesus Christ* (1880), 45.

Reynolds, H. R., *John the Baptist* (1874).

Robertson, A. T., *John the Loyal* (1912).

Robertson, F. W., *The Human Race* (1886), 252.

Scott, E. F., *The Kingdom and the Messiah* (1911), 58.

Simpson, W. J. S., *The Prophet of the Highest* (1895).

Skrine, J. H., *Saints and Worthies* (1901), 46.

Stalker, J., *The Two St. Johns* (1895), 189.

Taylor, W. M., *The Silence of Jesus* (1894), 17.

Whyte, A., *Bible Characters* : Joseph and Mary to James (1900), 26.

Wood, H. G., *The Kingdom of God in the Teaching of Jesus* (1914), 33.

Catholic Encyclopædia, viii. (1910) 486 (C. L. Souvay).

Dictionary of the Bible, ii. (1899) 677 (Ll. J. M. Bebb).

„   „   „   (Single-volume, 1909), 474 (J. G. Tasker).

Dictionary of Christ and the Gospels, i. (1906) 861 (J. C. Lambert).

Encyclopædia Biblica, ii. (1901), col. 2498 (T. K. Cheyne).

Smith's Dictionary of the Bible, i. (1893) 1736 (E. Hawkins).

JOHN AND THE JEWS.

Verily I say unto you, Among them that are born of women there hath not arisen a greater than John the Baptist.—Matt. xi. 11.

EVERYTHING that we are told of John the Baptist is unique. The asceticism of his life in the desert, the startling message with which he broke the silence maintained by the spirit of prophecy for four hundred years, the incorruptible sincerity of his humility, out of which no allurement could bribe him, the fearless honesty of his words, and the tragic horror of his death—all combine to give him a peculiar and distinctive place on the page of Scripture. But these things were, after all, only the indications and accompaniments of the singularity of his official position ; for he stands alone among the servants of God. He came, no doubt, in the spirit and power of Elijah, and his dress is not the only thing about him that reminds us of the prophet of Gilead ; but yet, take him for all in all, there is no one to whom he can be properly compared. He stood between the Jewish and the Christian dispensations, having much that connected him with both, and yet belonging exclusively to neither. He had more knowledge of the nature of the person and work of the Messiah than any of his predecessors among the prophets, and yet "he that is least in the kingdom of heaven is greater than he."

For centuries the thoughts and passion of the prophets had streamed into and filled the Jewish heart. They kindled there vague desires, wild hopes of a far-off kingdom, passionate discontent with things as they were. At last, about the time of the birth of Christ, these scattered dreams and hopes concentrated themselves into one desire, took form and substance in one prophecy—the advent of the anointed King. It was the blazing up of an excitement which had been smouldering for a thousand years ; it was the last and most powerful of a long series of oscillations which had been gradually increasing in swing and force. Now two things are true: first, wherever there is this passion in a people, it embodies itself in one man, who is to be its interpreter; secondly, wherever a great problem of the human spirit is growing towards its solution, and the soil of humanity is prepared for new seed from heaven, God sends His chosen creature to proclaim the truth which brings the light.

So a great man is the product of two things—of the passion of his age, and of the choice of God. So far as he is the former, he is but the interpreter of his own time, and only the highest man of his time; so far as he is the latter, he is beyond his age, and points forward to a higher revelation.

Such was the Baptist's position—the interpreter of the spiritual wants of the Jewish people, the prophet of a greater revelation in the future.

¶ There is something which touches in us that chord of sadness which is always ready to vibrate, when we think that John the Baptist was the last of all the heroes of the Old Dispensation, that with him closed the goodly fellowship of the prophets. For we cannot look at the last lighting up of the intellect of a man, the last effort for freedom of a dying nation, or the last glory of an ancient institution like that of the Jewish prophets, without a sense of sadness.

Men are we, and must grieve when even the shade
Of that which once was great hath passed away.

But if there be some melancholy in the feeling with which we view the Baptist, there is also much of enthusiasm. If he was the last, he was also the greatest, of the prophets. That which all the others had dimly imaged, he presented in clear light; that which they had spoken in parables, he declared in the plainest words.[1]

I.

AT HOME.

1. As the traveller emerges from the dreary wilderness that lies between Sinai and the southern frontier of Palestine—a scorching desert, in which Elijah was glad to find shelter from the sword-like rays in the shade of the retem shrub—he sees

[1] Stopford A. Brooke.

before him a long line of hills, which is the beginning of "the hill country" of Judæa. In contrast with the sand wastes which he has traversed, the valleys seem to laugh and sing. Greener and yet greener grow the pasture lands, till he can understand how Nabal and other sheep-masters were able to find maintenance for vast flocks of sheep. Here and there are the crumbled ruins which mark the site of ancient towns and villages tenanted now by the jackal or the wandering Arab. Among these, a modern traveller has identified the site of Juttah, the village home of Zacharias and his wife Elisabeth.

Zacharias was a priest, "of the course of Abijah," and twice a year he journeyed to Jerusalem to fulfil his office, for a week of six days and two Sabbaths. There were, Josephus tells us, somewhat more than 20,000 priests settled in Judæa at this time; and very many of them were like those whom Malachi denounced as degrading and depreciating the Temple services. The general character of the priesthood was deeply tainted by the corruption of the times, and as a class they were blind leaders of the blind. Not a few, however, were evidently deeply religious men, for we find that "a great number of the priests," after the crucifixion, believed on Christ and joined His followers. In this class we must, therefore, place Zacharias, who is described as being "righteous before God."

2. The parents were old, and had ceased to have the hope of children. In similar circumstances, the Father of the Faithful, in times remote, received the promise of a son; and the special favour of God, thus indicated, heightened his sense of gratitude and strained his anticipations to the utmost as to the issues bound up in his son's life. Zacharias and Elisabeth, in like manner, must have felt that their child was in a peculiar way a gift of God, and that a special importance was to attach to his life. When anything has been long desired, but hope of ever obtaining it has died out of the heart, and yet, after all, it is given, the gift appears infinitely greater than it would have done if received at the time when it was expected. The real reason, however, why in this case the gift was withheld so long was that the hour of Providence had not come. The fulness of time, when the Messiah should appear, and therefore when His forerunner

should come into the world, was settled in the Divine plan and could not be altered by an hour. Therefore had Zacharias and his wife to wait.

One memorable autumn, when the land was full of the grape-harvest, Zacharias left his home, in the cradle of the hills, some three thousand feet above the Mediterranean, for his priestly service. Reaching the Temple, he would lodge in the cloisters and spend his days in the innermost court, which none might enter, save priests in their sacred garments. Among the various priestly duties, none was held in such high esteem as the offering of incense, which was presented morning and evening, on a special golden altar, in the Holy Place at the time of prayer. "The whole multitude of the people were praying without at the time of incense." So honourable was this office that it was fixed by lot, and none was allowed to perform it twice. Only once in a priest's life was he permitted to sprinkle the incense on the burning coals, which an assistant had already brought from the altar of burnt-sacrifice, and spread on the altar of incense before the veil.

"And there appeared unto him an angel of the Lord standing on the right side of the altar of incense." How circumstantial the narrative is! There could be no mistake. He stood—and he stood on the right side. It was Gabriel, who stands in the presence of God, that had been sent to speak to the priest to declare the good tidings that his prayer was heard; that his wife should bear a son, who should be called John; that the child should be welcomed with joy, should be a Nazirite, should be filled with the Holy Spirit from his birth, should inherit the spirit and power of Elijah, and should go before the face of Christ, to prepare His way, by turning the hearts of the fathers to the children, and the disobedient to walk in the wisdom of the just.

3. As a rule, the naming of children takes place in haphazard fashion, the child receiving a certain name simply because some relative has borne it before him, or because the sound has pleased the fancy of father or mother, or for some similar reason. But on this occasion the name was Divinely decided beforehand; and this was an indication that this child was created for a special purpose. The name "John" signifies, "The Lord is favourable,"

or, put more briefly, " The Gift of God." He was a gift to his
parents, but also to far wider circles—to his country and to
mankind.

Not only was this child to be a gift, he was also to be gifted;
so the father was informed: "He shall be great in the sight of
the Lord." To be a great man is the ambition of every child of
Adam; and the thought of having as a son one who is a great
man is a suggestion which thrills every parent's heart. Greatness is, indeed, an ambiguous word. Who is great? To be
notorious, to be much in the mouths of men, to have a name
which is a household word—this is the superficial conception of
greatness. But such greatness may be very paltry; to as much
greatness as this, multitudes of the meanest and most worthless of
mankind have attained. But John was to be great "in the sight
of the Lord." This is a different matter; it implies not only
genuine gifts, but gifts employed for other than selfish ends.

4. It was an atmosphere of reverence, conscientiousness, and
refinement that John breathed from the first. He belonged to
the choicest caste of the chosen people, using the word without
its stigma. The son of a priestly race, a race which held the
chief and most unquestioned position in the nation, he inherited
its seclusive tendencies, and to his opening mind its quiet and
retirement must have been congenial. He was of the priestly
race on both sides, for his mother was "of the daughters of
Aaron." Heredity and its bias count for much in the inclination
of the developing life. The fineness of grain that comes from a
godly and cultured ancestry, especially when there is no concern
about the basal questions, "What shall we eat, what shall we
drink, and wherewithal shall we be clothed?" constitutes a
mental and spiritual capital of the golden denomination, a capital
whose value can hardly be overestimated.

John's recollections in after years would be of the constant
perusal by his father of the sacred books, and of his patient
teaching of their contents to him. To no ordinance of the Lord
was the devout Hebrew parent more faithful than to that which
enjoined the careful catechizing of his children in the first
principles of their faith and first records of their history: "These
words, which I command thee this day, shall be in thine heart:

and thou shalt teach them diligently unto thy children, and shalt talk of them when thou sittest in thine house, and when thou walkest by the way, and when thou liest down, and when thou risest up" (Deut. vi. 6, 7).

Family worship is also a strong and sacred power. We can almost see the small group in the eventide reverently laying aside other duties, while "the sire turns o'er wi' patriarchal grace," or rather unrolls, some copy of the Law or of the Prophets:

> The priest-like father reads the sacred page,
>   How Abram was the friend of God on high;
> Or, Moses bade eternal warfare wage
>   With Amalek's ungracious progeny;
>   Or, how the royal bard did groaning lie
> Beneath the stroke of Heaven's avenging ire;
>   Or Job's pathetic plaint, and wailing cry;
>   Or rapt Isaiah's wild, seraphic fire;
> Or other holy seers that tune the sacred lyre.[1]

Happy is he or she who has such a father and mother, and whose childhood is nurtured in such a home. Out of such homes have come the men who have been the reformative and regenerative forces of the world. The influence of the mother is especially noteworthy; nearly all men who have been conspicuously great and good have owed much to their mothers. In this narrative the mother is less prominent than the father; but enough is told to show of what manner of spirit she was. One likes to think of the three months spent by Mary under her roof. The homage paid by Elisabeth to her on whom had been bestowed the greater honour of being the mother of the Lord was an anticipation of the humility of her son, when he said, "He must increase, but I must decrease."

¶ In Phillips Brooks the power of observation, which constitutes the basis of the imaginative faculty, was fused with the vast power of feeling which came from his mother. She had the spirit of the reformer, who is born to set the world right and cannot contemplate with serenity the world as it is. She hungered and thirsted for righteousness whose coming is so slow. So strong was her will, so intense her nature, that she grew impatient with the obstacles in the way. Phillips Brooks knew

[1] Burns, *The Cotter's Saturday Night.*

the facts of life with his father's eyes, and the hopes and possibilities of life through the eyes of his mother. Had he received by transmission only the outlook of his father without the inspired heroism of his mother, he would not have risen to greatness. But, on the other hand, had he inherited from his mother alone, he might have been known as an ardent reformer, not wholly unlike his distinguished kinsman, Wendell Phillips,—a type familiar in New England; but the wonderful fascination of his power for men of every class and degree, the universal appeal to a common humanity, would have been wanting.[1]

II.

IN THE WILDERNESS.

I think he had not heard of the far towns;
Nor of the deeds of men, nor of kings' crowns:
  Before the thought of God took hold of him,
  As he was sitting dreaming in the calm
Of one first noon, upon the desert's rim,
  Beneath the tall fair shadows of the palm,
  All overcome with some strange inward balm.

So wrote the Irish poet, Arthur O'Shaughnessy, of John the Baptist; and so writing he touched two matters which are very important to any man who would understand the desert prophet. The first is that nature had a great share in making him. The sights and sounds of the solitary wilderness were for years familiar to him. The expansive sky above, the pure air to breathe, and all the wide outdoor life of the desert became a part of the very character of John. The physical health which nature gives to those who live on most intimate terms with her was his. The quick eye, the direct and incisive habit of mind, the freedom from all the graceful deceptions of civilization, the rugged, expressive speech which might have been taken fresh from the soil —all these were the contributions of that life in the desert which was a school to John.

1. In the meagreness of the historic record, no mention is made of the occasion on which John definitely left his home and

[1] A. V. G. Allen, *Phillips Brooks: Memories of His Life*, 344.

betook himself to the open country of the southern borderland. But most probably it was on the death of one of his now aged parents. As a Nazirite, he was not to "come near to a dead body." "He shall not make himself unclean," said the Law, "for his father, or for his mother, for his brother, or for his sister, when they die: because his separation unto God is upon his head." And if we suppose that he afterwards returned home, it would be but for the short time his other parent lived, on whose death he, having no near relatives or close personal friends (for he was, and probably always had been, of a solitary habit), and having, moreover, his manner of life shaped out for him, partly by his vow, and partly by those growing thoughts within him which drove him out, would finally leave "the hill country of Judæa." Then he made his dwelling-place far from the homes and haunts of men, among "the deserts and mountains, and dens and caves of the earth."

¶ "Oh, how often, when living in the desert, in that extensive solitude which, dried up by the burning rays of the sun, offered a frightful dwelling-place to the monks, it seemed to me that I was in the midst of the pleasures of Rome." Here in these brief words St. Jerome has revealed to us his abode, bereft of all the comforts which are needed for the miserable life of man! The ground dry and burnt up, without a vestige of verdure, no plants, no trees to afford a shade from the noonday heat. There were no towering cedars, no luxuriant palms, nor stately trees affording fruit, pleasing the eye by their beauty, no running waters, no refreshing streams to cool the air and afford a soothing murmur to the ear, no kind of rest or refreshment—in a word, a desert very much deserted of men. I mean men whose desires go no farther than the earth, yet as such even do not seek so unfertile a land. Here, indeed, did this great man fix his dwelling-place, he who pretends to no one thing of earth. Here did that divine youth imprison himself of his own free will, and here did that clear light of the Church bury the best and most flourishing days of his life, fully resolved upon spending it all here, had Heaven not designed otherwise, and brought him forth for the good of the world to be its great and most brilliant beacon of light. Nevertheless, we might well say that although the body was as a fact in so rough a place, yet the soul was in the enjoyment of supreme delight.[1]

[1] De Sigüenza, *The Life of Saint Jerome* (ed. 1907), 146.

2. Why did John go to the wilderness? Hermits went to the wilderness of Judæa, as Josephus tells us about Banus, who "lived in the desert, and used no other clothing than grew upon trees, and had no other food than grew of its own accord, and bathed himself in cold water frequently." Josephus "imitated him in those things" for three years. Keim thinks that John also led a "hermit life." Certainly he lived a solitary life, but, when he comes forth at last, it is not as a hermit or man of the woods. He did indeed lead "a rural life away from the capital," but it is by no means clear that he was an anchorite, though many of them came to these regions. It has, indeed, been urged that John went into the desert, like Josephus, to study the doctrine of the Essenes, and that he became one. But there is no foundation for this idea. These cenobites had monasteries along the shores of the Dead Sea. They numbered some four thousand in all. The Essenes were an offshoot of Pharisaism with ascetic tendencies concerning animal food, marriage, and animal sacrifices, but with an admixture of the philosophy of Parseeism and Pythagoreanism, including the worship of the sun. But there is no real reason for thinking that John had any contact with them; certainly he did not accept their cardinal tenets about animal food (he ate locusts), or marriage, which he did not condemn, or about sun-worship, which he did not practise. He did practise the ascetic life, as was true of many others not Essenes, but he came forth and lived among men. "He preached the Kingdom of God; they preached isolation. They abandoned society; he strove to reform it."

His predecessor Amos had been a herdsman and a dresser of sycomores in that very region eight centuries before. Like Amos, also, he would meditate upon his high calling better in this wild and desolate region. But John was no mere imitator of anyone. He was *sui generis*, and all the more so because of his grapple with himself in the wilderness. He went apart, not, as the usual monastic does, to gain merit with God, but to face his life problem and to adjust himself to it. His going was "an absolute break with the prevalent Pharisaic type of piety." He went, not to stay, but to get ready to come back, to come back to save his people. But John "learned his lesson at the feet of no human teacher." Reynolds has a fine word: "His education was the memory of his childhood and the knowledge of his commission, and was effected by the Spirit of the living God. His school-masters were the rocks of the desert of Judæa, the solemn waters of the Dead Sea, the eternal Presence that fills the solitudes of nature, the sins, the shame, the vows, the hopes, the professions of his countrymen."

¶ Over against the Baptist's desert and cave stands a contrasted landscape as attractive as the desert is repellent. It is the land-scape of this natural human life, the life which the hand of God made when He made the earth and the creatures, and then made man after His own image and breathed into his clay the breath of life, and bade him dwell on the earth and eat its fruits and have dominion over all its living kinds. The life of man, even as we know it, strangely marred by some malign influence in things that make for famine, and mischance, and pain, and strife, even so has much of beauty and delight and interest in it. Are we not to enjoy this charm and joy? Did not God who made it look on it, and behold it was very good? Why indeed was human life, with its activities, concerns, and pleasures created at all if it was not to be lived, and lived at the best and fullest? Is it not to the glory of God that we men should exercise all our powers of body, although to exercise be also to enjoy; that we should taste all the savours of this earthly existence, perceive with eye and ear its beauty and its music; that we should let the mind range and the passion play, and not be scared from using these energies just because in them there is delight? We look on this landscape of the smiling human life, and the Baptist's desert and cave wear a most grim, squalid, repulsive look, and we cannot believe God meant these places for the residence of the human spirit, or designed that narrowed, starved existence of the ascetic for the life of His children.[1]

3. With his principles fixed by long meditation, John came forth among men (as our Lord said), not a reed shaken with the wind, swayed this way or that by the opinions of others, but firm, even if he should be solitary, in his own opinions; not clothed in soft raiment, but a protest against the luxuriousness that ever threatens to smother our life, and a proclamation that a man's life consists not in the abundance of the things which he possesseth —one who, both by his appearance and by his words, drew men away from conventionalities to what was real and abiding in human life.

[1] J. H. Skrine, *Saints and Worthies*, 47.

His appearance must have been very striking. His hair was long and unkempt, and his features were tanned with the sun and the air of the desert. Probably they were thinned, too, by austerity; for his habitual food was of the simplest order, consisting only of locusts and wild honey. Locusts, dried and preserved, form still, at the present day, an article of food in the East, but only among the very poor; people in the least degree luxurious or scrupulous would not look at it. Wild honey, formed by hives of bees in the crevices of rocks or in rifted trees, abounds in the desert-places of Palestine, and may be gathered by anyone who wanders there. The raiment of the Baptist corresponded with his food, consisting of a garment of the very coarsest and cheapest cloth, made of camel's hair. The girdle of the Oriental is an article of clothing on which a great deal of taste and expense is laid out, being frequently of fine material and gay colouring, with the added adornment of elaborate needlework; but the girdle with which John's garment was confined was no more than a rough band of leather. Everything, in short, about his external appearance denoted one who had reduced the claims of the body to the lowest possible terms, that he might devote himself entirely to the life of the spirit.

¶ Some preachers derive a certain amount of influence from the impression made by their personal appearance. When, as in the case of Chalmers, on the broad and ample forehead there rests the air of philosophic thought, and in the liquid eye there shines the sympathy of a benevolent nature, the goodwill of the congregation is conciliated before the word is uttered. Still more fascinating is the impression when, as in the case of Newman, the stern and emaciated figure suggests the secret fasts and midnight vigils of one who dwells in a hidden world, out of which he comes with a Divine message to his followers.[1]

4. The long silence of the desert was broken by a ringing call of no uncertain sound, the call of one sure of his message, and burning to deliver it. We can see the tall, gaunt figure of the roughly-clad recluse entering one of the scattered hamlets of the borderland, standing like an apparition as he cried out the short, sharp sentence which pierced each of its quiet homes, and penetrated every heart that heard it—"Repent! the kingdom of

[1] J. Stalker, *The Two St. Johns*, 204.

heaven is at hand!" We can see the groups of people too, children in the foreground, flocking round him wonderingly. To them he is a new embodiment of the Law and the Prophets. His "Repent!" is an appeal to the former, a demand for a moral "baring" until the bed-rock is reached upon which Jehovah can build; while his statement that "the kingdom of heaven is at hand" is a re-affirmation of old and cherished prophecies.

(1) "Repentance" is perhaps not the best rendering of the first note of John's message; "conversion" would be a more literal trans-lation. It was for an entire change in the habits of thought and conduct that John called; and this change included not only the forsaking of sin but the seeking of God. Still, the forsaking of sin was very prominent in John's demands; for we are told how pointedly he referred to the favourite sins of different classes.

Nor has repentance in the mind of John to do only with the past, as his anticipations of the New Kingdom are conversant with the future. No: his preaching of repentance has to do with the future, and is full of animation and brightness, from the sight he has of the coming of Jesus Christ. Repentance with him means the personal equipment of the man for taking his part in the construction of this New Kingdom.

> Also of John a calling and a crying
>   Rang in Bethabara till strength was spent,
> Cared not for counsel, stayed not for replying,
>   John had one message for the world, Repent.
>
> John, than which man a sadder or a greater
>   Not till this day has been of woman born,
> John like some iron peak by the Creator
>   Fired with the red glow of the rushing morn.
>
> This when the sun shall rise and overcome it
>   Stands in his shining desolate and bare,
> Yet not the less the inexorable summit
>   Flamed him his signal to the happier air.[1]

(2) The other note of John's preaching was the Kingdom of God. This was not a novel watchword. The ideal of the Jews had always been a theocracy. When Saul, their first king, was

[1] F. W. H. Myers, *Saint Paul.*

appointed, the prophet Samuel condemned the act of the people as a lapse: they ought to have desired no king but God. And when, in subsequent ages, the kings of the land with rare exceptions turned out miserable failures, the better and deeper spirits always sighed for a reign of God, which would ensure national prosperity. The deeper the nation sank, the more passionate grew this aspiration; and, when the good time coming was thought of, it was always in the form of a Kingdom of God.

Alongside the proclamation of the Kingdom was the uncompromising insistence on "*the wrath to come.*" John saw that the advent of the King would bring inevitable suffering to those who were living in self-indulgence and sin. There would be careful discrimination. He who was coming would carefully discern between the righteous and the wicked; between those who served God and those who served Him not; and the preacher enforced his words by an image familiar to Orientals. When the wheat is reaped, it is bound in sheaves and carted to the threshing-floor, which is generally a circular spot of hard ground from fifty to one hundred feet in diameter. On this the wheat is threshed from the chaff by manual labour, but the two lie intermingled till the evening, when the grain is caught up in broad shovels or fans, and thrown against the evening breeze, as it passes swiftly over the fevered land; thus the chaff is borne away, while the wheat falls heavily to the earth. Likewise, cried the Baptist, there shall be a very careful process of discrimination before the unquenchable fires are lighted, so that none but chaff shall be consigned to the flames—a prediction which was faithfully fulfilled.

¶ In considering the wrath of God as always and at all times working with His love, the preaching of John the Baptist is a great assistance. The Jews, even in their most degenerate times, seem to have never doubted that all the tribulation which as a nation they had ever borne was part of that special care and government of God of which they were so justly proud. They acknowledged, not without awe and reverence, that a wrath to come was essentially bound up with their best hopes and their highest aspirations. They were to pass, as a people, through great suffering into noblest exaltation. We, under the Christian dispensation, have throughout our history greatly lost by inadequately realizing that same conception. In regard both of our individual and of our national life, we have even more reason than the Jews ever had to look upon Divine wrath as only the sterner and more solemn aspect of Divine love. "The wrath of God which is revealed from heaven against all ungodliness and unrighteousness of men" (Rom. i. 18) is a principal means whereby, in time or eternity, to bring sinners back to Him, and to prepare the way for the fulness of the Kingdom.[1]

5. His words rang like peals of thunder over the mountains and reverberated down the wadys to the Dead Sea. They echo yet through the centuries, the words of this Voice in the Wilderness. It was mighty preaching that smote the hearts of men. Some were superficial, as always, and the words passed over their heads. Others had only a secular notion of the Kingdom, and began to dream of place and power in that Kingdom. The self-indulgent began to hope for change, for a new king who would destroy the Law and the prophets. The poor and downtrodden would hope for better times somehow. But the devout and deeply spiritual were stirred to the very heart. Men and women talked religion under the trees, by the river brink, on the rocks of the desert, by the roadside, at home. A new day had come to Israel; a real preacher of righteousness had spoken again.

¶ True preaching struggles right away from formula, back into fact, and life, and the revelation of God and heaven. I make no objection to formulas; they are good enough in their place, and a certain instinct of our nature is comforted in having some articulations of results thought out to which our minds may refer. Formulas are the jerked meat of salvation—if not always the strong meat, as many try to think—dry and portable and good to keep, and when duly seethed and softened, and served with needful condiments, just possible to be eaten; but for the matter of living, we really want something fresher and more nutritious. On the whole, the kind of thinking talent wanted for a great preacher is that which piercingly loves; that which looks into things and through them, ploughing up pearls and ores, and now and then a diamond. It will not seem to go on metaphysically or scientifically, but with a certain roundabout sense and vigour. And the people will be gathered to it because there is a gospel fire burning in it that warms them to a glow. This is power.[2]

(1) "Many of the Pharisees and Sadducees" came. These two religious parties disliked one another very much, but they

[1] C. J. Abbey, *The Divine Love*, 17.
[2] Horace Bushnell, *Pulpit Talent*, 187.

are both deserving of John's condemnation. They will later be found working hand in hand to compass the death of Jesus. For the moment they bury their theological differences and rivalry for place and power in the common curiosity about John. By their distinctive dress, their separateness from the multitude among whom they slowly moved ; by the superiority of their demeanour, and by that air of refinement which can come only from culture, although the culture may be narrow both in base and super-structure, the penetrative eye of John singled them out. Like the Master who came after him, he employs terms that are hot and scathing. " O offspring of vipers,—O viperous brood,—who hath warned you to flee from the coming wrath ? " It was bitterly, it was uncourtly,—but oh, it was truly said ! They *were* the off-spring of vipers, for often had their fathers stung to death the benefactors, the saviours, sent from heaven to save the nation ; and soon were the children to show themselves born in the like-ness of their sires, by stinging with persecution and death that greater One whose shoe-latchet he was not worthy to unloose.

(2) While John has been anathematizing Pharisees and Sadducees, various questions have been rising in various minds as to the bearing of the Kingdom upon themselves, and what manner of men they ought to be to enter into it. Did they also come under the lash ? " And the multitudes asked him, saying, What then must *we* do ? " John's answer is plain, direct, and pointed : " He that hath two coats, let him impart to him that hath none ; and he that hath food, let him do likewise."

(3) Then the publicans come with their question : " Teacher, what shall *we* do ? "—by no means an idle question, put for the sake of hearing what kind of an answer the prophet will make in reply, but one that had behind it the sincere purpose of entering the Kingdom, for they came " to be baptized." John's reply to their question was not a summons to Temple service or sacrifice, nor was it ascetic or revolutionary in its tone. " Exact," said he, " no more than is appointed you." Extortion was the fierce temptation of the class. It would have been easier for the publicans to keep all the ritual than radically to change the whole spirit of their lives. He tested sincerity in a manner at once definite and practical. His answer involved no doctrine of human brotherhood or Divine Fatherhood ; it was a dogmatic

appeal to the conscience of men who had laid their ethical sense
to sleep. So they received *their* answer—one so complete and
self-evident that from it there was no appeal.

(4) Then came the soldiers. Apparently careless, but alert,
they move about in small groups among the people, and, coming
near the prophet, break a lance with him: "And what shall
we do?" His reply is personal, not national. The careless
soldiers must have been surprised at its pointedness. Its three
parts were short, sharp home-thrusts—"Do not extort money by
threats or violence from any man." It was not easy for quiet
civilians to resist the demands, although unjust, of trained soldiers,
strong in physique, and without effeminate pity for those from
whom money might be extracted. Mercy, consideration for
such, had but small weight with them. "Do not cheat by false
accusation ; be too honest to act as mere informers ; do not bleed
people's purses by threatening to lay fictitious charges." On the
other hand, "Be content with your pay, and as you agreed to it,
when you went into the service, let it serve you."

This was the style of John's preaching. However various the
classes of people or the types of character, his "exhortation" took
them back to righteousness of conduct, to the first principles
of ordinary morality. There was with him no slight or hasty
dealing with sin ; he required evidences of reform in character, in
"good works."

¶ It was a solemn scene, doubtless, when crowds from every
part of Palestine gathered by the side of Jordan, and there
renewed, as it were, the covenant made between their ancestor
and Jehovah. It seemed the beginning of a new age, the restoration of the ancient theocracy, the final close of that dismal period
in which the race had lost its peculiarity, had taken a varnish of
Greek manners, and had contributed nothing but a few dull
chapters of profane history, filled with the usual chaos of faction
fights, usurpations, royal crimes, and outbreaks, blind and brave,
of patriotism and the love of liberty. But many of those who
witnessed the scene and shared in the enthusiasm which it
awakened must have remembered it in later days as having
inspired hopes which had not been realized. It must have seemed
to many that the theocracy had not in fact been restored, that the
old routine had been interrupted only for a moment, that the
baptized nation had speedily contracted new pollution, and that

no deliverance had been wrought from the "wrath to come." And they may have asked in doubt, Is God so little parsimonious of His noblest gift as to waste upon a doomed generation that which He did not vouchsafe to many nobler generations that had preceded them, and to send a second and far greater Elijah to prophesy in vain?

But if there were such persons, they were ignorant of one important fact. John the Baptist was like the Emperor Nerva. In his career it was given him to do two things—to inaugurate a new régime, and also to nominate a successor who was far greater than himself. And by this successor his work was taken up, developed, completed, and made permanent; so that, however John may have seemed to his own generation to have lived in vain, and scenes on the banks of Jordan to have been the delusive promise of a future that was never to be, at the distance of near two thousand years he appears not less but far greater than he appeared to his contemporaries, and all that his baptism promised to do appears utterly insignificant compared with what it has actually done.[1]

6. The prophets of Israel were poets as well as preachers; and one way in which they displayed their poetical endowment was by the invention of physical symbols to represent the truths which they also expressed in words. Thus, it will be remembered, Jeremiah at one period went about Jerusalem wearing a yoke on his shoulders, in order to impress on his fellow-citizens the certainty that they were to become subject to the Babylonian power; and similar symbolical actions of other prophets will occur to every Bible reader. In the Baptist, ancient prophecy, after centuries of silence, had come to life again; and he demonstrated that he was the true heir of men like Isaiah and Jeremiah by the exercise also of this poetical gift. He embodied his teaching not only in words but in an expressive symbol. And never was symbol more felicitously chosen; for baptism exactly expressed the main drift of his teaching.

It has been well established, in the light of modern research, that John was by no means the originator of the rite of baptism, which has its counterparts in the Greek mysteries, in the religions of India, Persia, Egypt, Asia Minor. The washing of the body with running water expressed by a natural symbolism that cleansing from inward defilement without which there could be

[1] J. R. Seeley, *Ecce Homo*, chap. i.

no access to the Divine Presence. Judaism itself affords several analogies to the rite of baptism. We need instance only the lustrations demanded by the Mosaic law, the ceremonial washings of the Essenes, the purification by water which was part of the ritual employed in the admission of proselytes. It is more than probable that John ascribed a real validity to his baptism, apart from its symbolic meaning. He undoubtedly sought, in the first instance, to effect a moral change, and administered the rite only to those who professed repentance; yet the inward process required to be completed and sealed by the visible rite. When baptism meets us later in the New Testament, as an ordinance of the Christian Church, we find even Paul describing it as a mystery, by which the Spirit is, in some actual sense, imparted. He assumes that this view is shared, in still larger measure, by those whom he addresses; and it probably had attached itself to the rite from the beginning. Ancient religion made little attempt to discriminate between a symbol and its spiritual content. Just as the spoken word was vaguely identified with the person or thing that it designated, so the outward sign was confused with the reality, and was supposed to carry with it a religious worth and power. That a value of this nature was generally attributed to John's baptism may be inferred from the question with which Jesus, at a later day, silenced the priests and elders: "The baptism of John, was it from heaven or of men?" The question, it will be observed, refers to the baptism, not merely to the religious teaching, of John. It would have been meaningless if John had claimed to be nothing more than a preacher of righteousness, enforcing by symbol what he had taught in words. But he had offered his baptism as an actual means of obtaining a certain grace from God; and hence a controversy had arisen as to his sanction and authority.

¶ Baptism, when administered to an adult, is a visible assurance of the same great blessings that it assures to a child. It does not confer on him the blessings of the Christian redemption, but declares that they are his. It is a wonderful gospel—a gospel to him individually. If he has genuine faith he will receive it with immeasurable joy. He will look back upon the day of his baptism as kings look back upon the day of their coronation. It was the visible, external transition from awful peril to eternal safety in the love and power of Christ. It divided his old life in sin from his new life in God. He will speak of the hour when he was "baptized into Christ" (Gal. iii. 27), was "cleansed by the washing of water with the word" (Eph. v. 26), was "buried with [Christ] in baptism" (Rom. vi. 4; Col. ii. 12), and was "raised with him through faith in the working of God, who raised him from the dead" (Col. ii. 12). But kings are not made kings by being crowned; they are crowned because they are already kings: their coronation is only the assurance that the power and greatness of sovereignty are theirs. And it is not by baptism that we are made Christ's inheritance; it is because we are Christ's inheritance that we are baptized.[1]

> I think, perhaps, this trust has sprung
> From one short word
> Said over me when I was young,—
> So young, I heard
> It, knowing not that God's name signed
> My brow, and sealed me His, though blind.[2]

[1] *The Life of R. W. Dale*, 362.   [2] H. H. Jackson.

JOHN THE BAPTIST.

II.

JOHN AND JESUS.

LITERATURE.

Andrews, S. J., *The Life of Our Lord* (1892), 215.

Blakiston, A., *John Baptist and his Relation to Jesus* (1912).

Brooke, S. A., *Sermons Preached in St. James's Chapel*, i. (1873) 148.

Cumming, J. E., *John: The Baptist, Forerunner, and Martyr.*

Davidson, A. B., *The Called of God* (1902), 229.

Dawson, W. J., *The Man Christ Jesus* (1901), 29.

Edersheim, A., *The Life and Times of Jesus the Messiah*, i. (1887) 260, 275.

Farrar, F. W., *The Life of Christ* (1894), 272.

Feather, F., *The Last of the Prophets* (1894).

Ferguson, F., *A Popular Life of Christ* (1878), 79.

Furse, C. W., *The Beauty of Holiness* (1903), 47.

Higginson, E., *Ecce Messias* (1871), 247.

Hough, L. H., *The Men of the Gospels* (1913), 7.

La Farge, J., *The Gospel Story in Art* (1913), 180.

Lange, J. P., *The Life of the Lord Jesus Christ*, ii. (1864) 324.

Lee, F. T., *The New Testament Period and its Leaders* (1913), 56.

Meyer, F. B., *John the Baptist* (1911).

Moberly, R. C., *Christ Our Life* (1902), 106.

Neander, A., *The Life of Jesus Christ* (1880), 213.

Reuss, E., *History of Christian Theology in the Apostolic Age*, i. (1872) 119.

Reynolds, H. R., *John the Baptist* (1872).

Robertson, A. T., *John the Loyal* (1912).

Scott, E. F., *The Kingdom and the Messiah* (1911), 58.

Selwyn, E. C., *The Oracles in the New Testament* (1912), 179.

Simpson, W. J. S., *The Prophet of the Highest* (1895).

Stalker, J., *The Two St. Johns* (1895), 189.

Taylor, W. M., *The Silence of Jesus* (1894), 17.

Vaughan, D. J., *The Present Trial of Faith* (1878), 358.

Whyte, A., *Bible Characters*: Joseph and Mary to James (1900), 26.

Baptist Review and Expositor, xi. (1914) 41 (W. Lock).

Catholic Encyclopædia, viii. (1910) 486 (C. L. Souvay).

Dictionary of the Bible, ii. (1899) 677 (Ll. J. M. Bebb).

    ,,   ,,   ,,   (Single-volume, 1909), 474 (J. G. Tasker).

Dictionary of Christ and the Gospels, i. (1906) 861 (J. C. Lambert).

Encyclopædia Biblica, ii. (1900), col. 2498 (T. K. Cheyne).

Expository Times, xii. (1901) 312 (J. Reid); xv. (1904) 5; xviii. (1906) 193 (R. H. Kennett).

Lay Sermons from the Spectator (1909), 8.

Smith's Dictionary of the Bible, i. (1893) 1736 (E. Hawkins).

JOHN AND JESUS.

And this is the witness of John, when the Jews sent unto him from Jerusalem priests and Levites to ask him, Who art thou? And he confessed, and denied not; and he confessed, I am not the Christ. And they asked him, What then? Art thou Elijah? And he saith, I am not. Art thou the prophet? And he answered, No. They said therefore unto him, Who art thou? that we may give an answer to them that sent us. What sayest thou of thyself? He said, I am the voice of one crying in the wilderness, Make straight the way of the Lord, as said Isaiah the prophet.—John i. 19-23.

1. FROM ancient times it has been the custom with Oriental monarchs, when about to travel through any part of their dominions, to send heralds before them to announce their coming and to see that the roadways over which they were to pass were in order. All obstacles had to be removed, and rough places made smooth. If no roadway existed, one had to be made, even if it required the filling of valleys and the levelling of hills and mountains. In this way an easy and pleasant highway was provided for the royal travellers. This custom is alluded to in Is. xl. 3, 4: "The voice of one that crieth, Prepare ye in the wilderness the way of Jehovah; make level in the desert a high way for our God. Every valley shall be exalted, and every mountain and hill shall be made low; and the uneven shall be made level, and the rough places a plain." In the New Testament this passage is applied to John the Baptist as the herald or forerunner of the Messiah.

John himself originated the idea that he was the forerunner of the Messiah, the voice crying in the wilderness, for he quoted Is. xl. 3 to the embassy from Jerusalem, and applied it to himself. It is possible that in Matt. iii. 3 also we have the language of John, but it is more probable that it is that of the Evangelist. All four Gospels thus bear witness to this "primitive interpretation" that John is the forerunner described by Isaiah.

(1) We know that the Jewish people as a whole were not

prepared to receive Jesus as their Saviour; for they rejected and crucified Him. Still, much was done by the testimony of John. At the very last, when the enmity of the scribes and Pharisees was at its highest, we find they dared not insinuate that the baptism of John was not from heaven but of men,—because all the people held John for a prophet. Now what a vast advantage it must have given the early preachers of the gospel, to have had to do with a people who held John for a prophet! For John's testimony to Jesus was matter of notoriety. Our Lord appeals to it, in the face of the Jews themselves. How easy to lead on any candid mind from belief in John to belief in Jesus! And consequently we find, when the Church assembled to fill up the place of the traitor Judas, St. Peter specifying, as the qualification of a candidate for the Apostleship, that he must have companied with them all the time that the Lord Jesus went in and out among them, "beginning from the baptism of John." Again, in the only detailed sermon of St. Paul to Jews in their synagogue, we have him distinctly appealing to the testimony of John among the proofs of the Messiahship of our Lord.

(2) And if John thus prepared the way by witnessing to Jesus in person, he also prepared many of the children of Israel in spirit to receive the message of life by Him. In such an age of worldliness and hypocrisy, to hear " there is a prophet among us," to see once more the garb of Elijah in the desert, to hear once more that voice, clear as when it rang among the cliffs of Carmel, " How long halt ye between two opinions ? "—that must have gone into the depths of many a heart in Israel, and called up again the almost forgotten presence of Israel's covenant God. And then, when they stood and listened to the wonderful messenger of repentance, how the words of their old prophets, long wrapped in the napkin of formalism, and heard muffled through the drawl of the scribe in the synagogue, must have leapt out into life, and gone right to their hearts !

And again, when, confessing their sins, they were baptized by John in Jordan, must we not believe that many of those thousands who received the outward rite became deeply humbled within ? that many reeds were bruised, whom the Redeemer came not to break but to heal ? And if John was made the discloser of pain that he could not assuage, the discoverer of burdens that he could not remove, for whom was this a preparation but for Him who cried, "Come unto me, all ye that labour and are heavy laden, and I will give you rest"?

¶ John the Baptist is the supreme example of a general law; of the fact that all great changes in the worlds of spirit and of thought have their forerunners; minds which perceive the first significant movement, the sword of the spirit stirring in its sheath, long before the new direction is generally perceived or understood. John was a "prophet"—that is to say, a spiritual genius—with that intuitive knowledge of the immediate tendencies of life often found in those who are possessed of an instinct for Transcendent Reality. The span of a great mind, a great personality, gathers up into its "Now," and experiences "all at once," a number of smaller rhythms or moments which are separate experiences for lesser men. As we, in our wide rhythm of perception, gather up the countless small and swift vibrations of the physical world and weld them into sound or light; so the spiritual genius gathers up into his consciousness of a wide present, countless little tendencies and events. By this synthetic act he transcends the storm of succession, and attains a prophetic vision, which seems to embrace future as well as past. He is plunged in the stream of life, and feels the way in which it tends to move. Such a mind discerns, though he may not understand, the coming of a change long before it can be known by other men; and, trying to communicate his certitude, becomes a " prophet " or a " seer." [1]

2. John is not only called Christ's forerunner; he is also spoken of as Elijah. In what sense was he Elijah? Everything in him recalled the great prophet of action. Elijah did not write a single page in the Book of God; his book was himself, his prophecy was his life; it was enough for him to appear, to call up before degenerate Israel the living image of holiness. There runs a real parallel between the careers of the two men. It is strikingly put by Edersheim. "John came suddenly out of the wilderness of Judæa, as Elijah from the wilds of Gilead. John bore the same ascetic appearance as his predecessor; the message of John was the counterpart of that of Elijah; his baptism that of Elijah's novel rite on Carmel." It is true that John pointedly disclaimed being Elijah; but what he denied was the exaggerated expectations of the people, not the real promise of the prophet. Indeed, it was probably some word of John about this very matter

[1] E. Underhill, *The Mystic Way*, 83.

that had led the Sanhedrin to make this inquiry, a word which had been misunderstood and which John now bluntly corrects. Jesus expressly says that John was the real fulfilment of the prophecy, he was the Elijah that was to come; he was to come in the spirit and power of Elijah, as Gabriel had said. That is all that ever was meant, but it had been grossly misunderstood again.

¶ If we except Moses, who was the real founder of the nation, there is no man in Jewish history whose fame stands so high as Elijah's. What story is there so thrilling, so impressive, at times so overwhelmingly dramatic, as the story of this Bedouin of the desert, sweeping down in fire and thunder from the caves of Carmel, to subdue kings and terrify a whole people into submission by the force of a single imperious will? The very name of Elijah is to this day terrible in the East; never was there memory so potent and implacable. The manner of his removal from the earth added to the superstitious awe which clothed his name. He was believed not to have died; to have vanished from the earth only to halt upon some dim borderland between life and death, ready to reappear at any time; to have become a supernatural man, who might return, and assuredly would return in his chariot of flame, when some great national crisis called for him. Such legends are common; they are associated with King Arthur, and even with Sir Francis Drake. It is a curious testimony to man's inherent conviction of immortality, that he finds it difficult to believe that a great hero is really dead. But to the Jew, the sense of Elijah's real presence in the national life, his incompleted work upon the national destiny, was not so much a legend as a creed. It was an impassioned belief, increasing in vehemence as the times grew darker. The deeper the despair and impotence of the nation the more eager became the hope that Elijah would return. He would surely come again and smite the house of Herod as he had smitten the house of Ahab. The desert would once more travail in strange birth, and from it would come the redeeming Titan.[1]

¶ From the time that the Jewish nation had begun to reflect upon its destiny with a kind of despair, the imagination of the people had reverted with much complacency to the ancient prophets. Now, of all the personages of the past, the remembrance of whom came like the dreams of a troubled night to awaken and agitate the people, the greatest was Elias. This giant of the prophets, in his rough solitude of Carmel, sharing the life

[1] W. J. Dawson, *The Man Christ Jesus*, 32.

of savage beasts, dwelling in the hollows of the rocks, whence he came like a thunderbolt, to make and unmake kings, had become, by successive transformations, a sort of superhuman being, sometimes visible, sometimes invisible, and as one who has not tasted death. It was generally believed that Elias would return and restore Israel. The austere life which he had led, the terrible remembrances he had left behind him,—the impression of which is still powerful in the East,—the sombre image which, even in our own times, causes trembling and death,—all this . . . vividly struck the mind of the people, and stamped as with a birth-mark all the creations of the popular mind. Whoever aspired to act powerfully upon the people must imitate Elias; and, as solitary life had been the essential characteristic of this prophet, they were accustomed to conceive "the man of God" as a hermit. They imagined that all the holy personages had had their days of penitence, of solitude, and of austerity. The retreat to the desert thus became the condition and the prelude of high destinies.[1]

I.

JOHN'S BAPTISM OF JESUS.

To Jesus, in His obscure and humble home, the thrill which passed through every section of society at the voice of the Baptist, and the appearance of a true man among the ignoble shadows and self-satisfied hypocrisies, came as a sign from His Heavenly Father that the time had arrived for His manifestation to the world. For now, by John's work as an avowed forerunner, the long-slumbering hope was aroused, and "with mighty billows the Messianic movement surged through the entire people."

In going to listen to the preaching of John, our Lord doubtless followed that inward guidance which was the supreme law of His life. He offered Himself for baptism. The full meaning of this act is beyond our apprehension. The baptism of John was no mere Essene or Levitical ablution. It was accompanied with the confession of sins. It was not "a laver of regeneration" (Tit. iii. 5), but "a baptism of repentance." It was a sign that a man desired to cleanse himself from moral defile-

[1] Renan, *The Life of Jesus*, chap. vi.

ment, to abandon all righteousness of his own, and "to draw near" unto God "in full assurance of faith, having his heart sprinkled from an evil conscience, and his body washed with pure water." How, then, could it be accepted by the Divine and sinless Son of Man? To others—but not to Him—could have been applied the words of Ezekiel, "Then will I sprinkle clean water upon you, and ye shall be clean." All that we know is what the Gospels tell us. We see that the stern prophet, who was no respecter of persons but had dared to address scribes and Pharisees in words of scornful denunciation, was overawed before the innate majesty of the Son of God. This new Elijah, in his shaggy robe of camel's hair, with its coarse leathern girdle—this ascetic dweller in the deserts—this herald whose voice rang with sternest rebukes to startle drowsy souls, and stir them to repentance—is at once hushed into timidity at the presence of the Lord of Love. So far from welcoming the acknowledgment of his ministry by one whom he instinctively recognized as his Lord, he made an earnest and continuous effort to prevent Him from accepting his baptism. He even said, "I have need to be baptized of *thee*, and comest *thou* to *me*?" But the only explanation given to us is in the words of our Lord Himself. He overcame John's hesitating scruples by saying, "Suffer it to be so now: for thus it becometh us to fulfil all righteousness." "He placed the confirmation of perfect righteousness," says St. Bernard, "in perfect humility."

Everyone who accepted baptism at the hands of John accepted it in its general meaning and purpose, and applied it to his own spiritual condition. In fact, he would accept it in no other way. And there must have been a variety of spiritual conditions as great as the individual cases that presented themselves. To some the meaning of the rite would be a strong but diffused desire with vague ideas; to others, material and social progress and national aggrandizement would loom the largest; while to others, again, the spiritual would be the most prominent part of the conception. We cannot reduce all the adherents of new movements to the same unbroken level of spiritual nature or expectation. And many a man who attaches himself to such movements does so accepting the general *motif*, but by no means pledging himself to every tenet and position.

How didst thou start, thou Holy Baptist, bid
 To pour repentance on the Sinless Brow!
Then all thy meekness, from thy hearers hid,
 Beneath the Ascetic's port, and Preacher's fire,
Flow'd forth, and with a pang thou didst desire
 He might be chief, not thou.

And so on us at whiles it falls, to claim
 Powers that we dread, or dare some forward part;
Nor must we shrink as cravens from the blame
 Of pride, in common eyes, or purpose deep;
But with pure thoughts look up to God, and keep
 Our secret in our heart.[1]

1. Of the intercourse of John with Jesus the Fourth Gospel
gives an account which differs widely from that presented in
the Synoptics; but, apart from the Johannine colouring of the
later narrative, the difference is sufficiently explained on
the ordinary view that the Synoptists describe the meeting
between the two at the time of our Lord's baptism, while the
Fourth Evangelist concerns himself only with John's subsequent
testimony to the now recognized Messiah (cf. John i. 7 f.). There
is no real discrepancy between John's, "I knew him not," reported
in the Fourth Gospel (i. 31), and the representation of Matthew
(iii. 13 ff.) that, when the Man from Nazareth presented Himself
at the Jordan, John declined at first to baptize Him, on the
ground of his own unworthiness in comparison. Even if we
suppose that, in spite of their kinship and the friendship between
their mothers, the two had not met before, the fact that John's
baptism was a baptism of repentance and confession seems to
imply a personal interview with applicants previous to the
performance of the rite—an interview which in the case of
Jesus must have revealed to one with the Baptist's insight the
beauty and glory of His character. On the other hand, the "I
knew him not" of the last Gospel, as the context shows, means
only that John did not know that Jesus was indeed the Messiah
until he received the promised sign.

2. All the Evangelists unite in telling us that Jesus, as soon
as He was baptized, went straightway up out of the water, as

[1] J. H. Newman.

MARY—SIMON—6

if to intimate that it was chiefly for others, and not from any
personal necessity, that He had submitted to the rite. Luke tells
us that as He ascended the shelving bank of the Jordan our
Lord was engaged in prayer. We need not be surprised at
this fact. On his ordination day a minister of the Gospel, if
he enters at all into the spirit of the ceremony, will be in a
praying frame from morning to night. How much more, then,
would we expect this "Minister of the sanctuary, which the Lord
pitched and not man," to be found in a Jacob-like wrestling of
spirit on the occasion of His baptismal ordination

What was Christ's prayer ? Edersheim says that one prayer,
the only one which He taught His disciples, recurs to our minds.
We must here individualize and emphasize in their special application its opening sentences: "Our Father which art in heaven,
Hallowed be thy name. Thy kingdom come. Thy will be done
in earth, as it is in heaven." The first thought and the first
petition had been the conscious outcome of the Temple-visit,
ripened during the long years at Nazareth. The others were now
the full expression of His submission to baptism. He knew His
mission; He had consecrated Himself to it in His baptism:
"Father which art in heaven, Hallowed be thy name." The
unlimited petition for the doing of God's will on earth with the
same absoluteness as in heaven, *was* His self-consecration—the
prayer of His baptism, as the other was its confession. And the
"hallowed be thy name" was the eulogy, because the ripened and
experimental principle of His life. *How* this will, connected with
"the kingdom," was to be done by Him, and *when,* He was to
learn *after* His baptism. But it is strange that the petition
following those which must have been on the lips of Jesus in
that hour should have been the subject of the *first temptation* or
assault by the Enemy; strange also that the other two temptations should have rolled back the force of the assault upon the
two great experiences which He had gained, and which formed the
burden of the petitions, "Hallowed be thy name. Thy kingdom
come." Was it then so, that all the assaults which Jesus bore
concerned and tested the reality only of a past and already
attained experience, save those last in the Garden and on
the Cross, which were "sufferings" by which He "was made
perfect"?

3. As the prayer of Jesus winged heavenwards, His solemn response to the call of the Kingdom—"Here am I"; 'Lo, I come to do thy will"—the answer came, which at the same time was also the predicted sign to the Baptist. Heaven seemed cleft, and, in bodily shape like a dove, the Holy Ghost descended on Jesus, remaining on Him. The Jewish imagination, fastening on that passage in the first chapter of the Book of Genesis which speaks of "the Spirit of God brooding upon the face of the waters," according to the Rabbinical comment, "like a dove hovering over its young," loved to figure the Spirit as a dove. And there was another idea which had lodged itself in the minds of the later Jews. The voice of prophecy was mute, and men, longing to hear the silence broken, and remembering perhaps how their poets in old days had styled the thunder the Voice of Jehovah, persuaded themselves that ever and anon God spoke from Heaven, sending forth at perplexing crises what they called *Bath Kol*, the Daughter of a Voice.

Being a child of his age and people, the Baptist shared those ideas, and God employed them to reveal the Messiah to him. As Jesus after His baptism stood praying on the river bank, "Lo, the heavens were opened unto him, and he saw the Spirit of God descending as a dove, and coming upon him; and lo, a voice out of the heavens, saying, This is my beloved Son, in whom I am well pleased." It was a distinct attestation of His Messiahship, since "the Son of God" was a Jewish title for the Messiah. The vision was seen and the voice was heard by Jesus and by John, and by no others. Even so it was when the Lord manifested Himself after the Resurrection: His glorified body was invisible to the eye of sense, and only those perceived Him who were endowed with the gift of spiritual vision. Jesus and John were thus enlightened, and they beheld the vision and heard the voice, while the multitude saw nothing and heard nothing. It was fitting that it should happen thus. For them alone was the revelation designed—for Jesus, that He might know that His hour had come, and for John, that he might recognize the Messiah.

¶ If this vision were objective, would it not mark a new departure in the method by which Jehovah communed with His servants the prophets? The "voice of the Lord," or the "word of God," *came* to them and spoke in their exalted, inspired, and sensitized consciousness. It was "a conviction of surprising force and intensity"; and when it was a message for the people, it became, by thought and communion with God, at length too great and strong for retention, and burst forth in "Thus saith the Lord." Moses and all the prophets heard, believed, and obeyed these voices and uttered their messages, as the slightest examination of the records would amply show; and had they been objective, open to the eyes and ears of all and sundry, they must seriously have militated against the prophets' sacredness, their separateness of office and function as Jehovah's representatives and heralds. Micaiah said to the king of Israel: "I saw the Lord sitting on his throne, and all the host of heaven standing by him on his right hand and on his left." In like manner, Isaiah declares: "I saw the Lord sitting upon a throne, high and lifted up, and his train filled the temple. Above him stood the seraphim,"—and the prophet goes on to describe the scene in the heaven that is at once the throne-room and the temple. No one seriously considers that these visions, and others like them, existed anywhere else save in the inspired consciousness and sublime imagination of the prophets themselves. This is placed beyond doubt by the vision of Stephen at his martyrdom. Surrounded by his persecutors, he declared he saw the heavens opened, and Jesus standing on the right hand of God. Not when they saw the vision, but when they heard the testimony, they cried out, and stopped their ears, and ran upon him with one accord and stoned him. Stephen alone saw it. We cannot but conclude, then, that the vision of John and Jesus was subjective.[1]

¶ Matthew and Mark made clear the subjective nature of the vision by saying, "*He* saw the Spirit of God descending," and "*He* saw an opening in the sky." Moreover, the words of the message are compounded of two texts from the Hebrew Scriptures, suddenly heard within the mind and invested with a special meaning and authority. They are instances of audition, of the "distinct interior words" whereby the spiritual genius commonly translates his intense intuition of the transcendent into a form with which his surface mind can deal. The machinery of this whole experience is in fact natural and human machinery, which has been used over and over again in the course of the spiritual history of mankind.[2]

> And once again I saw him, in latter days
> Fraught with a deeper meaning, for he came
> To my baptizing, and the infinite air
> Blushed on his coming, and all the earth was still;

[1] J. Feather.   [2] E. Underhill, *The Mystic Way*, 87.

Gently he spake; I answered; God from heaven
Called, and I hardly heard him, such a love
Streamed in that orison from man to man.
Then shining from his shoulders either-way
Fell the flood Jordan, and his kingly eyes
Looked in the east, and star-like met the sun.
Once in no manner of similitude,
And twice in thunderings and thrice in flame,
The Highest ere now hath shown him secretly;
But when from heaven the visible Spirit in air
Came verily, lighted on him, was alone,
Then knew I, then I said it, then I saw
God in the voice and glory of a man.[1]

II.

JOHN'S TESTIMONY TO JESUS.

The culmination of the Baptist's personal experience was
reached when, standing in the water of Jordan, he saw and heard
the signs with which the baptism of Jesus was accompanied.
But he had still a great work to do in bearing testimony to the
Messiah. There are three recorded occasions on which he did so
—the first when a deputation was sent to him from Jerusalem
by the Jewish authorities; the second when he pointed Jesus
out to his own disciples as the Messiah; and the third when he
rebuked the attempt of his disciples to stir up rivalry between
Jesus and himself. And on each of these occasions John not
only bore conscious witness to Christ, but at the same time
unconsciously revealed his own character.

1. Farrar is very precise as to the time of the embassy, fixing
it "the day previous to our Lord's return from the wilderness."
That is possible, of course, if Jesus came directly to Bethany,
where John was now baptizing. The location of this Bethany
beyond Jordan is unknown. It was somewhere on the eastern
side of the river, probably about half-way between the Dead Sea
and the Sea of Galilee. We do not at all know that John had
remained in the same place during the forty days while Jesus was

[1] F. W. H. Myers, *Saint John the Baptist.*

in the wilderness. It is more than probable that John had kept moving up the river, having crossed over to the eastern side.

The "priests and Levites" who formed the deputation were the Temple dignitaries, regarded by all, and regarding themselves, as custodians of the Law and all matters religious. They were the ecclesiastics of their time, who, in their narrow conscientiousness, were sent to know who the prophet really professed to be, and what his mission was. There is no need to assume that they had prejudged him and sought only his condemnation, though the Pharisees who sent them still smarted under the castigation they had received from him in the face of the people. Probably the whole of them would be ready to welcome him, and to sanction his movement, if they could be satisfied of his credentials.

There was a profound silence, and men craned their necks and strained their ears to see and hear everything, as the deputation challenged the prophet with the inquiry, "Who art thou?" There was a great silence. Men were prepared to believe anything of the eloquent young preacher. "The people were in expectation, and all men reasoned in their hearts concerning John, whether haply he were the Christ." If he had given the least encouragement to their dreams and hopes, they would have unfurled again the tattered banner of the Maccabees; and beneath his leadership would have swept, like a wild hurricane, against the Roman occupation, gaining, perhaps, a momentary success, which afterwards would have been wiped out in blood. "And he confessed, and denied not; and he confessed, I am not the Christ."

If a murmur of voices burst out in anger, disappointment, and chagrin, as this answer spread from lip to lip, it was immediately hushed by the second inquiry propounded, "What then? Art thou Elijah?" (alluding to the prediction of Malachi iv. 5). If they had worded their question rather differently, and put it thus, "Hast thou come in the power of Elijah?" John must have acknowledged that it was so; but if they meant to inquire if he were literally Elijah returned again to this world, he had no alternative but to say, decisively and laconically, "I am not."

There was a third arrow in their quiver, since the other two had missed the mark; and amid the deepening attention of the listening multitudes, and in allusion to Moses' prediction that

God would raise up a prophet like to himself (Deut. xviii. 15; Acts iii. 22, vii. 37), they said, "Art thou the prophet?" and he answered, "No."

(1) Observe the *simplicity* of John's answer. "He confessed, and denied not." He was not thinking about himself, except as one of manifold things in God's world. So when they asked him about himself, he answered just as he would about anything else, outside of himself, on which they questioned him. He thought neither too much nor too little about himself. So when his own disciples got into trouble with the Jews, he gave no opinion, as we should say, but answered so simply—"A man can receive nothing, except it be given him from heaven."

¶ It is a good rule, "If anything comes to your mind which seems a good answer to anything you don't like, suppress it." There is sure to be something of self in it. It is pride putting down pride.[1]

(2) Then its *clear-sightedness*. He knew at once what he was, and what he was not. "He confessed, and denied not." Is not our trouble often that we do *not* know? And this haziness, is it a moral or an intellectual defect? Is it want of luminous judgment? or is it a double-mindedness? Certain it is that there are few notes of character more evident than this clear sight. It is like the purity of a child's vision in matters of conscience: knowledge without the trouble of thought, intuition, the action of light, quick, instantaneous, delicate, irresistible, and pure.

¶ The seer, what is he? Is he not just the man who sees deeper than others, more clearly than others; sees right into the heart of things, into the essential equality of being; one who, from an accurate knowledge of the great spiritual forces at work in the world, can predict how they will act, and what results will come from this action? This it is which has made the prophets —the true ones—the great moral authorities of the world. . . . Their insight, you may say, was a scientific one. It was the result of a true diagnosis. Just as the modern researcher, probing and testing the qualities of radium, can give his forecast of what it is to accomplish, so the prophet, the moral genius, whether he lived three thousand years ago or is among us to-day, predicts

[1] *Spiritual Letters of E. B. Pusey*, 72.

what the spiritual will do from his knowledge of what it contains.[1]

(3) Look in the third place at the *disinterestedness* of the Baptist's answer. He emptied himself into the fulness of Christ. All colour of self, deep-dyed as it was in the intensely characteristic life of the desert, was quenched in the burning light of his Lord. There was nothing in him of his own. "I am the voice of one crying in the wilderness, Make straight the way of the Lord, as said Isaiah the prophet." A voice—not a word; a voice crying only because God had foretold that it should cry; a voice crying in the wilderness, needing no audience; enough if it be heard by God and accepted as the true echo of His own word; a voice careless whether or not it make present impressions; a voice going out into the future, foretelling the mind of the Eternal, who is and is to come.

¶ In a sermon that he preached in Union Chapel on the Sunday that concluded the fortieth year of his ministry there, he insisted that the preacher's business was not to establish a set of theological principles or to proclaim simply a morality, but to proclaim a living Person and a historical fact. He frequently referred to John the Baptist's answer to the question "Who art thou?" "I am a voice," as being the model for all time. Most truly he took to himself the advice he gave: "We must efface ourselves if we would proclaim Christ."[2]

2. It may have been whilst Jesus was away in the wilderness, into which He plunged immediately after His baptism, to endure the forty days' temptation, that the deputation from Jerusalem came to John. It is easy to conceive that, after so unique and prolonged an experience as Jesus had passed through in the wilderness, there may have been in His aspect something unusually impressive; and, when He came suddenly again into the circle where the Baptist was standing, the first look at Him sent through the forerunner's soul a revealing shock; whereupon, with outstretched finger pointed to Him, he cried, "Behold the Lamb of God, which taketh away the sin of the world."

One stood among the people whom they knew not; but John knew and perceived features of the glory which was veiled from

[1] J. Brierley, *Faith's Certainties*, 85.
[2] Dr. McLaren of Manchester, 211.

others. He saw the beauty which the scribe and Pharisee neither saw nor desired. What were these features?

(1) He recognized *the purity of Christ's humanity.*—"Behold," he said, "the Lamb." Whatever else may be signified in this phrase, and the phrase has many meanings, none can doubt that the idea of the blamelessness and spotlessness of Christ's character is suggested; the notion is drawn from the paschal lamb, the lamb which must be "without blemish and without spot." When, then, John the Baptist, looking with loving regard upon Christ as He walked, said, "Behold the Lamb of God" (whatever anticipations of sacrifice might pass through his mind), he seems at that moment to be occupied chiefly with the thought of the beauty and the purity of Christ's character. If John's knowledge of our Lord began in early life, then we must suppose that the unsullied character of Christ, known to the Baptist through so many years, at last forces upon his mind the thought that this pure humanity is a revelation of something Divine. But in any case, John recognizes the moral beauty and dignity of our Lord when he counts it fitting to describe Him as the Lamb of God.

¶ In his conception of Christ the humanity was the thing on which Denny laid chief stress. He did not intrude into the region of dogmatic theology either in a heterodox or in an orthodox interest; but I think he would have agreed, at least substantially, with the opening words of Hinton's "Law-breakers": "If I believe that Christ is Divine, that is of no moment. We all wish to know what *man* He was."[1]

(2) He recognized *His pure Divinity.*—Think for a moment of that token of Divine anointing of which John spoke. "Upon whomsoever thou shalt see the Spirit descending, and abiding upon him, the same is he that baptizeth with the Holy Spirit." The advent of this Divine anointing, the sign of the Spirit descending like a dove, came within the range of John's experience. Whatever the historical circumstances connected with this descent of the Spirit may have been, the ethical meaning surely is clear. John recognized in Christ more than the mere purity of a beautiful human character; he recognized the fire of that Divine life which glowed within Him. He saw, too, that that fire was not a fire to glow unused upon the altar of Christ's manhood, but was destined

[1] A. B. Bruce, *Life of William Denny*, 282.

to be a kindling fire setting aflame the hearts of men and purifying the order of the world. He was not only anointed with the Holy Ghost, He was also destined to baptize the world with the Holy Ghost and with fire.

¶ Christ either deceived mankind by conscious fraud, or He was Himself deluded and self-deceived, or He was Divine. There is no getting out of this trilemma. It is inexorable.[1]

(3) He recognized *the work of Christ as one of suffering and love.*—He not only said, "Behold the Lamb of God," but he said, "the Lamb which taketh away the sin of the world." It is difficult to believe that the prophecy of Isaiah was not in his mind. If so, and we can hardly doubt it, the whole range of that wondrous prophecy is gathered up in the utterances of John the Baptist; and in his view Christ was "the servant of the Lord" who was to "see of the travail of his soul" and was to "be satisfied." He was One upon whose life was to fall sorrow, and yet in whose sorrow the world was to find life. He was to accomplish the reconciliation which should make the world glad. He was to achieve that work which would inaugurate among men a new era of love and a noble principle of sacrifice.

¶ That by the title "the Lamb of God" the Baptist meant only to designate Jesus as a person full of gentleness and innocence is out of the question. The second clause forbids this. He is the Lamb that takes away sin. And there is only one way in which a lamb can take away sin, and that is, by sacrifice. The expression no doubt suggests the picture in the fifty-third of Isaiah of the servant of Jehovah meekly enduring wrong. But unless the Baptist had been previously speaking of this chapter, the thoughts of his disciples would not at once turn to it, because in that passage it is not a lamb of sacrifice that is spoken of, but a lamb meekly enduring. In the Baptist's words sacrifice is the primary idea, and it is needless to discuss whether he was thinking of the paschal lamb or the lamb of morning and evening sacrifice, because he merely used the lamb as the representative of sacrifice generally. Here, he says, is the reality to which all sacrifice has pointed, the Lamb of God.[2]

3. John was but a herald voice; and his work was but a symbol. He but drew diagrams to suggest the realities that were

---

[1] John Duncan, *Colloquia Peripatetica*, 109.
[2] Marcus Dods, *The Gospel of St. John*, i. 46.

coming. Water will wash the body, but it will not purify the spirit. The spirit is like a precious metal, from which water will run off, leaving all its impurities and dross still there. The spirit must be baptized with fire, suffused with heat, penetrated, even melted, with the fire of God, that it may be cleansed; and He who would thus set aglow the spirit of man was at hand. Thus John, in the midst of his popularity, remained unaffected. He passed through all its temptations unchanged. But it began to appear that his day was over. People wearied of him. The fashion changed. The thunder and the earthquake had lost their terrors. Men revenged themselves upon him for the terrors he had caused them, and because he brought them to their knees, by ridiculing him and his manner. They had recovered from the fright he gave them, and they vented their dislike in mockery. John came neither eating nor drinking, and they said he had a devil. "The man," they said, "is touched in the head, and why mind him?" They forsook him. Another voice had begun to be heard, a still small voice; and some found it had a greater charm than the thunder of John's, and they flocked to listen to its gentle tones.

It was a trying hour for John; and there were some who rubbed the salt into the wound. Whether they were sympathizers, or candid friends, or busybodies pleased to make mischief, it is hard to say. "Rabbi," said they, "he that was with thee beyond Jordan, to whom thou barest witness, behold, the same baptizeth; and all men come to him." Professional jealousy is said to breed the deadliest rancour known; when one hears praise bestowed on another of the same cloth, it is said to run through the veins like poison. John heard the words that told him that his sun was setting, and that a brighter star had risen on the horizon, and he answered not with chagrin, but with joy: "A man can receive nothing, except it be given him from heaven. He must increase, but I must decrease." Surely nothing greater or nobler was ever said. A man has nothing except it be given him of God. What I have, God has given me. What my professional brother has, God has given him. If he can alleviate human pain and distress with more skill than I, it is from God he has the gift; if he can speak to men's consciences with greater power than I, it is of God. A spark of goodness or power from God animates us all. It is God in us. Let us see God in each other, and rejoice.

¶ By far the very best thing that the Baptist ever said or did was what he said to his jealous disciples: "A man can receive nothing," he said, "except it be given him from heaven. He that hath the bride is the bridegroom. He must increase, but I must decrease." I would rather have had the grace from God to say that than have been the greatest man ever born of woman. For he who thinks, and says, and does a thing like that is born, not of blood, nor of the will of the flesh, nor of the will of man, but of God.[1]

¶ Perhaps the secret of Father Stanton's success as a preacher is told in the advice he once gave to all his fellow-preachers, and most steadily followed in his own ministry: "Remember, our Lord and Saviour Jesus Christ has made you fishers of men, and a good fisher keeps himself well out of sight. Let your Master be always to the fore and yourself in the background. Then, when the time comes for you to go behind the scenes, and for others to take your place, you will be comforted by the words of the greatest among men of all the preachers, *Illum oportet crescere, me autem minui.*"[2]

¶ Writing of the festival of the Nativity of John the Baptist, which is celebrated on June 24th, Baring-Gould says: "A mystical signification may have attached to the position of this day in the kalendar. For in the months of June and December are the solstices,—with the first, the days decrease, with the latter they increase. In connection with this the words of the Baptist, 'He must increase, but I must decrease,' acquire a new and fanciful significance. S. Augustine says: 'At the nativity of Christ the days increase in length, on that of John they decrease. When the Saviour of the world is born, the days lengthen; but when the last prophet comes into the world, the days suffer curtailment.'"[3]

[1] A. Whyte.
[2] J. Clayton, *Father Stanton of St. Alban's, Holborn,* 83.
[3] S. Baring-Gould, *The Lives of the Saints* (ed. 1898), vi. 332.

JOHN THE BAPTIST.

III.

JOHN AND HEROD.

LITERATURE.

Andrews, S. J., *The Life of Our Lord* (1892), 276.
Carpenter, W. B., *The Son of Man among the Sons of Men* (1893), 235.
Clow, W. M., *The Secret of the Lord* (1910), 255.
Cumming, J. E., *John: The Baptist, Forerunner, and Martyr.*
Davidson, A. B., *The Called of God* (1902), 229.
Dawson, W. J., *The Man Christ Jesus* (1901), 29.
Edersheim, A., *The Life and Times of Jesus the Messiah,* i. (1887) 654.
Farrar, F. W., *The Life of Lives* (1900), 227.
Feather, J., *The Last of the Prophets* (1894).
Ferrier, J. T., *The Master: His Life and Teachings* (1913), 65.
Furse, C. W., *The Beauty of Holiness* (1903), 47.
Greenhough, J. G., in *Men of the New Testament*: Matthew to Timothy (1905), 71.
Higginson, E., *Ecce Messias* (1871), 247.
Holtzmann, O., *The Life of Jesus* (1904), 127.
Lange, J. P., *The Life of the Lord Jesus Christ,* iii. 98, 108; v. 322.
Mackay, D. S., *The Religion of the Threshold* (1908), 260.
Meyer, F. B., *John the Baptist* (1911).
Reynolds, H. R., *John the Baptist* (1874).
Robertson, A. T., *John the Loyal* (1912).
Robertson, F. W., *Sermons,* iii. (1876) 270.
Simpson, W. J. S., *The Prophet of the Highest* (1895).
Smith, D., *The Days of His Flesh* (1905), 221.
Stalker, J., *The Two St. Johns* (1895), 189.
Watson, J., *The Life of the Master* (1902), 77, 89.
Dictionary of the Bible, ii. (1899) 677 (Ll. J. M. Bebb).
  „   „   „   (Single-volume, 1909), 474 (J. G. Tasker).
Dictionary of Christ and the Gospels, i. (1906) 861 (J. C. Lambert).
Encyclopædia Biblica, ii. (1901), col. 2498 (T. K. Cheyne).
Smith's Dictionary of the Bible, i. (1893) 1736 (E. Hawkins).

John and Herod.

For Herod had laid hold on John, and bound him, and put him in prison for the sake of Herodias, his brother Philip's wife. For John said unto him, It is not lawful for thee to have her.—Matt. xiv. 3, 4.

1. When we last heard of John he was baptizing in Ænon, near to Salim. The scene has changed. The Baptist has become the prisoner of Herod Antipas. Herod has two palaces in Peræa, one at Julias, the other at Machærus. John was imprisoned at Machærus.

Machærus had been built by Alexander Jannæus, but destroyed by Gabinius in the wars of Pompey. It was not only restored but greatly enlarged by Herod the Great, who surrounded it with the best defences known at that time. In fact, Herod the Great built a town along the shoulder of the hill, and surrounded it by walls fortified by towers. From this town a farther height had to be climbed, on which the castle stood, surrounded by walls and flanked by towers one hundred and sixty cubits high. Within the inclosure of the castle Herod had built a magnificent palace. A large number of cisterns, storehouses, and arsenals, containing every weapon of attack or defence, had been provided to enable the garrison to stand a prolonged siege. Josephus describes even its natural position as unassailable.

2. What was the reason of John's imprisonment? According to the Synoptists, it was due to the spiteful hatred of Herodias because he had rebuked Herod for making her his wife in flagrant defiance of the law of Israel. Josephus, on the other hand, says that Herod put the prophet to death because he "feared lest the great influence John had over the people might put it in his power and inclination to raise a rebellion; for they seemed ready to do anything he should advise." The two statements, however, are not irreconcilable; and certainly the evidence of Josephus, whose

interests as an historian lay altogether in the political direction, is not such as to cast any suspicion on the trustworthiness of the more detailed and more intimate Gospel narrative. It may very well have been the case that, while John's death was really due to the implacable hate of Herodias, Herod felt that this was hardly an adequate ground, or one that he would care to allege, for the execution of the Baptist, and so made political reasons his excuse. Assuredly there was nothing of the political revolutionary about John; yet his extraordinary influence over the people and the wild hopes raised among certain classes by his preaching might make it easy for Herod to present a plausible justification of his base deed by representing John as a politically dangerous person.

3. We might wonder how it could happen that a man like Herod, who notoriously lived in a glass house, so far as character went, should be willing to call in so merciless a preacher of repentance as John the Baptist was—before whose words, flung like stones, full many a glass house had crashed to the ground, leaving its tenant unsheltered before the storm. But it must be remembered that most men, when they enter the precincts of the court, are accustomed to put velvet in their mouths; and, however vehement they may have been in denouncing the sins of the lower classes, they change their tone when face to face with sinners in high places. Herod, therefore, had every reason to presume that John would obey this unwritten law; and, whilst denouncing sin in general, would refrain from anything savouring of the direct and personal. But John said to Herod, " It is not lawful for thee to have her."

"It is refreshing," says Robertson of Brighton, "to look upon such a scene as this—the highest, the very highest moment, I think, in all John's history; higher than his ascetic life. For, after all, ascetic life such as he had led before, when he fed upon locusts and wild honey, is hard only in the first resolve. When you have once made up your mind to that, it becomes a habit to live alone. To lecture the poor about religion is not hard. To speak of unworldliness to men with whom we do not associate, and who do not see *our* daily inconsistencies, *that* is not hard. To speak contemptuously of the world when we have no power of commanding its admiration, *that* is not difficult. But when God has given a man accomplishments or powers which would enable him to shine in society, and he can still be firm, and steady, and uncompromisingly true; when he can be as undaunted before the rich as before the poor; when rank and fashion cannot subdue him into silence; when he hates moral evil as sternly in a great man as he would in a peasant, there is truth in that man. This was the test to which the Baptist submitted." So John was cast into prison.

¶ When staying at a country house, amongst men of great literary reputation, when the host, then but slightly known to him, made use of some Rabelaisian expression—unaware perhaps for the moment that he was entertaining a clergyman—Jowett said quite simply, "Mr. ——, I do not think myself better than you, but I feel bound to disapprove of that remark." This attitude was maintained consistently in later life, but with differences of method, in accordance with his increasing knowledge of men and things. At a Scotch shooting lodge, somewhere in the sixties, he insisted on going down to the smoking-room with the others at a late hour, and when the conversation of the younger men took a doubtful turn, the small voice that had been silent hitherto, was suddenly heard—"There is more dirt than wit in that story, I think." Once again, in the eighties, when at Balliol after dinner some old companion ventured on dangerous ground, he quietly said, "Shall we continue this conversation with the ladies?" and rose to go.[1]

I.

THE DEPUTATION TO JESUS.

1. The imprisonment was a weary time, and its protraction was due to the play of opposing influences on the mind of the vacillating tyrant. In the first flush of his resentment, Antipas would have had him executed had he dared; but, knowing how greatly the multitude revered the prophet, he dreaded an insurrection should he destroy their idol. He therefore kept John under arrest, and presently a still more powerful dread took possession of him. He had repeated interviews with the prisoner, and his guilty soul quailed before that fearless man, so helpless yet so majestic. "He was much perplexed, and gladly listened to him."

[1] *The Life and Letters of Benjamin Jowett,* i. 84.

It was the supreme crisis in the tetrarch's life. His conscience was stirred, and he was disposed to obey its dictates and yield to the importunities of the Holy Spirit; but, alas, he was hampered by his evil past. Herodias held him back. For her sake he had sinned, and now that he was minded to repent, he was fast bound by the fetters which he had himself forged. She was bitter with all a bad woman's bitterness against the Baptist for his denunciation of her infamous marriage, and clamoured for his death. Torn this way and that, the tetrarch had neither executed his prisoner nor set him at liberty, but had held him in durance all that weary time. It seems that he showed him not a little indulgence and made his captivity as easy as possible, allowing his disciples free access to their master. Imprisonment was not, indeed, in the ancient world exactly the same thing as it is among us. A prisoner frequently enjoyed a great deal of freedom, and he could generally be visited by his friends, as is indicated in the parable which says, "I was in prison, and ye came unto me." Hence the Baptist received information of what was taking place outside, and he was able to send messages to whomsoever he desired.

¶ People were kinder in these old days, and did not throw men into the lowest dungeons of towers, as happens with us. Captives were simply guarded, in places where others could approach them. Such was the prison of Joseph in Egypt and of Paul the Apostle in Rome. Many sat with them, and conversation went on. Others stood about the doors and exchanged remarks with the prisoners. We read in Demosthenes that Æschines, when in prison, was boycotted by the remaining captives, so that no one would eat with him or light his lamp. From this we see that even prisoners had their rules of government. Briefly, then, prisons in former times were merely places of secure guardianship, as even the lawyers say: A prison should be a place of ward, and not a torture house.[1]

2. It is very touching to remark the tenacity with which some few of John's disciples clung to their great leader. The majority had dispersed: some to their homes, some to follow Jesus. Only a handful lingered still, not alienated by the storm of hate which had broken on their master, but drawn nearer, with the unfalter-

[1] Melanchthon, *Corpus Reformatorum*, vol. xxiv. col. 33.

ing loyalty of unchangeable affection. They could not forget what he had been to them—that he had first called them to the reality of living; that he had taught them to pray; that he had led them to the Christ: and they dare not desert him now, in the dark sad days of his imprisonment and sorrows. These heroic souls risked all the peril that might accrue to themselves from this identification with their master; they did not hesitate to come to his cell with tidings of the great outer world, and especially of what *He* was doing and saying whose life was so mysteriously bound up with his own. "The disciples of John told him of all these things" (Luke vii. 18, R.V.). It was to two of these choice and steadfast friends that John confided the question which had long been forming within his soul, and forcing itself to the front. "And John calling unto him two of his disciples sent them to the Lord, saying, Art thou he that cometh, or look we for another?"

> From first to last I knew I must decrease:
> This in the Wilderness hath been my peace.
> Now in my cell He hath deserted me. . . .
> I wonder, is He Christ—can it be He?
>
> I have sent messengers to ask Him plain
> Is He the Christ? Before they come again
> I see Him on the road . . . I am sufficed!
> He is the Lamb of God, He is the Christ.
>
> I pointed others to Him and they went;
> I was deserted, yet in heart content:
> Now He deserts me, as His pleasure is—
> His pleasure, stricter than His promises.
>
> So bold I spoke to sinners of the axe,
> Who am just now a bit of smoking flax—
> He would but quench me if I saw Him nigh
> . . . Far off let Him abide, and I will die![1]

3. Doubt was in the question; and let none wonder that this man of energy and faith should doubt. The agony of doubt is often the portion of the highest faith. Job took the honest complaint of his spirit to God, and the love of God did not refuse him. So it proved with John. In his lone hour of doubt he

[1] Michael Field, *Mystic Trees*, 118.

turned to Christ, as naturally as Job in the hour of his doubt turned to God. And he did not turn in vain.

Now here is a man pre-eminently fitted to stand alone—a man who at first might be deemed independent of the assistance of inward or spiritual strength. Yet this man leans on Christ. He recognizes Christ as his superior, not merely in the way in which a man might recognize another from a literary or intellectual point of view as his superior; he recognizes Christ as a very present help in trouble, as One from whose life he can derive life, as One who can solve his doubts, as One who is the bridegroom of the spirits of men. An ascendancy like this may rebuke the imagination of those who think that religion is all very well for the weak, but that the strong can stand alone. It is a mistake to suppose that the mighty men of the earth need no help from the power of faith. It is indeed true that for a while men may live without realizing their need, but there are times in which the strongest are weak. If a man is noble he feels it when temptation is upon him; if he is hopeful he feels it when failure is his portion; if he is loving he will feel it in the hour of sorrow ; if he is hungering for righteousness he will feel it in the presence of sin. And if not at such times as these, yet afterwards, when the joys of life decrease, and our powers of enjoyment grow feeble; when success falls from our side; or when even our pleasure in success dies into nothingness; then, when we are face to face with the remediless weakness of humanity, we

> Stretch lame hands of faith, and grope
> And gather dust and chaff, and call
> To what we feel is Lord of all,
> And faintly trust the larger hope.

Something of this sort probably passed through John's mind in his prison at Machærus. He felt that the joy of life had vanished with his opportunity of activity, and, like so many from whose life sunlight has passed away, he found it hard to believe that the sun was shining anywhere.

¶ Nothing, to my mind, in the whole history of the Baptist is half so tragical as that. And why ? Because it is the man parting from his innermost self. It is as if Shakespeare had lost his passion, as if Tennyson had lost his culture, as if Keats had lost his colouring. If this man had kept his confidence undimmed we should have looked in vain for the element of tragedy; not the dungeon, not the persecution by Herod, not the axe of the headsman, could have made the final scene other than glorious. But when a cloud fell over his innermost self, when in the flood he lost sight of the bow, when his *faith* wavered, when his one strong and seemingly invincible possession received damage on a rock of earth—this is the crisis of the drama, this is the tragedy of the scene![1]

4. Christ's answer was one well fitted to the character and disposition and faith of John. " Go your way, and tell John what things ye have seen and heard; the blind receive their sight, the lame walk, the lepers are cleansed, the deaf hear, the dead are raised up, the poor have good tidings preached to them. And blessed is he whosoever shall find none occasion of stumbling in me." In other words, " Go and report to John that God is still actively working in the world, that the needs of humanity are not forgotten, that the sorrows of humanity are consoled. Tell John that though there may be darkness in Machærus, and deep darkness in the heart of the captive there, yet God's sunlight of love is still shining in the world. Tell him that the faith which can live only in the sunlight is not the faith which he himself once possessed. Tell him that the joy of souls that are noble may be found in suffering. Tell him that the delay and the seeming heedlessness of Divine power is never a loveless or unwise delay. Blessed is he whose heart does not stumble because Divine love does not act as selfishness or as despair may desire; blessed is he who in darkness can trust the Divine wisdom of the Divine love. Blessed is he whosoever shall not be offended in Me."

Such a message implied the highest trust in him to whom it was sent. It was a salutary message, for it carried comfort and invigoration. It did not merely console and soothe; it was calculated to stimulate and to inspire. It was just what the Baptist needed; it spoke to his manhood and to his faith. It was like the call of the officer on the field who bids his troops stand in the hour of danger. It was the message which, calling to courage and high trust, fell upon the captive's ear as the hour

[1] G. Matheson.

of his martyrdom drew nigh. He was to suffer as well as to serve; and his faith at the last is sustained by the message which assured him that God's love was not dead, and that patience as well as courage was needed in the discipline and education of faith. "Blessed is he who is not offended in me."

¶ Christianity not only lives, but it grows and holds the field. It lives, despite all the mistakes of its theology, notwithstanding all the persevering efforts of the Church to misrepresent and to falsify it. What is the meaning of all this? There seems only one explanation. Christianity came not as a theory but as a life —a new kind of life. And its fortune has been like that of a savage who is indeed alive, but whose explanation of his life, of his body and his soul, is the most grotesque misrepresentation of the reality. When he gets some anatomy and physiology he will find some better though still inadequate theories. Christianity has persisted because men, apart from their crude thinking about it, have felt the thrill of its life. It has persisted because age after age it has offered to the soul its hidden manna; has ministered as nothing else has done to its moral and spiritual hunger. Have we not here another illustration of our doctrine of loose ends? Are not the evidences left in this condition in order that we each may find our own evidences, may become men of faith by taking all the risks of it, the risk-taking being part of our spiritual education? Coleridge in his *Aids to Reflection*, has put it all in a nutshell : "Evidences of Christianity? I am weary of the word. Make a man feel the want of it, and you may safely trust to its own evidences!"[1]

5. John had often borne testimony to Jesus, and Jesus now bears glad witness to his great worth and work. In society men are commonly praised to their face, or the faces of their friends, and blamed behind their backs. Jesus does the opposite in the case of John. Gossip waits only till the door is shut behind a visitor before canvassing every defect in his appearance and ripping up the seams of his character. Jesus probably knew that the bystanders were charging the Baptist with vacillation and cowardice. His faith, once so assured, was shaken; adversity had broken his spirit. In the minds of the people, now that the messengers of John are gone, Jesus will not seem to be using words of fulsome flattery. It is clear that Jesus was not willing for the inquiry of John and his reply to have the effect on the

[1] J. Brierley, *Faith's Certainties*, 44.

crowd of depreciating John. Jesus was not willing for the people to draw injurious inferences from what had just occurred, so He began at once, as the messengers departed, His defence of John.

The opening words—"What went ye out into the wilderness for to see? A reed shaken with the wind? But what went ye out for to see? A man clothed in soft raiment? Behold, they which are gorgeously apparelled, and live delicately, are in kings' courts"—appear intended to protect John from the unfavourable impressions which may have been made by his own message. The question, "Art thou he that should come, or look we for another?" might have suggested in John a certain fickleness, when contrasted with the emphasis of his earlier testimony; and it suggested an impatience which might be attributed to dissatisfaction with the hardships which he was enduring. Was John, then, a changeable mortal, sighing for release and comfort? From such a caricature Jesus lifted the minds of the listeners to the image of the real John, as he appeared in the days of his prime.

¶ How little can we realize what a tremendous force is wielded by the concentrated will of a man wholly convinced of the Supreme Reality before whom he stands, and bending all his deepest faculties in a mighty longing for an object "inwrought" within his soul by the Spirit of God! A force as real as that which bears the electric message through the ether, and far more wonderful, is in the hands of God to direct at His will. Is it strange that it should prevail? Describing the pre-eminent greatness of John the Baptist, our Lord singled out the fact that he first taught men to "force on" the Kingdom of heaven (Matt. xi. 12). He and those who entered into his teaching were not minded to wait passively for a heavenly inheritance that might or might not come after long ages: like bandits they would "take it by force." The original form and meaning of this saying cannot be recovered with certainty, but the paraphrase I have given seems to present the most probable view of it.[1]

II.

The Death of John.

The final scene presented in the narrative of John is the one preceding and immediately connected with his martyrdom.

[1] J. H. Moulton, *Religions and Religion*, 200.

1. Herod Antipas, to whom, on the death of Herod the Great, had fallen the tetrarchy of Galilee, was about as weak and miserable a prince as ever disgraced the throne of an afflicted country. Cruel, crafty, and voluptuous like his father, he was, unlike him, weak in war and vacillating in peace. In him, as in so many characters which stand conspicuous on the stage of history, infidelity and superstition went hand in hand. But the terrors of a guilty conscience did not save him from the criminal extravagances of a violent will. He was a man in whom were mingled the worst features of the Roman, the Oriental, and the Greek.

Yet even this man heard John gladly, and did many things because of him. Even Herod was not all bad. Deep down, under all the hard crust of evil that had covered over his life, there was something that could yet be touched. His eye could be made to see fair visions of a life unlike his own, visions which he would long to clutch and keep. He was able to wish his past undone. Moods of tenderness, for long unwonted, returned. There were moments when he felt broken. He longed to escape the entanglements which bad men and worse women had woven around him. Such moods were perhaps temporary ; he forgot them, and became again what he had been before. Such moods we all have at times ; and we often wonder what their meaning may be, what worth they have in God's sight, what possibilities may be in them for ourselves.

But "our pleasant vices," it has been well said, are made "instruments to plague us." From the moment that he carried away his brother's wife there began for Herod Antipas a series of annoyances and misfortunes which culminated only in his death, years afterwards, in discrowned royalty and unpitied exile.

2. The Baptist had no cause to apprehend immediate danger from Herod; but behind the tetrarch there stood another figure, whose attitude was ominous. This was Herodias. What Jezebel was to Elijah in the Old Testament, Herodias was to the Elijah of the New Testament. She was worse. Elijah escaped from the deadly hate of Jezebel, and, as he had prophesied, her bones were devoured by the dogs of Jezreel; but John did not escape the vengeance of his enemy.

¶ It has often been said that women are like the figs of

Jeremiah : when good, they are very good, but when bad, they are very bad.

> For men at most differ as heaven and earth,
> But women, worst and best, as heaven and hell.[1]

3. Herodias had very good reasons for hating John ; for if Herod put her away as John advised, where was she to go ? For her the enjoyment and glory of life were over for ever. A woman's hatred is different from a man's. It sees its purpose straight before it, and no scruple is allowed to stand in its way. Herod, bad man as he was, feared John and reverenced him. Not so Herodias ; for her there was no halo round the prophet's head. Either he must die or she be banished from the sunshine, a disgraced and ruined woman ; and she did not hesitate a moment between the alternatives.

The birthday of Antipas had come round, and, to celebrate the occasion, he summoned his leading nobles and officers to a banquet in the princely castle of Machærus. In the midst of the revel an unexpected diversion was introduced by Herodias. She had, by the husband whom she had so shamelessly abandoned, a daughter named Salome, who by and by became the wife of Philip the tetrarch of Trachonitis. The young princess, a mere girl some seventeen years of age, was sent by her wicked mother into the banquet-chamber to entertain the wine-inflamed company by executing a lewd dance before their lascivious eyes. It was a shameless performance, unbefitting alike a princess and a maiden. Nevertheless it evoked rapturous applause, and the gratified host assumed an air of maudlin magnificence. He was only a humble vassal of Rome, but in popular parlance he was styled " the King," a reminiscence of the days of Herod the Great ; and his vain soul loved the title. He summoned the girl before him, and, sublimely oblivious of the fact that he durst not dispose of a single acre of his territory without the Emperor's sanction, vowed, in a strain of Oriental munificence, to grant whatever boon she might crave, were it half of his kingdom. She went out and consulted with her mother, and that wicked woman, exulting in the success of her stratagem, bade her request the head of John the Baptist served up, like some dainty viand, on a trencher. The tetrarch

[1] J. Stalker, *The Two St. Johns*, 277.

was deeply distressed, and would gladly have withdrawn from his engagement; but, according to that age's code of honour, he durst not, and sorely against his will he sent an executioner to behead the prophet in his cell.   The deed was done, and the dripping head was brought on a trencher into the banquet-hall and presented to Salome.   She bore the ghastly trophy to Herodias; and it is said that, not content with feasting her eyes upon it, that she-devil emulated the barbarity of Fulvia and pierced with a bodkin the once eloquent tongue which had denounced her sin.

> Just for the sake of them that sat with him
>   At meat, King Herod kept his sinful oath
>   And slew the Baptist, though his heart was loth
> To crown his record with a crime so grim.
> We live in fuller day; his light was dim:
>   Yet oftentimes we make high heaven wroth
>   By deeds which stay our souls' eternal growth,
> To satisfy some senseless, social whim.
> We laugh with flippant scorn at what full well
>   We know we should adore on bended knees;
>   We trample our ideals 'neath our feet:
> And this for no great cause approved of hell,
>   Which devils might applaud; but just to please
>   The whims of them that sit with us at meat.[1]

4. Wherein lay the greatness of John, and what was the work he did?   His greatness lay largely perhaps in his genuineness, in the grasp of reality which he had of human life.   He saw it in its simplicity and its reality.   He laid an emphasis on sin and duty. He was a man who looked behind conventionalities, and stripped off coverings, and showed men as they are.   But if this had been all, he would not have been the greatest of those born of women. The painter who paints reality merely, however graphic and power-ful his delineation may be, fulfils only half his task.   He must also teach us by showing us what should be, what might be.   Nay, we look that he should be in some sense prophetic, and encourage us with visions of what will be in a better future.   It is not the real, but the ideal, in art and in all things, in which power to make us better resides.

And John did not merely show what men are, or what they

[1] E. T. Fowler, *Love's Argument*, 136.

should be ; he had visions of what they were to be, of what God
was about to make them. He had presentiments of a Divine
day, which was about to dawn. He did not tell men their duty
merely, and leave them with the impossible task of fulfilling it.
He knew that power to fulfil it came from on high ; and he was
gifted to perceive that the power was at hand, and about to be
revealed. He showed men not earthly things only, but heavenly
things. He did not say "Repent," but "Repent, for the kingdom
of heaven is at hand." "I baptize with water : but there standeth
one among you, who will baptize with the Holy Ghost and with
fire. Behold the Lamb of God, which taketh away the sin of the
world," he said, pointing to Christ.

Like Moses preparing Joshua to lead his people into a land
which he himself may see only from afar; like David preparing
the materials with which Solomon may build the temple which he
himself had longed to build, but which is never to bear his name ;
like every true prophet who has the "intuitive grasp of novelty,
whose mind discerns, though it may not understand, the coming
of a change long before it can be known by other men," John the
Baptist, that strange figure watching and waiting in the desert for
some mighty event which his heightened powers could feel in its
approach, but could not see, remains the type of self-effacement,
the type of a passing generation which can recognize the rise of
new ideals and nobler aims, and leave them room to develop in
God's own time.

It is this that makes men great, whatever they be, whether
inventors or statesmen—the vision of the future, of possibilities
which men cannot yet realize. And especially here lies the
greatness of the preacher—in his sensibility to the nearness of
something not yet manifest, to a revelation of Christ which
is at hand—that, in all he is doing, he feels himself on the
marge, on the outskirts, of a great manifestation of Christ,
when He shall baptize with the Holy Ghost, and take away the
sin of the world. And this is his message still to us. God has
come nigh. The Redeemer is here. Receive Him. The Kingdom
of God is among you. The door is open. Enter in, that you may
see the light.

"The word of God came to John in the wilderness." This is
the irony of the situation, that through this fanatic in the wilds of

Judæa came an uprising of spiritual force, a shattering word of God which has run on from that day to this. Not from the throne of all the Cæsars, not from the haughty tributaries of empire, not from the priestly circle at Jerusalem, although Herod's splendid temple was their shrine, and a great inheritance seemed to invest them with authority, but from a rude, passionate soul, touched with flame. Not all the dignities of that age could produce one authentic word of God possessing permanence and revelation; not one influence that had within it the powers of a world to come. But it was given to this man to see the heavens opened, and the Spirit descending like a dove upon the Son of Man. That was the supreme event, at that historical juncture, as the spiritual event must always be, even in the most dazzling periods of secular splendour. You may conclude that you have failed to analyze any great movement that means progress or enlightenment until you can lay your finger here and there and say, "There came the spirit and the word of God."

¶ John the Baptist, that strange figure watching and waiting in the desert for some mighty event which his heightened powers could feel in its approach but could not see, is the real link between two levels of humanity. Freed by his ascetic life from the fetters of the obvious, his intuitive faculties nourished by the splendid dreams of Hebrew prophecy, and by a life at once wild and holy, which kept him closer than other men to the natural and the supernatural worlds, he *felt* the new movement, the new direction of life. Though its meaning might be hidden, its actuality was undeniable. *Something* was coming. This conviction flooded his consciousness, "inspired" him; became the dominant fact of his existence. "A message from God came upon John," speaking without utterance in the deeps of his soul. He was driven to proclaim it as best he could; naturally under the traditional and deeply significant images of the Jewish Scriptures and apocalyptic books. Hence he was really its Forerunner, the preparer of the Way. . . . If he is to be taken as a true harbinger, as an earnest of the quality of the Christian life; then, how romantic, how sacramental—above all, how predominantly ascetic —that life must seem! Nothing here forecasts the platitudinous ethics of modern theology. Deliberate choice, deep-seated change, stern detachment, a humble preparation for the great re-making of things: no comfortable compromise, or agreeable trust in a vicarious salvation. As a matter of fact, in the lives of that small handful in whom the peculiar Christian consciousness has been developed, the demands of John the Baptist were always fulfilled before the results promised by Jesus were experienced. Asceticism was the gateway to mysticism; and the secret of the Kingdom was only understood by those who had (in the literal meaning of the Greek of Matt. iii. 2) "changed their minds."[1]

Thine, Baptist, was the cry,
In ages long gone by,
Heard in clear accents by the Prophet's ear;
As if 'twere thine to wait,
And with imperial state
Herald some Eastern monarch's proud career;
Who thus might march his host in full array,
And speed through trackless wilds his unresisted way.

But other task hadst thou
Than lofty hills to bow,
Make straight the crooked, the rough places plain:
Thine was the harder part
To smooth the human heart,
The wilderness where sin had fixed his reign;
To make deceit his mazy wiles forego,
Bring down high vaulting pride, and lay ambition low.

Such, Baptist, was thy care,
That no objection there
Might check the progress of the King of kings;
But that a clear highway,
Might welcome the array,
Of Heavenly graces which His Presence brings;
And where Repentance had prepared the road,
There Faith might enter in, and Love to man and God.[2]

[1] E. Underhill, *The Mystic Way*, 85.
[2] Richard Mant, in *Lyra Messianica*.

ANDREW.

LITERATURE.

Banks, L. A., *Christ and His Friends* (1895), 56.

Brooke, S. A., *The Spirit of the Christian Life* (1902), 294.

Cuckson, J., *Faith and Fellowship* (1897), 223.

Deane, A. C., *At the Master's Side* (1905), 1.

Greenhough, J. G., in *Men of the New Testament* : Matthew to Timothy (1905), 81.

Hancock, B. M., *Free Bondmen* (1913), 52.

Jones, J. D., *The Glorious Company of the Apostles* (1904), 87.

Lightfoot, J. B., *Sermons Preached on Special Occasions* (1891), 1ff.

Lovell, R. H., *First Types of the Christian Life* (1895), 82.

Maclaren, A., *A Year's Ministry*, ii. (1888) 127.

Morgan, G. C., *Discipleship* (1898), 1.

Pearce, E. H., *The Laws of the Earliest Gospel* (1913), 5.

Punshon, W. M., *Sermons* (1882), 1.

Purves, G. T., *Faith and Life* (1902), 271.

Rattenbury, J. E., *The Twelve* (1914), 91.

Sidey, W. W., *The First Christian Fellowship* (1908), 1.

Skrine, J. H., *Saints and Worthies* (1901), 15.

Biblical World, xxxiii. (1909) 314 (E. Gates).

Dictionary of the Bible, i. (1898) 92 (M. R. James).

Smith's Dictionary of the Bible, i. (1893) 128 (E. R. Bernard).

ANDREW.

And passing along by the sea of Galilee, he saw Simon and Andrew the brother of Simon casting a net in the sea : for they were fishers. And Jesus said unto them, Come ye after me, and I will make you to become fishers of men.—Mark i. 16, 17.

WHEN Jesus emerged from His private life to enter upon the work of His public ministry, He was without followers or adherents of any sort. No existing ready-for-work society or church awaited Him or welcomed His coming. A certain group of Jews had been aroused by the preaching of John the Baptist into a fresh Messianic expectancy of a moral rather than a political sort. In this circle Jesus first appeared, and here was the only soil in any wise prepared for His teaching. He did not so much as succeed to the leadership of the rudimentary society brought together by John. Out of this society, however, He gathered His first disciples. Probably most of the disciples of John passed over to the company of Jesus finally, but only after the gradual dissolution of John's society. One of the very first to pass from John to Jesus was Andrew.

In the first three Gospels Andrew is only a name. We know nothing more about him than that he was the brother of Peter; but, as in the case of several of the obscure Apostles, St. John gives us some insight into the character and work of Andrew. We know that he was a fisherman, the brother of Simon Peter, the son of Jonas. We know that he was already one of John the Baptist's disciples when Jesus began His work, and that he was one of the first two disciples of Jesus. He, along with John, heard the great words of the Baptist, " Behold, the Lamb of God, which taketh away the sin of the world "; and these two disciples, hearing him speak, followed Jesus. " Jesus turned, and beheld them following, and saith unto them, What seek ye? And they said unto him, Rabbi (which is to say, being interpreted, Master), where abidest thou? He saith unto them, Come, and ye shall see. They came therefore and saw where he abode; and they abode with him that day: it was about the tenth hour." Andrew thenceforth ranked himself as a believer in Jesus of Nazareth; and on the very day of his own acceptance of Jesus, he brought his brother Simon Peter to the Master.

Thereafter we hear of this Apostle on only four occasions. When the Galilæan ministry of Jesus was beginning, He called these men, whose faith He had already won, to be His constant followers; and He marked their call by the miraculous draught of fishes, which symbolized so well the task to which He was calling them and the power by which He would give them success. We are told that Andrew, as well as Peter, obeyed the summons, left all, and followed Jesus in order to be a "fisher of men." When, again, the public ministry of Jesus was about half finished, He performed on the east shore of the Sea of Galilee that wonderful act of feeding, from a few loaves and fishes, five thousand men. St. John, whose clear memory often appears in such particulars as this, tells us that when the disciples were asked by Jesus how that vast multitude could be fed, Andrew replied, with a vague feeling, probably, that, absurd as the provision seemed, it might be a help, or at least a starting-point, for other supplies: "There is a lad here, which hath five barley loaves, and two small fishes: but what are they among so many?" Again, when the ministry of Jesus was nearing its close, certain Greeks wished to see the new Messiah, and applied to Philip. Philip consulted Andrew and together Andrew and Philip told Jesus. And, finally, when Christ gave on Mount Olivet to a few disciples that solemn prediction of the future,—of the fall of Jerusalem, and the troubles and persecutions which were impending, and of the end of the world itself,—we read not only that Peter and John and James were present,—those three whom so often Jesus took into special confidence,—but also that Andrew shared on this occasion the sad privilege of listening to the terrible prophecy.

With these few items our knowledge of the Apostle Andrew ends. Let us consider him as Disciple, as Missionary, and as Brother.

I.

The Disciple.

" Disciple " is the term consistently used in the four Gospels to mark the relationship existing between Christ and His followers. Jesus used it Himself in speaking of them, and they in speaking of each other. Neither did it pass out of use in the new days of Pentecostal power. It runs right through the Acts of the Apostles. It is interesting also to remember that it was on this wise that the angels thought and spoke of these men : the use of the word in the days of the Incarnation is linked to the use of the word in the Apostolic Age by the angelic message to the women, " Go, tell his *disciples* and Peter " (Mark xvi. 7).

It is somewhat remarkable that the word is not to be found in the Epistles. This is to be accounted for by the fact that the Epistles were addressed to Christians in their corporate capacity as churches, and so spoke of them as members of such, and as the " saints," or separated ones of God. The term " disciple " marks an individual relationship ; and though it has largely fallen out of use, it is of the utmost value still in marking the relationship existing between Christ and each single soul, and suggesting our consequent position in all the varied circumstances of everyday living.

¶ Lads to be afterwards notable as Lord Palmerston, Lord John Russell, Lord Dudley and Ward, who had as class-mates Henry Brougham, Francis Horner, Henry Cockburn, and Francis Jeffrey, were among the students then attending Edinburgh University. These men looked fondly back in their older years to those delightful days of plain living and high thinking in Edinburgh, where they studied under Playfair and Robison and Dalziel. But it was Dugald Stewart, the Professor of Moral Philosophy, whom they regarded as their master, as he set forth fine moral aims and ideals—especially when discussing the application of ethics to the principles of government and the conduct of citizens in political life. As Henry Cockburn listened in his boyhood to the per- suasive eloquence, he felt his whole nature changed by his teacher : " his noble views unfolded in glorious sentences elevated me into a higher world." Francis Horner was touched and moved to admiration ; and it was the inculcating of high moral purpose on men and citizens which influenced young men who had a public career before them. As Sir James Mackintosh said, Dugald Stewart's disciples were his best works.[1]

1. Why did Jesus attach disciples to Him? The answer may be given that it was partly for His own sake and partly for theirs and for what they could do in the spread of the gospel.

(1) *What they could do for Him.*—He was not, indeed, one who needed attendance and service; His personal wants were few, His life the simplest. But there were many things in which they would minister to Him and aid Him, sparing His strength, relieving His toil, and so helping on His work. In the ardour of His Divine zeal He was capable of forgetting the claims of the body, and they had sometimes to constrain Him, saying, "Master, eat." If, after a day of labour and excitement, with heavy incessant demands upon Him, evening came and found Him spent and weary, He needed but to say, " Let us go over unto the other side," and they did all the rest: they brought the boat to the nearest landing-place, and He stepped aboard and was their passenger. Some of them were skilful fishermen as well as faithful friends, and He might trust Himself to their hands. If the wind served they would run up the sail; if not, they rowed, taking turns with the oars; and it pleased them well if, wearied with His work, and soothed by the motion of the boat and the breeze upon the lake, He fell asleep, to wake only when the boat's keel grated upon the shingle at the place where He would be.

Nor was this the only kind of service they could render Him. From a very early period He had enemies, and feeling was often stirred to violence as He spoke. Again and again there were fierce fanatics in the crowds that thronged and pressed Him. Sometimes, it may be, a solitary teacher would not have been safe, where He, with His Twelve about Him, was left in peace. Christ Himself, we know, was absolutely fearless, and had an extraordinary power of quelling the rising storm in men's hearts as well as upon the lake. Still, for the sake of His work—that He might finish it, and deliver all His message—it may be that it was well for Him that He sat surrounded by these staunch friends when He spoke the words which " half concealed and half revealed " His tremendous claims, or when He hurled His denun-

[1] H. G. Graham, *Scottish Men of Letters in the Eighteenth Century*, 426.

ciations at scribes and Pharisees. But probably such service was
not the best of the help they gave Him. Just to be with Him,
to make an atmosphere of sympathy about Him, to constitute a
spiritual home into which He could retreat from the strife of
tongues, and rest and recover Himself—perhaps this was the chief
of all the service by which they helped Him then.

(2) *What He could do for them.*—What they might do for Him,
however, does not explain the calling of the Twelve. For all the
personal service they rendered Him, fewer would certainly have
sufficed. It was much more for the sake of what He could do for
them, and with a view to a great service of the future, that they
were with Him. He was a Teacher; He traversed the land proclaiming to all men His gospel, and that Kingdom of which He
was the King; these went with Him that they might hear all
His truth. In place after place they listened while He taught.
They heard the gospel in Galilee; they heard it, in different
accents, in Samaria; they heard it in Judæa and in Jerusalem, and
again the tone was new, for it was a many-sided gospel. They
heard Him preach His Kingdom in various aspects: now it was
a spiritual state, a community in which God's will is done; now
it was a power which goes out in effort to get that will done, an
influence which had come into the world, mixing with human
affairs, permeating them, leavening them, charging them with its
own Divine redeeming qualities; and now again it was the prize
of life, man's chief good, his supreme treasure and reward. They
heard all His teaching; they alone of all His hearers obtained a
complete view of His truth.

Some part of it indeed was reserved specially for them. When
night fell, and the crowd of common hearers dispersed, they
gathered round Him in some humble home, and He taught them,
and His thought grew ever more luminous and wonderful. As
they journeyed from town to town, beguiling the tedium of the
way, He taught them, and the bright flowers bloomed unnoticed by
the wayside where they passed, for they hung upon Him listening, and their hearts burned within them while He spoke. It was
His will to entrust His truth to them, to make them the deposi-
taries and stewards of it, that through them, by and by, it might
be for all. Meanwhile they have to listen and learn, and store
up in heart and mind His teachings; and in order that they

may do so they must be with Him through all the days of His ministry.

And there is something else, of chiefest moment, yet unnamed. They were learning His truth. His mighty works were teaching them, but He Himself was greater than His words or His works; and as they lived with Him day by day they came to know Him, and His spirit penetrated them. That spirit showed itself not only in His public teachings, but sometimes more beautifully and impressively still in simple unconscious acts in the region of the private life, and always in the tone and character of their intercourse. Slowly, but surely, the disciples acquired His habits of thought, His point of view, His instinctive feeling. To the end the difference rather than the resemblance may strike us; nevertheless at the end the men are changed, the disciples are like their Master.

¶ Christ is not merely a truth to be believed, but a way to be trodden, a life to be lived. We get to know Christ, as fellow-travellers, fellow-workers, fellow-soldiers get to know one another, by mingling their lives together. It is ever in what we know to be our best moods that we find ourselves most in sympathy with Christ; when we work more faithfully by the light of conscience. It is in what we know are our worst moods that the light of faith begins to grow dim : when we are disturbed, tempted, distracted, out of sympathy with our conscience.[1]

2. Whom did He choose? Was it the wise and learned? They would have tormented the simplicity of His teaching with endless commentaries, and wrought it into intellectual schemes, so that the shepherd on the hill and the slave in the city could not have understood it. Too well we know what the wisdom of the world in the brains of the priesthood has made of the words of Christ. If the work of theologians had been done at the beginning of Christianity, we should have had no simple Christianity at all.

Then did He choose the rich and those in high position? No, truly, that would not have been wise. For they would have weighted His goodness with the cares and deceitfulness of wealth, with the ambition and meanness of society. And what could rich men have done with a doctrine which bade them give away wealth, which told the business man to take no thought for the morrow,

[1] George Tyrrell, *Oil and Wine*.

which said to the courtier, "There is only one King, and He is in heaven," which told the man in society, "There is only one nobility, and the slave who carries your litter may have it as well as you"? Did He choose the religious leaders? How could He? They would dissolve His charity, His mercy, and His tolerance, in the acid of their theological hatreds. They would cast His religion into a fixed form which would destroy its variety and flexibility so that it could not enter into the characters of diverse nations and become the universal gospel; they would subject it to their own ecclesiastical interests, and it would cease to be the interest of mankind.

Did He choose the politicians—those among the Jews who conspired against the Romans, or those who held to the Romans? Why should He? That would have made His gospel a gospel for the Jews only, and not for Greek and Roman and barbarian. To choose the politicians would have been to propagate His truth by political craft or by the sword. It was not the way of Christ to set up the Kingdom of God by the worship of the devil.

None of these He made His messengers. He chose the unlearned and the poor and the outcast of the theologians, and the uninterested in politics, and the men and women of whom society knew nothing; the fisherman and the publican, the Pharisee who left the priestly ranks, the rich who left their riches, the Israelite without guile, the cottager, the sinner and the harlot who were contrite, but chiefly—for with those in His favourite haunts He most companioned—the fishermen of the Lake of Galilee.

¶ All the world knows how in the fifth century a few fishermen driven from the mainland laid in reefs of mud and sand the foundation-stones of Venice. These heroic souls in deep desolation drove stakes and built their huts in the slime of the lagoon; then little by little a city of incomparable splendour rose out of the sea—a city of superb palaces, gorgeous temples, crowded marts, of museums, picture galleries, and libraries, of wonderful loveliness, power, and riches: the ideal shrine of poets and painters, of all worshippers of the perfect and Divine. So another handful of fishermen in great travail laid in the mud and misery of the old world the foundation-stones of the Church of Christ, the City of God, the spiritual Venice. It was built on the sea, established on the floods; it has been edified through ages of strife and conflict.[1]

3. Two things alone were necessary to discipleship.

(1) *Loyalty.*—The bond of union was to be nothing less than a personal attachment. It was not to be the interest which a thinker feels in his thought or a reformer in his principles, but the devotion of a disciple for his Master. Jesus of Nazareth, not the Messiah of Jewish expectation, or the Christ of later dogma, still less the floating ideal of ages of Christian sentiment, but the historical Person whose life is recorded in the Synoptic Gospels, exercised authority and commanded obedience. He made loyalty to Him the sovereign principle of discipleship.

The soul of all religion, and especially of the Christian religion, is loyalty to a great personality who images to the imagination and reverence of the race that still greater personality, otherwise unrevealed, and without a name. It is allegiance to truth and goodness, not as these are formulated in abstract propositions and maxims, but as they are incarnated in a noble life. And so it may be said that Christianity has not begun for the individual or the community until both have given to its Founder a confidence and personal attachment they would be ashamed to limit, and equally ashamed not to confess before all the world. Nothing can take the place of this high-born fealty. It is the very life of the Christian faith, the inspiration to service and sacrifice without which men will never be induced to bear loss and suffering, grief and reproach, with resignation and heroism.

(2) *Teachableness.*—The loyalty of discipleship must precede understanding, and not understanding discipleship. No one would pretend, of course, that the closest companionship with our Lord in this life will completely solve the problems which human existence presents. In part it does actually solve them; for the rest, it enables us, as nothing else can do, to acquiesce in their being, for the time, insoluble. The Christian alone can rest content to see now "through a glass darkly," because he alone can hope to see hereafter "face to face." Yet even here the revelation given to those who persist in discipleship is wonderfully full. To them, in a very real sense, it is given to know the mysteries of the Kingdom of God, but to others in parables. Intellectually,

[1] W. L. Watkinson, *The Supreme Conquest*, 33.

these others may be much superior to many of the disciples. They may take a real interest in religious questions. They may have studied the historical and moral evidence for Christianity with scrupulous care. They may have the language of theology in familiar use. And yet all this amounts to so many parables for them; the spiritual words they utter are but counters in a game of logic, they do not stand for glowing realities which penetrate every moment of life. And so these people are still dissatisfied. When this or that difficulty is fully explained, then, they declare, they will be only too glad to be disciples. Alas, they still regard understanding as the antecedent condition instead of the ultimate result of discipleship! Only to those who have sojourned at the Master's side is it given to know the mysteries.

Andrew's lesson began the very first day he spoke to Jesus. " I should like," says Dr. J. D. Jones, " to have had some record of what took place in our Lord's humble lodging that night. When I think of our Saviour's wonderful conversation with Nicodemus, and His equally wonderful conversation with the Samaritan woman at the well, I feel I would give worlds to have had a report of the conversation that took place between Jesus and these seeking souls that night. It would be a never-to-be-forgotten conversation, I know; and just as Paul used to look back to the great light on the way to Damascus as the supreme experience of his life, so Andrew and John used to date everything back to this their first conversation with Jesus. I do not know what He said; but as they listened to Him, their hearts— like that of John Wesley in the Moravian meeting-house—were strangely warmed, and before they left that night they had found their Messiah."

¶ More than two hundred years ago there was a young probationer in the Church of Scotland named Thomas Boston. He was about to preach before the parish of Simprin. In contemplation of the eventful visit he sat down to meditate and pray. "Reading in secret, my heart was touched with Matthew iv. 19: 'Follow me, and I will make you fishers of men.' My soul cried out for the accomplishing of that to me, and I was very desirous to know how I might follow Christ so as to be a fisher of men, and for my own instruction in that point I addressed myself to the consideration of it in that manner." Out of that honest and serious consideration there came that quaint and spiritually profound and suggestive book, *A Soliloquy on the Art of Man-Fishing*. All through Thomas Boston's book one feels the fervent intensity of a spirit eager to know the mind of God in the great matter of fishing for souls. Without that passion our inquiry is worthless. "The all-important matter in fishing is to have the desire to learn."[1]

> Of all the honours man may wear,
>   Of all his titles proudly stored,
> No lowly palm this name shall bear,
>   "The first to follow Christ the Lord."
>
> Such name thou hast, who didst incline,
>   Fired with the great Forerunner's joy,
> Homeward to track the steps divine,
>   And watch the Saviour's best employ.[2]

II.

THE MISSIONARY.

The day after Andrew's conversion was the day on which he became a soul-winner. The new-found life in Christ always longs to impart itself. The wonderful things which Christ whispers to a man in secret burn within him until he can tell them to other ears. When the pilgrim in Bunyan's story had been relieved of his burden, as he knelt before the Cross, his joy was so great that he wanted to tell it to the trees and stars and water-brooks and birds; to breathe it out to everything and every one.

¶ "Let the redeemed of the Lord *say so*," sings one Psalmist; and the redeemed, I will add, simply cannot help saying so. "I have not hid thy righteousness within my heart, I have declared thy righteousness and thy salvation," sings another Psalmist. Yes, when a man has experienced the salvation of God the word is like a fire in his bones, and *he must declare it.*[3]

¶ I received a letter from a very sagacious Scotch friend (belonging, as I suppose most Scotch people do, to the class of persons who call themselves "religious"), containing this marvellous enunciation of moral principle, to be acted upon in diffi-

---

[1] J. H. Jowett, *The Passion for Souls*, 59. [2] Dean Alford.
[3] J. D. Jones, *The Glorious Company of the Apostles*, 99.

cult circumstances, "Mind your own business." It is a serviceable principle enough for men of the world, but a surprising one in the mouth of a person who professes to be a Bible obeyer. For, as far as I remember the tone of that obsolete book, "our own" is precisely the last business which it ever tells us to mind. It tells us often to mind God's business, often to mind other people's business; our own, in any eager or earnest way, not at all. "What thy hand findeth to do." Yes; but in God's fields, not ours. One can imagine the wiser fishermen of the Galilean lake objecting to Peter and Andrew that they were not minding their business.[1]

1. What was the power that made Andrew a missionary? It was the intensity of spirit that Christ stirred in His followers. He had the prophet's power of kindling passion, of awaking youth in those who loved Him. When He spoke, men rose from the dead! And of course they did great things. All their powers put forth leaves and blossoms and flowers. These who saw and heard men who had come under the influence of Christ wondered, as one who has seen a wood in winter wonders when he sees the same wood in spring. They took notice of them, it is said, that they had been with Jesus. The mocking crowd thought it was new wine, but it was the new wine of a new life. It made men a new creation in Christ Jesus.

And that is our work. Are we doing it with all our heart? Is it our first thought? Does it possess our soul with passion? Is it our greatest and divinest joy to save and rescue men for God to a life of love, purity, sacrifice, progress, and immortality? My work! I say. How can that be? I am not an apostle, not a preacher, not authorized; and I have my own work in the world to do. Not a preacher? If we know God and love Him, how can we help telling men about Him; how can we help saving men whom we see lost, suffering, and sinful? Not authorized? The Apostles were not set apart as a special class, nor do their so-called descendants form one. Ministers are set apart, not to be a class, but as representatives of that which all men should be. They are specially called to be fishers of men in order that they may teach all who hear them to be fishers of men. We *know* that is true when we think about it, when we begin to care for doing the thing itself. The moment a man asks himself what he can do

[1] Ruskin, *Letters on Public Affairs* (*Works*, xviii. 540).

in this way, he finds the work ready to his hand, close beside him. The moment we have the heart to do it, do we mean to say that we can help doing it? Not save, help, console, uplift, teach the sinful, the weak, the pained, the broken-hearted, the ignorant; not rush into this work with joy? We cannot help being fishers of men, and we ask no authority for that Divine toil. It is human work, and it makes us men to do it. It is Divine work, and it makes us one with God to do it.

¶ "Oh, for a church of Andrews!" I do not know that many ministers would want a church of Peters; it would be too quarrelsome. I am quite willing for Thomas to go to the City Temple and Simon Zelotes to Whitefield's. Let me have a church of Andrews—of simple, loving men, content to bring people to Jesus. Men like Andrew are so valuable because everybody can be a man like Andrew. Not a greatly gifted man, but a greatly faithful man; not a man who would dispute with Peter as to who should be primate, or with John and James as to who shall sit on the left hand of Christ and who on the right, but a man who simply and humbly and lovingly does the work that lies nearest to him. He surely is of those last in the world's estimate who are first in the Kingdom of God.[1]

2. Andrew began his missionary activity *in his own home.* This is what the Gospel says: "He findeth first his own brother Simon, and saith unto him, We have found the Messiah. He brought him unto Jesus." Young men and young women are ambitious to engage in missionary work or to enter the ministry. They are all on fire with the romance of missions; they want to go to those vast mysterious regions where multitudes sit in darkness, or to prove their preaching gifts before great audiences at home; and, meanwhile, they almost despise the humbler evangelical work which is waiting at their own doors. But the first proof that they are fit for the larger call is found in their willingness to answer the smaller and immediate call.

Every zealous Christian should begin at home. He wants to make his light shine as a witness there among his own kinsfolk. For these are, and must be, more to us than others—children, brethren, parents, husband, and wife. No one, whether young or old, can rejoice in the light and love of God without anxiety and

[1] J. E. Rattenbury, *The Twelve,* 95.

intense desire to make every member of the home circle partner with him in these things. It is always painful to think that they are separated from us by a barrier of unbelief; that they who have so many dear things in common with us have no communion with us in the best and dearest thing of all. And every Christian who thinks seriously of this finds it such a trouble to him that he cannot help bearing some sort of witness for Christ in the home. Never does he kneel in prayer without supplicating for the near and dear ones. He longs to have them persuaded. Oh yes, and he will endeavour, God helping him, to make his whole life in the home a speaking witness for Christ—a gospel that utters itself either in words or without words, a gospel that shows itself in sympathy, forbearance, kindly actions, gentleness, cheerfulness, unselfishness. You remember what Jesus said to the man out of whom He had cast a legion of devils, and who, in his gratitude, wished to remain at Jesus' side: "Go home," said Jesus, "go home to thy friends, and tell them how great things the Lord hath done for thee." He was to become a missionary, and his first sphere of service was to be *his own home*. That is exactly what Andrew did without being ordered—he became a missionary to his own home.

The first member of a family who is brave enough to show his religion where all around in the household is indifference and worldliness; the first little boy in the school dormitory who— like Arthur in the story of *Tom Brown's Schooldays*—dares to kneel down and say his prayers by his bedside, as he had knelt in his nursery at home; the first soldier in the barracks who has the courage to rebuke the profanity and impurity which prevail around him; the first pitman who raises his voice against the gambling and the intemperance of his companions—these, and such as these, are the true heroes of God, of whom Andrew was the forerunner.

¶ The Rev. J. W. Dickson, of St. Helens, who was one of Dr. Paton's students at Nottingham Institute, in his notes of the Principal's *obiter dicta*, quotes him as saying: "There is no place so difficult to begin work for Jesus as the home. Said a servant-girl of her master, a Wesleyan minister: 'Many conversions at chapel, but never a word for poor Polly; I do wish I could find Jesus.' We [ministers] think of congregations, of young men, of the outsider; but we need to think of home and of ourselves."[1]

[1] J. Lewis Paton, *John Brown Paton*, 359.

3. But Andrew's labours were not confined to his own home. We read in the Gospels that he was the means of introducing to Jesus those *Greeks* who were so anxious to see Him. Nothing stirred our Lord's soul as did the coming of those Greeks. They were the first-fruits of the Gentiles, and in vision Christ saw the Kingdom stretching from shore to shore and from the river unto the ends of the earth. And it was Andrew who brought them.

We find in this incident a repetition of the characteristic which Andrew had showed at the first. He is the man who quietly and by personal efforts brings men to Jesus. Some of the disciples would have hesitated to introduce foreigners to Christ. They would, perhaps, have rejected the notion that the Messiah was sent to the Gentiles, or at least would have feared the possible effect on the populace of throwing Christ into association with outsiders. Philip was undecided what to do till he had consulted Andrew. But the latter seems to have better understood his Master. He felt that Jesus would be glad to help and save any; and it was just in the line of his habits to be thus the medium of leading inquiring minds to the Saviour of them all.

¶ St. Andrew is styled by the Greeks Protoclet, or first-called : and by the Venerable Bede, Introductor to Christ, a name aptly assigned to that large-hearted Saint who at the outset of his ministry brought St. Peter to the Messiah, and at subsequent periods introduced to his Lord's notice not only certain Greek suppliants, but even a lad who had five loaves and two small fishes. After the apostolic dispersion from Jerusalem, St. Andrew, preaching the Crucified from place to place, travelled, according to tradition, into Russia, and as far as the frontiers of Poland. At Patrae in Achaia, having kept the faith and exasperated the Proconsul by a harvest of souls, he finished his course. On an X-shaped cross, constructed as is alleged of olive-wood, and to him the pledge of assured peace; to his yearning soul less the olive-twig of the pilgrim dove than the very ark of rest; on such a cross after ignominious scourging he made his last bed, and from such a bed he awoke to that rest which remaineth to the people of God. The outburst of his joy on beholding his cross has been handed down to us: " Hail, precious cross, consecrated by my Lord's Body, jewelled by His Limbs. I come to thee exultant, embrace thou me with welcome. O good cross, beautified by my Lord's beauty, I have ardently loved thee, long have I panted seeking thee. Now found, now made ready to my yearnings, embrace thou me, separate me from mankind, uplift me to my Master, that He who redeemed me on thee may receive me by thee."[1]

III.

THE BROTHER.

1. There are many very useful people in the world who are not appreciated because they are overshadowed by someone especially conspicuous. They are dwarfed by comparison with a giant. They are forgotten because the attention of men is fixed on the greater one near them. They are like tall trees and huge rocks on a mountain side: tall and huge though they be, they look small by contrast with the great peak itself. Such people may be really useful, worthy of study and imitation; their lives may be terrible tragedies; the pathos of their existence may be unutterable, or the value of their work may be actually more than that of another who towers over them; but by reason of the other's nearness they are passed by without notice.

We are often quite arbitrary in the selection of our models and heroes. We confine our admiration to a few whom, indeed, it is scarcely possible to imitate, while scores of others present excellences which are not less worthy of praise, and which may be more nearly within our reach. They are cast into the shade, however, by the more conspicuous object near which it is their fortune to be. So was it with Andrew. He was Simon Peter's brother. He was more distinguished, therefore, by his connexion with Simon than by what he was or did. No figure stands out more prominently in the annals of the Early Church than that of Peter. How often his name is mentioned in the Gospels! How much we hear of him in the earlier part of the Book of Acts! What a great number of precious practical lessons has he been the means of our learning! What a mighty character was his— that Luther of the Apostolic Age—towering, as Luther did, above all but a few of his fellow-Christians! But the very fact that to distinguish Andrew more clearly it was easiest to call him Simon Peter's brother has tended to obscure the merit of the less renowned disciple. He is presented to us in the gospel history

[1] Christina G. Rossetti, *Called to be Saints*, 3.

in the shadow of his brother's giant shape. This puts him at a disadvantage.

Not that Christian historians have been wrong in their estimate of the two—Peter was the greater; but that Christ, by choosing Andrew also to the apostleship, recognized his worth, where history has scarcely done so. He is a fair type, we doubt not, of multitudes of useful people whose worth is unrecognized because men either see or are looking for someone of very extraordinary characteristics.

2. Thus Andrew occupied an uncertain and most difficult position. If we look at the lists of the Apostles given to us in the Gospels, we find Andrew's name always mentioned in the first group, along with those of Peter and James and John. And yet, when we come to examine the gospel history, we discover that he was certainly not on an equality with the great three. He was not admitted into the intimacy of Christ; he was not made a witness of the great experiences of Christ as were they. Andrew was left behind when Jesus took Peter and James and John to witness His first struggle with the power of death in Jairus' house. Andrew was left behind when Jesus took Peter and James and John to behold His transfiguration glory on the Holy Mount. Andrew was left behind when Jesus took Peter and James and John to share His sorrow in the garden.

Of all places in the Apostolate, this that Andrew held was the most calculated to test the qualities of a man's soul. Andrew was "betwixt and between." He was above the second, and not quite in the first rank. And of all places to test a man's character, *that* was the place. It would have been an intolerable place for James and John. With their keen and absorbing desire to be first they would have turned sick with envy had they occupied Andrew's position. But it is to Andrew's everlasting credit and honour that, in this most trying and terrible place, he preserved the sweetness and serenity of his temper. He did not mope or murmur when Peter and James and John were taken and he was left. No trace of jealousy found a lodging in his large and generous heart. He was content to be passed over; he was content to fill a subordinate place.

He was not as gifted as Peter or James or John. But he had

that rare ornament, the brightest gem in the whole chaplet of Christian graces—he had the ornament of a meek and quiet spirit. And in that great day when judgment will go by character and not by gifts, when first shall be last and last first, it may be that this man Andrew, this self-forgetful, self-effacing Andrew, will be found among the chiefest in the Kingdom of God.

¶ The longer I live, the more I learn to dread and hate that ugly, universal and well-nigh ineradicable sin of *envy*. "Love *envieth* not," says Paul. Applying that test, how many of us can lay claim to the possession of Christian love? [1]

¶ Lord, I read at the transfiguration that Peter, James, and John were admitted to behold Christ; but Andrew was excluded. So again at the reviving of the daughter of the ruler of the synagogue, these three were let in, and Andrew shut out. Lastly, in the agony the aforesaid three were called to be witnesses thereof, and still Andrew left behind. Yet he was Peter's brother, and a good man, and an apostle; why did not Christ take the two pair of brothers? was it not pity to part them? But methinks I seem more offended thereat than Andrew himself was, whom I find to express no discontent, being pleased to be accounted a loyal subject for the general, though he was no favourite in these particulars. Give me to be pleased in myself, and thankful to Thee, for what I am, though I be not equal to others in personal perfections. For such peculiar privileges are courtesies from Thee when given, and no injuries to us when denied. [2]

3. Andrew appears a faithful, useful man, doing good work in a quiet way, even in advance of Peter in practical suggestions and, perhaps, in the understanding of Christ's mission; not fitted, indeed, to fill his brother's place, not the man to stand up at Pentecost and preach to thousands, but the man to add by constant, personal, practical work to the power of the common cause. Every Simon Peter needs an Andrew, every preacher needs the practical workers to unite with him, just as every general needs subordinate officers. If Andrew be undervalued because of his brother's brilliance and publicity, he will not be when we remember how little the latter could have done, humanly speaking, without the aid of the former. Beyond doubt the Master's choice was good. Simon Peter's brother was as useful in his way and as truly an Apostle as Simon Peter himself.

[1] J. D. Jones.   [2] Thomas Fuller, *Good Thoughts for Bad Times.*

¶ There are some men who will only work if they are put into prominent positions ; they will not join the army unless they can be made officers. James and John had a good deal of that spirit; they wanted to be *first* in the Kingdom. They and Peter and the rest were always wrangling which should be greatest. But Andrew never took part in those angry debates; he had no craving for prominence. Andrew anticipated Christina Rossetti, and said to his Lord—

Give me the lowest place; not that I dare
Ask for that lowest place, but Thou hast died
That I might live and share Thy glory by Thy side.

Give me the lowest place : or if for me
That lowest place too high, make one more low
Where I may sit and see my God and love Thee so.[1]

¶ Mark Guy Pearse is an expert fisher, and rarely does a year pass without his paying a visit to the rivers of Northumberland. And he has more than once laid down what he considers to be the three essential rules for all successful fishing, and concerning which he says, " It is no good trying if you don't mind them. The first rule is this: keep yourself out of sight; and secondly, keep yourself further out of sight; and thirdly, keep yourself further out of sight ! " Mr. Pearse's counsel is confirmed by every fisher. A notable angler, writing recently in one of our daily papers, summed up all his advice in what he proclaims a golden maxim : " Let the trout see the angler, and the angler will catch no trout." Now this is a first essential in the art of manfishing : the suppression and eclipse of the preacher.[2]

[1] J. D. Jones.   [2] J. H. Jowett, *The Passion for Souls*, 62.

JAMES THE APOSTLE.

LITERATURE.

Adeney, W. F., in *Men of the New Testament* : Matthew to Timothy (1905), 14ᵗ.

Banks, L. A., *Paul and His Friends* (1898), 169.

Durell, J. C. V., *The Self-Revelation of Our Lord* (1910), 145.

Godet, F., *Studies on the New Testament* (1879), 218.

Greenhough, J. G., *The Apostles of Our Lord* (1904), 63.

Jones, J. D., *The Glorious Company of the Apostles* (1904), 46.

Lovell, R. H., *First Types of the Christian Life* (1895), 57.

Maclaren, A., *The Wearied Christ* (1893), 51.

Plummer, A., *The Humanity of Christ*, 144.

Rattenbury, J. E., *The Twelve* (1914), 111.

Stanley, A. P., *Sermons and Essays on the Apostolic Age* (1874), 284.

Watson, J., *Children of the Resurrection* (1912), 129.

Dictionary of the Bible, ii. (1899) 540 (J. B. Mayor).

Dictionary of Christ and the Gospels, i. (1906) 846 (H. W. Fulford).

Encyclopædia Biblica, ii. (1901), col. 2317 (O. Cone).

JAMES THE APOSTLE.

And going on from thence he saw other two brethren, James the son of
Zebedee, and John his brother, in the boat with Zebedee their father, mend-
ing their nets; and he called them.—Matt. iv. 21.

And he [Herod] killed James the brother of John with the sword.—
Acts xii. 2.

1. THE first three Lives of our Lord—the Synoptic Gospels—as
well as the Acts of the Apostles contain lists of the Twelve, in
which the name of James stands nearly always between those of
Peter and John. But he is sometimes ranked after, instead of
before, his brother (see Luke viii. 51, ix. 28; Acts i. 13 R.V.), and
it would appear that his early death, with the subsequent prominence of the disciple whom Jesus loved, had by the time the
Gospels were written already begun to throw his name into the
shade. His death in the prime of his manhood strikingly illustrates his Master's words, "The one shall be taken, and the other
left." While John remained to teach and inspire the Apostolic
Church until the reign of Domitian in the last decade of the first
century, James was taken full half a century earlier to join the
Church triumphant in heaven, being the first of the "glorious
company of the apostles" to be numbered likewise with the
"noble army of martyrs." And not only was his career soon
ended, but no adequate record of it was preserved.

How we should like, in particular, to possess some authentic
account of his latest days and hours, some mirror of his mind in
the ultimate ordeal, some human document worthy to compare
with the last speech of St. Stephen or the last letters of St.
Ignatius, some pen-and-ink portrait for the Church on earth to
cherish and contemplate till the end of time! History has done
but scant justice to this Apostle, epitomizing the story of his
martyrdom in one brief sentence and the beginning of a second.
King Herod Agrippa, we are told, "killed James the brother of

John with the sword. And when he saw that it pleased the
Jews, he proceeded to seize Peter also." And then the chapter
goes on to relate, with a wealth of charming incidents, the story
of the rescue of St. Peter from prison and from death. But no
word of embellishment is spared for the story of the Apostle who
was *not* rescued. The historical style was never more bare and
unadorned than here. The sword, we learn, did its work, and
the work pleased the Jews, and that is all. That is all, but the
imagination is not satisfied with a gleaming sword and a vampire
smile. How it longs to recreate a whole psychological drama of
heroic faith and spiritual passion on the one hand, of sinister
policy and fanatical hate on the other!

But regrets are vain. We shall never know how the brave
Apostle received his sentence of death, how he prepared himself—
if any time was allowed—for the moment of his departure, or
how he fared in his swift passage through the valley of the
shadow. Perhaps the historian himself did not know. Perhaps
it was all done so stealthily and so suddenly that nothing ever
leaked out. And so the Church could only guess with what feelings the Apostle stepped into the river of death, just as it could
only imagine with what a storm of jubilation he was welcomed on
the other side. How true it is that the place which a man fills
in history, the meed of honour and applause which he receives
among his fellows, is but a poor index of his worth in the eyes of
God! For every hero who receives the Victoria Cross how many
others just as brave—the flower of a nation's chivalry—sleep their
last earthly sleep in unknown graves! Is it "just their luck"?
Say rather that not one of them is forgotten before God. The
names which have not become famous on earth are written in
heaven, and "many that are first shall be last; and the last shall
be first."

¶ According to the legend of Saint Iago, the patron saint of
Spain, the gospel was first preached in Spain by St. James, who
afterwards returned to Judæa, and, after performing many miracles
there, was finally put to death by Herod. His body was placed
on board ship at Joppa and transported to Iria in the north-west
of Spain under angelic guidance. The surrounding heathen were
converted by the prodigies which witnessed to the power of the
saint, and a church was built over his tomb. During the barbarian
invasions all memory of the hallowed spot was lost till it was

revealed by vision in the year 800. The body was then moved by order of Alphonso II. to the place now called Compostella (abbreviated from Jacomo Postolo), which became famous as a place of pilgrimage throughout Europe. The saint was believed to have appeared on many occasions mounted on a white horse, leading the Spanish armies to victory against their infidel foes. The impossibilities of the story have been pointed out by Roman Catholic scholars.[1]

2. Although this Apostle is referred to after his decease as "James the brother of John," as if that were his chief title to fame, yet there are evidences, slight and easily overlooked but quite convincing, that during his lifetime he was the more prominent, just as he was probably the elder, of the two sons of Salome and Zebedee. In the Gospel of St. Matthew we find the order of the two names inverted, for we read twice of "James the son of Zebedee and John his brother" (iv. 21, x. 2), and once of "James and John his brother" (xvii. 1). In the Gospel of Mark we hear of "James and John his brother," and of "John the brother of James" (i. 19, iii. 17, v. 37). In the earliest list of the Twelve, contained in Mark iii. 16–19, Peter's name stands first, James's second, and John's third. It is true that the lists in Matthew and Luke begin with the brothers Peter and Andrew, but it is probable that this arrangement was an afterthought, and that during the whole of our Lord's earthly ministry Peter, James, and John were recognized in this order, as the three foremost and most highly privileged disciples. Just as Jesus selected from the wide outer circle of His followers twelve disciples who formed an inner circle, so from among the Twelve He chose three intimate human friends who formed an innermost circle of His Apostles. These three were with the Master on great and memorable occasions—at the healing of Peter's wife's mother, at the raising of Jairus' daughter, at the Transfiguration, at the Mount of Olives during the great discourse on the Last Things, and at the Agony in the Garden of Gethsemane. How many sermons and studies, how many theological, ecclesiastical, and mystical books have been devoted to Peter and John, but how few to the second of that great Triumvirate! Yet it is by no means impossible to gain such a knowledge of James the

[1] J. B. Mayor, in Hastings' *Dictionary of the Bible*, ii. 541.

Apostle as must constrain us to love him; for, if only a few rays of light have been thrown upon his character and career, yet each of them is so beautifully illuminative that with the exercise of a little historical imagination we can see him again, as he lived and as he died, a noble and alluring type of Christian manhood.

When we ask what manner of man he was in his youthful, formative years, we soon find that he had three natural enough human propensities, each of which required, not to be eradicated, but to be touched to finer issues, before he could become a disciple after Jesus' own heart, worthy at length to wear a halo as the first martyr among the Apostles. By nature he was zealous, jealous, and ambitious in the pursuit of earthly ends; and by grace he became so true-hearted and whole-hearted in the service of Christ—so zealous in His cause, so jealous of His honour, so ambitious to follow in His steps—that Herod Agrippa, king of the Jews, could think of no surer way of pleasing his subjects than by offering him as the first victim to their fanatical hate.

¶ The Bishop lost no opportunity of impressing upon his clergy the need of kindling in themselves, from the altar of God, the flames of fervid enthusiasm, and prophetic fire. The people are not saved by the keenness of a cold philosophy, but by the affection of an inspiring faith. Preaching upon this subject at St. Peter's, Little Oakley, March 30, 1882, the Bishop said:

"The ministers of the Church of England have many gifts and graces, but they too seldom have fervour, which, for the work they have to do, is, perhaps, the most needed of all. The common people rarely have subtle minds. Laboured expositions, an elaborated style, dogmatic precision, rarely touch and certainly do not affect or move them. They ask for some potent tokens of the presence of the Spirit of God. Churchmen shrink, and rightly so, from extravagances, and lament to see some strange, and to them startling, things done in the name and for the cause of Christ. They naturally, and properly, like quiet, sober, and well-ordered ways. But all these things are compatible with fervour. If the clergy wish to reach the mass of the people—and to do so would be the greatest glory and stability of the Church—I venture to assert it will never be done except by fervour." [1]

[1] J. W. Diggle, *The Lancashire Life of Bishop Fraser,* 346.

I.

Zealous by Nature and by Grace.

1. James's character is strikingly indicated by the surname which the Lord bestowed on him and his brother—"Boanerges, which is, Sons of thunder." This strange appellation is found in Mark iii. 17, and nowhere else in the New Testament. The derivation of the word is uncertain, some scholars holding that it means "sons of tumult" or "sons of rushing" (*bĕnē-rĕgĕsh*), others that it means "sons of anger," "soon angered" (*bĕnē-rōgĕz*). In any case, it seems to have been suggested to Jesus by the intense and enthusiastic nature, the fervent and irascible temper, of the two brothers. There is no reason whatever to suppose that it referred to the quality of their voices, though the name Boanerges is now popularly applied to a loud and powerful preacher. It did not once denote any physical trait, or any single characteristic of any kind, but referred to the whole disposition of the men—the ardent vehement spirit often latent in the depths of still and reserved natures, ordinarily held in strict control, but flaming forth on occasion with fierce, volcanic energy.

¶ Dr. John Brown, author of *Rab and His Friends*, writing of his granduncle, Ebenezer Brown, the Seceder minister at Inverkeithing, whose gifts as a preacher so impressed Lord Jeffrey and Lord Brougham, says : "Uncle Ebenezer was always good and saintly, but he was great once a week ; six days he brooded over his message, was silent, withdrawn, self-involved ; on the Sabbath, that downcast, almost timid man, who shunned men, the instant he was in the pulpit, stood up a son of thunder. Such a voice! such a piercing eye! such an inevitable forefinger, held out trembling with the terrors of the Lord ; such a power of asking questions and letting them fall deep into the hearts of his hearers, and then answering them himself, with an 'ah, sirs !' that thrilled and quivered from him to them."

¶ An extract from the Meditations and Devotions which Newman wrote from time to time may be set down as having much of self-revelation :—

"Breathe on me with that Breath which infuses energy and kindles fervour. In asking for fervour, I ask for all that I can need, and all that Thou canst give ; for it is the crown of all gifts and all virtues. It cannot really and fully be, except where all are present. It is the beauty and the glory, as it is also the continual safeguard and purifier, of them all. In asking for fervour, I am asking for effectual strength, consistency, and perseverance; I am asking for deadness to every human motive, and simplicity of intention to please Thee; I am asking for faith, hope, and charity in their most heavenly exercise. In asking for fervour I am asking to be rid of the fear of man, and the desire of his praise; I am asking for the gift of prayer, because it will be so sweet; I am asking for that loyal perception of duty, which follows on yearning affection; I am asking for sanctity, peace, and joy all at once. In asking for fervour, I am asking for the brightness of the Cherubim and the fire of the Seraphim, and the whiteness of all Saints. In asking for fervour, I am asking for that which, while it implies all gifts, is that in which I signally fail. Nothing would be a trouble to me, nothing a difficulty, had I but fervour of soul."[1]

2. Jesus did not avoid fervent men; on the contrary, He enlisted them in His service, He chose them as His intimate friends. What a work for His Kingdom they could do, if once the impetuous current of their lives was turned into another channel! Harness the forked lightning that flashes from a storm-cloud, or the raging torrent that thunders over a precipice, and these mighty forces will beneficently light and heat whole cities. And man's native endowment of untamed energy, like Nature's own mechanical powers, is at first neutral in quality, all its moral value depending on the character of his aims or ideals, and the spirit in which he pursues them. Remember how the same Jew of Tarsus who confesses that his zeal at one time made him a persecutor of the Church yet declares that "it is good to be zealously sought in a good matter at all times," and that Christ's purpose in giving Himself for us is to purify unto Himself a people for His own possession, zealous of good works. The passionate heart, therefore, needs only to find its destined object, its true affinity, in order to purify and hallow and perfect itself. Then the enthusiastic temperament will resemble that of Jesus Himself, of whom it is recorded that the zeal of God's house consumed Him.

Jesus, let it be repeated, chose as His favourite disciples men of a fervent spirit, capable of an intense devotion and a self-sacrificing love. And has not all the best work ever attempted

[1] W. Ward, *The Life of John Henry Cardinal Newman*, i. 367.

for humanity—the quiet, steady, patient, unintermittent labour
which has made the world a better place for us all to live in—
been done by men and women in whose hearts has burned
a hidden fire, purified into a passion of holy love for Christ and
His Kingdom? Therefore in days of doubt we must ever pray—

> Oh, bring us back once more
> The vanished days of yore,
> When the world with faith was filled;
> Bring back the fervid zeal,
> The hearts of fire and steel,
> The hands that believe and build.

¶ Dr. Chalmers was an *enthusiast* in its true and good sense;
he was "entheat," as if full of God, as the old poets called it. It
was this ardour—this superabounding life, this immediateness of
thought and action, idea and emotion, setting the whole man
agoing at once—that gave a power and a charm to everything
he did. . . . His energy, his contagious enthusiasm—this it was
which gave the peculiar character to his religion, to his politics, to
his *personnel*; everything he did was done heartily—if he desired
heavenly blessings, he "panted" for them—"his soul broke for
the longing." To give the words of the spiritual and subtle
Culverwel in his " Light of Nature ": " Religion (and indeed everything else) was no matter of indifferency to him. It was θερμὸν τι
πρᾶγμα, a certain fiery thing, as Aristotle calls love; it required
and it got, the very flower and vigour of the spirit—the strength
and sinews of the soul—the prime and top of the affections—this
is that grace, that panting grace—we know the name of it and
that's all—'tis called zeal—a flaming edge of the affection—the
ruddy complexion of the soul." [1]

II.

JEALOUS BY NATURE AND BY GRACE.

1. The zeal of James for the Christ had at first more of heat
than of light, and nothing in the world is more dangerous than
a blind zeal which takes the form of religious fanaticism. St.
Paul testifies that the Jews of his time had a zeal for God, but
" not according to knowledge," and the words well describe the

[1] Dr. John Brown, *Horæ Subsecivæ*, ii. **127.**

zeal of the two sons of Zebedee at the beginning of their career as followers of Jesus.

That it was an intemperate and misguided zeal is proved by the familiar story of their passing with the Lord through Samaria on the way to the Holy City. He sent messengers to a village of the Samaritans which lay in His path, to make ready for His coming, *i.e.*, to seek lodgings for the night, and the villagers would not receive Him, simply because His face was directed towards Jerusalem. Their refusal of hospitality was no unheard-of rudeness, but one of those acts of resentment and retaliation which were constantly occurring in the Holy Land. If the Jews, whether of Galilee or of Judæa, would have no dealings with the Samaritans, the Samaritans could equally refuse to have any dealings with the Jews. Against Jesus personally they had no possible grudge, and had they known Him better, had they welcomed Him for a night, they would have found out how friendly were His feelings to the Samaritans. But they did not know Him, and it was enough for them that He belonged to the hated race. When therefore He came through their territory, seeking shelter and rest and food, they could not deny themselves the spiteful pleasure of bidding Him go and seek entertainment among His own countrymen. The feud of Jew and Samaritan was centuries old, and very little was ever needed to fan the embers of strife into a new flame. And on that particular evening it almost appeared as if there were no fiercer fanatics among all the Galilæan pilgrims than the two sons of Zebedee. But it was not any theological dispute or racial difference that roused their wrath; it was jealousy for the honour of their Lord. The night was falling fast, and they could not brook the idea of their Master spending it under the stars, or trudging on weary foot till He came to some more hospitable hamlet or village. And they felt that people who could be so insufferably rude to the best of men deserved no mercy. "Wilt thou," said James and his brother in their blazing wrath, "that we bid fire to come down from heaven and consume them?"

¶ It is one thing to be a Son of Thunder, another to become a father of lightning. Some even edifying examples must be copied, though in the spirit yet not in the letter: thus what Elias did St. James must forbear to do. When Christ sends down fire

upon His flock, it is for salvation not for destruction, as St. John
Baptist aforetime prophesied : "He shall baptize you with the
Holy Ghost, and with fire"; a promise both visibly and invisibly
fulfilled to the Apostles, when at Pentecost the Holy Ghost
descended upon them in the likeness of fiery tongues. For us to
covet and compass revenge might make us indeed like lightning : but
how ? by making us like Satan, who "as lightning" fell from heaven.[1]

2. The two brothers had in their hearts that evening the very
spirit of persecutors, who do not hesitate to inflict pain and death
in the name and for the sake of Jesus.   They did not yet realize
what depths of mercy were in their Master's great soul, or how
wide a gulf still separated His spirit and theirs.   *He* never made
fire or sword the instrument of His will.   He said on one occasion
that He could have summoned twelve legions of angels to be His
bodyguard, but He did not summon them.   He saw that evening,
as clearly as the sons of Zebedee did, how cruel, how vindictive,
how inhuman the Samaritans were; but to His mind the only
victory worth gaining over such men was the victory of love.
Fire could never work His will, for it was not His will that any
should perish; He "came not to destroy men's lives but to save
them."   (Whether these words are part of the original text or a
marginal comment, they at any rate rightly represent the tenor of
the passage.)   And in rebuking His jealous disciples, Jesus rebuked
the persecutors of all ages, teaching that it is His purpose to win
mankind without coercion, by that sweet reasonableness, that
Divine patience, that redeeming love, which beareth, hopeth,
believeth, and endureth all things, and never faileth.

> "Oh, for a two-edged sword, my God,
>   That I may swiftly slay
> Each foe of Thine—that I may speed
>   Thy universal sway!"
> "Put up thy sword within its sheath;
> My gift is life; would'st thou deal death?"
>
> "Oh, for the fire from heaven, my God,
>   That it may fiercely burn
> All those who, following not with me,
>   To other masters turn";
> "With scorching flame would'st thou reprove,
> But I must win by fire of love!

[1] Christina G. Rossetti, *Called to be Saints*, 344.

"My son, art thou above thy Lord?
A greater one than He?
When callèd I for fire or sword?
Thou hast not learnt of Me:
Make 'truth thy sword, and love thy flame,
Then battle in thy Master's name.'"[1]

¶ "I beseech you," said Paul, "by the mildness and gentleness of Christ." The word which our Bible translates by "gentleness" means more properly "reasonableness, with sweetness," "sweet reasonableness." "I beseech you by the mildness and sweet reasonableness of Christ." This mildness and sweet reasonableness it was which, stamped with the individual charm they had in Jesus Christ, came to the world as something new, won its heart and conquered it. Every one had been asserting his ordinary self and was miserable; to forbear to assert one's ordinary self, to place one's happiness in mildness and sweet reasonableness, was a revelation. As men followed this novel route to happiness, a living spring opened beside their way, the spring of charity; and out of this spring arose those two heavenly visitants, Charis and Irene, *grace* and *peace*, which enraptured the poor wayfarer, and filled him with a joy which brought all the world after him. And still, whenever these visitants appear, as appear for a witness to the vitality of Christianity they daily do, it is from the same spring that they arise; and this spring is opened solely by the mildness and sweet reasonableness which forbears to assert our ordinary self, nay, which even takes pleasure in effacing it.[2]

3. As "it was the custom of the Galilæans, when they came to the Holy City at the festival, to take their journey through the country of the Samaritans" (Josephus, *Antiq.* xx. vi. 1), it seems somewhat strange if the mere fact of Jesus' face being directed towards Jerusalem was the sole occasion of the Samaritan rudeness; and Dr. A. B. Bruce suggests that "perhaps the manner of the messengers had something to do with it. Had Jesus gone Himself the result might have been different. Perhaps He was making an experiment to see how His followers and the Samaritans would get on together." If the experiment failed, it may have been because the disciples had not yet enough of the mind and spirit of the Master. Their devotion to Him was unquestionable, but there was still too much unchristian heat, unholy fire, in their

---

[1] W. Chatterton Dix.
[2] Matthew Arnold, *St. Paul and Protestantism.*

fervour. They had not yet discovered that the Christian wins his triumphs, not by returning evil for evil, but by overcoming evil with good. They had still much to learn and unlearn before they could understand the precept, "Love your enemies, do good to them that hate you, bless them that curse you, pray for them that despitefully use you."

In a sense it was, of course, quite natural that James and his brother that evening should feel their hearts grow hot within them, and that their indignation should flame out so fiercely against the churlish Samaritans. In a sense it is always natural for strong men to be intolerant of those who oppose and thwart them. But things are not always right because they are natural. The end and aim of true religion is to transcend the natural by the supernatural, to lift us above ourselves by making us partakers of the Divine nature, to subdue the wrath of man by giving him a vision and an experience of the love of God. When James and his brother had that vision and that experience they fulfilled their destiny, not by seeking to destroy the lives of others, but by giving their own lives, as Christ gave His, and so helping to create that new spirit of brotherly love which will in the long run break down all the barriers between Jew and Samaritan, Greek and barbarian, Slav and Magyar, Celt and Teuton, black man and white, making them all one man in Christ Jesus. To-day it may seem almost as impossible as it seemed twenty centuries ago. But with God all things are possible, and all things are possible to them that believe. "That stupid word *impossible*," said Napoleon, "is not in my vocabulary"; but he had to admit it at last. Christ alone has never admitted it. Listen to His language: "If ye have faith as a grain of mustard seed, ye shall say unto this mountain, Remove hence to yonder place; and it shall remove," and again, "If ye have faith as a grain of mustard seed, ye would say unto this sycamine tree, Be thou rooted up, and be thou planted in the sea; and it would have obeyed you."

¶ Faith, no larger than the tiniest mustard-seed, but able to toss the mountains, as pebbles, from their foundations, into the sea, is the determination to do the thing chosen to be done or to die—literally to die—in the trying to do it. Death is farther from most of us than we fancy, and if we would but risk all, to win or lose all, we could almost always do the deed which looks so grimly impossible. Those who have faced great physical dangers, or who have been matched by fate against overwhelming odds of anxiety and trouble, alone know what great things are to be done when men stand at bay and face the world, and fate, and life, and death, and misfortune, all banded together against them, and say in their hearts, "We will win this fight or die." Then, at that word, when it is spoken earnestly, in sincerity and truth, the iron will rises up and takes possession of the feeble body, the doubting soul shakes off its hesitating weakness, is drawn back upon itself like a strong bow bent double, is compressed and full of a terrible latent power, like the handful of deadly explosive which, buried in the bosom of the rock, will presently shake the mighty cliff to its roots, as no thunderbolt could shake it.[1]

III.

AMBITIOUS BY NATURE AND BY GRACE.

1. Ambition was the third trait in the character of James which needed to be transmuted. Ambition is the strong and inordinate desire for preferment, honour, pre-eminence, superiority, power, or fame. Conscious of a great enthusiasm in the service of Jesus, and assured that He was Israel's promised Messiah, James and his brother imagined that, as the privileged disciples and intimate friends of Jesus, they had an incontestable claim to the highest rank and the noblest titles in the coming Kingdom. Nothing less would satisfy James than that he should be Christ's grand vizier. And when he heard the Lord say to Peter at Cæsarea Philippi, "Thou art Peter, and upon this rock I will build my church," the words sent a pang to his heart, because he mistook the great promise for a personal slight. Brooding over the thought that Peter might stand highest in honour and power, he and his brother determined to prevent it.

And there was another who shared their ambition, thinking nothing too good for them. This was their mother Salome, the sister of Mary the mother of Jesus. Accompanied by her, the two disciples came and cast themselves before Jesus in an attitude of worship; and when He asked them what they desired, they answered, "Grant unto us that we may sit, one on thy right hand,

---

[1] F. Marion Crawford, *The Cigarette-Maker's Romance*, chap. ix.

and one on thy left hand, in thy glory." According to Matthew it was the ambitious mother who said on their behalf, "Command that these my two sons may sit, one on thy right hand, and one on thy left hand, in thy kingdom."

Thus they all laid bare their jealous, envious hearts, revealing at the same time their blindness to spiritual values, their ignorance of the true nature of honours and rewards in Christ's Kingdom. In asking for the first places there, they did not know what they were saying. If even in the kingdoms of this world, won and maintained by the sword, the post of honour is often the post of danger, what is the law of promotion in the kingdom of love? In that kingdom every true and faithful follower of Jesus has in some sense to drink of His cup and to be baptized with His baptism.

2. Jesus asked the sons of Zebedee if they were able to fulfil these conditions of service. Had they the moral and spiritual power to walk in His footsteps? It was a searching question, and it brought out again the nobler side of the men's character. Even if their unhesitating and confident answer betrayed an imperfect knowledge of what the cup and the baptism meant, it at any rate proved their implicit faith in Christ, and their splendid devotion to His cause. Whatsoever He saw fit to require of them they were convinced that they could fulfil. To walk in His steps and share His experiences, to be with Him in doing or in suffering, to be at all costs identified with His cause and Kingdom —that was the only life they cared to live, and for that service they believed they had the power, as they certainly had the will. Not therefore with foolish boasting, but with the daring of a great love, they answered, "We are able."

It was a noble and a moving answer; and even if there was still some dross in the gold, some forgetfulness of men's need of heavenly power to help them in the evil hour, it was essentially the right answer. For the humility that makes a man say, "*I* can never walk in the steps of Christ; I can never drink of His cup or be baptized with His baptism," is a humility which Jesus not only does not love but entirely repudiates. In truth He loves ambition if it is of the right kind—the ambition which makes men aspire to be fellow-workers with Him and fellow-sufferers with Him, the ambition which both expects great things from Him and attempts great things for Him. There is no limit to the ability of those who are vitalized by His spirit, quickened by His grace. "I can do all things," said Paul to the Philippians, "through Christ which strengtheneth me." To the students of Edinburgh, Henry Drummond used to say, "You have all omnipotence behind you, and you cannot fail." "Domine," said Augustine, "da quod jubes, et jube quod vis"—"Lord, give what Thou commandest, and command what Thou wilt."

3. Well pleased with the confident answer of James and his brother, Jesus took them at their word. He knew better than they did what the cup and the baptism meant, but He believed that they would not shrink from the ordeal. And before the testing day came to James the Apostle, he was prepared for the destiny that awaited him. Till the day of his death he was evidently regarded as one of the "pillars" (στύλοι) of the Church in Jerusalem, a designation afterwards reserved for James the Lord's brother, and Peter, and John. And there must have been a reason why King Herod Agrippa pitched on him rather than any of the other Apostles as his first victim. James was chosen because he was the foremost in zeal and the most valiant in utterance among them all. Though still in the prime of life, he was now an older man than he was on the unforgotten day when Jesus spoke of the cup and the baptism. Twelve years had passed, and he was changed. He had lost all his intolerance, except the intolerance of sin; all his ambition, except the ambition to serve Christ; and if he retained his old zeal, it was now a pure and holy flame. On himself, not on the Samaritans, had fallen the fire of heaven—the Pentecostal fire of Christian love. It is said that no heart is pure which is not passionate, and if the question was asked in those great days which of all the Apostles had the most passionate heart and the most fervent speech, everyone answered without hesitation, "James the son of Zebedee." Therefore when Herod, in the spirit of his grandsire, who half a century before decreed the massacre of the innocents, resolved to destroy the Church in Jerusalem, he was well advised in beginning as he did with James the brother of John. And if James heard any rumour of the danger which his burning evangelism was making for himself, he was in no wise perturbed, and never dreamed of

fleeing from the Holy City. He only preached the more earnestly, and besought men the more fervently to accept the Messiah, until suddenly the blow fell. And then, having drunk the Lord's cup and received His baptism, he went to be for ever with Him.

4. Whether he took his seat at the Lord's right or left hand, as he once desired, is not told. His reward was doubtless such as his imagination had never conceived, but nothing is said of that. History emphasizes the bare fact of his death, saying nothing of the crown of life which he won. Enough that by his example he inspired one knows not how many others in the Early Church to endure scorn and hatred and shame and death, teaching them that they were able to face the worst that man could do, since all things, including love's final sacrifice, are possible to them that believe. Pioneer in the as yet almost untrodden path of suffering for Christ's sake, he left a name which inspired, and may still inspire, the manhood of Christendom to bear the cross, not seeking deliverance.

> They climbed the steep ascent of heaven,
> Through peril, toil, and pain :
> O God, to us may grace be given
> To follow in their train.

¶ The Church, by the martyrdom of St. James, lost in her infancy one of her main pillars; but God was pleased that His name should be glorified by so illustrious a testimony, and that it should appear He was the immediate supporter and defender of His Church. For when it was deprived of its chief members and pastors, it remained no less firm than before ; and even grew and gathered strength from the most violent persecutions. The apostle with confidence committed his tender flock to God, and commended to them his own work, whilst he rejoiced to go to his Redeemer, and to give his life for Him. We all meet with trials; but can we fear or hesitate to drink a cup presented to us by the hand of God, and which our Lord and Captain, by free choice, and out of pure love, was pleased Himself to drink first for our sake ? He asks us whether we can drink of His cup, He encourages us by setting before our eyes the glory of heaven, and He invites us by His own divine example. Let us humbly implore His grace, without which we can do nothing, and take with joy this cup of salvation which He presents us with His divine hand.[1]

[1] Alban Butler, *The Lives of the Fathers, Martyrs and Other Saints*, ii. 97.

Two brothers freely cast their lot
  With David's royal Son;
The cost of conquest counting not,
  They deem the battle won.

Brothers in heart, they hope to gain
  An undivided joy;
That man may one with man remain,
  As boy was one with boy.

Christ heard; and will'd that James should fall,
  First prey of Satan's rage;
John linger out his fellows all,
  And die in bloodless age.

Now they join hands once more above,
  Before the Conqueror's throne;
Thus God grants prayer, but in His love
  Makes times and ways His own.[1]

[1] J. H. Newman.

PHILIP.

LITERATURE.

Banks, L. A., *Christ and His Friends* (1895), 70, 81.
Black, H., *Edinburgh Sermons* (1906), 164.
Brooke, S. A., *The Spirit of the Christian Life* (1902), 123.
Creighton, M., *The Heritage of the Spirit* (1896), 129.
Davies, D., *Talks with Men, Women and Children*, v. (1893) 591.
Drummond, R. B., *The Christology of the New Testament* (1901), 97.
Edwards, F., *These Twelve* (1895), 7.
Gladden, W., *Where does the Sky Begin?* (1904), 286.
Greenhough, J. G., *The Apostles of Our Lord* (1904), 75.
Hankey, W. B., *The Church and the Saints* (1907), 111.
Hodges, G., *The Human Nature of the Saints* (1905), 102.
Holden, J. S., *Redeeming Vision* (1908), 63.
Jones, J. D., *The Glorious Company of the Apostles* (1904), 109.
Liddon, H. P., *Sermons on Some Words of Christ* (1892), 311.
    „   „   *University Sermons*, ii. (1879) 1.
Lightfoot, J. B., *Cambridge Sermons* (1890), 129.
Lilley, J. P., *Four Apostles* (1912), 17.
Lovell, R. H., *First Types of the Christian Life* (1895), 145.
Maclaren, A., *A Year's Ministry*, ii. (1888) 155.
Matheson, G., *Representative Men of the New Testament* (1905), 160
Milligan, G., *The Twelve Apostles*, 49.
Pearson, J. B., *Disciples in Doubt* (1879), 1.
Plummer, A., *The Humanity of Christ*, 80.
Rattenbury, J. E., *The Twelve* (1914), 155.
Simon, D. W., *Twice Born*, 60.
Skrine, J. H., *Saints and Worthies* (1901), 20.
Stimson, H. A., *The New Things of God* (1908), 169.
Telford, J., *The Story of the Upper Room* (1905), 115.
Trench, R. C., *Studies in the Gospels* (1867), 66.
Westcott, B. F., *Village Sermons* (1906), 236.
Dictionary of the Bible, iii. (1900) 834 (H. Cowan).
Dictionary of Christ and the Gospels, ii. (1908) 359 (G. Milligan).
Encyclopædia Biblica, iii. (1902), col. 3697 (P. W. Schmiedel).
Expositor, 1st Ser., i. (1875) 29 (T. T. Lynch); vi. (1877) 445 (A Roberts).

PHILIP.

1. WE know but little about the characters of the companions of Jesus. We reverence them because they were chosen by Him to be His witnesses; but we have little means of comparing their lives with ours, or drawing from their experiences anything that may help ourselves. They are almost as remote from our struggles as the chieftains of the heroic age are remote from the problems of modern warfare. They stand by themselves as examples of the thoroughness and sufficiency of the life in Christ. They stand unapproachable patterns of quiet strength, of unfailing joyousness, of large hopefulness, or perfect trust. They had no room for the doubts, the questionings, the despondencies, the sense of struggle, the feelings of sadness, which overpower the modern mind, and were inevitable as soon as the Church came into conscious antagonism with the society and speculations of the world.

Yet though this is the great lesson to be learned from reflection on the companions of Jesus, further curiosity about them is at least pardonable. We may collect the brief and fragmentary notices of them which occur in the gospel narratives, and so construct some view of the chief characteristics of thought of those among them who have left no written records of themselves. In this attempt our criticism unconsciously follows the example set by pictorial art. It was natural for the painter to use the figures of the Twelve as types of different temperaments. It was natural that a belief in the universality of the gospel message should lead to a pious wish to discover in the earliest disciples signs of varied characters and divergent impulses. It was natural to group round the Person of the Redeemer men of every sort, as Leonardo set the example in his picture of The Last

Supper. Though it may be little else than a fancy, it is a fancy which embodies an eternal truth—the truth that Jesus draws all manner of men unto Him, and can satisfy the cravings of all manner of minds.

2. Philip was one of the Twelve; and that is all that we learn about him from the first three Gospels. It is the Fourth Gospel that brings him before us as an individual with his own life and character. There are four occasions on which he comes into notice—first, at his call; next, in connexion with the feeding of the five thousand; thirdly, when certain Greeks came to him and said, "Sir, we would see Jesus"; and lastly, during the discourse in the Upper Room when he said to Jesus, "Lord, shew us the Father, and it sufficeth us." We shall take these occasions in order, and when we have observed Philip's behaviour on each occasion we shall say what manner of man we think he was.

3. But first of all let us notice that he came from Bethsaida in Galilee and that he was probably one of the disciples of John the Baptist.

(1) He came from Bethsaida. "Now Philip was from Bethsaida, of the city of Andrew and Peter," says John; and as we read that sentence we are inclined at first glance just to regard it as a geographical note—Philip's postal address, so to speak. But this is more than a geographical note; it is a link in Philip's spiritual history. This is more than the mention of the place of Philip's abode; it gives us the clue and key to Philip's religious development. The important part of the sentence is not that Philip was from Bethsaida, but that Bethsaida was the city of Andrew and Peter. This sentence links Philip with Andrew and Peter. It reveals to us not his mere dwelling but—what is infinitely more important—his friendships, the friendships that shaped and moulded his character, and so led to his new birth and his Apostolic calling. It was Philip's good fortune, it was his happy lot, to live in the same town and to count among his friends those two eminent saints of God, Andrew and Peter, the sons of Jonas.

(2) Again, Philip was probably one of John the Baptist's disciples. He always stands fifth in the list of the Twelve,

though in point of time he was fourth to receive the call, which
came to him the day after Jesus had enlisted Andrew and Peter
(John i. 43). It is probable that he, like many of the others, had
been a disciple of the Baptist, or at least had felt the stirrings of
that prophet's words, and had thus been prepared for a higher
service. The work of that God-sent messenger had been avowedly
to prepare the way of the Lord, and not the least effective part of
it had been done upon these men by impressing them with the
conviction that the coming of the Messiah was at hand, and
opening their minds for the reception of Him. We can trace his
influence in their subsequent thoughts and questionings. His
zeal had kindled zeal in them which was not always in accord
with Christ's gentler spirit; but his courage and love of righteousness and stern hatred of wrongdoing had infused an element of
strength into their character which Jesus was able to temper and
subdue to His own finer mind. He "rested from his labours, but
his works did follow him"; and it was to him doubtless, along
with others, that our Lord referred in the words, "I sent you to
reap that whereon ye bestowed no labour: other men laboured,
and ye are entered into their labours."

L.

PHILIP AND THE MESSIAH.

1. Jesus was forming an inner circle of disciples who should
come out more openly on His side than the majority of those who
heard His teaching. Already in a single day He had gathered
three from among the disciples of the Baptist, namely, Andrew
and his brother Simon and another unnamed, doubtless the
Evangelist John himself; for here he writes as an eye-witness.
But Jesus felt that He needed more followers, and after
deliberation He, the next day, moved northward from Bethabara
in search of other candidates. In the course of His journey He
remembered Philip; and, finding him, He addressed to him the
same call as He had given to the others.

¶ Andrew and John sought Christ and found Him. To them
He revealed Himself as very willing to be approached, and glad

to welcome any to His side. Peter, who comes next, was brought
to Christ by his brother, and to him Christ revealed Himself as
reading his heart, and promising and giving him higher functions
and a more noble character. But "Jesus findeth Philip," who
was not seeking Jesus, and who was brought by no one. To him
Christ reveals Himself as drawing near to many a heart that has
not thought of Him, and laying a masterful hand of gracious
authority on the springs of life and character in that autocratic
word, "Follow Me." So we have a gradually heightening revelation of the Master's graciousness to all souls, to them that seek
and to them that seek Him not.[1]

2. "Jesus findeth Philip, and said unto him, Follow me."
No doubt a great deal more passed, but no doubt what more
passed was less significant and less important for the development of faith in this man than what is recorded. The word of
authority, the invitation which was a demand, the demand which
was an invitation, and the personal impression which He produced
upon Philip's heart, were the things that bound him to Jesus
Christ for ever. "Follow me," spoken at the beginning of the
journey of Christ and His disciples back to Galilee, might have
meant merely, on the surface, "Come back with us." But the
words have, of course, a much deeper meaning. They mean—Be
My disciple.

We lose the force of the image by much repetition. Sheep
follow a shepherd. Travellers follow a guide. Here is a man
upon some dangerous cornice of the Alps, with a ledge of
limestone as broad as the palm of your hand, and perhaps
a couple of feet of snow above that for him to walk upon, a
precipice on either side; and his guide says, as he ropes himself
to him, "Now, tread where I tread!" Travellers follow their
guides. Soldiers follow their commanders. There is the hell of
the battlefield; here a line of wavering, timid, raw recruits.
Their commander rushes to the front and throws himself upon
the advancing enemy with the one word, "Follow!" And the
weakest becomes a hero.

"Follow me," says Christ to you and me. We may not have
mastered all the subtleties of theology; like Philip, we may not
even realize to the full the glory of Christ, but at any rate we see

[1] A. Maclaren, *A Year's Ministry*, ii. 156.

in Him the one Leader and Guide of souls. Let us follow Him, therefore. Let us say with the American poet—

> If Jesus Christ is a man,—
> And only a man,—I say
> That of all mankind I cleave to Him,
> And to Him will I cleave alway.

> If Jesus Christ is a God,—
> And the only God,—I swear
> I will follow Him through heaven and hell,
> The earth, the sea, and the air!

And following Him, like Philip, we shall come into the light. "He that followeth me shall not walk in darkness, but shall have the light of life."

¶ In an address on "Some Types of Student Life," Professor Charteris instanced Henry Martyn and John Mackintosh ("the Earnest Student") as cases of University men that took time to cultivate their souls whilst doing something for others all the while. "The law of the Life of God is," he added, "as inexorable as any law which natural science has disclosed in the strata of the earth or in the mechanism of an animal frame. That law is —that we follow Christ, that we seek not our own things but the things of others. He came not to be ministered unto, but to minister. And you, to whom professors minister, to whom relatives minister, to whom vast libraries minister, to whom do you in return minister of such things as ye have? Not for your own sakes at all, but because you are possessed by the sense of others' need; not for the return you will get, but for the relief you can render; you follow Him

> Who gave Himself most earnestly away,
> Not thinking of the grandeur of the deed,
> But of the souls dying for need of Him.

You will have your reward if you don't think of it at all; your souls' peace will be promoted if ye are peacemakers for others; your hold of Christ's hand will make you follow whither He draws, where ignorance has to be taught, and pain has to be soothed, and sorrow brightened. Would you like to learn how little you know? Try to teach a Sunday class. Would you like to be sure of your grip of the truth? Visit that artisan who doubts it. Would you like to follow Christ closely? Then you must go where He still goes, as in Palestine—to the needy, the suffering, and the poor."[1]

3. Whenever our Lord receives a new disciple, He at once gives him something to do. So we read that "Philip findeth Nathanael." One cannot help thinking that he went in search of his friend at the instance of Jesus Himself. The Lord may have known Nathanael in private life as one who stood far above his associates. Philip at least knew him, and was fortunate enough to meet him on the journey north.

How intensely interesting is the meeting of the two friends. Nathanael had evidently been a keen student of the Scriptures. He, too, was eagerly longing to see the great One of whom the Baptist spoke. At this very time he seems to have been making a strenuous personal preparation to receive Him aright, when lo! Philip meets him, and, with the radiance of the new disclosure of Jesus still fresh upon his heart, tells him that at last the object of their quest has been discovered. "Philip findeth Nathanael and saith unto him: Him of whom Moses in the Law and the Prophets wrote have we found, Jesus the son of Joseph, the man from Nazareth"—for thus, following the order of the original Greek, we may render the statement.

Thus the Church begins. One man makes the supreme discovery and comes into acquaintance with Jesus of Nazareth, and straight he goes and tells his new truth to another. Read the first chapters of the history of the Christian Church as they are written at the beginning of the New Testament, and see how many times this incident is repeated. It is characteristic of Christianity. It is the instinctive motion of the Christian. One finds another, and thus the Kingdom of God comes.

Nathanael was not so easily won by Philip as Simon was by Andrew. Pious in heart as he was, and ready to accept the fulfilment of Scripture, he had certain preconceived ideas which prevented his immediately assenting to Philip's good tidings. For the present, however, we must leave Nathanael's prejudices alone. What we have to deal with now is the method Philip took to disarm him of his objection. Slow, deliberate men can be very decided when fairly roused, and this is the very spirit in which

[1] A. Gordon, *The Life of Archibald Hamilton Charteris*, 500.

Philip acts here. With an alacrity quite equal to that of Andrew, he said to Nathanael, "Come and see."

Observe Philip's way of dealing with Nathanael. Philip might have argued, either that the popular prejudice against Nazareth, which Nathanael quoted, rested on no sure foundation, or that, whatever its truth, Jesus belonged to Nazareth in so limited and temporary a sense that the reputation of the place did not touch Him or His claim to fulfil the Messianic prophecies. This, perhaps, would have been our modern plan of meeting the objection. Philip takes a shorter course. His object is not to put himself argumentatively in the right by vindicating Nazareth, or by showing that it does not stand in his way; he only wants to bring Nathanael into the Presence, ay, close to the Person of the Son of God. He is convinced that if Nathanael can only see Him, speak with Him, breathe the atmosphere that surrounds Him, feel the Divine majesty and tenderness which had already won himself, the prejudice against Nazareth will simply be forgotten. "Philip saith unto him, Come and see."

¶ Philip's answer, "Come and see," is at once the simplest and profoundest apologetics. To every upright heart Jesus proves Himself by showing Himself.[1]

II.

PHILIP AND THE MULTITUDE.

1. Jesus has crossed the Sea of Tiberias and has reached its eastern shore. Great crowds are coming in the same direction— some from the scattered ranks of the Baptist, some consisting of the pilgrims to the Passover at Jerusalem. Both are naturally drawn to Jesus—the disciples of the Baptist by a kindred association, the Passover pilgrims by a spirit of devotion. We should have thought Jesus would have grasped the moment as one eminently adapted to the spread of His doctrines. Strange to say, His whole interest seems bent upon something else. He thinks of the *physical* well-being of that crowd. They must already be hungry and faint with their journey. If they are to interrupt that journey to listen to Him, they will be more faint

[1] F. Godet, *Commentary on the Gospel of St. John*, i. 450.

and hungry still. Accordingly, Christ's primal care is for their bodies, their food, their nourishment. He intends that before all things they shall receive provision for their *temporal* wants. But He is not content to achieve that; He wishes His disciples to go along with Him, to sympathize with Him. And so He starts a problem of political economy—How shall we procure food for this multitude ?

2. It was to Philip that Jesus put the question. Philip answered Him, " Two hundred pennyworth of bread is not sufficient for them, that every one may take a little." This was an eminently practical answer. Philip was evidently a practical man. He was acquainted with the cost of things. He knew how much money the Apostolic brotherhood had in their scanty treasury. He decided at once that this generous thought of Christ's could not be executed. It would take too much money. Philip was a man who had some idea of money. What he would have said to St. Teresa's project, who started out, it is said, to build a hospital having two halfpence in her pocket, and saying, " Two halfpence with God can build a city "—what Philip would have said to that sort of financing we cannot say. At any rate, there is no mention of God here. The bread will cost so much money. We have not that amount of money; the plan cannot be carried out.

3. But Jesus was quite prepared. As John puts it, " He himself knew what he would do "—knew, that is, at first sight of the crowds as they came up the hill from the shore of the lake. When, therefore, towards the close of the day, the disciples—and Philip doubtless with the rest—came to Jesus and said, " Send the multitudes away, that they may go into the villages, and buy themselves food," Jesus had His answer ready: " They have no need to go away; give ye them to eat." We can imagine the surprise that swept over the heart of Philip as he heard these words. Such a saying looked like urging them to do what they knew to be utterly impossible. He said that even two hundred pennyworth of bread would not suffice. Andrew supported Philip in this contention, for he added, " There is a lad here, which hath five barley loaves, and two fishes : but what are these among

so many ? " Yet Jesus did not swerve from His purpose. The multitudes were to be fed, and the disciples themselves were to do the work. His only reply to them was that they should bid the multitudes recline on the green grass and prepare for a meal.

Let us not forget Christ, as Philip did. That was the very heart of his failure, and the secret and explanation of his hasty and self-sufficient answer. He forgot Christ. We must remember Him. In all the difficulties that press upon us in our generation, some of them sociological, some of them theological; some touching the problem of poverty, some touching the problem of belief; some tempting us to hasty answer, others tempting us to a self-sufficient answer; let us find our refuge and our help in the sure word of the Lord Jesus Christ.

> Herein you proudly erred,
> Here may the source of woe be found,
> You . . .
>   deemed that in our own heart's ground
> The root of good was to be found,
> And that by careful watering
> And earnest tendance we might bring
> The bud, the blossom, and the fruit
> To grow and flourish from that root.
> You deemed we needed nothing more
> Than skill and courage to explore
> Deep down enough in our own heart,
> To where the well-head lay apart,
> Which must the springs of being feed,
> And that these fountains did but need
> The soil that choked them moved away,
> To bubble in the open day.
> But, thanks to heaven, it is not so,
> That root a richer soil doth know
> Than our poor hearts could e'er supply,
> That stream is from a source more high;
> From God it came, to God returns,
> Not nourished from our scanty urns,
> But fed from His unfailing river,
> Which runs and will run on for ever.[1]

[1] R. C. Trench, *Poems*, 7.

III.

PHILIP AND THE GREEKS.

Philip, in the latest days of Christ's ministry, was made the instrument of a wondrously practical work quite on the lines of his search for Nathanael. If we were suddenly asked the question, Which of the Christian disciples brought the earliest help to the Gentiles? we should probably say "Paul" or "Peter" or "Stephen." But in truth there was one before any of these—it was Philip. After our Lord Himself, the first who spoke a word to the Gentiles was this obscure man of Bethsaida. Before Peter had called Cornelius, before Stephen had lifted his voice, before Paul had raised his banner, Philip had brought a Gentile band into the presence of Jesus. True, they were the descendants of Jews; but they had been born in a foreign land, bred in a foreign culture, trained in foreign ideas. They had become Greeks in nationality, Greeks in education, Greeks in taste, Greeks in manner. But they had heard of the fame of Jesus, and they longed to see Him. Their pride in the old ancestry was not dead. They were glad that where their fathers' homes had been there had risen a great light. How were they to gaze upon that light? The Jews would now despise them, count them aliens. Yet they would try. The Passover Feast was coming on; they would go up to Jerusalem; perchance someone might show them the new star. They came; and they are gladdened by a discovery. Among the names of Christ's inner circle they heard of one which was Greek—Philip. They were attracted by the kindred sound. Is not *this* the man to lead them to Jesus—a man with an affinity of name to the names of their own countrymen? And so Philip becomes the medium of the first Gentile wave. To him is it granted to open the door. To him is committed the privilege of unveiling the Christ to the eyes of other lands. To him, above all, is assigned the glory of performing the great marriage between the East and the West, and of joining the hand of Europe to the hand of Asia!

Philip did not lead them at once to the Master, but first consulted Andrew and acted in harmony with him. In this action we find at once a fresh revelation of this Apostle's character

as well as a new stage in his missionary training. Philip
gathered confidence as he drew near to a man who appears to
have been more closely associated with him than the rest, and
who, as stated, bore not a Jewish name—though both were Jews
—but Greek, like himself. "Philip cometh and telleth Andrew."
As the Greeks watched, they saw the two men among the Twelve
who bore Greek names talking the matter over. What additional
confidence they would gain from that incident! Observe that
Andrew at once takes the precedence in the record. Philip was
all very well when alone, but when he came into touch with
Andrew he immediately became second.

¶ I shall never forget when Mr. Spurgeon came to this chapel
one week-day. He looked round, and, standing in this very place,
said to me, "Brother Davies, it is not every stylish chapel that I
like, but I like this." He had just been in the caretaker's house,
and admired it, and, in his own inimitable fashion, then added,
"Look here, will you have me as a caretaker?" I replied
emphatically, "No; you stay where you are. I know who the
caretaker will be if you come." I acted instantly on the instinct
of self-preservation. I knew into what position I should very
soon subside if he were here. Mr. Spurgeon away, I might do
for pastor; but, with Mr. Spurgeon here, I should naturally fall
into the post of caretaker.[1]

IV.

PHILIP AND THE FATHER.

1. The last time that we hear the voice of Philip is the most
memorable of all. It was in the Upper Room in Jerusalem.
Our Lord was seeking to comfort His disciples at His approaching
departure. Thomas asked for fuller information when the Master
spoke about going somewhere, which He calls the Father's House.
Part of Christ's reply was that to know Himself was to know the
Father also. "And from henceforth," He added, "ye know him
and have seen him." Philip's request shows that he did not
understand the inference of these words; for he interrupted with
the prayer, "Lord, shew us the Father, and it sufficeth us."
Now in that prayer Philip expressed a longing that is not only

[1] D. Davies, *Talks with Men, Women and Children*, v. 595.

legitimate, but really irresistible, in every quickened soul. It is simply the desire to get at the fountain-head of the Divine life. In the ministry of Jesus Philip saw the clearest tokens of the presence of God; but like the ardent explorer who looks at the lower reaches of a stream and wishes that he could ascend to the great lake amidst the mountains where it takes its rise, Philip longs to have some nearer, fuller manifestation of the holy and blessed Father, in whom Jesus, His Son, lived and spoke and wrought.

¶ Someone told Tennyson that his chief desire was to leave the world a little better than he found it. Tennyson replied, "My chief desire is to have a new vision of God."

A touch divine—
And the scaled eyeball owns the mystic rod;
Visibly through his garden walketh God.[1]

2. It was a devout and sincere wish, but in a disciple of Jesus it was a very disappointing one; for it put the emphasis on the wrong thing. It asked for some startling outward revelation that would convince every observer, without thinking how little such a revelation was worth. The revelation that Jesus was making was one of God's nature and character and essential being, not an outside attestation of His existence, which from the point of view of religion meant nothing. It was not unbelief that prompted Philip's difficulty. It was slowness of understanding, defective spiritual apprehension, obtuseness, ignorance.

The answer of Jesus was not a refusal, but it was a suggestive rebuke: "Have I been so long time with you, and dost thou not know me, Philip?" Philip had not understood the difference between the revelation of the Lord and the revelation of the Father. God, as the Lord, was made known by the thunders and lightnings and trumpet-blast of Sinai. God, as the Lord, spoke by the mouth of a human prophet, whom the vision of His glory might strengthen for the accomplishment of his high mission. God, as the Father, was made known by the human life of His Son, which was to carry home to the hearts of men the sense of their own share in that sonship. The revelation of Jesus was not

[1] Browning, *Sordello*, bk. i. l. 502.

a renewal of the former revelation of the "Lord of the whole earth," but was an extension of that revelation: "God with us." The request of Philip was not merely an unauthorized tempting of God, not merely a demand that something should be done specially for his own individual satisfaction; it involved a contradiction of all that Jesus had come to declare. The glory of the Lord, the power of the Lord, the majesty of the Lord—these might be made known by the sign which Philip sought. But the love of the Father could not be made known by any awful or commanding vision. It had been made known already by the life of Jesus; it was to be further manifested by His death. Jesus was preparing His disciples for His approaching departure, was summing up the meaning of all that He had done and said: "From henceforth ye know the Father, and have seen him." Philip's request showed that his mind was travelling along a mistaken road. He had failed to grasp the meaning which underlay the whole message of Jesus: "Have I been so long time with you, and dost thou not know me, Philip?"

¶ The love of God is the love of Christ. How can I love Nature? Yet—look at an open wild-rose.[1]

¶ I read of a boy who found himself alone during a nutting expedition. It was at a spot where no one had been before him. Not a branch was broken; the nuts hung in great clusters. He sat down and tried to enjoy the pleasures of anticipation. Overhead, the branches were so closely intertwined that no sky was to be seen. He heard the ripple of the little burn. He could not see it. But he cared not; he just kept thinking for a minute or two what a "ripping" time he was going to have. Then he rose, tore down the hazel branches, roughly spoiled them of their nuts, ate, and pocketed. He was rich beyond the wealth of kings. But when at last he sat down, he looked up to see the broken branches. The clear blue sky looked down upon him. The world was bigger than he thought. It was God's world.[2]

> With thoughts too lovely to be true,
> With thousand, thousand dreams I strew
> The path that you must come. And you
>   Will find but dew.

[1] Mark Rutherford, *Last Pages from a Journal*, 301.
[2] *The Expository Times*, October 1915, p. 18.

I set an image in the grass,
A shape to smile on you. Alas!
It is a shadow in a glass,
And so will pass.

I break my heart here, love, to dower
With all its inmost sweet your bower.
What scent will greet you in an hour?
The gorse in flower.[1]

3. Here, then, is the place to review the character of Philip.
We have seen him on four occasions, all interesting and revealing,
but the last occasion is the most revealing of all. We notice three
characteristics.

(1) Philip was plainly an inquirer. The patient inquirer comes
out in the description of Jesus he gives to Nathanael. "We have
found him," says Philip, "of whom Moses in the law and the
prophets did write." Andrew and John followed Christ on the
testimony of the Baptist and at the bidding of their own hearts.
But Philip accepted Him, and followed because he found that
Christ satisfied the descriptions given in the Old Testament. Yes,
Philip brought out Moses and the prophets and tested Christ by
them and accepted Him because he saw that what they had
written was fulfilled in Him. The same habit of patient and
accurate examination and inquiry comes out in the incident of
the feeding of the five thousand. Jesus, at a certain point in the
day's proceedings, turned to Philip with the question, "Whence
are we to buy bread, that these may eat?" And this He said to
prove him. Jesus knew His disciple; He knew his inquiring
mind. He knew that Philip would have been making his
computations. And so he had. "Two hundred pennyworth of
bread," answered Philip promptly, "is not sufficient for them, that
every one may take a little." Philip had been working it all out
in his head, and was ready with his answer. It was for his
inquiring and candid mind, probably, that the Greeks chose him
out of all the Apostles as the one to whom they would make their
request to see Jesus. "Their turning to him," says Lange,
"depended upon a law of kindly attraction." His own inquiring
spirit would naturally put him in sympathy with these inquiring

[1] *The Collected Poems of Margaret L. Woods*, 142.

Greeks. And the same inquiring temper comes out in that memorable request which Philip made in the Upper Room on the night in which He was betrayed: "Lord, shew us the Father, and it sufficeth us." That, then, is the Philip of the Gospels—a man of inquiring and interrogative mind, a man intent upon proving and testing everything.

An inquiring spirit—properly so called—is of the utmost importance in every department of human activity and achievement. It is those who have been in the habit of asking questions of Nature, and pressing for answers to them, that have been chiefly instrumental in extending the boundaries of knowledge. Others have been satisfied with what was already ascertained. They have been content to be hemmed in by that circle of darkness which surrounded them, and have made no attempt to explore its mysteries, or to widen the circumference within which the light of science is enjoyed. But inquisitive and reflecting minds, by the unceasing questions which they put, have laboured to add something to the amount of man's knowledge, and have thus, at times, been led by the simplest incidents to a discovery of some of the most dominant and comprehensive laws of the universe. It is those who follow up science to her most advanced outpost, and who, while standing there, inquire if it be not possible to take yet a further step, and to bring something more of earth and heaven within the domain of human cognizance, that are the real contributors to the advancement and elevation of our race. Others may conserve, but they, as it were, create. Others may be silent and receptive, but they are inquiring and communicative. And although many of their inquiries may not be answered by themselves, or in their own day, yet, by instituting them, they have given an impulse and direction to the human mind, which will, in all probability, hereafter lead to the desired success. Again and again has this proved to be the case. All those marvellous discoveries and equally marvellous applications of science, as also all those social improvements, those deliverances from long-prevalent errors and superstitions, which our own day has so largely witnessed, have flowed from the efforts of men who were bold enough to put some question which others had never asked, or to follow out to their proper results inquiries which had been suggested by their predecessors.

Now this spirit of reflection and inquiry, so valuable in other departments, is also of great importance within the province of religion. It is melancholy to think of the multitudes who hold what faith they have in the gospel simply as a matter of tradition. They have shown none of the spirit of Philip in examining into the grounds on which their belief rests; and hence they have not attained an intelligent and established faith. The evil consequence is twofold. On the one hand, many of the class referred to cling to their traditional beliefs with an obstinacy which takes no account of reason, and which is fatal to all progressive spiritual enlightenment. On the other hand, numbers who have taken no pains to be able to "give a reason of the hope that is in them" are apt to be carried away by any wind of doctrine which happens, for the time, to prevail—by any sort of heresy or scepticism which enjoys a temporary power and popularity. Nothing, then, is more important than to cherish a spirit of earnest and sustained inquiry with respect to all that falls within the domain of religion. There should be a sincere desire for "light," and for "more light."

¶ In nature we see no bounds to our inquiries. One discovery always gives hints of many more, and brings us into a wider field of speculation. Now, why should not this be, in some measure, the case with respect to knowledge of a moral and religious kind. Is the compass of religious knowledge so small, as that any person, however imperfectly educated, may comprehend the whole, and without much trouble? This may be the notion of such as read or think but little on the subject; but of what value can such an opinion be?

If we look back into ecclesiastical history, we shall see that every age, and almost every year, has had its peculiar subjects of inquiry. As one controversy has been determined, or sufficiently agitated, others have always arisen; and I will venture to say there never was a time in which there were more, or more interesting, objects of discussion before us than there are at present. And it is in vain to flatter ourselves with the prospect of seeing an end to our labours, and of having nothing to do but to sit down in the pleasing contemplation of all religious truth, and reviewing the intricate mazes through which we have happily traced the progress of every error.[1]

(2) But secondly, Philip was a practical, straightforward. common-sense man. This emerges without its limitations in his

[1] Dr. Joseph Priestley, *Theological and Miscellaneous Works*, xv. 72.

interview with Nathanael. Nathanael was a dreamer, a fine and beautiful soul, but lacking activity. Philip shows his common sense in declining to argue with him. Nathanael could have proved to his own satisfaction that it was utterly impossible for the Messiah to come from a place like Nazareth; and since he had a far better knowledge of the Scriptures than Philip, Philip would have been confounded if he had entered into that argument. He knew what type of man Nathanael was, and he knew it was not very safe to enter into an argument with him. He positively refuses to argue with the theoretical man, the mystical man, the dreamer. He lays rough hands upon him and says, " Come and see!" There you have the practical attitude, and that practical attitude of a man like Philip, who knows a fact, who has realized the truth in Jesus, is entirely admirable.

We see Philip's common sense again in the feeding of the multitudes. There are five thousand people. Now, what would a church treasurer be likely to say if there were five thousand people to feed, with five loaves and two small fishes? Have you ever known a church treasurer who would say anything but "Impossible!" He would do precisely what Philip did. Philip made a quick, probably accurate, common-sense calculation of the material resources at hand. It would cost two hundred pence to feed that multitude, and they had not two hundred pence. It simply could not be done.

His character is again revealed in the interview with the Greeks. It is the attitude of a man who could be depended upon for carrying out instructions exactly, that he should be doubtful about bringing these Greeks to Jesus. What Jesus had said had seemed so definite, so plain, so clear. He came to seek the lost sheep of the house of Israel. The Greeks were eager to get to Jesus, but Philip was very doubtful how they should be treated.

And finally, in the Upper Room, we see precisely the same explicit temper. He is a man who wants to handle and feel and see. He wants something tangible. The impalpable, shadowy things are so difficult to grasp, so difficult for him to interpret and explain; let the whole thing be put into a revelation of the Father, let him see with his own eyes, handle with his own hands, and then it will be sufficient for him.

¶ How little of that which makes up life is visible or tangible! We habitually speak and act as if there were certain realities with which we are in such immediate contact that we constantly see and touch them; they exist beyond all question because their existence is evident to the senses. The man who is willing to accept nothing of the being and nature of which he has not ocular or tangible proof accepts these things as realities; all the rest he dismisses as dreams, or rejects as incapable of demonstration. And he does this, in many cases, because he believes that this is the only course open to one who means to preserve absolute integrity of intellect and to be entirely honest with himself and with life. A man of this temper is ready to believe only that which he thinks he knows by absolute contact; there is much else he would like to believe, but he will not permit himself a consolation or comfort based on a hope which the imagination, or the heart or the mind working without regard for certain laws of evidence, which he arbitrarily makes, has turned into a reality. Many honest men go through life and will not see God because they have bolted all the doors through which God can enter and reveal Himself.

Dr. Bushnell, in a moment of insight, once pictured to a friend with whom he was talking the making of man. And after man was made in His own image God said, "He is complete"; and then He added: "No; there is no way in which I can approach him. I will open the great door of the Imagination in his soul, so that I may have access to him." And this great door, which opens outward upon the whole sweep and splendour of the universe, some men bolt and bar as if it were an unlawful and illicit entrance to the soul![1]

(3) Now the inquiring, straightforward, practical mind is excellent in its way, but it has limits of its own creation which prevent it from discerning the deeper truths of man's spiritual life.

There are always men and women who are like Philip in their practical enlightenment. Sometimes a little more, sometimes a little less, and the gospel of Christ would suffice them. There are sincere, serious, thoughtful souls, who claim to have thought things out for themselves. All fits together, and points clearly in one direction; the last remaining conclusion only needs to be clearly stated, and all will be well. The Christian system will then be in accordance with the needs of the highest minds,

[1] H. W. Mabie, *The Life of the Spirit*, 222.

and will be unassailable. There is always a cry for this step to be taken, this compromise made. There is always the honest, heartfelt plea, "One further admission, and it sufficeth us." We have need to recall the words of Jesus: "Have I been so long time with you, and dost thou not know me?" We can give no other account of Jesus than St. Paul gave—to some a stumbling-block, to others foolishness, but to those who receive Him, the power of God and the wisdom of God. The Church rests on a definite foundation, Jesus Christ, the Son of God, the one revelation of the Father. Those who demand some modification of this basis urge the needs of their individual satisfaction. It has been well said, "They confound the right of the individual, which is to be free, with the duty of an institution, which is to be something." Philip thought that he was justified in making a small demand for the satisfaction of his own honest, upright, conscientious soul. He did not see that his demand involved a contradiction of all that Jesus had come to declare. With all his reasonableness, he had taken only an outside view of the matter. He needed some glow of enthusiasm, some spark of emotion, some touch of his spiritual being to raise him to a higher level, to make him capable of a larger view. Then he could understand that Jesus had not come to satisfy the outworn traditions of his early training, the problems of society or politics among which he lived, the questionings which outward circumstances suggested. He had come to raise him to newness of life, to carry him into a higher world than the world of sense, where, moving in a larger sphere, he might feel and know that "God is light, and in him is no darkness at all." So it is still, and so it must ever be. There are limits to the sensible, practical spirit as applied to religion. It deals admirably with outlying points of doctrine or of organization. When it reaches the centre it is powerless, and the answer to its earnest and well-meant demands must ever be the same: "Lift up your hearts."

It was a spiritual density and obtuseness on Philip's part, a want of insight; but when we make this charge against Philip, are we not made to pause by the thought of our own obtuseness? May not the charge be made against us, with less excuse in our case than in Philip's, "Have I been so long time with you, and dost thou not know me?" To the Church as well as to the world may the Baptist's words be often said in sorrow and in surprise, "There standeth one among you whom ye know not."

¶ To those who are worth most there comes home early in life the conviction that, in the absence of a firm hold on what is abiding, life becomes a poorer and poorer affair the longer it lasts. And the only foundation of what is abiding is the sense of the reality of what is spiritual—the constant presence of the God who is not far away in the skies, but is here within our minds and hearts.[1]

¶ We are just as much in the presence of the Lord here to-day, this hour, as we shall ever be, except that as one grows more spiritual and less material, as his perceptions are opened to spiritual things and his temperament becomes more responsive to spiritual influences he is, of course, more in the presence of the Lord than when he was steeped and stifled in the material life. The man who can see possesses the sunshine more than the man who cannot see, although the sunshine is the same all the time. We are spirits now, or we are nothing. We are dwelling in the body as an instrument through which the spirit must work in order to work in a physical world. We are spirits, but spirits embodied. Does not this realization invest this part of our life with a new dignity, as well as a new responsibility? This world, so far as it is anything, is a spiritual world now, though in a cruder and lower state of development than that which the spirit enters after leaving the body. But the forces that govern it are of spirit; for there is no force but spirit.[2]

> Why of hidden things dispute,
> Mind unwise, howe'er astute,
> 　　Making that thy task
> Where the Judge will, at the last,
> When disputing all is past,
> 　　Not a question ask?

> Folly great it is to brood
> Over neither bad nor good,
> 　　Eyes and ears unheedful!
> Ears and eyes, ah, open wide
> For what may be heard or spied
> 　　Of the one thing needful![3]

[1] Lord Haldane, *The Conduct of Life*, 15.
[2] Lilian Whiting, *The World Beautiful*, 187.
[3] George MacDonald, *Poetical Works*, i. 438.

THOMAS.

I.

WHO WAS HE?

LITERATURE.

Adeney, W. F., in *Men of the New Testament* : Matthew to Timothy (1905), 221.

Arnold, T., *Sermons*, vi. (1878) 172.

Bernard, J. H., *Via Domini* (1898), 165.

Bickersteth, C., *The Gospel of Incarnate Love* (1906), 88.

Bramston, J. T., *Fratribus* (1903), 104.

Butler, H. M., *University and Other Sermons* (1899), 43.

Cooke, G. A., *The Progress of Revelation* (1910), 139.

Davidson, A. B., *The Called of God* (1902), 319.

Drysdale, A. H., *Christ Invisible Our Gain* (1909), 87.

Ealand, F., *The Spirit of Life* (1908), 69.

Ellis, P. A., *Old Beliefs and Modern Believers* (1909), 166.

Greenhough, J. G., *The Apostles of Our Lord* (1904), 93.

Gwatkin, H. M., *The Eye for Spiritual Things* (1907), 131.

Hodges, G., *The Human Nature of the Saints* (1905), 79.

Hough, L. H., *The Men of the Gospels* (1913), 32.

Jeffrey, J., *The Personal Ministry of the Son of Man* (1897), 276.

Jones, J. D., *The Glorious Company of the Apostles* (1904), 172.

Keble, J., *Sermons for the Christian Year* : Miscellaneous (1880), 177.

Liddon, H. P., *Forty-Two Sermons Selected from "The Penny Pulpit,"* iv (1886), No. 1100.

Lilley, J. P., *Four Apostles* (1912), 95.

Lynch, T. T., *Sermons for My Curates* (1871), 33.

MacDonald, G., *Unspoken Sermons*, i. (1890) 50.

Mackennal, A., *Christ's Healing Touch* (1884), 115.

Martyn, H. J., *For Christ and the Truth* (1898), 128.

Matheson, G., *The Representative Men of the New Testament* (1905), 137.

Mortimer, A. G., *Jesus and the Resurrection* (1898), 184.

Rattenbury, J. E., *The Twelve* (1914), 193.

Stanford, C., *From Calvary to Olivet* (1893), 157.

Stone, D., *The Discipline of Faith* (1904), 131.

Stubbs, W., *Ordination Addresses* (1904), 325.

Tuckwell, W., *Nuggets from the Bible Mine* (1913), 223.

Vaughan, R., *Stones from the Quarry* (1890), 97.

Waller, C. H., *The Silver Sockets* (1883), 302.

Whyte, A., *Bible Characters* : Joseph and Mary to James (1900), 159.

Wright, D., *Waiting for the Light* (1875), 34.

Young, D. T., *The Crimson Book* (1903), 53.

Dictionary of the Bible, iv. (1902) 753 (J. H. Bernard).

Dictionary of Christ and the Gospels, ii. (1908) 728 (E. H. Titchmarsh).

Encyclopædia Biblica, iv. (1903), col. 5057 (E. Nestle).

Who was Thomas?

Thomas, one of the twelve, called Didymus.—John xx. 24.

The name Thomas in English, as in Greek, is just a reproduction, with the addition of a single euphonic letter, of the original Syriac name, Thoma. This is derived from the Hebrew word for "twin." Hence when he is also called Didymus he does not receive an additional name. Nor is there, as so many suppose, any attempt to indicate his character. He does not get this name because he was a doubter or ready to halt betwixt two opinions, but simply because this word in Greek expresses the fact, already indicated in the Syriac form of his name, that he was one of twin children.

Thomas appears in all the lists of the Apostles. But we have no account of his call. In Matthew's arrangement of the Twelve as couples he is associated with Matthew — "Thomas, and Matthew the publican" (Matt. x. 3); and this fact has led to the suggestion that possibly the two were twins. But that is not likely, because in the case of two earlier instances the relationship of brotherhood is stated—"Simon, who is called Peter, and Andrew *his brother*"; "James the son of Zebedee, and John *his brother.*" If there were another pair of brothers it would be natural to go on and read, "Thomas and Matthew *his brother.*"

Our knowledge of Thomas is derived from the Fourth Gospel. In the first three he is named as one of the twelve Apostles and no more. In the fourth, however, he appears on four occasions. He utters memorable words on each occasion, and it is by these words that we know both who and what he was.

I.

AT THE RAISING OF LAZARUS.

Let us also go, that we may die with him.—John xi. 16.

The first scene in which he becomes prominent is the narrative of the raising of Lazarus from the dead.

1. There had been a commotion in the streets of Jerusalem. The transition of Jesus from the work of a reformer to the work of a theologian had produced also a transition in the feelings of the multitude. They passed at a bound from applause to reprobation. Goaded by the suggestion of heresy in His teaching, they assailed Him with stones. The majesty of Christ's presence saved Him—paralyzed the directness of their aim. Evading the fury of the populace, He retired into a secluded place, and for some time was visible only to His disciples. At last, to this desert spot came tidings of the death of Lazarus. Then Jesus resolved to return. The disciples were startled—on His account and their own. They were very unwilling to come into the vicinity of a place which had been so fraught with fear, so full of danger. Jesus, for His part, is determined. He says, " I go." He does not ask anyone to accompany Him; He simply expresses His personal resolve. Then through the silence one man speaks out for the company—" Let us also go, that we may die with him." It is the voice of Thomas.

¶ I have always felt that is one of the greatest and noblest things any human being ever did say. You talk about the martyrs—well, the martyrs were noble people and they nobly died, but if you read the records of the martyrs you will find that they were often sustained wonderfully by their faith, and that in the act of martyrdom they were often so lifted up above the common and the material that the common and material things seemed hardly to touch them. If you know anything of the records of the martyrs, you will know that the very flames seemed warm and beautiful to them, that they saw the chariots and horses ready to take them away straight to heaven, and notwithstanding their courage there is a gladness of heart that lifts them up, and enables them to endure material pangs. Just as artists have delighted to depict Saint Sebastian stuck all over with arrows, and yet with a beatific smile on his face as if he were enjoying it. You find that continually in the history of the martyrs—they are elevated by their faith above the things they see. For religious faith Wesley's words are true :

> Lo ! to faith's enlightened sight,
> All the mountain flames with light;
> Hell is nigh, but God is nigher,
> Circling us with hosts of fire.

But Thomas was not like that at all. He had no exaltation, or, as I think he would have put it, he suffered from no illusions. He simply saw the material things. He knew the jaws of death would devour him. He thought a stone was a stone, and that the stones would hurt and kill that would be flung at him. He took no rosy, optimistic, religious view of the scene. He simply saw all the crude material forces. It was a cruel death, and his flesh shrank from it. He was under no illusions, or, to put what I mean from the point of view of faith, which indeed is the true point of view, he had not the faith that exalted him above the material world, and made him realize the powers of the world to come. He saw death in all its hardness and cruelty and pain; and yet notwithstanding that he says, " Let us also go, that *we* may *die* with him." [1]

2. Now that which the Lord Jesus expects is a service according to the measure of each man's capacity, a service according to the character and disposition of each disciple. He requires from each man his own service, not that of his brother. This He demands, and will be content with nothing less. We may be dull-witted, with no splendid vision breaking in upon our imagination, and yet may possess a clear sense of duty, a true knowledge of our appointed way, and the loyal devotion that is ready to follow Christ whithersoever He may lead, though it be into the midst of foes. Devoid of the impetuous outflow of love, such as Simon Peter knew, there are disciples of Christ, like Thomas, who in quiet, undemonstrative fidelity are prepared for the hardest lot this fidelity may bestow. There are some whose lives never rise above the common level, hardly reach thereto, they may think—men with limited capacities for service, with meagre intellectual and emotional endowments, whose labours never

[1] J. E. Rattenbury, *The Twelve*, 197.

strike the imagination of their fellows, whose professions never thrill and move the multitude. They may hear voices that would undermine their faith, and see the gilded bait set to allure them from their service; they may be unduly despondent of themselves, of their fellows, and of the trend of things around them, and may exaggerate the perils and losses of their association with Christ, His Church, His Kingdom. Yet in their deepest heart there may dwell a quiet fervour of love that will be faithful unto death, a loyal devotion that only in the presence of peril asserts its full strength and nobility, as it says, in the spirit of consecration that moved St. Thomas, "Let us also go, that we may die with him."

¶ Erasmus confessed that he was not constituted of the stuff of which martyrs are made, and many of us feel a similar misgiving concerning ourselves. But if we resolve to be on the Lord's side He will wonderfully strengthen and deliver. The golden-crested wren is one of the tiniest of birds; it is said to weigh only the fifth part of an ounce, and yet, on frailest pinions, it braves hurricanes and crosses northern seas. It often seems in nature as if Omnipotence worked best through frailest organisms; certainly the omnipotence of grace is seen to the greatest advantage in the trembling but resolute saint. Give me the spirit of those who are faithful unto death![1]

II.

In the Upper Room.

Lord, we know not whither thou goest; how know we the way?—John xiv. 5.

The next time that Thomas speaks is when Jesus and His disciples are still in the Upper Room where the last Passover had just been celebrated and the Lord's Supper instituted. "In my Father's house are many mansions; I go to prepare a place for you. And whither I go, ye know the way." The other disciples may know whither their Master is going, and they may know the way, but Thomas knows neither. "His Father's house?" said Thomas to himself. "What does He mean? Why does He not speak plainly?" Thomas must understand his Master's meaning.

[1] W. L. Watkinson, *The Gates of Dawn*, 311.

Thomas is one of those unhappy men who cannot be put off with mere words. Thomas must see to the bottom before he can pretend to believe. Thomas was the first of those disciples, and a primate among them, in whose restless minds

> doubt,
> Like a shoot, springs round the stock of truth.

The question was natural; it argued no want of loyalty; and the Master answered it with one of His greatest and deepest sayings: "I am the way, and the truth, and the life." In leading His disciples on to a higher level of discipleship, He would lead them to Himself.

In our own lives there are many places where there is nothing for us but that word of Jesus. We have our doubts and our difficulties. We look to the future. We argue about immortality; we see something to be said for it, and something against it; we express the mind of the twentieth century, the feeling of our times, and when we are baffled and confused and troubled with the problems of the mind what comfort is there for us? There is this—that One stands before us and says, "I am the way," and if He be not there in whom our hearts can trust then we are of all men the most miserable. The hand of God is laid heavily upon us. We suffer bereavement or affliction or trouble. Dear ones are taken away from our family circle; the chairs are left vacant; those upon whom we depend are moved from us; our whole life is altered; we have to reshape it at some bitter hour of tragedy, when one or another has been removed to another sphere of service; and in a moment like that we are confused and troubled. We know not which way to go, or how to find our way; but there is One who stands before us and says, "I am the way," and in the confusion of our brain, in the cloudy days of mental trouble and distraction that come to us, has not the Christian in all ages found to his supreme comfort and victory that Christ is the Way, and that He opens to him the gates of life, and makes time and eternity a possible thing for him to contemplate?

¶ Much may remain dark to us; but the purposes of life receive a clear and powerful direction the moment we believe that the one supreme Way of life is Jesus Christ, God's Son, our Lord. No other single way, capable of uniting the whole nature and life of man, has yet been discovered or devised which does not tend to draw us down rather than lift us up. But if in Him is shown at once the Way of God, so far as it can be intelligible to man, and the Way of man according to God's purpose, then many a plausible and applauded way stands condemned at once as of necessity leading nowhither; and many a way which promises little except to conscience is glorified with Him, and has the assurance of His victory. Yet, when the primary choice has once been made, the labour is not ended. The Way is no uniform external rule. It traverses the changes of all things that God has made and is ever making, that we may help to subdue all to His use; and so it has to be sought out again and again with growing fitnesses of wisdom and devotion. Thus the outward form of our own ways is in great part determined for us from without, while their inward coherence is committed to our own keeping; and the infinite life of the Son of man can transmute them all into ways of God. . . . But we shall never reach the full measure of the word, Christ is the Way, till the journey itself is ended, and with thankful wonder we find ourselves wholly gathered to Him in the place and presence assigned from the beginning by the heavenly Father's will.[1]

III.

ABSENT.

Except I shall see . . . I will not believe.—John xx. 25.

1. The remaining incidents in which Thomas appears followed one another closely. They belong to the forty days during which Christ showed Himself alive after His resurrection. On the first occasion when Jesus appeared to the Apostles after His resurrection, Thomas was not with them. When he heard of what the others had seen during his absence, he could not believe it. He repudiated the notion as absurd. The vehemence of his language shows us how gladly he would have welcomed the news, if only he had been able to accept it as true. But to him it is too good to be true. He cannot submit to a delusion simply because it would be very delightful. He must have truth—truth at any price. For this, however, he declares that he will be satisfied with nothing less than the most convincing sense perception, the

[1] F. J. A. Hort, *The Way, the Truth, the Life*, 38.

sense of touch. "Except I shall see in his hands the print of the nails, and put my finger into the print of the nails, and put my hand into his side, I will not believe."

¶ In the *Lives of the Saints* it is related that one day when St. Martin of Tours was praying in his cell, the devil came to him, arrayed in light, clothed in royal robes and wearing a crown of gold. Twice the devil told the saint he was Christ. "I am come in judgment," he said. "Adore me." "Where," asked Martin, "are the marks of the nails? Where the piercing of the spear? Where the crown of thorns? When I see the marks of the Passion I shall adore my Lord." At these words the devil disappeared.[1]

2. How shall we account for the absence of Thomas? It could not have been by accident. He must have been told that the ten astounded, overwhelmed, and enraptured disciples were to be all together that wonderful night; astounded, overwhelmed, and enraptured with the events of the morning. What conceivable cause, then, could have kept Thomas away? Whatever it was that kept Thomas away, he was terribly punished for his absence. For he thereby lost the first sight of his risen Master, and His first benediction of peace. Not only did He lose that benediction, but the joy of the other disciples who had received it filled the cup of Thomas's misery full. And, besides that, had not Jesus promised a spiritual presence in the assembly of His people, assuring them that wherever two or three of them were met together in His name, He would be in the midst of them? Thomas missed that. All Christians who neglect the assembly of the Church, carelessly or wilfully, may expect to miss many blessings which can be enjoyed only in fellowship. Christianity is a social religion; it attains its perfection in brotherhood. With the solitary it shrinks and withers.

¶ "Old Father Morris," says his American biographer, "had noticed a falling off in his little village meeting for prayer. The first time he collected a tolerable audience, he took occasion to tell them something 'concerning the conference meeting of the disciples' after the resurrection. 'But Thomas was not with them.' 'Thomas not with them!' said the old man in a sorrowful voice; 'why, what could keep Thomas away? Perhaps,' said he, glancing at some of his auditors, 'Thomas had got cold-hearted, and was

[1] S. Baring-Gould, *Lives of the Saints*, xiii. 251.

afraid that they would ask him to make the first prayer; or, perhaps,' he continued, looking at some of the farmers, 'he was afraid the roads were bad; or, perhaps,' he added, after a pause, 'he thought a shower was coming on.' He went on significantly summing up common excuses, and then with great simplicity and emotion he added, 'But only think what Thomas lost, for in the middle of the meeting the Lord Jesus came and stood among them!'" [1]

¶ Now you will think me a worldling—I am—but you made me feel sorry a little for the "large and fashionable congregation." There are sad hearts under fashionable clothes as well as under rags. There were kings in the Bible whose prayers were heard, as well as beggars. Why may we not

> Go together to the kirk
> In a goodly company?

There is something in the mere fact of numbers when they sing—when they are silent—that makes the hymn or the prayer different from that at home—more inspiring to some people and less of an effort. And though our Lord said so much about private prayer He went often to the public service in the Temple or the Synagogue, and did He not mean us to learn from His life as well as from His words? I do not care for crowded services—nor for frequent services of any kind—but there was a time when I did, and I understand the feelings of those who do. [2]

> O faithless found when all believed,
> Where wast thou, Thomas, then;
> Not with the rout that raged without,
> Not with the faithful Ten?
> Why not with friends sure counsel take,
> Who sought the House of Prayer;
> O why, the first Lord's-day, forsake
> The first assembling there?
>
> Not hear the word, when first the Lord
> His preachers' flag unfurl'd
> And lit their torches at the flame
> Which overshone the world!
> Not there, when each became—to preach
> The Cross from pole to pole,—
> Breath'd on with breath which conquer'd death,
> An ever living soul!

[1] C. Stanford, *From Calvary to Olivet*, 163.
[2] *Gathered Leaves from the Prose of Mary E. Coleridge*, 242,

Thou could'st the Jewish stones defy
For Him at danger's call:
O better far with Christ to die,
When Christ has died for all!
It was not fear, for all were near
Who closed the doors for fright,
Hid in that room, when e'en the tomb
Was full of living light.

Or had'st thou stray'd to see display'd
The Paschal barley-ears,
Heaved bright and high across the sky,
When harvest-time appears?
More blest were they that week's first day,
With Him the feast was kept,
Who came to wave, fresh from the grave,
First-fruits of them that slept.[1]

IV.

PRESENT.

My Lord and my God.—John xx. 29.

1. A week has passed, and without record. It is a blank on which a reverent imagination may dare to fasten. We might have been thankful if the same powerful and devout hand that drew for us the picture of "A Death in the Desert" could have drawn this also—the agony of suspense in such a heart and such a mind as that of the Apostle who had so lately said, "Let us also go, that we may die with him." Two things we may say with certainty. That week was a week of strong crying and prayer, as when Jacob wrestled with God and became Israel. Again, such a man in such a brotherhood would not have suffered quite alone. Who that has ever pondered on the character of the disciple whom Jesus loved, and noted the fact that he and he alone records all these details in the life of his brother Apostle, Thomas, can doubt that these agonizing hours were cheered by the prayers and the sympathy of at least one earthly friend?

At last the suspense ended. Again the first day of the week returned. Again the disciples were together, this time Thomas

[1] Herbert Kynaston.

with them. Again the same Master stood among them, with the old message of Peace. We can imagine, with reverent awe, with what eyes *one* of those present gazed upon Him, "looking unto Jesus," even as *he* had never looked before. "Then saith he to Thomas, Reach hither thy finger, and see my hands; and reach hither thy hand, and put it into my side: and be not faithless, but believing." Thus the evidence that a week before was granted to the others, the evidence that he was certain he needed for himself, was now offered him. There it stood within his grasp. Which of us believes that he grasped it? No, surely no. If *before* his words had done his heart some wrong, *now* his heart was better than those words. In the full tide of a satisfied faith, he saw, we may believe, even more than they all. "Thomas answered and said unto him, My Lord and my God."

Thomas "the doubter" is the first to pronounce the great word "God," the first to confess the full Divinity of Christ. This rebound from despair to faith carries the soul farther at one leap than the position reached by more placid minds after long experience. Here is the compensation of the questioning mind. The restlessness of dissatisfaction in the conventional or traditional is very painful. Doubt is always distressing, and when it is carried far into regions of vital importance, agonizing. But when it is dispelled, and sure conviction takes its place, that conviction is more clear and more assured than the faith of unquestioning minds. There is no faith so strong as that of a man who has fought his doubts and conquered them by honest means.

It was his heart that conquered. "My Lord and my God." It was the deep spiritual life of Thomas that overcame; and in that supreme revelation it was not that he put his brain aside as useless, but that in the deepest revelation—the revelation that comes not to the wise and prudent but to the little child—there is such a degree of certainty that rational methods, however they may substantiate, will make no difference whatever to the assurance of the man who comes into living contact with the Lord Jesus Christ. "My Lord and my God."

¶ Thomas is the apostle for our century. He has the critical, sceptical mind of the time, but he has the loving heart, the simple heart that will always conquer. I do not think that the brain and the heart are in necessary conflict, because I am quite sure that when Thomas entered into that supreme knowledge of Jesus Christ his brain was no longer in conflict with his heart. He realized the truth, and his brain would give its witness to the truth that had been realized—on a higher spiritual plane the two concurred, " My Lord and my God!"[1]

2. We must not treat him harshly whom Jesus treated gently. In him the triumph of faith was delayed only that it might be thorough. Think rather how fully he now believes than how slowly he came to his faith.

But what says the Saviour to him? " Because thou hast seen me, thou hast believed : blessed are they that have not seen, and yet have believed!" As he heard these words, Thomas perhaps said in his heart: " Henceforth this blessedness shall be mine. Last week it might have been mine, for I only heard of that which the rest saw. How happy had I been could I have then believed! But, having now received this great 'sign,' henceforth I will live by a faith confirmed by sight, but not dependent upon it."

How are *we* to take these words of Christ? Do they commend those who believe without having seen? or do they, as it were, congratulate them on being able to do so? They teach us to regard such persons as both happy and approved. But they do not imply that it is well to believe without evidence, or that the sight of that which nevertheless we believe without seeing will not afford us peculiar joy. Happy, how happy, are they who see the good days, the good fruits, for which they have long waited! He indeed is blest who trusts an absent God ; but how blest is he who opens the door when at last it pleases God to knock thereat as a visitor! They were blest who could calmly believe, when Peter lay in prison awaiting death, that God would provide for His servant whether in death or by deliverance ; but how happy were they to find Peter standing at the door, and to know that their prayer was answered! " Blessed are *your* eyes, for they *see*," said our Lord to the disciples. Not thus blest were the righteous men and prophets who had desired to see. And yet to these holy and faithful men belonged the very blessing of which Christ spoke to Thomas. They *believed* that God would do great things for Israel and the world, that a glorious time was coming; but they knew not when God would work, and only very obscurely

---

[1] J. E. Rattenbury, *The Twelve*, 208.

how. They believed that God would make of the wilderness "a garden," and in the desert would give "water springs"; but they did not *see* these happy changes, or know the time and way in which they would be effected. These men were approved of God; and they were happy as well as approved: for often by faith alone were they rescued from the despair into which others sank, and many of their days were passed in peaceful hope.

Let us then dare something. Let us not always be unbelieving children. Let us keep in mind that the Lord, not forbidding those who insist on seeing before they will believe, blesses those who have not seen and yet have believed—those who trust in Him more than that, who believe without the sight of the eyes, without the hearing of the ears. They are blessed to whom a wonder is not a fable, to whom a mystery is not a mockery, to whom a glory is not an unreality.

¶ St. Jane Frances Chantel never cared to hear of miracles in confirmation of the Faith, nor revelations, and occasionally she made them pass them over while they were reading in the refectory the *Lives of the Saints*. She resembled in this the great St. Louis of France, who, once when he was called into his private chapel to see some miraculous appearance which had taken place at Mass, refused to go, saying, that he thanked God he believed in the Blessed Sacrament, and should not believe it more firmly for all the miracles in the world, neither did he wish to see one, lest he should thereby forfeit Our Lord's special blessing on those who have not seen, and yet have believed.[1]

3. The adoring confession of Thomas, "My Lord and my God," is the climax of the Gospel of St. John. He has led us from confession to confession, steadily upward from Nathanael to Peter, from Peter to Martha, and now from Martha to these culminating words of Thomas. With these he stops, as though his work was done when the loftiest confession of all burst out from the soberest and most cautious of the Twelve.

And to these words of Thomas all Christian life must come. We know well enough what we ought to do. What can be simpler than to do justly, and to love mercy, and to walk humbly with thy God? But where in the wide world shall we find strength to do so? It is not enough to hear of Christ, or to confess Him

[1] *The Spirit of Father Faber,* 77.

along with others as our Lord and our God. The belief of others
will do you no good, for no truth is truly yours till you have made
it yours by labour and toil, and found its echo in your own heart.
You are not truly Christ's till you let the world drop out of sight
and take Him for your own with the Apostle's cry, " My Lord and
my God." " Whom have I in heaven but thee? and there is none
upon earth that I desire beside thee." This is the cry which the
Saviour delights to hear; and in it you shall find for yourself a
never-failing well of life, and a never-failing stream of blessing
for those around you.

¶ Dr. Pusey's daughter (Mrs. Brine), in her description of her
father's last moments, says : " I spent the morning either kneeling
by his side or leaning over him, and holding his dear hand.   It was
about ten o'clock that I heard the faint but distinct utterance,
'Thou Lord God of Hosts,' as if he were conscious of a Presence
we could not see.   Later on there came a sort of triumphant burst,
with the words, 'My Lord and my God.'   He said the words with
an emphasis of victorious, *assured* faith, as if the vision were
revealed to him of the Master he had loved and served so faithfully.
One must have heard it to enter into what I mean."[1]

> The bonds that press and fetter,
> That chafe the soul and fret her,
> What man can know them better,
>   O brother men, than I?
>
> And yet, my burden bearing,
> The five wounds ever wearing,—
> I too in my despairing
>   Have seen Him as I say ;—
> Gross darkness all around Him
> Enwrapt Him and enwound Him,—
> O late at night I found Him
>   And lost Him in the day!
>
> Yet bolder grown and braver
> At sight of One to save her
> My soul no more shall waver,
>   With wings no longer furled,—
> But cut with one decision
> From doubt and men's derision
> That sweet and vanished vision
>   Shall follow thro' the world.[2]

[1] *The Story of Dr. Pusey's Life*, 552.   [2] F. W. H. Myers, *A Vision*.

THOMAS.

II.

WHAT WAS HE?

LITERATURE.

Adeney, W. F., in *Men of the New Testament* : Matthew to Timothy (1905), 221.

Alexander, S. A., *Christ and Scepticism* (1894), 293.

Arnold, T., *Sermons*, v. (1878) 223.

Bernard, J. H., *From Faith to Faith* (1895), 263.

Calthrop, G., *In Christ* (1893), 205.

Campbell, R. J., in *Sermons by Congregational Preachers*, i. 9.

Carpenter, W. B., *The Son of Man among the Sons of Men* (1893), 117.

Curzon, J. E., in *Sermons on the Gospels* : Advent to Trinity (1896), 284.

Davidson, A. B., *The Called of God* (1902), 319.

Dawson, W. J., *The Church of To-Morrow* (1892), 83.

Gwatkin, H. M., *The Eye for Spiritual Things* (1907), 131.

Hadden, R. H., *Selected Sermons* (1911), 12.

Hardy, E. J., *Doubt and Faith* (1899), 104.

Henson, H. H., *The Value of the Bible* (1904), 182.

Ingram, A. F. W., *Friends of the Master* (1898), 60.

„   „   *A Mission of the Spirit* (1906), 149.

Jones, J. D., *The Glorious Company of the Apostles* (1904), 172.

Lilley, J. P., *Four Apostles* (1912), 95.

Macnutt, F. B., *The Riches of Christ* (1903), 34.

Magee, W. C., *Growth in Grace* (1892), 81.

Maggs, J. T. L., *The Spiritual Experience of St. Paul* (1901), 195.

Rattenbury, J. E., *The Twelve* (1914), 193.

Robertson, F. W., *Sermons*, ii. (1875) 268.

Ryle, H. E., *On the Church of England* (1904), 125.

Temple, W., *Studies in the Spirit and Truth of Christianity* (1914), 121.

Thew, J., *Broken Ideals*, 141.

Tholuck, A., *Light from the Cross* (1869), 99.

Whyte, A., *Bible Characters* : Joseph and Mary to James (1900), 159.

Wilkinson, G. H., *Some Laws in God's Spiritual Kingdom* (1909), 280.

Williams, C. D., *A Valid Christianity for To-Day* (1909), 124.

Williams, T. R., *Belief and Life* (1898), 99.

Dictionary of Christ and the Gospels, ii. (1908) 728 (E. H. Titchmarsh).

WHAT WAS THOMAS?

Except I shall see in his hands the print of the nails, and put my finger into the print of the nails, and put my hand into his side, I will not believe.— John xx. 25.
My Lord and my God.—John xx. 28.

IT is probable that, as Jesus chose only twelve Apostles, He chose persons of distinct and marked character, in order that the truth of the gospel might in after ages shine among men, not with one colour of light, but in many colours. Now, in judging men's conduct, we need to know not only their circumstances but, above all, their kind of mind. We need this even in judging of their religious conduct. For religion does not alter the natural cast of a man's mind; it only sanctifies and consecrates the natural disposition. The man who was impulsive before he was impressed with the truth remains impulsive still, and will act impulsively even in religious things, although he may be taught gradually to guard against his impulsiveness. The man who is despondent by nature will not be immediately transported by his faith into a clear air and sunny sky, although his natural disposition may be, to some extent, corrected by the many hopes set before him in the gospel, and even more by the healthy activity into which it sets all his feelings. At all events, in forming an opinion of men's actions, we should endeavour, if we have the means, to get behind their actions and look at themselves.

Now, while there are many wonderful portraits in the portrait-gallery of St. John's Gospel, there is no figure more distinctly drawn than that of the Apostle Thomas. And yet, strange to say, it is possible that great injustice has been done to him. His name has become, in Church history, a proverb for unbelief. Among the typical characters that surround our Lord in the gospel story, he has always been regarded as the type of the doubter; he is known as the doubting or unbelieving Thomas. Why should he be so called? It is true that he doubted; but his doubt does not seem either so very unreasonable or so very obstinate that he should be called, by way of distinction, *the* doubter, *the* unbeliever. It was not unreasonable, on the contrary it was reasonable and natural, that he should feel some doubt respecting the resurrection of Jesus Christ. Others had doubted as well as he, and they were called " fools, and slow of heart to believe " ; and yet they did not inherit the name of the doubters. Nor was his disbelief of a very obstinate kind. It seems to have yielded almost instantaneously to evidence, and immediately after he had seen what he asked to see, he gave utterance to a confession of faith which was really in advance of his time—he said more for Christ than many others of His disciples perhaps would then have said—he said, " My Lord and my God." He not only admitted Christ's resurrection but acknowledged His Divinity ; and yet he is called " Thomas the doubter—the sceptic."

I.

Was He a Doubter?

1. Thomas was a man of positive temperament, thoughtfulness, and caution : he was unwilling, with a not improper unwillingness, to accept any fact except upon sufficient evidence. Nor indeed do we find any strong condemnation of his attitude from Christ's own lips—certainly not the sharp censure with which, once and again, He had rebuked Peter, James, and John. He does not dismiss him from His presence ; He does not tell him that the spirit which inspires his conduct is an unrighteous spirit; He does not even turn upon him a look of sorrowful reproach. On the contrary, as though admitting the naturalness and justice of his demand, He gives the proof required, only adding, as if those piercing eyes were looking out over the centuries to far-distant times, " Blessed are they that have not seen, and yet have believed." Thomas's scepticism was due simply to the fact that the evidence offered him was not, in his judgment, satisfactory ; when stronger evidence was given, we read that his scepticism at once disappeared.

He is called the doubter because he alone of the eleven Apostles questioned the fact of his Lord's resurrection. But he was the only one who had not seen the risen Christ. For anything we know to the contrary, if he had been present, he would have been convinced; and for anything we know to the contrary, if any one of the others had been absent, that disciple would have been equally sceptical. As it is, none of them had believed the reports of previous appearances. What the women said appeared to them all but idle tales, and the appearance to Peter had only filled the rest with perplexity. It was Christ's appearance to them that convinced the Ten; on the next occasion, Thomas being present, he too was convinced. In all this, then, they seem to have been on a level as to previous unbelief and the belief that came with the first sight of Christ. It may be that Thomas's different position was due only to the accident of circumstance. He was exceptional in not being present. Therefore he was also exceptional in not believing. How much scepticism and even unbelief on which the Church has looked so sternly is really due to some misfortune of environment! how much peaceable acquiescence in established convictions has no merit, because it has been nursed in favourable circumstances that have made it seem quite natural and simple and without any difficulties!

2. The truth is, that doubt is a stream with many sources. There is the doubt of indifference, and there is the doubt of pretentiousness. There is also the doubt of deep earnestness, of jealous affection, of intense agonizing love of truth.

(1) There is the doubt of *the indifferent*—that which finds its type in the man who said, "What is truth?" That is, who knows? Who cares? What does it matter? That which in strict accuracy is the simple absence of all care, all interest, and all conviction. Such was not the doubt of Thomas.

¶ I remember talking to a nice young fellow in Bethnal Green. "Well, now," I said, "what do you think about religion?" "Well, Mr. Ingram," he replied, "to tell you the truth, I never think of it from one end of the year to the other." He was a Bethnal Green boy, hardly grown up. We cannot blame him; he was never brought up to anything better, but we taught him something better later on. If any of you have given up prayer, and have come to church to-day for the first time perhaps for many years, and long ago gave up your Communion (even supposing you ever came to Communion); if you never kneel down and say a prayer at home, I ask you, brother, in all love, Can you wonder that the face of God has gone farther and farther from you, and that Jesus Christ has become a far-off figure in the distance? and that the Holy Spirit who is so strong to help you, to heal you, to cleanse you, and guide you in life, has less and less power over you every year? and that your conscience now scarcely speaks to you at all? Of course, you doubt; it is the doubt of blank indifference.[1]

(2) Then there is *shallow scepticism*; and you can always tell the shallow sceptic first by his conceit. He is rather proud of being a doubter, he is rather proud of being a little more knowing than other people, he is rather proud of sneering at his brother's or sister's faith. You know him by the almost certain mark that he knows very little about that at which he is sneering. As Bacon so beautifully says, "A little philosophy inclineth man's mind to atheism; but depth in philosophy bringeth men's minds about to religion." The shallow sceptic is irreverent; he does not realize the sanctity of life or the awfulness of death, he does not realize what the issues are; and while he is in that state of shallow scepticism he will not see the light. He may be brought to his knees, by God's mercy, by being face to face with death; he will see, perhaps, his nearest and dearest cut down before his eyes; he will see, perhaps, his wife or his child at the point of death, because God will use almost any means if only He can bring the truth to a soul before it is too late. But the shallow sceptic, as he does not want the light, will not get the light.

¶ It is perfectly true that no true man can really avoid altogether the gravest spiritual issues, and that when he is in contact with these issues, especially when he is dealing with the personal issue of right or wrong for his own will, he begins to realize the meaning of the unseen world in the very sense in which the Christian apostles and evangelists realized it, and then perhaps he knows what religious certainty means. But the meaning and measure of certainty in that region are very different from the meaning and measure of certainty in that world of understanding in which so large a part of the better human life is now passed. And I do not hesitate to say that, quite apart from the intrinsic difficulties of religious questions, one of the chief bewilderments of modern life in relation to religion is this—that men have learnt most of their tests of certainty in a region which is not spiritual at all, and in which certainty hardly involves the

[1] A. F. W. Ingram, *A Mission of the Spirit*, 152.

inward judgment of the true man, but only, at most, a kind of shadow of the man. [1]

(3) But Thomas, to use a phrase of Plato's, "doubted well." His was the doubt of *deep earnestness.* He realized what was involved in his doubts: there was not a grain of affectation about him. He was not like the dilettante doubters we sometimes meet to-day, who brush the whole thing lightly aside with the superior air of those who have outlived old-fashioned superstitions; he was in dead earnest. He knew perfectly well that if this Sun set no other sun was likely to rise; he knew perfectly well that if this Man failed him he would never have the heart to trust another; and he was quite aware, in his grim and silent way, that what he doubted was life or death, not only to himself but also to a dying world.

And then, again, Thomas doubted well because he was loyal, not only to Christ but also to the Church. He was found with all the rest of the disciples, in spite of his doubt, at the next meeting: he was not one of those who at the first difficulty fling off their old friends, throw over their Communions, and turn their back on the Church. He had a steadier judgment; he knew there must be difficulties in religion, and, painful as they were, the place where he would be most likely to have them solved would be where he had received so much help and light before; and because he kept with the Church Jesus found His friend in his old place when He came to help him.

¶ Whilst minister of the Evangelical Union Church at Bathgate, Fairbairn went through a spiritual crisis, in which, as he said, "My faith broke down." In his despair, he went abroad, where he studied for a year, and where he came to realize doubt was not sin, but rather a growing pain of the soul, a means to a wider outlook and a clearer faith. . . . What he learned in Germany and the change it produced in his relation to the problems of religious thought may best be stated in his own words: "(1) The doubts which had been hidden like secret sins lost their power to harm, and ceased to cause shame. Freedom of expression had taken from them their sting. And with freedom there had come a new personal conviction. So (2) a simple and wonderful thing happened: theology changed from a system doubted to a system believed. But the system believed was not

[1] R. H. Hutton, *Aspects of Religious and Scientific Thought,* 29,

the old system which had been doubted. (3) And so a third and more wonderful thing happened: theology was reborn and with it a new and higher faith. God seemed a nobler and more majestic Being when interpreted through the Son: the Eternal Sonship involved Eternal Fatherhood. Since God had created out of love, He could not so suddenly turn to hate. Since His grace was His glory, He could not and would not use the ill-doing of ignorance or inexperience to justify His dislike. (4) Nor could the old narrow notion which made salvation rather an affair of a future state than of this life survive on the face of those larger ideas. Redemption concerned both the many and the one, the whole as well as the parts, the unity as much as the units. I believed then what I still believe, that the Christ I had learned to know represents the largest and most gracious truth God has ever communicated to man."[1]

¶ With Clough this sort of large, half-genial suspense of judgment, that looks upon natural instincts with a sort of loving doubt, and yields with cautious hand a carefully stinted authority to human yearnings in order not wholly to lose a share in the moving forces of life, was unfortunately not supplemented by any confident belief in a Divine answer to those vague yearnings, and consequently his tone is almost always at once sweet and sad. It is saturated with the deep but musical melancholy of such thoughts as the following, whose pathos shows how much more profoundly and deeply Clough thirsted for truth than many of even the most confident of those of us who believe that there is a living water at which to slake our thirst:—

> To spend uncounted years of pain,
> Again, again, and yet again,
> In working out in heart and brain
>   The problem of our being here;
> To gather facts from far and near,
> Upon the mind to hold them clear,
> And, knowing more may yet appear,
> Unto one's latest breath to fear
> The premature result to draw—
> Is this the object, end, and law,
> And purpose of our being here?[2]

3. But the fact remains, says the conventional Christian apologist, that he doubted, and that, then as now, doubt is

---

[1] W. B. Selbie, *The Life of Andrew Martin Fairbairn*, 39.
[2] R. H. Hutton, *Literary Essays*, 305.

sinful Is that quite so? We remember with what gentleness
and strength Tennyson resisted the same suggestion as it came
to him from his sister, who was to have been Arthur Hallam's
bride. Read the 96th canto of *In Memoriam*, especially these
lines:

> He fought his doubts and gather'd strength,
> He would not make his judgment blind,
> He faced the spectres of the mind
> And laid them: thus he came at length

> To find a stronger faith his own;
> And Power was with him in the night,
> Which makes the darkness and the light,
> And dwells not in the light alone.

¶ It can be readily conceived how a serious student like
Flint, possessed of a wealth of knowledge exceptional for his
years, with powers of thought equal to his learning, impelled
by moral earnestness and with a conscience quick to take
offence at the slightest deviation from truth, was bound to come
into conflict with the official orthodoxy of his day; and that
is what really happened. Before he reached his twentieth year
he had to fight his battle of the soul, and he did not conquer
without experiencing those mental pangs which have been the
lot of all earnest spirits that have passed through similar
troubles. What the particular nature of the conflict was, we
do not exactly know. He has left no record. But in an address
which he delivered to the Young Men's Christian Association, in
connection with the East Church, when he was on the eve of
leaving Aberdeen, he thus refers to this time of mental conflict:
"Almost ever since I can remember, the great spiritual
questions which agitate society, which harass young men most
of all, sometimes even under seeming levity of disposition, have
been of vital interest to me; and whatever of solid footing
in Divine truth I seem to myself to have found has been gained
with a struggle and a pain which I thank God devoutly for; so
that with the deeper trials of young and earnest spirits I do
feel in sympathy through every fibre of my being."
Now it seems to me that these are words which those who
knew Flint in after years, when he was regarded as the "Defender
of the Faith," might well ponder. A tradition had grown up
round him which shadowed him forth as one who from earliest
years had his feet planted firmly on the foundations of truth,
and who had never felt these foundations sinking under him.
While many have admired, and others have been grateful for,

the masterly way in which he re-establishes the main doctrines of religion, very few were aware that his power was the fruit of a great conflict which raged in his student days, and that the firm land on which he stood had been reached only after struggling through the breakers.[1]

¶ When I think of Thomas I always think of an incident of a Methodist, a man with a bright, joyous experience, in the North of England, a man who could shout with gladness:

> O for a thousand tongues to sing
> My great Redeemer's praise!

who never had the slightest difficulty in reading "his title clear to mansions in the sky." He married a wife who had a great deal of difficulty in all these things, and who could not follow him in his Methodist raptures. She was greatly troubled because of her lack of experience, and he was greatly troubled because of her lack of experience and her good character, and he was not able to reconcile the two. She came to die, and when she was dying he was in great distress. He knelt by her bedside and prayed that God would give her some revelation of His love that she might have an experience like his joyous experience. He turned to her and asked her whether she could not leave some testimony behind of God's love, but her only reply was " It's very dark! It's very dark!" The man was in an anguish by her bedside, and pleaded with God that light might come, but she only said, " It's very dark! It's very dark!" He said, " Your character is beautiful. Everybody knows you are better than I am, and I certainly know the joy of the Lord and have experienced His pardoning love. Why is it? Why should He leave you in this dimness and mist and darkness?" but she only replied, " It's very dark!" Then just before the light of life went out altogether, she clasped his hand and said, " It's very dark, but God sometimes puts His children to sleep in the dark, and they wake up in the morning."[2]

II.

Was He a Pessimist?

1. When Thomas is not called the doubting disciple, he is singled out as the despondent disciple. As the evidence for

[1] D. Macmillan, *The Life of Robert Flint*, 64.
[2] J. E. Rattenbury, *The Twelve*, 200.

his doubt is found in the saying, "Except I see in his hands the print of the nails, and put my finger into the print of the nails, and put my hand into his side, I will not believe"; so the evidence for his despondency is found in the previous saying, "Let us also go, that we may die with him."

Accordingly Prebendary Calthrop speaks of his "despondent character," and "what we may perhaps call his pessimistic bias." And even Dr. A. B. Davidson says: "The prevailing character of the man was this proclivity to despond, a certain want of buoyancy of mind, coupled perhaps with a feminine tenderness and sensitiveness, and, it may be, not without that self-will and obstinacy and love of solitude which many times go along with too great delicacy of feeling. He was the kind of man whom one often observes in the East, of a gloomy dark exterior, to appearance emotionless and with a bent to melancholy, yet fervid and fiery within, like a stream of lava over which there gathers a hard black crust, but within there rolls a red molten stream of fire."

"The doubt of Thomas," says Dr. W. J. Dawson, "is the despondence of a great spirit. It breathes like a gentle sigh through that other saying of his: 'Lord, we know not whither thou goest; how know we the way?' He was, perhaps, one of those men through whose natures a vein of tender melancholy runs. Such men are like delicate musical instruments, the brilliance of whose tone suffers by the slightest change of temperature; they often suffer by the physical oppression of the robust, who little know how their unsympathetic brusqueness sets sensitive nerves jarring, and how their rough touch sets old bruises aching; their life moves in an orbit where transitions are rapid and frequent; they have their bright moments and their dark; they are of unequal temperament; they receive all impressions acutely because they are acutely sensitive; their joy is ecstasy, their suffering is agony, their disheartening is despair. Think of such men as Dr. John Brown, the author of *Rab and His Friends*, in whom humour and melancholy lay so close together; of Charles Lamb, whose laughter is the foil to such unutterable despair; of Coleridge with his gleams of celestial light breaking out of bitter darkness; of Johnson, with his sturdy faith ever struggling through the inertia and gloom of hypochondriac fancies; of Cowper, who can write with such delicate humour, such freshness of touch, such inspired faith and joy, and yet can die saying, 'I feel unutterable despair.' Think even of a man of action, and heroic action, like Abraham Lincoln, whose laughter was the relief of hereditary brooding melancholy, and was, as he said, 'the vent,' which saved him from a frenzied brain or broken heart. Such men may furnish us with a hint of what Thomas called Didymus may have been. I think that his, too, was a tender, brooding, intensely sensitive nature. He dwelt in the exceeding brightness or the blackness of darkness. His quick intelligence perceived things with an infinite clearness of vision, and they were things which often he would rather not have seen. He had none of the blindness of Peter to the shadow of coming events. He never debated as John did who should be the first in the Kingdom. He followed Christ because he could not help it; but he knew it was to judgment and death. He doubted, not because he would, but because he must; and it was out of that cloud of unutterable misgiving that he sent forth this heroic cry, 'Let us also go, that we may die with him.'"

¶ There are two classes of minds which habitually stand in the post of outlook—the man of the laurel and the man of the cypress. The first sees the world as rose-coloured. It is all brightness, all beauty, all glory—a scene of splendid possibilities which is waiting to open for him its gates of gold. The second, on the other hand, approaches it with dismay. To him the prospect looks all dark. He is a pessimist previous to experience. He is sure he will never succeed. He is sure the gate will not open when he tries it. He feels that he has nothing to expect from life. He hangs his harp upon a willow, and goes forth to sow in tears.

And each of these has a representative in the New Testament. I think the man of the laurel is the evangelist John. From the very beginning he is optimistic. Even when Christ was on the road to that martyrdom of which He had warned His disciples, John is so sanguine of success that he applies for a place in the coming kingdom. And through life this optimism does not desert him. His very power to stand beside the cross was a power of hope. It was not that he excelled his brother-disciples in the nerve to bear pain. It was rather that to him the spectacle conveyed an impression of less pain—that he saw in it elements of triumph as well as trial, signs of strength along with marks of sacrifice.

But if the man of the laurel is John, the man of the cypress is assuredly Thomas. There are men whose melancholy is the result of their scepticism; Thomas's scepticism is the result of his melancholy. He came to the facts of life with an antecedent prejudice; he uniformly expected from the banquet an inferior menu. It is a great mistake to imagine that the collapse came with the Crucifixion. Strictly speaking, there was no collapse. If I understand the picture aright it represents the figure of a man who could never stand at his full stature but was always bent towards the ground. It was not from timidity. He was a courageous man, ready to do and dare anything even when he was most downcast. It was not from a mean nature. He was a man of the noblest spirit—capable of the most heroic deeds of sacrifice. That which gave him a crouching attitude was simply a constitutional want of hope—a natural inability to take the bright view. It was this which made him a sceptic.[1]

2. Thomas's melancholy is given as the explanation of his absence when first the risen Lord appeared to the disciples. "When the last terrible tragedy came," says Hough, "Thomas sank into misanthropy and despair. It was not so much a reaction with him as with the others. He had had his deep misgivings, and lately they had grown stronger. Now his sober judgment was vindicated. His Master had failed. He had been killed. Thomas would never see Him again. It was small comfort, however, that Thomas had expected some tragic end to the ministry of his Master. He had loved Jesus, and now that face of glowing, eager friendliness and lofty love would never be seen again. His heart bled at the thought. He had nothing to look forward to. He had only wonderful memories. He sat nursing them in silent gloom. He had not heart enough to meet with the disciples as in mutual fellowship they tried to comfort one another. Thus he missed the first appearance of Jesus to the company of the disciples."

¶ The character of Thomas is an anatomy of melancholy. If "to say man is to say melancholy," then to say Thomas, called Didymus, is to say religious melancholy. Peter was of such an ardent and enthusiastical temperament that he was always speaking, whereas Thomas was too great a melancholian to speak much, and when he ever did speak it was always out of the depths of his hypochondriacal heart.[2]

[1] G. Matheson, *The Representative Men of the New Testament*, 137.
[2] A. Whyte, *Bible Characters*, 159.

¶ In that Inferno of his, which is simply the subterranean chambers of the soul thrown upon a screen, Dante places the doubters, the deniers, next to the slothful, on the side farther from the light, nearer to the uttermost state of darkness. In his view, that is to say once again, doubt or denial may creep upon the human soul and harden over it like a crust, not so much in consequence of this or that particular incident in the man's intellectual life, but as the last result of his permitting the disheartening things in human experience to weigh unduly upon him, to dwell habitually with him. According to Dante, one may sink into an invincible attitude of doubt or denial, by simply encouraging within oneself the sad or dismal view of things, by refusing to entertain the evidence on the other side, giving it equal weight: nothing worse than that. But there is not anything which *could* be worse for beings such as we are, who have been sent into the world, not to hesitate about things, but to live our life once for all, with all our strength.[1]

3. Now these despondent men are sometimes lifted to the mountain-tops of faith and confidence by the surprising joys which come to them. Their moods change rapidly. From the deep Valley of Humiliation and the grounds of Giant Despair they are raised to the Delectable Mountains and the height of celestial vision. So it was with Thomas, when the risen Christ was truly revealed to him and proved. He who had believed not at all believed most then, and passed into a radiant confidence and joy ; and we may well suppose that the pessimism of the man was thoroughly cured by the sweet medicine which had been administered to it, and that afterwards his love and courage and faith were brightened and strengthened by a hopefulness and cheerfulness as great as any other of the disciples showed.

¶ Not only did Stevenson diligently seek out the encouraging and bright aspects of experience as he actually found them. Jesus Christ once said to a doubting apostle, "Blessed are they that have not seen, and yet have believed." Stevenson believed through many an hour when he had not seen, and so was blessed. When all was dark, he pointed his telescope right into the blackness, and found a star. It is thus that faith may imitate the Master's work, calling things which are not as though they are, and find that the dark world has no power to resist faith's command when it boldly says, Let there be light.[2]

[1] J. A. Hutton, *Pilgrims in the Region of Faith*, 24.
[2] J. Kelman, *The Faith of Robert Louis Stevenson*, 253.

So now, thy Lord, thy God confess,
Believe and worship, too,
And first adore,—yet they have more
Who deem the witness true.
Thy faith has seen but what was seen,—
Blest they who still believe
What eye nor ear shall see or hear,
Nor heart of man conceive.

O, in my body, not in Thine,
Lord Jesus, let me see
The blessed marks of love divine,
Which Thou hast borne for me;
Compunction sweet on hands and feet,
The pierced, the open heart;
Or e'er, without one faithless doubt,
I see Thee as Thou art.[1]

III.

WAS HE A HEROIC LOVER?

We may say, then, that Thomas was a doubter, but we must not mistake the nature of his doubt. So we may say that he was a pessimist. But to say that he was a doubter or a pessimist is not to explain altogether his conduct or to do justice to his character.

1. It is manifestly unfair to find the proof of his pessimism in the words, "Let us also go, that we may die with him." Is there any evidence that the other disciples were a particle more hopeful? Nay, as regards the matter of this saying, was Jesus Himself more hopeful? Jesus had told His friends before this that He would have to die when He went up to Jerusalem. Thomas takes no more gloomy a view of the situation than his Master had taken. Indeed, he simply accepts Christ's own prediction, and bases his proposal upon it. And he was right in his anticipation. It is true Jesus did not die immediately He went up to Judæa on this errand of mercy. There was another brief respite. But Jerusalem meant death sooner or later, and it was not long before the net was drawn round the Victim, and His own

[1] Herbert Kynaston.

forecast verified. Jesus did die in Jerusalem only two or three months after Thomas had spoken of the coming event. We may even say that his words showed his faith and insight. Thomas had now accepted what Peter had previously rejected. The notion that Jesus should suffer and die had been repudiated by the leading Apostle with indignation; it was accepted by his humbler companion with settled resignation.

There is another side to Thomas's utterance, which gives it an entirely different character. Instead of taking it as a confession of despondency we may treat it as a note of heroism. It is a bugle call to his shrinking comrades. They are terror-stricken at their Master's determination, frozen into silence by fear. Thomas breaks the cowardly silence. There is no denying it: Jerusalem spells death. But Jesus will face this fate that awaits Him there. Then He must not go alone. His little remnant of followers, the few faithful disciples still left when so many have forsaken Him and fled, must not desert Him in this desperate extremity. To follow Him still would seem to involve sharing His fate. Be it so, thinks Thomas. Is He to die? Then let us die with Him. Christ's courage is infectious, and Thomas is the first to catch the infection. From him it spreads through all the circle of disciples. Braced by this one man's example, they too follow Jesus, making straight for the centre of peril, for the goal of doom. That is heroic. For the moment, at least, Thomas is a hero, and his heroism passes into the whole band. Under his inspiring influence, they all feel ready to leap into the jaws of death.

¶ You will have heard the story which Napier relates of a young officer riding down into his first battle, with pale face and trembling hand, when a companion, looking at him, said, "Why, man, you're pale; you're afraid!" "I know I am," he quietly rejoined; "and if you were half as much afraid as I am you would run away." That was courage, the higher courage; the flesh failing for fear, every nerve trembling, loosened, unstrung, but the soul resolved and calm, ordering the body to its duty. And that was the spirit of Thomas: he can at least die with Christ.

> Shall Jesus bear the Cross alone
> And all the world go free?
> No; there's a Cross for every one
> And there's a Cross for me.

That is the meaning of Thomas's speech, and the very fact that he thinks that the peril and the cross should be avoided invests with a sublimer glory his sacrifice of self in facing them. Few more heroic sayings have ever been recorded in history than this: "Let us also go, that we may die with him!"[1]

¶ In every earnest life there are weary flats to tread, with the heavens out of sight—no sun, no moon, and not a tint of light upon the path below; when the only guidance is the faith of brighter hours, and the secret Hand we are too numb and dark to feel. But to the meek and faithful it is not always so. Now and then something touches the dull dream of sense and custom, and the desolation vanishes away: the spirit leaves its witness with us: the divine realities come up from the past and straightway enter the present: the ear into which we poured our prayer is not deaf; the infinite eye to which we turned is not blind, but looks in with answering mercy on us.[2]

2. Now this heroism sprang out of love to Christ. If Thomas was a doubter or despondent, he conquered his doubts and his despondency because he never lost his love. Who can miss the deep love that breathes in the words which have been quoted? Thomas was a thorough disciple: for he not only trusted the saving power of Jesus, but loved Jesus Himself. Separation from home and kindred this loyal soul could bear, but not separation from Jesus. What caused him anxiety was nothing relating to his own prospects, but only the Master's safety. He is knit to Jesus with so pure a love that he will incur the risk of death rather than suffer Him to take the journey to Judæa alone. It was probably the discernment of this affection in Thomas's heart that led John to give him such a prominent place in the later pages of his Gospel.

¶ For devotion and heroic love I know of no one to excel Thomas. "As the Lord liveth," said Elisha in answer to Elijah's appeal to him to leave him, "as the Lord liveth, and as thy soul liveth, I will not leave thee." "Intreat me not to leave thee," said Ruth, the Moabitess, to Naomi her mother-in-law; "whither thou goest, I will go; and where thou lodgest, I will lodge; where thou diest, will I die, and there will I be buried: the Lord do so to me, and more also, if aught but death part thee and me." Those are moving and pathetic instances of loyalty, but they are

[1] W. J. Dawson, *The Church of To-Morrow*, 98.
[2] James Martineau.

not more moving and pathetic than the loyalty with which Thomas was ready to dare anything for his Master. "Let us also go," said this man of the devoted heart, "that we may die with him." And this, as it is Thomas's chief characteristic, is also his crowning glory. Of Thomas it might be said, as of that woman who was much forgiven, that "he loved much." He loved Christ with all the fervour and passion of his deep and sorrowful heart.[1]

3. But is this moral heroism compatible with the signs of doubt which are seen in Thomas? We think it is. Thomas was a man who desired certitude. His love led him to recognize the greatness of the issues which the life and words of Christ put before him, and he was restless under vagueness or uncertainty. Too many people view all things through a mental haze. They cannot tell what they see and what they do not see. It would be impossible for them to make a clear confession of faith, for they do not know what they believe, although they honestly think they believe all that it is right and proper to believe. Such faith is nearly worthless. At all events it is blind. But worse than this, there are people who are content with mere phrases that convey no meaning whatever to their minds. It is enough for them that the words sound pious, or are familiar from religious association, or come with the sanction of venerated authority. Thomas would never sink down to the mental indolence of such torpid minds. He would welcome Dr. Johnson's famous advice to clear our minds of cant. Even if the words we hear are quite sincere and full of meaning, such as the words of Christ, if we cannot see the drift of them and yet settle down in lazy satisfaction, we degrade them to the level of the unreal, and our use of them is no better than what Dr. Johnson so justly stigmatized. There is a sickly state of mind which disgusts all healthy natures. To Thomas this would be an abomination. He may not be able to see far; but what he does see, he must see clearly.

"I will not believe," he said; for he had been at the crucifixion, and witnessed all that went on there. He saw the Saviour raised upon the tree. He saw the nails driven home, and the spear thrust in. He saw it all, and felt it all. And he saw the Lord bleed and die. The whole picture fastened itself upon his

[1] J. D. Jones, *The Glorious Company of the Apostles*, 180.

mind; it was a constant impression which he carried about with him, and at which he shuddered every moment. And it is from this vivid impression that he speaks. He reads off the whole outline of it from his mind, feature after feature—the nails, the spear, the hands, the side: all the evidence of death. And until this impression be removed by another impression, nothing will make the man believe.

Thus Thomas was just what some of our triflers would like to be thought—a sober, truthful man who insists on facing the facts he sees before he goes a step farther. Such a man is slow to move: no passing enthusiasm can stir him, only the gravest sense of duty. And faith is none the worse for counting the cost before it gives itself to Christ. When Wellington saw a man turn pale as he marched up to a battery, he said, "That is a brave man. He knows his danger, and faces it notwithstanding."

¶ Those Christians are blessed who need to leave their simple views of childhood's faith no more than the field-lark does her nest—rising right over it to look at God's morning sun, and His wide, beautiful world, singing a clear, happy song, and then sinking straight down again to their heart's home. But those are not less blessed who, like the dove, lose their ark for a while, and return to it, having found no rest for the sole of their foot save there. They have a deeper experience within, and carry a higher and wider message to the world. The olive leaf in the mouth, plucked from the passing flood, is more than the song at coming daylight. It is as Paul's "Thanks be to God who giveth us the victory," compared with the children's "Hosannah."[1]

[1] John Ker, *Thoughts for Heart and Life*, 24.

MATTHEW.

LITERATURE.

Bruce, A. B., *With Open Face* (1896), 107.

Carpenter, W. B., *The Son of Man among the Sons of Men* (1893), 141.

Cone, O., *Gospel-Criticism and Historical Christianity* (1891), 173.

Conybeare, F. C., *Myth, Magic, and Morals* (1909), 60.

Cox, S., *A Day with Christ*, 67.

Greenhough, J. G., *The Apostles of Our Lord* (1904), 84.

Haweis, H. R., *The Story of the Four* (1886), 39.

Jones, J. D., *The Glorious Company of the Apostles* (1904), 150.

Lilley, J. P., *Four Apostles* (1912), 69.

Lovell, R. H., *First Types of the Christian Life* (1895), 120.

Matheson, G., *The Representative Men of the New Testament* (1905), 183.

Milligan, G., in *Men of the New Testament* : Matthew to Timothy (1905), 1

Rattenbury, J. E., *The Twelve* (1914), 213.

Skrine, J. H., *Saints and Worthies* (1901), 33.

Whyte, A., *Bible Characters* : Joseph and Mary to James (1900), 63.

Christian World Pulpit, lxxviii. (1910) 77 (L. B. Phillips).

Dictionary of Christ and the Gospels, ii. (1908) 142 (J. Herkless).

MATTHEW.

And as Jesus passed by from thence, he saw a man, called Matthew, sitting at the place of toll : and he saith unto him, Follow me. And he arose, and followed him.—Matt. ix. 9.
Matthew the publican.—Matt. x. 3.

I.

MATTHEW THE PUBLICAN.

IT is a profoundly significant fact that the first of the four Gospels, which is for ever associated with the name of Matthew, is the only one that contains the phrase "Matthew the publican" (Matt. x. 3). He did not himself coin the phrase, which must at one time have been on many lips. But he alone has introduced it into the Scriptures, and we may be sure that he did so with a definite purpose. The Church in all ages might call him "Matthew the Apostle," or "Matthew the Evangelist," but he was determined to let every reader of his book know that in his pre-Christian days he was known, and well-known, as "Matthew the publican." That was his occupation; and more, that was his character; therefore let that still be his name. Neither Mark nor Luke nor John sets that mark of ignominy upon him; he brands himself with it. He might, one would have thought, have preferred to bury his past. He could have been a truthful enough evangelist without that personal reference and that melancholy confession. But evidently he had other thoughts on the matter. He probably felt an overmastering necessity laid upon him. Impelled by the Spirit to which he owed his inspiration, he realized somehow that he could not write the Gospel truly without telling the truth about himself.

And in telling it he inscribes in his book—a monument more enduring than bronze—his own name with a word of dishonour and shame beside it. Not with any desire to attract attention to himself, but in deep humility, and for the encouragement of others as steeped in worldliness and sin as he had been, he gives himself the name he bore before he knew the Lord. Once Matthew the publican, he will always be Matthew the publican. It would have been discourteous and ungenerous had any of his fellow-Apostles continued to use that name, either in their ordinary talk or in their writings; but it is the surest indication of the greatness as well as the lowliness of Matthew's own soul that he published and perpetuated the stigma by inserting it in the Holy Scriptures. For the glory of his Lord, who redeemed him from the service of mammon and received him into the circle of His disciples and friends, he kept up, as a Christian, the old name which other New Testament writers left in oblivion. Matthew the publican, like Paul the persecutor, Augustine the libertine, Bunyan the blasphemer, and many another sinner snatched as a brand from the burning, felt the impulse, when he became a Christian writer, to return to the penitent-form and remain there, uttering his confession in a phrase which will be read with wondering awe and adoring gratitude as long as the world lasts.

His confession is contained in three words. When he had called himself "Matthew the publican," he needed to say no more. For the Jew who demeaned himself to become a publican—a *telōnēs* or farmer of the Roman revenues—paid a great price for his lucrative office. He sold his country and his soul for gold. He was in the first place a traitor to his country, trampling his nation's ideals in the dust. In order to enrich himself, and to do so as quickly as possible, he joined hands with the oppressors of his people. And what was still worse, he deliberately chose a calling in which it was impossible to be an honest man. In our country the scale of taxation is fixed by law, and any tax-gatherer who appropriated a part of the revenue would be held guilty of fraud and severely punished for his crime. But in ancient Palestine the business of collecting the revenue was let to the highest bidder, who did his duty if he paid a lump sum into the Roman exchequer, pocketing the surplus of the profits, or who received a certain percentage of whatever he contrived to extort from the long-suffering populace. In either case the system evidently lent itself to all kinds of abuses. The more exacting a farmer of the revenue was—the more he gave the rein to his avarice, grinding the faces of the poor, hardening his heart and stifling his conscience—the more certain was he to become a rich man. But he was equally certain to lose what, in the estimation of all good men, alone makes life worth living—the honour, affection, and friendship which wealth can never buy. He could make no friends among the Romans, by whom he was regarded merely as a useful tool; and he made nothing but enemies among his own people, who despised and scorned him as a traitor while they hated and feared him as an extortioner.

When a wave of religious revival swept over the Holy Land in the days of John the Baptist, the publicans came among the rest to receive the baptism and listen to the counsels of the stern prophet, who laid the axe at the root of their besetting sin by bidding them extort no more than what was appointed them (Luke iii. 12, 13). The words indicate clearly enough that in his opinion the ordinary publican was an extortioner. When Zacchæus, the chief publican (*architelōnēs*) of Jericho, was deeply moved by the presence and spirit of Jesus, and called Him for the first time "Lord," he at once felt a pang of remorse at the thought of all his ill-gotten wealth, and promised to restore it fourfold. And Matthew and Zacchæus were but two of a crowd of Jews who had taken service under the Romans in order to feather their nests at the expense of their own countrymen.

Many taxes had to be collected—a heavy poll-tax, customs duties payable at the frontiers, land taxes, road taxes, and many others. Hence the publicans (*telōnai*) were very numerous, and each had his office where he sat and collected his own special tax, either alone or in company with others, for associations of *telōnai* sometimes united to make the contract. And every penny paid to the Romans in this way was, in the eyes of Jewish patriots, a sign and symbol of Israel's shame; for the Jews regarded it as a fundamental principle of their religion that they should pay no money except to the Temple and to the priests.

¶ Along the north end of the Sea of Galilee, there was a road leading from Damascus to Acre on the Mediterranean, and on that road a customs-office marked the boundary between the territories of Philip the tetrarch and Herod Antipas. Matthew's occupation was the examination of goods which passed along the road, and the levying of the toll. The work of a publican excited the scorn so often shown beyond the limits of Israel to fiscal officers; and when he was a Jew, as was Matthew, he was condemned for impurity by the Pharisees. A Jew serving on a great highway was prevented from fulfilling requirements of the Law, and was compelled to violate the Sabbath law, which the Gentiles, who conveyed their goods, did not observe. Schürer makes the statement that the customs raised in Capernaum in the time of Christ went into the treasury of Herod Antipas, while in Judæa they were taken for the Imperial *fiscus*. Matthew was thus not a collector under one of the companies that farmed the taxes in the Empire, but was in the service of Herod. Yet the fact that he belonged to the publican class, among whom were Jews who outraged patriotism by gathering tribute for Cæsar, subjected him to the scorn of the Pharisees and their party; and his occupation itself associated him with men who, everywhere in the Empire, were despised for extortion and fraud, and were execrated.[1]

II.

MATTHEW THE CHRISTIAN.

1. Matthew had his "receipt of custom" at Capernaum, by the Lake of Galilee. And Capernaum in his time was famous for other things than its exquisite scenery and its thriving trade and its rapidly made fortunes. It was a city exalted to heaven in privilege, inasmuch as it was the second home of Jesus of Nazareth. Not that all the inhabitants of Capernaum knew what that meant. There were many Jews in that busy town whom the holy presence and the mighty works of Jesus did not lead to repentance; many who never understood their privilege or knew the day of their visitation—many, but not all. For the words and the deeds of Jesus soon began to make a profound impression upon the mind of Matthew the publican, reawakening his better nature and making him ashamed of his nefarious trade. Some of those sayings (*logia*) of our Lord which he afterwards recorded so faithfully were in the first instance sharp arrows piercing his own heart and conscience. We can easily imagine what were the winged words that came to him with convicting power, and so *found* him. They were the words which told him that the life is more than meat,

[1] J. Herkless, in the *Dictionary of Christ and the Gospels*, ii. 142.

that a man is not profited if he gain the whole world and lose his own soul, that a man's chief business is to lay up treasures for himself not on earth but in heaven, and that it is easier for a camel to go through the eye of a needle than for a rich man to enter the Kingdom of God. Words like these destroyed his peace.

¶ Our veritable birth dates from the day when, for the first time, we feel at the deepest of us that there is something grave and unexpected in life. . . . We can be born thus more than once; and each birth brings us a little nearer to our God. But most of us are content to wait till an event, charged with almost irresistible radiance, intrudes itself violently upon our darkness, and enlightens us, in our own despite. We await I know not what happy coincidence, when it may so come about that the eyes of our soul shall be open at the very moment that something extraordinary takes place. But in everything that happens is there light; and the greatness of the greatest men has but consisted in that they had trained their eyes to be open to every ray of this light.[1]

¶ We have been watching successive men following after the ideal, which, like some receding star, travelled before its pilgrims through the night. In Francis Thompson's *Hound of Heaven*, the ideal is no longer passive, a thing to be pursued. It halts for its pilgrims—"the star which chose to stoop and stay for us." Nay, more, it turns upon them and pursues them. . . . *The Hound of Heaven* has for its idea the chase of man by the celestial huntsman. God is out after the soul, pursuing it up and down the universe—God,—but God incarnate in Jesus Christ, whose love and death are here the embodiment and revelation of the whole ideal world. The hunted one flees, as men so constantly flee from the Highest, and seeks refuge in every possible form of earthly experience. . . . The soul is never allowed, even in dream, to rest in lower things until satiety brings disillusion. The higher destiny is swift at her heels; and ever, just as she would nestle in some new covert, she is torn from it by the imperious Best of all that claims her for its own. . . . Thus has he compassed the length and breadth of the universe in the vain attempt to flee from God. Now at last he finds himself at bay. God has been too much for him. Against his will, and wearied out with the vain endeavour to escape, he must face the pursuing Love at last. . . .

[1] M. Maeterlinck, *The Treasure of the Humble*, 173.

Finally, we have the answer of Christ to the soul He has chased down after so long a following:

"Strange, piteous, futile thing!
Wherefore should any set thee love apart?
Seeing none but I makes much of naught" (He said),
"And human love needs human meriting:
How hast thou merited—
Of all man's clotted clay the dingiest clot?
Alack, thou knowest not
How little worthy of any love thou art!
Whom wilt thou find to love ignoble thee,
Save Me, save only Me?
All which I took from thee I did but take,
Not for thy harms,
But just that thou might'st seek it in My arms.
All which thy child's mistake
Fancies as lost, I have stored for thee at home:
Rise, clasp My hand, and come!"
Halts by me that footfall:
Is my gloom, after all,
Shade of His hand, outstretched caressingly?
"Ah, fondest, blindest, weakest,
I am He whom thou seekest!
Thou dravest love from thee, who dravest Me."[1]

2. The conversion which seems sudden, and which is indeed consummated by an instantaneous act of the will, is never without its antecedent and preparatory train of events. It is extremely probable that in Matthew's case, as in Paul's, there was a season in which he was "kicking against the goads." Every time he saw Jesus pass his toll-booth, his heart felt a pang. Every time he stood on the edge of a crowd, listening to that thrilling and soul-awakening voice, he was conscious of a growing hatred of the life to which he was bound by interest and habit. Every time he heard the solemn call to repentance, he despised himself as a man lost to faith and honour. Until Jesus had come into his life, he had had the comfortable feeling that he was getting rich, that he was increased in goods and would soon have need of nothing; but now he knew that he was poor and miserable and blind and naked. For now he knew that a man's life does not consist in the abundance of the things which he

[1] John Kelman, *Among Famous Books*, 302.

possesses. Now that he began to look at life through Christ's eyes, he saw what a glorious thing it might be made, and what an inglorious thing he was making it. And his discontent with himself made him the most unhappy of men. Such a state of things could not last, and it was well for him that the kind but searching eyes of Jesus saw what was going on in the depths of his soul. And that was the gladdest day in his life when Jesus, once more passing the place of custom, where he was miserably and mechanically gathering in the taxes, said to him in a voice of irresistible authority, "Follow me." And without a moment's hesitation, Matthew arose, left all, and followed Him. In doing so he began the new life. He came to himself. Stepping out of his toll-booth he stepped out of bondage into liberty and peace and joy.

¶ While I was making myself acquainted with the work of the West London Mission I came across a man so much out of the common, and with so original a view of the religious life, that I turned aside from my researches to cultivate his sympathy and learn his story. . . . On the subject of conversion he had his own particular view. The narratives in Professor James's wonderful book moved him to no admiration. "The best model for a story of conversion," he said, "is to be found in Matthew, nine, nine—*He saith unto him, Follow Me. And he arose, and followed Him.*"[1]

¶ "If we had to choose one out of all the books in the Bible for a prison or desert friend the Gospel according to St. Matthew would be the one we should keep." So remarks Ruskin in speaking of Carpaccio's picture of the calling of Matthew; and the great art critic adds, "We do not enough think how much the leaving the receipt of custom meant as a sign of the man's nature who was to leave us such a notable piece of literature. . . . Matthew's call from receipt of custom, Carpaccio takes for the symbol of the universal call to leave all that we have, and are doing. 'Whosoever forsaketh not all that he hath, cannot be my disciple.' For the other calls were easily obeyed in comparison of this. To leave one's often empty nets and nightly toil on sea, and become fishers of men, probably you might find pescatori enough on the Riva there, within a hundred paces of you, who would take the chance at once, if any gentle person offered it them. James and Jude—Christ's cousins—no thanks to them for following Him; their own home conceivably no richer than His. Thomas

---

[1] Harold Begbie, *In the Hand of the Potter*, 207.

and Philip, I suppose, somewhat thoughtful persons on spiritual matters, questioning of them long since; going out to hear St. John preach, and to see whom he had seen. But *this* man, busy in the place of business—engaged in the interests of foreign governments — thinking no more of an Israelite Messiah than Mr. Goschen, but only of Egyptian finance, and the like "—[at the time Ruskin wrote, Mr. (afterwards Lord) Goschen had gone to Cairo to reorganize the public debt of Egypt]—"suddenly the Messiah, passing by, says, 'Follow me!' and he rises up, gives Him his hand. 'Yea! to the death;' and absconds from his desk in that electric manner on the instant, leaving his cash-box unlocked, and his books for whoso list to balance!—a very remarkable kind of person indeed, it seems to me."[1]

> So Matthew left his golden gains,
> At the great Master's call;
> His soul the love of Christ constrains
> Freely to give up all.
>
> The tide of life was at its flow,
> Rose higher day by day;
> But he a higher life would know
> Than that which round him lay.
>
> Nor Fortune, bright with fav'ring smile,
> Can tempt him with her store;
> Too long she did his heart beguile,
> He will be hers no more.
>
> To one sweet Voice his soul doth list,
> And, at its "Follow Me,"
> Apostle, and Evangelist
> Henceforth for Christ is he.
>
> O Saviour! when prosperity
> Makes this world hard to leave,
> And all its pomps and vanity
> Their meshes round us weave:
>
> Oh grant us grace that to Thy call
> We may obedient be;
> And, cheerfully forsaking all,
> May follow only Thee.[2]

[1] Ruskin, *St. Mark's Rest*, § 173 (*Works*, xxiv. 344).
[2] J. S. B. Monsell.

3. Forthwith Jesus made Matthew the publican one of His disciples. In doing so He set every consideration of worldly prudence at defiance. He outraged public opinion, and earned for Himself the scornful title, "a friend of publicans and sinners." But no title ever bestowed on Him on earth or in heaven, by adoring saints and angels, proclaiming His eternal power and honour and glory, ever gave Him greater joy than that name which was first flung at Him in mockery, by jibing and jeering enemies. For that name told exactly what He was; it indicated the whole end and aim of His life on earth. Of Him more truly than of any other teacher it might have been said, "He was a man, and nothing human was alien to Him." He knew best what was in man—all the weakness and all the sin—yet He was the greatest of all optimists. He saw infinite possibilities in those whom the official teachers of the time—the scribes and the Pharisees—had given up in despair. And He was able to awaken in the publicans and sinners a twofold faith—faith in Himself as the Saviour and Friend of mankind, the Physician of all sick souls, and faith in themselves, which they needed no less. And to the end of their lives they never for a moment imagined that what was high and pure and good in them had come there through their own efforts or achievements; they knew that it had all come through the love of God revealed to them in the friend-ship of Jesus of Nazareth. Among them was Matthew the publican, drawn by the love of Christ into the Kingdom of God. And it was because he wished to make his own conversion an object-lesson which might help to convince his readers of the freeness and richness of Divine grace, and so assure the most doubting and despairing of a welcome into the same Kingdom, that he persisted in calling himself, even after many years of Christian apostleship, "Matthew the publican."

¶ "I have loved thee with an everlasting love, therefore with lovingkindness have I drawn thee." After long conscientious serving of God, refreshed by little feeling of joy or comfort, there are moments when the soul seems suddenly made aware of its own happiness. . . . Such moments are surely more to us than a passing comfort. Do they not teach us something of the depth of those words, "We love him because he first loved us"? For is not this also of the Lord—this tender attraction, this warmth, at which the frozen waters of the heart break up and flow forth as at the breath of spring? And does not this seeking of our love on Christ's part convince us that He is ever loving us in our colder as well as more fervent seasons, and that in being drawn by His lovingkindness we have laid hold on His everlasting love —a chain which runs backwards and forwards through all eternity? [1]

III.

MATTHEW THE EVANGELIST.

1. It is St. Luke who informs us that before Matthew became a disciple of Jesus he was known as Levi, the son of Alphæus. We may perhaps infer that he was a brother of James, the son of Alphæus (Acts i. 13). "Matthew," which means "the gift of God," corresponding to the Greek "Theodore" (fem. "Dorothea"), was probably the surname which he assumed or received when he became a Christian. And in the Third Gospel we learn that Levi, after forsaking all, and rising up and following Christ, "made him a great feast in his house: and there was a great multitude of publicans and of others that were sitting at meat with them."

Being no ascetic like John the Baptist, Jesus was often seen at feasts, and no banquet which He ever attended—not even the marriage feast at Cana of Galilee—gave Him greater happiness than the festal gathering in the house of Levi. That feast had a profound significance for Levi himself, and the day on which it took place must have been ever afterwards the red-letter day in his calendar. For not only was the feast of Levi, now to be called Matthew, the instinctive offering of a glad and grateful heart, but it gave him the opportunity of telling his own companions— publicans and "others," as Luke says with characteristic reticence —that he had broken with his past, renouncing for ever a life in which he could not be true to God and his conscience. And best of all, it enabled him to gather for Jesus just such an audience as He loved to have around Him.

In rendering such a service to Christ, Matthew was only obeying, with a fine originality, the impulse which every new convert to Christianity immediately and inevitably feels—the impulse of evangelism. No one ever believed in the glad tidings

[1] Dora Greenwell, *The Patience of Hope*, 120.

of the gospel—in the forgiveness offered to all sinners who repent of their sin and resolve to live a new life—without at once desiring the same tidings to be proclaimed to all the world. Nothing creates altruists—men and women who "live no longer unto themselves"—like an experience of Divine love in Jesus Christ. Matthew, till lately so hard and unmerciful, now felt his heart overflowing with pity and compassion. He knew well that many a publican of Galilee was just as unhappy as he had been, and would be just as happy to have done for ever with that shameful and degrading business.

¶ There was more than universalism latent in the mission of Christ to the publicans. It was the cradle of Christian civilization, which has for its goal a humanized society from whose rights and privileges no class shall be hopelessly and finally excluded. It was a protest in the name of God, who made of one blood all the nations and classes, against all artificial or superficial cleavages of race, colour, descent, occupation, or even of character, as of small account in comparison with that which is common to all— the human soul, with its grand, solemn possibilities. It was an appeal to the conscience of the world to put an end to barbarous alienations and heartless neglects, and social ostracisms, cruelties, and tyrannies; so making way for a brotherhood in which "sinners," "publicans," and "Pharisees" should recognize one another as fellow-men and as sons of the one Father in heaven.[1]

2. Whether Matthew himself gave his old companions what would now be called his "testimony" is not told. It was strange if he did not. For when the heart is full the lips become eloquent, and even if a convert does not possess the distinctive gifts, he at any rate has the spirit, of an evangelist. He can no longer be dumb; he regards silence as a sin; he is impelled to say to all with whom he comes in contact, "Come and hear, and I will declare what God hath done to my soul." The oral invitation to Matthew's feast, which was at once his farewell to the old life and his welcome of the new, probably included an intimation that he wished his old comrades and friends to meet and to hear Jesus the prophet of Nazareth. And "a great multitude" came so that the court of his villa by the Galilæan lake was full of "publicans and others." And it was with the memory of such a day and such an audience that Jesus afterwards said to the chief

[1] A. B. Bruce, *With Open Face*, 119.

priests and elders of the Jews, "Verily I say unto you, that the publicans and the harlots go into the kingdom of God before you." Matthew did not call his friends merely that he and they might once more feast together. He invited them with the secret hope and prayer that after eating his bread and drinking his wine they might find spiritual food in the words of grace which would, he was sure, fall from the lips of Jesus. He wanted to give them something far better than the feast of reason and the flow of soul. He wished to receive, as he had received, the bread of life, whereof if a man eat he shall never hunger. And it is more than probable that both Matthew and his chief Guest were satisfied with the work done that day for eternity in the court of his house. And, having left all, he felt that he had already received his hundred-fold. His cup was running over.

¶ The hostility [of the Jews to Jesus] recorded in the Gospels arose in connection with the class of persons to whom He made the offer of entry into the Kingdom, and the practical interpretation which He gave to repentance as the necessary condition for this entry. So far as the Scribes were concerned, the teaching of Jesus as to the class of persons who could be admitted to the Kingdom was wholly unacceptable. In their eyes this was the especial privilege of the righteous and pious in Israel; but Jesus announced that He had come to call sinners. In the later forms of the text this is softened by changing the phrase to "call sinners to repentance." In one sense, no doubt, this change is justified: Jesus did not tell sinners to continue sinning, and nevertheless offer them entry into the Kingdom. But it obscures the full importance of the message. The Scribes did not seriously consider the possibility that a " Publican " or a " Sinner "—that is to say, anyone who did not observe all the obligations of the Scribes' interpretation of the Law—would be admitted to the Kingdom, nor did they take any special pains to convert these despised elements among the people. Jesus, on the other hand, regarded Himself as having a special mission to those classes, and offered to those who would follow Him in His mission of preaching and preparation the certainty of entry into the Kingdom.[1]

3. The multitude whom he entertained, and whom Jesus addressed, were regarded as outcasts, but they were outcasts of a peculiar type.

The outcast with us usually means someone who has impover-

[1] Kirsopp Lake, *The Stewardship of Faith*, 27.

ished, and demoralized, and debauched himself with indolence and with vice till he is both penniless in purse and reprobate in character. We have few, if any, rich outcasts in our city and society. But the outcast publicans at that feast were well-to-do, if not absolutely wealthy, men. They were men who had made themselves rich, and had at the same time made themselves outcasts, by siding with the oppressors of their people and by exacting of the people more than was their due. And they were, as a consequence, excommunicated from the Church, and ostracized from all patriotic and social and family life. What, then, must the more thoughtful of them have felt as they entered Matthew's supper-room that night and sat down at the same table with a very prophet, and some said—Matthew himself had said it in his letter of invitation—more than a prophet ? And, then, all through the supper, if He was a prophet He was so unlike a prophet ; and, especially, so unlike the last of the prophets. He was so affable, so humble, so kind, so gentle, with absolutely nothing at all in His words or in His manner to upbraid any of them, or in any way to make any of them in anything uneasy.

If Jesus saw how hard it was for such men to enter the Kingdom of Heaven, He did not despair of them. It was in reference to the special difficulty of saving the rich that He said, "With men this is impossible; but with God all things are possible."

¶ With some the love of accumulation has a strange power of materializing, narrowing, and hardening. Habits of meanness—sometimes taking curious and inconsistent forms, and applying only to particular things or departments of life—steal insensibly over them, and the love of money assumes something of the character of mania. Temptations connected with money are indeed among the most insidious and among the most powerful to which we are exposed. They have probably a wider empire than drink, and, unlike the temptations that spring from animal passion, they strengthen rather than diminish with age. In no respect is it more necessary for a man to keep watch over his own character, taking care that the unselfish element does not diminish and correcting the love of acquisition by generosity of expenditure.[1]

[1] W. E. H. Lecky, *The Map of Life*, 287.

IV.

MATTHEW THE WRITER.

Dr. Whyte says finely that " when Matthew rose up and left all and followed the Lord, the only things he took with him out of his old occupation were his pen and ink. And it is well for us that he took that pen and that ink with him, since he took it with him to such good purpose." Early in the second century, Papias of Hierapolis wrote regarding the first of the four Evangelists: " Matthew put together and wrote down the Divine utterances (τὰ λόγια) in the Hebrew (Aramaic) language, and each man interpreted them as he was able." From the Aramaic these priceless sayings are translated into New Testament Greek, and from the Greek they have been, or they are being, translated into all the languages of the earth. And the words which Christ spoke and Matthew recorded differ from all other words ever spoken or written, in that they are spirit and they are life. Tennyson says of the words of certain would-be comforters that they were " vacant chaff well meant for grain," and that figure of speech might well have been applied to the teaching of the Rabbis in the beginning of our era. But the words of Christ were and are the bread of life. They are worth more than all the facts of science and speculations of philosophy put together. To receive them and to believe them is to have an education such as is provided in no school or college or university of secular learning, for it makes men wise unto salvation. It was Matthew's supreme merit that he recognized the importance of the written word. What he heard he committed to rolls or tablets which were his priceless legacy to the Apostolic Church and to all the Churches of all ages. *Litera scripta manet*—the written word abides.

After the record of his feast Matthew disappears from history ; he is heard of no more in the New Testament. But in virtue of the Gospel which he was inspired to write, he is to-day one of the chief benefactors of the human race.

¶ Oh thou who art able to write a book, which once in the two centuries or oftener there is a man gifted to do, envy not him whom they name city-builder, and inexpressibly pity him whom they name conqueror or city-burner ! Thou, too, art a conqueror and victor ; but of the true sort, namely, over the Devil. Thou, too, hast built what will outlast all marble and metal, and be a wonder-bringing city of the mind, a temple and cemetery and prophetic mount, whereto all kindreds of the earth will pilgrim.[1]

¶ Traditions clash and contradict each other in relating to us the career of St. Matthew subsequent to the point at which Holy Writ leaves him. The year in which he wrote his Gospel is held to tally with that of the Apostolic Evangelist's departure from Jerusalem to a wider field of missionary enterprise; thus, on quitting his Jewish flock, he bequeathed to them in lieu of his actual presence the written Word of God. Like so many points of his life his death remains unascertained. One ancient authority is quoted in favour of his having died a natural death, and the antiquity of such a view lends it weight. A contrary tradition, widely adopted both by early and later writers, shows us our Saint invested with the crown and palm-branch of martyrdom. In preparation for so glorious an end we mark him toiling to save the lost in Persia, Parthia, and other places; and in barbarous regions making converts among the actual Anthropophagi. Persia, or Parthia, or Caramania then held in subjection by the latter country, is fixed upon as the scene of his violent death; which some, again, assign to Ethiopia. Nor are legends unanimous as to the mode of his martyrdom. One avers that he was beheaded in requital for having warned Hyrtacus, King of Ethiopia, against contracting an unlawful marriage; others relate that he died by fire; or that a fire kindled around him being first extinguished by his prayers, he gave up the ghost in peace.[2]

[1] Carlyle.   [2] Christina G. Rossetti, *Called to be Saints*, 381.

NATHANAEL.

LITERATURE.

Bain, J. A., *Questions Answered by Christ* (1908), 127.

Brent, C. H., *The Consolations of the Cross* (1904), 81.

Carpenter, W. B., *The Son of Man among the Sons of Men* (1893), 165.

Cox, S., *Biblical Expositions* (1884), 204.

Davies, J. A., *Seven Words of Love* (1895), 98.

Edwards, F., *These Twelve* (1895), 25.

Greenhough, J. G., *The Apostles of Our Lord* (1904), 74.

Hull, E. L., *Sermons Preached at King's Lynn*, ii. (1869) 167.

Huntington, F. D., *Christ in the Christian Year* : Trinity to Advent (1882), 196.

Jones, J. D., *The Glorious Company of the Apostles* (1904), 130.

„ „ *The Hope of the Gospel* (1911), 139.

Jowett, J. H., *The Silver Lining* (1907), 1.

Knight, G. H., *The Master's Questions to His Disciples* (1903), 101.

Liddon, H. P., *Sermons Preached before the University of Oxford*, ii. (1879) 1.

Lilley, J. P., *Four Apostles* (1912), 51.

Lovell, R. H., *First Types of the Christian Life* (1895), 70.

Lucas, B., *Conversations with Christ* (1905), 1.

McDougall, J., *The Ascension of Christ* (1884), 171.

Maclaren, A., *A Year's Ministry*, ii. (1888) 169.

Matheson, G., *The Representative Men of the New Testament* (1905), 71.

Newman, J. H., *Parochial and Plain Sermons*, ii. (1868) 333.

Parker, J., *City Temple Pulpit*, iii. (1900) 252.

Rattenbury, J. E., *The Twelve* (1914), 175.

Rix, H., *Sermons, Addresses and Essays* (1907), 40.

Rowland, A., in *Men of the New Testament* : Matthew to Timothy (1905), 95.

Skrine, J. H., *Saints and Worthies* (1901), 52.

Thom, J. H., *Laws of Life after the Mind of Christ*, i. (1901) 43.

Trench, R. C., *Studies in the Gospels* (1867), 66.

Wilberforce, A. B., *The Trinity of Evil* (1888), 3.

Woodhouse, F. C., *The Life of the Soul in the World* (1914), 131.

Expositor, 5th Ser., viii. (1898) 336 (W. D. Ridley).

Expository Times, xiii. (1902) 432 (E. Nestle).

Journal of Biblical Literature, xvii. (1898) 21 (R. Rhees).

NATHANAEL.

Behold, an Israelite indeed, in whom is no guile!—John i. 47.

WHAT story in the New Testament has a more modern character than the story of how Nathanael came to believe? Ours is an age much given to psychology, the study of the facts of the human mind, how it does its thinking; and how fascinating a problem is here for a psychologist!

The name of Nathanael occurs in two separate parts of John's Gospel, but it does not occur at all in the other Gospels. He is introduced to us at the beginning and at the close of our Lord's ministry. We may reject as improbable the tradition that he was the bridegroom at the marriage in Cana of Galilee, as well as the other one, that he was one of the two disciples who journeyed towards Emmaus. All that we know positively about him is found in these two references to him by John. The question naturally arises, Was he an Apostle? He had the highest praise given him by the Lord; did it end there? Against that idea is the fact that the earliest of our Lord's disciples became Apostles, and that in the second reference to him he is found in company with those who are known to have been Apostles. The question, however, is a legitimate one: How is it, if Nathanael was an Apostle, that his name does not occur either in the Gospels or in the Acts, where the Apostles are enumerated? The explanation may be that he bore a double name, and that he is referred to in them as Bartholomew.

The identifying of the two, which, when once suggested, carries so much probability with it, and which in modern times has found favour with so many, was quite unknown to the Early Church. Indeed Augustine more than once enters at large into the question, why Nathanael, to whom his Lord bore such honourable testimony, whom He welcomed so gladly, was *not* elected into the number of the Twelve. The reason he gives is curious. He sees evidence in Nathanael's question, "Can any good thing come out of Nazareth?" that this disciple was a Rabbi, learned in the wisdom of the Jewish schools (that he should be numbered among fishermen [John xxi. 2] makes this unlikely, yet not impossible); and such the Lord would in no case choose to lay the foundations of His Church (cf. 1 Cor. i. 26), lest that Church might even seem to stand in the wisdom of man rather than in the power of God. The arguments for the identity of the two, which identity was first suggested by Rupert of Deutz in the twelfth century, are very strong. They are mainly these: that Nathanael's vocation here is co-ordinated with that of Apostles, as of equal significance; that on a later occasion we meet him in the midst of apostles, some named before him, some after (chap. xxi. 1, 2); that the three earlier Evangelists never mention Nathanael, the fourth never Bartholomew; that Philip and Bartholomew in the catalogue of the Apostles are grouped together, as a pair of friends, but with Philip first, even as he is here the earlier in Christ (Matt. x. 30; Mark iii. 18); that the custom of double names seems to have been almost universal at that time in Judæa, so that all or well-nigh all the Apostles bore more than one; to all which may be added that Bartholomew, signifying "son of Tolmai," is of itself no proper name. All these arguments in favour of the identity, with nothing against it, bring it very nearly to a certainty that he to whom the promise of the vision of an opened heaven, with angels ascending and descending on the Son of man, was vouchsafed, was no other than Bartholomew the Apostle.

¶ Christina Rossetti devotes two little poems in "Some Feasts and Fasts" to St. Bartholomew. The shorter, relating to his martyrdom, is as follows:—

> He bore an agony whereof the name
>   Hath turned his fellows pale:
> But what if God should call us to the same,
>   Should call, and we should fail?
>
> Nor earth nor sea could swallow up our shame,
>   Nor darkness draw a veil:
> For he endured that agony whose name
>   Hath made his fellows quail.[1]

[1] Christina G. Rossetti, *Poetical Works*, 177.

I.

NATHANAEL'S CALL.

1. It is a quiet Syrian scene of sunlight falling upon the landscape, and of soft and grateful shadows cast by the broad-leaved trees. The spot is on the western side of the Lake of Tiberias, and not far from the city of Capernaum. It is, in fact, in the village of Bethsaida, where dwelt, in the Saviour's youth, Andrew and Peter, fishermen of Galilee. The village lay on the shore of the little inland sea on which they plied their occupation as fishermen. The name itself means " fishing-town," and we know that it must have been the frequent resort of our Lord Himself. Alas that, like so many of what would be to us holy places, this tiny fishing-town has disappeared! Its site is guessed at, but cannot be precisely fixed. All that people now living in the district know about it is its New Testament name. Andrew and Peter were certainly fishermen ; Philip and Nathanael were probably so—these four, with John, making the five disciples hitherto secured by Jesus. It is too soon to depict their individual characters, although Simon has already received that name which has given rise to endless debate amongst rival ecclesiastical leaders, and the Saviour emphatically calls him Simon the Stone, or Simon the Rock, and declares the rock-foundation of His Church in giving him the name of Peter.

Going forth on the day after Peter's designation, Jesus finds Philip, and calls him. Philip at once responds. These simple-natured fishermen, like all the truly faithful of their nation, were at this time full of an indescribable expectancy. They were looking and waiting for the appearing of the long-promised Messiah, the Great Comer who should deliver Israel, and whose most signal and convincing proof of Divine authority would be His power to "reveal all things." We may understand, therefore, how ingenuous and pious Jews who looked for the immediate "redemption of Israel" would glow with spiritual warmth as they came under the influence of Jesus of Nazareth ; and we cannot be surprised at the readiness which they exhibited to obey Him. There is also great naturalness in what Philip does. Once called and captured, as only profound conviction can capture a soul, what so probable as that he should desire to tell the new and startling fact to those nearest to him? Deep emotion is demonstrative. The man possessed with a really Divine emotion will display it.

¶ Dr. Paton felt that the Christian Endeavour movement would never realize its potentialities until it yoked itself to definite service and acted the Christian life as well as talked about it. In the course of an address to the Council at Portsmouth on 6th February, 1908, he said:

"The emotions are in themselves a source of pleasure, but they also incite to action and become a motive power. There is, however, a moral law according to which alone they can be healthily cultivated. Bishop Butler has enunciated this law. If emotions as passive impressions are freely indulged, they become gradually weaker and ebb away: or they may be continually stimulated; but in that case they always need a stronger stimulus, and this terrible result follows—that they become inoperant, and lose their power to incite to appropriate action. On the other hand, if these emotions, according to their healthful law, lead to action, the acts which they induce are more readily done by repetition. They then form habits, and habits form character, and character forms destiny. Now this great law, which applies to the training of our youth in the adolescent age, bears specially and with profound significance upon the Christian life. Emotions awakened in the Christian life are full of delight and blessing, but if they are indulged selfishly, without leading, as they are intended, to healthful and appropriate action, they will either ebb away, as has been seen so sadly in the great Welsh Revival, or they may be repeatedly stimulated until they become morbid and inoperant, having no effect upon conduct and character. Our Lord gave to His disciples the rapture of the Mount of Transfiguration, but only for a short time. They had soon to follow Him to the bottom of the Mount, where the poor epileptic child sought for healing, and thence to follow Him, bearing their cross —in training for service." [1]

2. Philip knows of one who will gladly hear what he has to tell. It is Nathanael, his quiet, thoughtful, modest friend, who is probably stretched, as may have been his habit, in meditative mood, beneath the shade of a fig-tree. And there indeed he is, pondering the crisis of his nation's history, as the incidents of the time float up in rumours more or less correct from the great centre

[1] J. Lewis Paton, *John Brown Paton*, 425.

of activity—Jerusalem. To him, as to every God-fearing soul, there is one subject of supreme anxiety, one question above all others to be solved—" When will Israel be redeemed by Messiah ? " The restoration of Israel to its proud place among the nations ; the resurrection of the Royal House of David from obscurity to greatness and pre-eminence ; above all, the supremacy of the faith of Israel, wait for the appearing of the Great Comer.

Absorbed in deep thought, as we may imagine Nathanael to have been, his friend Philip suddenly breaks in upon him with the astounding announcement—" We have found him, of whom Moses in the law, and the prophets, did write, Jesus of Nazareth, the son of Joseph." Nathanael's reply was a natural one, the reply of a sincere believer in Old Testament prophecy—" Can any good thing come out of Nazareth ? " Something of contempt, perhaps, for a not very reputable little city, mingled with his astonishment that Nazareth, of which nothing had been pre-dicted, should be named in connexion with the Hope of Israel. Philip has but one answer. He is in no mood to talk about Nazareth or to discuss its demerits. He is concerned only about a Person, who has strangely impressed him with His Messianic character and claims, and a sight of that Person will be the best reply to Nathanael's scepticism. " Come and see," exclaims Philip, and the dreamer in the shadow rises and follows his friend.

3. Notice two striking things: Nathanael's doubt (" Can any good thing come out of Nazareth ? "), and Philip's answer (" Come and see ").

(1) If we would appreciate Nathanael's doubt, we must remember that all the Galilæans were held in contempt by the Pharisees of Jerusalem, and that not altogether without cause. The province of Galilee was, practically, much farther from Jerusalem than the Highlands of Scotland are from London, although not half or quarter so many miles lay between the two. And, to reach the metropolis, the Galilæans had either to traverse the alien district of Samaria or to risk a somewhat perilous journey across the highlands and valleys on the other side of the Jordan. Hence many of them habitually absented themselves from the annual services and feasts of the Temple. To these every Jew was bound, by the law of Moses, to go up thrice every

year. Those who failed to "present themselves before the Lord" were held by the punctilious Pharisees and scribes to be little better than heathen.

The Galilæans, moreover, engaged in commerce with their Gentile neighbours, and especially with the wealthy merchants of Tyre and Sidon. Their commercial intercourse with heathen races had abated the edge and strictness of their ceremonialism, and, still worse, had also chilled the fervour of their piety. And here was another reason for holding them in contempt. Even the prophets described the Galilæans as a "people that sat in darkness"; and the Pharisees, instead of carrying them "a great light," were much more disposed to consign them to "Gehenna."

But besides the general prejudice against Galilæans which for these and other reasons possessed the minds of the Jews, there may have been and probably were special reasons for their contempt of Nazareth. This prejudice lingered long. To speak of the Christians as Nazarenes was to hold them up to contempt. The Talmudists call the Lord "Hannozeri," or "Ben Nezar." The Arabs call the Christians "En-Nusara" to this day.

¶ From its very position, Nazareth—the precious memories of which are entwined with our holiest thoughts, and whose name has become a household word to the ends of the earth—seems to covet obscurity and seclusion. Unlike Bethlehem and the cities of Judah and Benjamin, perched on the hill-tops; unlike Shechem, whose gushing fountains and perennial streams have invited the earliest settlements of man, the site of Nazareth (on the edge of a shallow basin in the low hills of Galilee) offers no natural advantages. Among the many smaller ridges which crowd round the platform, from which rises the mountain chain of Lebanon, several here are clustered, forming a wide natural amphitheatre, the crest of which rises round the basin of Nazareth, as though to guard it from intrusion: "enclosed by mountains as the flower is by its leaves." The town clings to the hillside, on a steep slope to the north-west of this hollow, unknown and unnamed in the Old Testament,—a place that had no history till He came who has hallowed and immortalized it.[1]

(2) Philip met Nathanael's doubt very wisely. He did not argue with him. He simply answered, "Come and see." Very likely he recognized in Nathanael a mood with which he himself

[1] H. B. Tristram, *Bible Places*, 291.

was familiar: for Philip also seems by nature to have been "slow of heart to believe." He had had his doubts, his prejudices, his fears; and probably he and his neighbour, Nathanael, had often sat under the fig-tree at Cana, talking sadly, and a little sceptically, over the affairs of the Jewish Church and State. Only in the light of one Presence had his prejudices vanished; only by the sound of one Voice had his doubts been charmed to rest. If he could bring Nathanael to that Presence, and within the sound of that Voice, he had no fear of the result.

Philip's "Come and see," which is all the reply he vouchsafes to the objection of his friend, is manifestly an echo of Christ's "Come and see" of the day preceding (ver. 39). That immediate personal intercourse which had proved so effectual in the case of Andrew and another shall not prove less effectual in the case of Nathanael. It was a wise answer then, and is often a wise answer now. The highest heavenly things are in their nature incapable of being uttered in words, and "Come and see, come and make proof of them," is sometimes the only true reply to difficulties about them, an indication of the only effectual way by which those difficulties shall be removed. There are truths in the heavenly world which, like the sun in the natural world, can be seen only by their own light; which in no other way will be seen at all.

¶ Among the cases of conversion recorded by Mr. Robertson, when working in the Pilrig district of Edinburgh, is one of a young girl who was induced by her companion to "come and see" for herself:—

Whilst the Saturday morning meetings were in progress, one girl, Jeannie, was on her way to the meeting, when she met a companion, Lizzie ——, whom she invited to come with her. "Gae wa' wi' yer meetin's; gaun tae a meetin' on a Saturday morning! No, I'm gaun tae nane o' yer meetin's," was the response, and she then commenced to call her names—hypocrite, Methodist, and such like.

Jeannie went quietly on to the meeting, not answering a word. On the following Saturday morning, on her way to the meeting, she saw the same girl coming down the lane. There was no escape, and she wondered what she should do. Having lifted up her heart to the Lord, praying to be helped, Jeannie went straight up to her friend and greeted her with these words, "Oh, Lizzie, will ye no come tae the meetin' this mornin'?"

Lizzie burst into tears and said, "Yes, Jeannie, I'll gang tae the meetin'. Oh, Jeannie, if ye only kent what a week I've had. I laughed at ye, and ca'ed ye names, when ye wanted me tae gang tae the meetin' last Saturday mornin', and ye never said a word. Oh, I've been sae wicked. I wanted tae meet ye and I hoped ye wad ask me. I'll gang tae the meetin'."

They were both present that morning, but I knew nothing of the proceeding till Lizzie and another girl came to my lodgings in great distress of soul. They both wished to give their hearts to Jesus. The last accounts we have heard about Jeannie are from America, where she is working in the Salvation Army.[1]

II.

NATHANAEL'S CHARACTER.

"Jesus saw Nathanael coming to him, and saith of him, Behold, an Israelite indeed, in whom is no guile!" The precise form of the Evangelist's statement is to be carefully noted. He does not say that Jesus addresses these words to Nathanael, but only that He spoke them in his presence, so as to be overheard. In truth, Jesus was at this time exercising that marvellous power of looking into the past history and experience and character of men which the Spirit of God vouchsafed to Him at every great crisis in His career. Never did He need it more than when He was choosing the companions of His ministry and the agents for the propagation of His gospel all over the world. In letting Nathanael hear these words, He was only giving that earnest soul the encouragement he needed, and preparing the way for the closest fellowship with Himself.

1. "An Israelite indeed." The reference is, no doubt, to the old story of the occasion on which Jacob's name was changed to Israel. Jacob had wrestled with God in that mysterious scene by the brook Jabbok, and had overcome, and had received instead of the name Jacob, "a supplanter," the name Israel, "for as a prince hast thou power with God and with men, and hast prevailed." And says Christ: This man also is a son of Israel, one of God's warriors, who has prevailed with Him by prayer.

¶ Ruskin's fragmentary and hitherto unpublished "Notes on

[1] *William Robertson of Carrubber's Close Mission*, 39.

the Bible" contain the following references to the earliest recorded words of our Saviour :—

"Third recorded words of Christ to the two disciples, to Peter, and to Nathaniel [John i. 39, 42, 47]. To the disciples, the ' Come and see ' as well as the command to Philip, ' Follow me ' [John i. 43], are both commands of *acts*: addressed to persons beginning to seek the right; and which commands by obeying, they would gradually find leading to more light. Nathaniel is already an ' Israelite indeed,' *i.e.*, keeping the law perfectly, and wholly upright, and then a miracle is vouchsafed to him, that he may understand that Christ is indeed his Lord. This is just as it seems to me God deals with all His people." [1]

2. " In whom is no guile "—Jacob in early life had been marked and marred by selfish craft. Subtlety and guile had been the very key-note of his character. To drive that out of him years of discipline and pain and sorrow had been needed. And not until it had been driven out of him could his name be changed from Jacob to Israel. This man has had the guile driven out of him. By what process? The words are a verbal quotation from Psalm xxxii. : " Blessed is he whose transgression is forgiven, whose sin is covered. Blessed is the man unto whom the Lord imputeth not iniquity, and in whose spirit there is no guile." Clear, candid openness of spirit, and the freedom of soul from all that corruption which the Psalmist calls " guile," is the property of him only who has received it, by confession, by pardon, and by cleansing, from God. Thus Nathanael, in his wrestling, had won the great gift. His transgression had been forgiven; his iniquity had been covered ; to him God had not imputed his sin ; and in his spirit, therefore, there was no guile.

¶ We felt—we could not but feel—the large, unhampered guilelessness in Mr. Gladstone which, in spite of obvious subtleties of intellectual dialectic in talk and discussion, still made itself known as the most radical and elemental characteristic of the man. He was transparent as a babe: even when he was most acute in framing puzzling distinctions, or hurrying us over the thinnest possible ice. You saw the man flinging himself into his case, with the keen abandonment of a child without reserves. You might hear endless stories of the versatilities and elasticities and shifts by which he had thrown his opponents in the public arena of debate ; but nothing could ever shake your

[1] Ruskin, *Works*, xxxiv. 680.

conviction that guilelessness was the main note of his character.
Deep down in the life there was the untouched heart of a little
child.[1]

"The childlike faith, that asks not sight,
Waits not for wonder or for sign,
Believes, because it loves, aright—
Shall see things greater, things divine.

"Heaven to that gaze shall open wide,
And brightest Angels to and fro
On messages of love shall glide
'Twixt God above, and Christ below."

So still the guileless man is blest,
To him all crooked paths are straight,
Him on his way to endless rest
Fresh, ever-growing strengths await.[2]

3. In Nathanael's response to the salutation of our Lord we
have a fine illustration of true, as distinguished from false,
modesty. Jesus had greeted him, with wonder and delight, as a
guileless Jacob, a genuine Israelite, as worthy therefore to receive
the visions and gifts vouchsafed to his father Israel. And
Nathanael does not disclaim the honour; he does not protest that
he is unworthy of it. He feels, apparently, that the Rabbi of
Nazareth has fairly summed up his spiritual history, that He has
expressed his true character in a single phrase. And he does not,
as surely false modesty would have done, pretend to put away the
honour from him. He tacitly admits the truth of Christ's description. The only thing that puzzles him is how a stranger should
know him so well. "Yes, Thou knowest me: but *whence* knowest
Thou me?" And yet, on the other hand, there is a true and
unfeigned modesty in this response. His words mean "Whence
knowest Thou one so little known, so inconspicuous, so obscure,
as I am." He has but a poor opinion of himself. He is conscious
that he has lived a quiet, retired, and meditative life, that he has
not attracted the public eye, and has done nothing great enough
to attract it; and it perplexes him to meet with One who seems
to know him altogether. Moreover, it perhaps irks and a little

[1] H. Scott Holland, *Personal Studies*, 31.
[2] Keble, *The Christian Year* (St. Bartholomew).

frightens him to find his inward life laid bare, to stand in the presence of One from whom nothing seems to be hid. He feels that his secret has been read, and he shrinks back with a touch of fear from an inspection so searching; not because he has anything to hide, for he is without guile, but because it is as terrible to him to find himself utterly known by One whom he knows not as it would be to us. One can fancy his recoiling form, and catch the tone of alarm in his voice, as he looks on the Teacher who had read his every heart, and cries, " Whence knowest thou me ? "

> " What word is this ?   Whence know'st thou me ? "
> All wondering cries the humbled heart,
> To hear Thee that deep mystery,
> The knowledge of itself, impart.
>
> The veil is raised : who runs may read,
> By its own light the truth is seen,
> And soon the Israelite indeed
> Bows down t'adore the Nazarene.
>
> So did Nathanael, guileless man,
> At once, not shame-faced or afraid,
> Owning Him God, who so could scan
> His musings in the lonely shade;
>
> In his own pleasant fig-tree's shade,
> Which by his household fountain grew,
> Where at noonday his prayer he made,
> To know God better than he knew.[1]

III.

NATHANAEL'S CONFESSION.

1. When Nathanael asked in surprise, " Whence knowest thou me ? " Christ answered, " Before Philip called thee, when thou wast under the fig tree, I saw thee " ; not the words only, but the voice and the tones of love, carried their message to Nathanael's soul. The meaning is clear to him. The message carries the authentication and claim of love. His prayers and desires are known and understood. He had thought of himself as alone,

[1] Keble, *The Christian Year* (St. Bartholomew).

struggling in prayer and surrounded by perplexity, living in an age when God seemed far off, and when there was no open vision for the sons of men. But, lo! there has been One near at hand who has known and understood. Like Jacob, he had deemed that he was an exile from the revelation of God and the ministry of His love; but, lo! like Jacob, too, he awakes, and finds that the Divine light is near. The spot where he had prayed was none other than the house of God, and the gate of heaven.

Obviously, Nathanael was moved to the very heart, and to the surrender of his heart; and even we, who are but bystanders, can hardly look on unmoved. In Nathanael's example we find our duty; and in the wisdom and grace of Him who spake to Nathanael we find, or may find, a sufficient motive for the discharge of that duty. We, like the son of Tolmai, are bound to surrender ourselves to the Son of God, the King of men. And what will move us to this surrender if the gracious wisdom of Christ will not? From many of the stories related in the Gospels, notably from the story of St. Peter's call, we learn that, as He looked on men, Christ could read the innermost secret of their being, and forecast their future destiny; that, as He turned His glance on this man and that, their whole future shot out in long perspective before His eye, brightening ever toward the eternal day, or sinking toward the darkness. And now we learn that He who could forecast the future of men could also recall the past; that on every countenance on which He looked He could trace and interpret every line inscribed by experience, deciphering every enigma, solving every problem figured thereon by Time. Our present character, our past experience, our future destiny, all are naked and open to Him. Before Him the hidden things of darkness are as the secrecies of light. We cannot hide ourselves from Him under any tree in the garden, however dense its shade. He looks on us, and, lo! He knows us altogether, even to the purpose, passion, desire we most scrupulously conceal. Such wisdom would be dreadful to us, were it not in the service of a love most tender and Divine.

¶ One of three letters, written at the beginning of 1886 to Miss Edith Rix, to whom he had dedicated "A Tangled Tale," is interesting as showing the deeper side of his character:—

"The Moral Science student you describe must be a beautiful

character, and if, as you say, she lives a noble life, then, even though she does not, as yet, see any God, for whose sake she can do things, I don't think you need be unhappy about her. 'When thou wast under the fig tree, I saw thee,' is often supposed to mean that Nathanael had been *praying*, praying no doubt ignorantly and imperfectly, but yet using the light he had: and it seems to have been accepted as faith in the Messiah. More and more it seems to me (I hope you won't be *very* much shocked at me as an ultra 'Broad' Churchman) that what a person *is* is of more importance in God's sight than merely what propositions he affirms or denies. *You*, at any rate, can do more good among those new friends of yours by showing them what a Christian *is* than by telling them what a Christian *believes.*" [1]

2. With this we are brought to the confession itself, and we must note that Nathanael's two declarations concerning Jesus form a poetic parallelism which is a marked anticlimax, unless the title "the Son of God" is taken as essentially equivalent to, and not as of signally higher dignity than, the other title, "King of Israel." If this anticlimax is to be avoided, we do wrong to read into this confession any of the more metaphysical content which has come to predominate in the Christian use of the term "the Son of God," notwithstanding the fact that that transcendental significance is quite at home in the circle of ideas which we meet in the Fourth Gospel.

That the expression "King of Israel" is a simple Jewish Messianic designation seems to be proved by the title mockingly affixed to the cross of Jesus, by the taunt of the multitudes who stood by, "Let the Messiah, the King of Israel, now come down," and by the other current title "Son of David." Mention only is needed of the Messianic picture of the theocratic king in the Second Psalm; of the prayer of the devout Jew in the first century B.C., "Behold, O Lord, and raise up unto them their King, the son of David"; and of the fact that in the Targums the Messiah is always called King Messiah.

It is not otherwise with the other term in this parallelism To the Jewish mind the title "the Son of God" served to designate one among men exalted to high dignity, either as God's chosen (so collectively Israel), or as God's representative (so the theocratic king, the Messiah). The collective use is not peculiar

---

[1] *The Life and Letters of Lewis Carroll*, 250.

to the Old Testament; it appears as well in the Psalms of Solomon. For the specific reference of the title to the Messiah it would seem to be conclusive to refer to the question of the high priest at the trial of Jesus, "Art thou the Messiah, the Son of the Blessed?" (Mark xiv. 61; Matt. xxvi. 63 has "the Son of God"); while the Book of Enoch (cv. 2) and the Fourth Book of Ezra (vii. 28, 29, xiii. 32, 52, xiv. 9) furnish extra-canonical confirmation from late pre-Christian and early post-Christian Jewish literature. The language of this confession of Nathanael appears thus to be simply and purely Messianic, in the sense in which this hope was held in the early decades of the first century A.D., and the incident depicts a devout Jew, who finds one who can read his inmost thoughts, which have been turned with longing towards the promised hope, and who is therefore moved to join with others in hailing the new Master as the expected King of Israel.

It is a great step when any soul can thus leave all its presumptions and difficulties behind and step into the presence of one whom it can recognize as the fulfilment of its dreams and the satisfaction of its desires. We may speak of the value of independence, and its value is great and its cultivation is needful for the maturing of the human spirit; but in its search for independence the soul is truly seeking also for that on which it can rest without the sacrifice of that which is greater than mere comfort, its moral and spiritual integrity. The great problem is how to find rest which can satisfy the spirit while maintaining its own inward uprightness. All the moral forces, all the better nature, as we say, must be reconciled, or peace and rest is impossible. But whoever comes with power to reconcile these and to bestow the gift of love is acknowledged as rightful lord of the soul. The spirit bows at once in homage to its king. Thus Nathanael gave his allegiance to our Lord. His spirit had found its Divine satisfaction, its teacher, its king. So complete was the victory expressed in his declaration of homage—"Rabbi, thou art the Son of God; thou art King of Israel."

¶ Only Owen's closing volumes on the Spirit and the Person of Christ do justice to this principle [the majesty and mystery of Jesus]; this awe and wonder which he felt before the glory of Jesus; this instinct for the magnificence and unspeakable worth of salvation as the one reality that endures amid the shows and shadows of the world. "Young man," said Owen once to a religious inquirer, "in what manner do you think to go to God?" "Through the mediator, sir." "That is easily said," replied the Puritan, "but I assure you it is another thing to go to God through the mediator than many who make use of the expression are aware of. I myself preached Christ some years, when I had but very little, if any, experimental acquaintance with access to God through Christ." The personal revelation of this truth in his own experience perhaps made him all the more eager and competent to enforce it in his writings, and many a passage attests the strength of his conviction on this point of Christianity. "O blessed Jesus," he ejaculates at one point, "how much better were it not to be than to be without thee—never to be born than not to die in thee!" And again: "The most superstitious love to Christ—that is, love acted in ways tainted with superstition—is better than none at all." "If Christ be not God, farewell to Christianity—as to the mystery, the glory, the truth, the efficacy of it! Let a refined heathenism be established in its room." [1]

When, o'er the primrose path, with childish feet
  We wander forth new wonderments to spell,
And, tired at length, to loving arms retreat
  To hear some loving voice old tales retell:
We know Thee, Lord, as our Emmanuel,
Who, lying in a manger cold and bare,
Brought Christmas music on the midnight air.

When fiercely throbs the pulse, and youthful fire
  Burns through the heart and kindles all the brain;
When overflows the cup of our desire
  With beauty and romance, and all in vain
  We strive the fulness of our joy to drain:
Thou art our Poet and our Lord of Love,
Who clothed the flowers and lit the stars above.

When, at life's noon, the sultry clouds of care
  Darken the footsteps of our pilgrim way,
And when, with failing heart, perforce we bear
  The heat and burden of the summer's day:
Thou, Man of Sorrows, knowest our dismay,
And, treading 'neath the heavens' burning arch,
Thou art our Comrade in the toilsome march.

[1] J. Moffatt, *The Golden Book of John Owen*, 89.

And when at length the sun sinks slowly west,
  And lengthening shadows steal across the sky;
When dim grey eyes yearn patiently for rest,
  And weary hearts for vanished faces sigh:
Then Thou, the Lord of Hope, art very nigh,
Thou, the great Conqueror in the ageless strife—
The Lord of Resurrection and of Life.[1]

[1] Gilbert Thomas, *The Wayside Altar*, 7.

JUDAS ISCARIOT.

I.

THE MAN.

LITERATURE.

Aitken, J. R., *The Christ of the Men of Art* (1915).

Andrews, S. J., *The Life of our Lord upon the Earth* (1892).

Baldwin, G. C., *Representative Men of the New Testament* (1859), 57.

Dawson, W. J., *The Man Christ Jesus* (1901), 358.

Deems, C. F., *Jesus* (1880), 603.

Donehoo, J. de Q., *The Apocryphal and Legendary Life of Christ* (1903).

Edersheim, A., *The Life and Times of Jesus the Messiah*, ii. (1887) 471.

Fairbairn, A. M., *Studies in the Life of Christ* (1881), 258.

Farrar, F. W., *The Life of Christ* (1894), 471.

Lange, J. P., *The Life of the Lord Jesus Christ*, vi. (1864).

Liddon, H. P., *Passiontide Sermons* (1891), 210.

Lightfoot, J. B., *Sermons Preached in St. Paul's Cathedral* (1891), 58.

Morrow, H. W., *Questions Asked and Answered by Our Lord*, 235.

Neander, A., *The Life of Jesus Christ* (1880), 123, 419.

Nicoll, W. R., *The Incarnate Saviour* (1897), 216.

Page, G. A., *The Diary of Judas Iscariot* (1912).

Rhees, R., *The Life of Jesus of Nazareth* (1900), 178.

Ross, J. M. E., *The Christian Standpoint* (1911), 103.

Stalker, J., *The Trial and Death of Jesus Christ* (1894), 110.

Stevenson, J. G., *The Judges of Jesus* (1909), 1.

Trench, R. C., *Shipwrecks of Faith* (1867), 59.

Catholic Encyclopædia, viii. (1910) 539 (W. H. Kent).

Dictionary of the Bible, ii. (1899) 796 (A. Plummer).

    ,,   ,, (Single-volume, 1909), 502 (D. Smith).

Dictionary of Christ and the Gospels, i. (1906) 907 (J. G. Tasker).

Encyclopædia Biblica, ii. (1901), col. 2623 (T. K. Cheyne).

Expositor, 3rd Ser., x. (1889) 161 (G. A. Chadwick).

Jewish Review, iv. (1913) 199 (S. Krauss).

Smith's Dictionary of the Bible, i. (1893) 1831 (J. M. Fuller).

THE MAN.

And Judas, which betrayed him, answered and said, Is it I, Rabbi? He saith unto him, Thou hast said.—Matt. xxvi. 25.

THROUGH the deep shadows that gather round the closing scenes of the life of Christ on earth one sinister figure has arrested every eye—Judas of Kerioth. On no human head has such a cloud of infamy descended: in all human history there is no man who has been regarded with such complete abhorrence. His entire biography is included in a dozen sentences, yet so vivid is each touch that the effect is of a portrait etched in "lines of living fire."

¶ Thus do the things that have produced fruit, nay, whose fruit still grows, turn out to be the things chosen for record and writing of; which things alone were great, and worth recording. The Battle of Châlons, where Hunland met Rome, and the Earth was played for, at sword-fence, by two earth-bestriding giants, the sweep of whose swords cut kingdoms in pieces, hovers dim in the languid remembrance of a few; while the poor police-court treachery of a wretched Iscariot, transacted in the wretched land of Palestine, centuries earlier, for "thirty pieces of silver," lives clear in the heads, in the hearts of all men.[1]

¶ I would fain see the face of him who, having dipped his hand in the same dish with the Son of Man, could afterwards betray Him. I have no conception of such a thing; nor have I ever seen any picture (not even Leonardo's very fine one) that gave me the least idea of it.[2]

1. The name Judas is the Greek form of the Heb. *Judah*, which, in Gen. xxix. 35, is derived from the verb "to praise," and is taken as meaning "one who is the subject of praise." The etymology is disputed, but in its popular sense it suggests a striking paradox when used of one whose name became a synonym for shame. Another Apostle bore this common Jewish name, but

[1] Carlyle, *On History Again.*
[2] Charles Lamb, in Hazlitt's *Table Talk.*

"Judas" now means the Betrayer of Jesus. His sin has stamped the word with such evil significance that it has become the class-name of perfidious friends who are "no better than Judases."

¶ It was over and over again forbidden by the Church that a child should be baptized by the name of Jude. To this day the name probably does not exist outside Mr. Hardy's novel. With regard to great sinners in general, and Judas in particular, the feeling was, "I will not make mention of their names within my lips," "Let his name be clean put out."[1]

2. Iscariot is understood to be equivalent to *ish-Kerioth*, that is, "man of Kerioth." The epithet is applied in the Gospels both to Judas and to his father Simon (John vi. 71, xiii. 26). Now Kerioth was a town in South Judæa. The other disciples were Galilæans all. The southern Jews regarded the northerners with a certain superiority. "Thou art a Galilæan. Thy speech be-wrayeth thee," said the town servants of the high priest. Is it possible to imagine that some of this spirit of superiority, utterly at variance with the ideal of fellowship, alienated Judas from his brethren? If it did, it is psychologically probable that Judas would attribute the lack of sympathy to them. They would appear reserved and unsociable, and in his own view he would seem the injured one. Such blindness is almost invariably characteristic of the pride which causes estrangement from one's fellows.

¶ We need not cross the English Channel in search of racial differences. We have them in our own island. Look at the Keltic fringe on the other side of Offa's Dyke. The Welsh are mystical, poetical, imaginative, and emotional. We Saxons, with our blend of Danish and Norman blood, are stolid, practical, tenacious, and indomitable. Dissimilarities quite as striking prevailed among the Jews in the Holy Land. The natives of the south were proud, dreamy, austere, and passionate. They were fired with an unquenchable hope to restore the power and the splendour of the reign of David and Solomon. A desire to repeat and surpass the exploits of the Maccabees tingled in their veins. The Judeans were fanatical patriots.[2]

3. When and where Jesus met Judas we cannot tell, but it was probably in the neighbourhood of Jerusalem. The unwritten

---

[1] R. L. Gales, *Studies in Arcady*, 181.
[2] W. Wakinshaw, *John's Ideal City*, 123.

chapters in the history of Judas may be easily supplied from what we know of the movements of the time, and of the relations of Christ with His other disciples. There was certainly an earlier and different Judas, who possessed some striking characteristics of mind and spirit, or he would never have been deliberately selected by Jesus for the toils and honours of the Apostolate. It is natural that John should speak of him in the bitterest terms, for he was deeply penetrated by a horror of his crime; but the action of Christ in calling Judas to the Apostolate must be weighed against the denunciation of his fellow-Apostle. Somewhere in the past, which can only be conjectured, we may discern a youthful Judas, growing up in the devout adherence of the Jewish faith, conscious of unusual powers and distinguished by a sombre heat of enthusiasm, filled with patriotic ardour and deeply moved by the Messianic hope. In due time this youth finds himself in the presence of Jesus of Nazareth. He listens to a voice which stirs his heart as no human voice has ever stirred it. He feels the eye of Jesus resting on him in solicitation and intimate appeal. The current of his life is turned instantly, and he leaves all to follow this new Divine Teacher.

¶ Smetham's perception of things in the Bible, his putting of them in a new light, is sometimes like an apocalyptic sunrise. Through the incumbent darkness of some grim episode he sends a shaft of unexpected light, which transfigures all our prepossessions. Here is a case in point. In St. John's Gospel, at the eighteenth chapter, is told the gruesome story of that arch-renegade Judas, in the act of treachery which has placed his name as a byword of heinous vice upon the page of universal history. There is no written comment. But the third verse is flanked by a master-stroke of pictorial suggestion: a tiny etching half an inch square depicts a child, lying upon its cradle-pillow, with a face of captivating infantile sweetness, and large wondering eyes. Underneath is written with laconic simplicity, "Judas Iscariot." What! Was that incarnation of treason ever a child? By some lapse of logic it has always seemed as though he had leaped in full-orbed criminality upon the world which he disgraced. It strains one's faculty of imagination to think of Judas and cradle-songs. Yet is the homiletic painter true. Stoddard the poet is also right:

We lie, in infancy, at heaven's gate;
Around our pillows, golden ladders rise.

The holy office of motherhood, since the betrayer's day, has wasted its sweetness a thousand times upon the embryo malefactor. Many a branded and blighted life to-day looks back with yearning, through a rain of scalding tears, at childhood's *Paradise Lost*, saying:

> Happy those early days,
> When I shined in my angel infancy;
> Before I taught my soul to fancy aught
> But a white celestial thought.
> Before I had the black art to dispense,
> A separate sin to every sense;
> But felt through all this fleshly dress
> Bright gleams of everlastingness!

Aye! "Judas also which betrayed him" was once a child. The childhood of Jesus, the infancy of the good, are phases of alluring charm in the life of man; but the childhood of Judas is a new thought in the old story of the Fall. It is an unaccustomed key in the broken music of our discordant existence.[1]

> Oh, a new star, a new star
> Blazed like a lamp of gold.
> For closely pressed to Mary's breast
> The Saviour Jesus lay at rest,
> As prophets had foretold.
>
> (But little Judas, as he slept,
> Stirred in his mother's arms and wept.)
>
> Oh, the night wind, the night wind
> A new song found to sing,
> Caught from the gleaming angel choir,
> With harps of light and tongues of fire,
> To praise the new-born King.
>
> (But little Judas, as he slept,
> Stirred in his mother's arms and wept.)
>
> Oh, the worship, the worship,
> And myrrh and incense sweet,
> Which shepherd kings from far away
> Had brought with golden gifts to lay
> At the Saviour Jesus' feet.
>
> (But little Judas, as he slept,
> Stirred in his mother's arms and wept.)

[1] W. G. Beardmore, *James Smetham*, 80.

Oh, the shadow, the shadow
Of the cross upon the hill!
But yet the Babe who was to bear
The whole world's weight of sin and care,
On Mary's heart lay still.

(But Judas' mother, with a cry,
Kissed him and wept, she knew not why.)

4. Judas is found among the twelve Apostles. Almost from
the first the man must have had a baffled sense of unfitness for
his calling, mingled with eager desire to secure the great things
which Jesus promised, and which the miracles attested His power
to grant. As each day led others up from their old levels, by the
purifying tidings of an unearthly kingdom, of vast rewards to be
received "with persecutions," and how they should be killed and
crucified, yet not a hair of their heads should perish, all was
assuredly a blind paradox to the earthly heart of Judas, causing
him to lie silent, warily abstinent from comment and from question,
feeling his way towards the position which would best suit him in
the expected kingdom by securing now the poor treasurership of
the Galilæan group. By what intrigues he excluded or ejected
from that post Matthew, whose experience as a publican fitted
him so specially for it, we cannot tell; but we can well imagine
that he would endeavour, by energy in the direction which gave
scope to his earthly instincts, to hide from others, and for a season
from himself, the lifelessness and lovelessness of his spirit. For
such is the method of all declining souls.

It is St. John who tells us that Judas carried the purse. After
describing the anointing of Christ's feet by Mary at the feast in
Bethany, the Evangelist continues: "But Judas Iscariot, one of his
disciples, which should betray him, saith: Why was not this ointment
sold for three hundred pence, and given to the poor? Now this
he said, not because he cared for the poor; but because he was a
thief, and having the bag, took away what was put therein" (John
xii. 4–6). This fact that Judas carried the bag is again referred
to by the same Evangelist in his account of the Last Supper
(xiii. 29). The Synoptic Gospels do not notice this office of Judas,
nor do they say that it was he who protested at the alleged waste
of the ointment. But it is significant that both in Matthew and

in Mark the account of the anointing is closely followed by the story of the betrayal: "Then one of the twelve, who was called Judas Iscariot, went unto the chief priests, and said, What are ye willing to give me, and I will deliver him unto you ?" (Matt. xxvi. 14, 15); "And Judas Iscariot, he that was one of the twelve, went away unto the chief priests, that he might deliver him unto them. And they, when they heard it, were glad, and promised to give him money" (Mark xiv. 10, 11). In both these accounts it will be noticed that Judas takes the initiative: he is not tempted and seduced by the priests, but approaches them of his own accord. St. Luke tells the same tale, but adds another touch by ascribing the deed to the instigation of Satan: "And Satan entered into Judas, who was called Iscariot, being one of the number of the twelve. And he went away, and communed with the chief priests and captains, how he might deliver him unto them. And they were glad, and covenanted to give him money. And he consented, and sought opportunity to deliver him unto them in the absence of the multitude" (Luke xxii. 3–6).

¶ The Golden Legend says : "Then it happed that he was angry and sorry for the ointment that Mary Magdalene poured on the feet and head of our Lord Jesus Christ, and said that it was worth three hundred pence, and so much he had lost, and therefore sold he Jesus Christ for thirty pieces of that money, of which every penny was worth tenpence, and so he received three hundred pence. Or after that, some say, he ought to have of all the gifts given to Jesus Christ the tenth penny, and so he recovered thirty pieces of that he sold Him." Legend has invested these thirty pieces with a long mysterious history. They were made of the precious metal brought by Adam out of Paradise, and were coined by Ninus, King of Assyria. Abraham carried them into the land of Canaan, and with them Joseph was bought by the Ishmaelites. They were in the treasures of Pharaoh, of Solomon, of Nebuchadnezzar. The Magi offered them to the Holy Child. At last, by command of Jesus Himself, they were given to the temple at Jerusalem, whence they were paid by the chief priests to Judas, and afterwards to the soldiers who watched the tomb.[1]

5. Is it to be wondered at that the bargain with the high priests should have seized on the imagination of Christendom ? Can we wonder that Dante should have placed Judas in the lowest

[1] R. L. Gales, *Studies in Arcady*, 176.

circles of the damned, sole partner with Satan of the uttermost dark ? But terrible as is the mere suggestion of the betrayal, its details are more repellent still. It was essential to the carrying out of his bargain that Judas should keep in close touch with our Lord and His disciples. So even when they went to the Upper Room to keep their last Passover together Judas went with them. His presence made impossible the harmony our Lord desired for their last meeting; and He was so troubled that He could not keep the guilty secret between Judas and Himself. So it came to pass, while they sat at meat, that the face of Jesus was shadowed with concern. With amazement the little circle of the disciples heard Him say, " Verily, I say unto you, that one of you shall betray me." The words moved the true comrades of the Christ to deep disquietude. Once again our Lord was hinting that one of them was a traitor. Reclining in the dim glow of the flickering lamps, they searched each others' faces in the endeavour to scrutinize each others' souls. While they were troubled thus, the Master determined on one fina' appeal to Judas. In the East it is a mark of special consideration to dip a piece of bread or meat in the sauce or gravy that forms part of a meal, and to pass it to the guest whom one has it in one's heart to honour specially. With a heart full of pity for the traitor, Jesus dipped in the dish and gave the sop to Judas Iscariot. Such an act was bound either to shame him out of his evil purpose or to harden perversity into determined wickedness. It was the latter that happened. The favour of his Lord did but confirm the evil in the heart of Judas ; and, recognizing the true inwardness of what had taken place, he rose from the couch and passed from the room. Sullen of soul and hardened of spirit, he passed down the steps and crossed the shadowed courtyard into the narrow and winding city street. Then in the darkness he was alone. " He then having received the sop went immediately out : and it was night." What else should it be ?

¶ When Jesus is speaking of His betrayal He uses two phrases calculated to aggravate, were that possible, the enormity of the offence. He describes the traitor as " he that eateth with me," " he that dippeth with me in the dish " (Mark xiv. 18, 20). These expressions are both designed to bring out the same fact, that the traitor is breaking the sacred bond of

table-fellowship. It is well known what importance was attached
to this law of table-fellowship in ancient times. Once a person
shared a meal with another, he became bound to him by closest
ties, and was required to protect him to the best of his ability.
Judas in betraying his Master is breaking this sacred bond. In
St. John's Gospel, Jesus quotes, with reference to him, the words
of the Psalmist who had bewailed like treachery on the part of
one who had broken the law of hospitality: "He that eateth
bread with me hath lifted up his heel against me."[1]

¶ The scene of the Supper has stamped itself upon men's
minds as few others in all history have done, and has evoked a
whole world of wonderment and fancy. It is unnecessary to
mention the superstition about the number thirteen. "He sat
down with the twelve." Judas sat on the right hand of Our Lord,
between St. John and St. Peter. One thinks of the last days
of those three comrades—of the hideous death of Judas, of the
world-making martyrdom of St. Peter, of the figure described
by the great Russian seer, the old St. John, all white, a keeper
of bees, smelling of wax and honey. In Leonardo's picture the
hand of Judas is upon the salt-cellar, which he upsets as he says,
"Lord, is it I ?" This little detail, carried all over Europe as the
Faith spread, may have given rise to the superstition expressed
in the proverb, "He who spills salt, spills sorrow." The idea that
the ill effects may be warded off by throwing the spilt salt over
the left shoulder is, no doubt, explained by the old belief that
the Good Angel is stationed on the right side of every man, the
Demon on the left.[2]

6. A few hours later, Judas led towards a garden which was
one of the favourite resting-places of his Lord a great multitude
with swords and clubs, with lanterns, torches, and weapons.
They were the myrmidons of the high priests ; and their instructions were to capture our Lord and to bring Him bound to
Annas. Out of the city gate, across the brook, into the shadow
of the trees they passed, the traitor leading the way. Then,
beneath the murky glare of the torches, he saw the face of
the Christ, white with spiritual strain. With an amazing refinement of villainy he kissed our Lord, that the band might know
whom to capture. The Master must have shuddered at his touch,
but even then He spoke kindly to him; and before long, with

---

[1] G. Wauchope Stewart, in *The Sunday Magazine*, March 1910, p. 389.
[2] R. L. Gales, *Studies in Arcady*, 177.

Jesus as prisoner, the melancholy procession started anew towards the city.

¶ Not only is kissing a mark of homage: it is still in the East the salutation of intimate friendship; and as a mark of affection, of respect, of condescension, is much more usual than among ourselves. Ordinary acquaintances touch each other's hand, and then kiss their own, and apply it to their forehead, lips, and breast. Inferiors kiss the back of the hand, or, if above the position of a servant, the palm. Slaves kiss the foot, and so do suppliants deprecating anger, or begging pardon. Kissing the hem of the garment expresses great reverence, and holy men or dervishes are especially so saluted. In the Greek Church, during grand ceremonials, the edge of the robe of the officiating priest is often kissed by the worshippers. I have seen Russian officers in Moscow kneel down in the mud of the street and kiss the hem of the robe of the priest who was conducting a holy picture in a procession. But the kiss on either cheek is the sign of close intimacy and warm affection among equals. It is the mark, not of gratitude nor of homage, but of unselfish love and esteem. Hence the betrayal by Judas with a kiss intensified the black act of treachery. It is only paralleled by the treacherous assassination of Amasa by Joab, taking him by the beard as if to kiss his cheek, while holding the sword with which he basely stabs him. I remember a sheikh of the Adwân tribe assassinating a rival in a similar manner, professing reconciliation and holding his beard with his left hand to kiss him, while he suddenly stabbed him over the shoulder with a dagger in his right hand.[1]

> Hail! Master mine! so did the viper hiss,
>   When, with false fang and stealthy crawl, he came
> And scorched Messiah's cheek with that vile kiss
>   He deemed would sojourn there—a brand of shame.
>
> Ah, no! not long! for soon, and face to face
>   With His world-shouldering Cross Lord Jesu stood.
> All hail! He said; and, with a proud embrace,
>   Fasten'd the traitor's kiss to that forgiving wood![2]

7. Satan must once more enter the heart of Judas at that Supper before he can finally do the deed. But, even so, we believe it was only temporarily, not for always—for he was still

---

[1] H. B. Tristram, *Eastern Customs in Bible Lands*, 204.
[2] Robert Stephen Hawker.

a human being, such as on this side eternity we all are—and he had still a conscience working in him. With this element he had not reckoned in his bargain in the high priest's palace. On the morrow of His condemnation it would exact a terrible account. That night in Gethsemane never more passed from his soul. In the thickening and encircling gloom all around he must have ever seen only the torchlight glare as it fell on the pallid Face of the Divine Sufferer. In the terrible stillness before the storm he must have ever heard only these words: "Betrayest thou the Son of man with a kiss?" He did not hate Jesus then—he hated nothing; he hated everything. He was utterly desolate as the storm of despair swept over his disenchanted soul and swept him before it. No one in heaven or on earth to appeal to; no one, angel or man, to stand by him. Not the priests, who had paid him the price of blood, would have aught of him, not even the thirty pieces of silver, the blood-money of his Master and of his own soul—even as the modern Synagogue, which approves of what has been done, but not of the deed, will have none of him! With their "See thou to it!" they sent him reeling back into his darkness. Not so could conscience be stilled. And, louder than the ring of the thirty silver pieces as they fell on the marble pavement of the Temple, rang it ever in his soul: "I have betrayed innocent blood!"

An ancient writer, impressed by the bitterness of Judas's grief and the sincerity of his confession, "I have sinned in that I have betrayed innocent blood," would interpret his suicide favourably. In the agony of his condition he could not bear to wait; his Master was doomed, and he would anticipate Him; he would rush at once into the world of the unseen, seek His presence there, and confess the heinousness of his guilt, and throw himself on His infinite compassion—"with his bare soul." It is a striking thought. "With his bare soul"—stripped of those hands which sealed the fatal compact by their grasp, of those eyes which gloated over the accursed gain, of those lips which gave the final, fatal, treacherous kiss. And yet this, we feel, is not the Judas of the Evangelists, the Son of Perdition. "With his bare soul." It had been bare enough throughout in the sight of God, with all its dark windings, all its treacherous subterfuges—bare with that blackened guilt, which a long life of penitence were too little to

wipe out, and which a suicidal death could only fix there the
more indelibly.

> I know not what I am—I saw Him there!
> I saw Him cross the brook,
> With feet that shook,
> And enter by the little garden-stair.

> Am I of those who watch Him to betray?
> That little garden-path,
> That way He hath—
> I know the very turn where He will pray.

> Judas I know . . . But who are these I mark,
> Who come with torches' flare?
> I weep and stare . . .
> Jesus is very safe, deep in the dark.

> He broke forth from the flowers,
> To front these hellish powers;
> A Rose of Sharon He,
> Uplifted from the tree.

> Oh, fair of Spirit He!
> As Venus from the Sea,
> So soft, so borne along,
> He drew to that mad throng.

> He questioned them; He thought
> He was the One they sought—
> He is the only One . . .
> They have bound Him, He is gone!

> Oh, Who is this they have crucified?
> They have not yet raised Him above:
> They are drawn in a group aside,
> His garments to divide:
> On the ground He lieth, crucified—
> Through the Heavens there beateth one wild Dove.[1]

8. A certain mystery broods over Judas's obscure and lonely
death, through which we dimly discern an unsteady attempt at
suicide, a treacherous knot or a cord that breaks, a heavy fall

[1] Michael Field, *Mystic Trees*, 25.

into the hollow whence the potters had long since dug out the clay, and last of all a hideous mass, the strange antithesis of that undesecrated Body which even then perhaps was being reverently laid in a new tomb, and which saw no corruption.

"He went to his own place"—this is St. Peter's simple phrase. The veil is drawn over his fate. We dare not, cannot, lift it. There let us leave him; there to the mercy of the Righteous Judge, and the justice of a merciful God; there "with his bare soul," in the presence of the Christ whom he betrayed and crucified. It is not ours to judge. Only his history remains; not as a discouragement, for that it cannot be, but as a warning to us, how the greatest spiritual privileges may be neutralized by the indulgence of one illicit passion, and the life which is lived in the face of the unclouded sun may set at last in the night of despair.

¶ Deeper—farther out into the night! to its farthest bounds—where rises and falls the dark flood of death. The wild howl of the storm has lashed the dark waters into fury: they toss and break in wild billows at his feet. One narrow rift in the cloud-curtain overhead, and in the pale, deathlike light lies the Figure of the Christ, so calm and placid, untouched and unharmed, on the storm-tossed waters, as it had been that night lying on the Lake of Galilee, when Judas had seen Him come to them over the surging billows, and then bid them be at peace. Peace! What peace to him now—in earth or heaven? It was the same Christ, but thorn-crowned, with nail-prints in His Hands and Feet. And this Judas had done to the Master! Only for one moment did it seem to lie there; then it was sucked up by the dark waters beneath. And again the cloud-curtain is drawn, only more closely; the darkness is thicker, and the storm wilder than before. Out into that darkness, with one wild plunge—there, where the Figure of the Dead Christ had lain on the waters! And the dark waters have closed around him in eternal silence.

. . . .

In the lurid morn that broke on the other shore where the flood cast him up, did he meet those searching, loving Eyes of Jesus, whose gaze he knew so well, when he came to answer for the deeds done in the flesh?

. . . .

And—can there be a store in the Eternal Compassion for the Betrayer of Christ?[1]

[1] A. Edersheim, *The Life and Times of Jesus the Messiah*, ii. 478.

JUDAS ISCARIOT.

II.

THE APOSTLE.

LITERATURE.

Andrews, S. J., *The Life of our Lord upon the Earth* (1892).

Blunt, J. J., *Plain Sermons*, ii. (1868) 256.

Burn, A. E., *The Crown of Thorns* (1911), 1.

Dawson, W. J., *The Man Christ Jesus* (1901), 358.

Edersheim, A., *The Life and Times of Jesus the Messiah*, ii. (1887) 471.

Fairbairn, A. M., *Studies in the Life of Christ* (1881), 258.

Holtzmann, O., *The Life of Jesus* (1904), 457.

Kemble, C., *Memorials of a Closed Ministry*, iii. 61.

Ker, J., *Sermons*, i. (1885) 282.

Lange, J. P., *The Life of the Lord Jesus Christ*, vi. (1864).

Liddon, H. P., *Passiontide Sermons* (1891), 210.

Lightfoot, J. B., *Sermons Preached in St. Paul's Cathedral* (1891), 58.

Maclaren, A., *Leaves from the Tree of Life* (1899), 153.

Moulton, J. H., *Visions of Sin* (1898), 93.

Neander, A., *The Life of Jesus Christ* (1880), 123, 419.

Page, G. A., *The Diary of Judas Iscariot* (1912).

Parker, J., *The Ark of God* (1877), 40.

Rhees, R., *The Life of Jesus of Nazareth* (1900), 178.

Ross, J. M. E., *The Christian Standpoint* (1911), 103.

Selwyn, E. C., *The Oracles in the New Testament* (1912), 214.

Stalker, J., *The Trial and Death of Jesus Christ* (1894), 110.

Trench, R. C., *Shipwrecks of Faith* (1867), 59.

Weiss, B., *The Life of Christ*, ii. (1884) 273.

Christian World Pulpit, lxxvii. (1910) 138 (G. Barratt).

Dictionary of the Bible, ii. (1899) 796 (A. Plummer).

Dictionary of Christ and the Gospels, i. (1906) 907 (J. G. Tasker).

Encyclopædia Biblica, ii. (1901), col. 2623 (T. K. Cheyne).

Expositor, 3rd Ser., x. (1889) 161 (G. A. Chadwick).

Homiletic Review, lxv. (1913) 311 (A. T. Cadoux).

Jewish Review, iv. (1913) 199 (S. Krauss).

The Apostle.

Jesus answered them, Did not I choose you the twelve, and one of you is a devil? Now he spake of Judas the son of Simon Iscariot, for he it was that should betray him, being one of the twelve.—John vi. 70, 71.

WE now come to the question which is in our minds through all the story of this man's career—Why was Judas called to be an Apostle? Jesus chose twelve that they might be with Him. He offered to them His friendship. He admitted them into the very closest intimacy. He lavished upon them all the wealth of His tender and gracious love. And from that little circle of twelve came forth the man who was to sell Him. "Did not I choose you the twelve, and one of you is a devil?" And that was the peculiar bitterness in the death of Christ. It was brought about by the *instrumentality of a friend*. The hate of the priests, the furious clamour of the mob, the pitiful cowardice of Pilate, the brutality of the soldiers—Jesus could contemplate the prospect of it all with a quiet heart; but the thought that one of His own beloved and cherished Twelve should sell Him to His deadly foes for a slave's ransom pierced Him to the quick. "Mine own familiar friend," was the cry of His outraged heart, "in whom I trusted, who did eat of my bread, hath lifted up his heel against me." "When Jesus had thus said, he was troubled in the spirit, and testified, and said, Verily, verily, I say unto you, that one of *you* shall betray me." And the one who thus returned treachery for love and pierced his Master's soul was Judas Iscariot, the son of Simon, one of the Twelve.

¶ The nethermost circle [of hell] is buried in the heart of the earth : it is the region of pitiless cold : every spark of warm love is banished from this spot where treachery is punished. When the false heart has sold itself to the deceit which works evil against those to whom it is bound by ties of blood or gratitude, love flies from it. In such a chill heart pity cannot dwell; and, alas! the penalty of evil is to place itself under influences which tend to perpetuate the evil. The false, cold heart dwells where the icy blast does but intensify its coldness; the breath which beats upon it freezes all it touches. This, the possession of a heart out of which love has perished, is the last doom of sin ! [1]

1. Now, first of all, observe that there are sayings about Judas which might seem to imply that his part in life was forced on him by an inexorable destiny. St. John says that Jesus knew from the beginning who should betray Him. Our Lord asked the assembled Apostles : " Have not I chosen you the twelve, and one of you is a devil ? " In His great Intercession, He thus addresses the Father : "Those that thou gavest me I have kept, and none of them is lost, but the son of perdition." And at the election of Matthias, St. Peter points to the destiny of Judas as marked out in prophecy : "His bishoprick let another take ": and he speaks of Judas as going to "his own place." This and other language of the kind has been understood to represent Judas as unable to avoid his part as the Betrayer: and the sympathy and compassion which is thus created for him is likely to blind us to a true view of his unhappy career.

The mistake has arisen from a confusion between foreknow-ledge and fore-ordaining. We know of many things that will happen to-morrow, but we cannot be said to bring them to pass. Further, the idea that our Lord allocated to Judas the part of the villain in the crucifixion drama is not consistent with the Master's constant attitude of rebuke. Had Judas been predestined to treachery, and had he had no choice in the matter, our blessed Lord would surely have pitied rather than blamed him. And our feelings towards Judas would necessarily be very different. For if we offer gratitude and praise to Him who by a perfect life and an atoning death wrought our salvation, what should be our attitude to one who, by the compulsory damnation of his own soul, contributed to the saving of his fellows? Further, with all reverence be it said, God Himself would have no right to condemn any child of His to so despicable a career. The fate of the traitor was the choice of Judas and not the will of God.

The truth is that the Bible looks at human lives from two very different and, indeed, opposite points of view. Sometimes it

[1] W. B. Carpenter, *The Spiritual Message of Dante*, 88.

regards men merely as factors in the Divine plan for governing the world—for bringing about results determined on by the Divine Wisdom; and when this is the case, it speaks of them as though they had no personal choice or control of their destiny, and were only counters or instruments in the Hand of the Mighty Ruler of the Universe. At other times Holy Scripture regards men as free agents, endowed with a choice between truth and error, between right and wrong, between a higher and a lower line of conduct; and then it enables us to trace the connexion between the use they make of their opportunities and their final destiny. Both ways of looking at life are, of course, strictly accurate. On the one hand, it belongs to the sovereignty of the Almighty and Eternal Being, that we, His creatures, should be but tools in His Hands; on the other, it befits His justice that no moral being, on probation, should suffer eternal loss save through his own act and choice. The language of Scripture about Pharaoh illustrates the two points of view. At one time we are told that the Lord hardened Pharaoh's heart, that he would not let the children of Israel go; at another, that Pharaoh hardened his own heart. The same fact is looked at, first from the point of view of what was needed in order to bring about the deliverance of Israel, and next from the point of view of Pharaoh's personal responsibility. St. Paul stands at one point of view in the ninth chapter of his Epistle to the Romans, and at another in the twelfth. It is no doubt difficult, if not impossible, with our present limited range of knowledge, to reconcile the Divine Sovereignty in the moral world with the moral freedom of each individual man. Some of the great mistakes in Christian theology are due to an impatience of this difficulty. Calvin would sacrifice man's freedom to the Sovereignty of God; Arminius would sacrifice God's Sovereignty to the assertion of man's freedom. We cannot hope here to discover the formula that combines the two parallel lines of truth, which meet somewhere in the Infinite beyond our point of vision; but we must hold fast to each separately, in spite of the apparent contradiction. If our Lord, looking down upon our life with His Divine intelligence, speaks of Judas, once and again, as an instrument whereby the redemption of the world was to be worked out, the gospel history also supplies us with materials which go to show that Judas had his freedom of choice, his opportunities, his warnings, and that he became the Betrayer because he chose to do so.

¶ No combination of all the natural forces in the planet can vie for one moment with the potentialities of the human volition. In its secret chamber we can force destinies. The combination of freedom and necessity that goes on there is a mystery we shall probably never explain. The nearest approach to it, perhaps, is in the formula of Hegel: "It is only as we are in ourselves that we can develop ourselves, yet is it we ourselves that develop ourselves." Despite the dense sophistical webs that have been woven round this subject, man has always believed in his freedom.[1]

2. The only reasonable account of the choice of Judas that we can form is this, that our Lord acted by Judas as He did by all the rest. He accepted him on the ground of a profession which was consistent as far as human eye could see. Christ Himself received members into His Church as He intended that we should receive them; for, had He used His Divine omniscience in His judgments, the whole structure of His life would have been out of our reach as an example. Judas accordingly entered among the Apostles, because, in all outward things, and even in some inward convictions, he was like them. He came under the same influences, listened to the same invitations and warnings, and they were meant as truly for Judas as for the rest. It would have gladdened the heart of Christ had Judas yielded to the voice of mercy. It is not any question for us how then the Saviour could have suffered for the sins of men, any more than it is a question how the history of the world would proceed without the sinful deeds which are permitted by God and gathered by Him into the final result. The plan of the universe, in its lowest or its highest part, does not rest on the doom of any man to be a sinner. God forbid! There are manifold doors in the Divine purpose which God may open or shut as He pleases, but there is one always shut —that God should tempt any man to evil,—and there is one for ever open—that He wills not the death of the sinner, but that he should turn and live. Whatever difficulties may be in these questions of freedom and decree, we can never permit the speck of one to touch the Divine purity and mercy. If Judas had come, he would have been welcomed as any other.

[1] J. Brierley.

If, when Judas was chosen to his high office, his heart had been already cankered with avarice, and his character debased, then indeed the difficulty would be great; then indeed his selection would have been (we cannot think the thought without irreverence) a solemn unreality, a mere dramatic display. But we have no reason to suppose this. When he was chosen, he was worthy of the choice; he was not a bad man; he had, we must suppose, considerable capacity for good; there was in him perhaps the making of a St. Peter or a St. John. His whole history points to this view of his character. Can we suppose that he alone had made no sacrifices, suffered no privations, met with no reproaches, during those three years, in which through good and evil report he followed that Master who was despised and rejected of men, who had not where to lay His head? Can we imagine that he alone had given no pledges of his earnestness, that he alone escaped the bitter consequences of discipleship, that from him alone Christ's unpopularity glanced off without leaving a bruise or a scar behind? And does not his terrible end read the same lesson? The sudden revulsion of feeling, the bitter remorse, the crushing despair, so fatal in its result, show what he might have been, if certain vile passions had not been cherished in him till they had eaten out all his better nature. And so it was that throughout the Lord's ministry, even to the last fatal moment, he seems to have been unsuspected by his brother-Apostles, moving about with them, trusted by them, appearing outwardly as one of them. On that night when the Master announced the approaching treachery, each asked sorrowfully, " Is it I ? "—not enduring to entertain the thought of himself, and yet not daring to suspect the evil in another. All this while Judas was on his trial, as we are on our trial. He was selected for the Apostleship, as we are called into Church-membership. But, like us, he was allowed the exercise of his human free will; he was not compelled by an irresistible fate to act worthily of his calling; he was free to make his election between good and evil; he rejected the good, and he chose the evil.

¶ Do not forget that Judas was once a little child, fondled and cherished by those who loved him. His mother probably spoke of him as " dear little Judas." He was not always the distracted man who committed suicide in despair:

I saw a Judas once,
It was an old man's face. Greatly that artist erred.
Judas had eyes of starry blue,
And lips like thine that gave the traitor's kiss.[1]

¶ Why did Jesus choose *you*? Could you ever make out *that* mystery? Was it because of your respectability? Was it because of the desirableness of your companionship? Was it because of the utter absence of all devilishness in your nature? What if Judas did for you what you were only too timid to do for yourself? The Incarnation, with a view to human redemption, is the supreme mystery; in comparison with that, every other difficulty is as a molehill to a mountain. In your heart of hearts are you saying, "If this man were a prophet, he would know what manner of man this Judas is, for he is a sinner?" O thou self-contented Simon, presently the Lord will have somewhat to say unto thee, and His parable will smite thee like a sword.[2]

3. Let us recall Christ's method. He did not receive recruits without caution. Take the case of the young and wealthy man who sought eternal life. Our Lord made the young man sift his heart. He brought him to the test: "Sell all that thou hast." It is a picture of our Lord's method. No man should join His band under any mistake if possible. Christ sought to arm with weapons against self-deception those who volunteered to follow Him. Above all things, He made it clear that riches and worldly wealth were not to be looked for by those who would come after Him. The incidents recorded in the close of Luke ix. are enough to convince us of this. "A certain man (was it Judas?) said unto him, I will follow thee whithersoever thou goest. And Jesus said unto him, The foxes have holes, and the birds of the heaven have nests; but the Son of man hath not where to lay his head." No words can point out more clearly that earthly advantage must neither be sought nor expected by those who would follow Him. If the certain man in this case had been Judas, full of speculative hopes and dreams of possible wealth and splendour, the answer of Christ is an explicit caution, nay, a rebuke of any such anticipations; but whether this "certain man" was Judas or not, it is enough to remind ourselves that our Lord's method was to place

[1] J. E. Rattenbury, *The Twelve*, 288.
[2] Joseph Parker, *The Ark of God*, 43.

before those who sought Him the need of complete self-surrender, and the banishing of worldly dreams and futile expectations of temporal glories. Not unwarned then (we may well conclude) did Judas attach himself to Christ's company.

Judas must once have had real faith in the Lord Jesus; for he, like the other Apostles, healed the sick and cast out devils in His Name; he preached that men should repent, and there is not a hint that he preached it less sincerely or less effectively than the rest. And more than that—he had left his home and all that he had, like the other Apostles, and it is scarcely possible that he should have done so unless he had, at the time, real love, as well as faith, toward the Lord Jesus Christ. Who would have guessed that he who had made such a sacrifice would ever fall through covetousness ? Who would have thought it possible that such a saint could become a devil ?

¶ If thou hast dipped thy foot in the brink, yet venture not over Rubicon. Run not into extremities from whence there is no regression. In the vicious ways of the world, it mercifully falleth out that we become not extempore wicked, but it taketh some time and pains to undo ourselves. We fall not from virtue, like Vulcan from heaven, in a day. Bad dispositions require some time to grow into bad habits; bad habits must undermine the good; and often-repeated acts make us habitually evil; so that by gradual depravations, and while we are but staggeringly evil, we are not left without thoughtful rebukes, and merciful interventions, to recall us unto ourselves.[1]

4. Let us conceive, then, a devout and patriotic young Jew, his hands busy all the week with honourable toil, his heart full of a fervent and honourable ambition to see Messiah in His glory, and Jerusalem once more a praise in the earth. And what should that Messiah be ? Surely the hero who reigned in the visions of a thousand other patriotic hearts—a mighty warrior to sit on the throne of David, and rule with empire that should crush as dust the iron power of Rome. Human, of course, he would be, and less than David; for to the Jew it was irreverent to imagine that the glory of the canonized past could ever be matched in the present, or that God could ever do again what He had done so often before. Antiquity alone was quite enough to

[1] Sir Thomas Browne, *Christian Morals*, 104.

invest those distant ages with grandeur altogether unapproachable in later and therefore inferior ages. Yet even within these limits there was room enough for a grand and soul-inspiring ideal; and we have at any rate no right to blame Judas and Peter and Philip if, in the fervour of patriotism, they forgot that six centuries ago a prophet had declared their ideal a "light thing" compared with the work which the Servant of Jehovah was in real fact to do. How far worldly and personal thoughts at first mingled with Judas's visions we cannot say. To fight his way to the front in the army of the conqueror of the nations, to take an honourable place in his councils, to share in the spoils he should wring from proud kings and warrior peoples—was it really such a degrading ambition? We do not use abusive names of a very similar ambition when we see it now in a young enthusiast who enters his profession with a conviction that there is glory to be won in it; and we do not always pour lofty scorn on him if he conceives the ignoble idea of making his fortune as well. The wrong of such an ambition comes only when a higher is presented and the soul chooses what, till that higher ambition came, was noble, but has now lost its lustre and become a sordid thing.

No doubt he shared with his fellow-Apostles in the great hopes of a kingdom, of that kingdom which David's Son and Israel's King should establish. But the fatal difference between him and them was this—they, in the presence and under the teaching of their Lord, suffered these expectations to be transformed and transfigured from earthly to heavenly. Translated by their Lord into a new world of righteousness and purity and truth, of fellowship with Him and through Him with the Father, that was indeed a kingdom to them, a kingdom which should one day immeasurably transcend even in outward splendour all the kingdoms of the earth, but for the outward glories of which they were content to wait. Not so he. The kingdom of One who had not where to lay his head, who was not ministered unto, but laboriously ministered to others, whom the princes of this world rejected and despised—that was no kingdom to him.

¶ It was certain, and is so for ever, that such Righteousness as Jesus set forth must be the essential requirement for admittance into God's Eternal Kingdom. Into it no sin can enter. The very existence of the perfected Kingdom depends on the exclusion

from it of all that is evil, self-seeking, or unloving. Admit sin,
and not only does all security for blessedness disappear, but the
Kingdom itself, as the Kingdom of *God*, has no longer any existence. It is not only that the Righteousness of God decrees this,
but that His Love for His children requires it. The Kingdom of
God as the final goal of man is a *society*, and in that society
perfect Love must rule—not only Love for God, but for one
another—Love itself—the Love that God is—such practical Love
as Christ pictured in His teaching and set forth in His Person.
Apart from the reign of such Love, there can be no eternal
blessedness for God's children, and no real Kingdom of God their
Father.[1]

> When Lazarus rose at Christ's command
> And God was glorified of men,
> The children cried Hosanna then,
> But Judas would not understand.
>
> When seated with Thy chosen band
> Thou didst to Thy disciples say
> That one, O Christ, would Thee betray,
> But Judas would not understand.
>
> The sop revealed the traitor's hand,
> In answer to the question made;
> They saw by whom Thou wert betrayed,
> But Judas would not understand.
>
> The Jews, O Christ, Thy life demand,
> 'Twas purchased for a price like this—
> For silver pieces and a kiss,
> But Judas would not understand.
>
> Thou, with Thine own unstainèd hand,
> Didst wash the feet, and humbly teach
> That such a task becometh each,
> But Judas would not understand.
>
> "Watch thou and pray," was Thy command,
> Lest, thoughtless, the disciples fall
> Beneath the tempter's bitter thrall;
> But Judas would not understand.[2]

[1] W. L. Walker, *The Cross and the Kingdom*, 187.
[2] J. Brownlie, *Hymns of the Greek Church*, 41.

5. The choice of one who subsequently fell is analogous with all the ways of God. Other ambassadors of Christ have fallen. In every age men have been endowed with mighty powers of genius and with vast resources, and yet their free will has not been cancelled. The marvellous brain of Napoleon could have permanently elevated all Europe if he had only been true to what is called one's better self, and yet he was not coerced. It remained open to Napoleon to drown the civilized world in blood, to compromise the future of history, and permanently to degrade the political aspirations of Frenchmen, by the abuse of powers which God, having given, did not paralyze. Nay, the meanest who rejects salvation has a soul for which Christ died; and that universal privilege, vastly greater than all special gifts which may be superadded, does not ensure heaven. Doubtless the treason of Judas remains unmatched in turpitude, but it is not in kind that it differs from many more; and sober commentators have believed that his guilt is yet to be overtopped by the "lawless one" of the last time.

If the further question is asked why Judas was entrusted with the purse, we may answer that when Judas was alienated and unfaithful in heart, his very gift became also his greatest temptation, and, indeed, hurried him to his ruin. And so, as ever in like circumstances, the very things which might have been most of blessing become most of curse, and the judgment of hardening fulfils itself by that which in itself is good. Nor could "the bag" have been afterwards taken from him without both exposing him to the others, and precipitating his moral destruction. And so he had to be left to the process of inward ripening, till all was ready for the sickle.

¶ Every power that is put into action goes on to a determined limit assigned by God. His judgments are not judgments that wait like thunderbolts under His throne ready to dart forth when He shall command; but they are accumulating in the soul of every man in the relation in which every man stands to his fellow-men. Every event which is going to happen to you next week, every coming event is prepared for by your inmost thought and interest for months and years past. God's judgments are instantaneous, present, growing.[1]

¶ The hardening effects of sin, which save from pain, are

[1] W. H. Channing.

worse judgments than the sharpest suffering. Anguish is, I am more and more sure, corrective; hardness has in it no Hope. Which would you choose if you were compelled to make a choice? —the torture of a dividing limb granulating again, and by the very torture giving indications of life, or the painlessness of mortification; the worst throb from the surgeon's knife, or ossification of the heart? In the spiritual world the pangs of the most exquisite sensitiveness cut to the quick by the sense of fault and aching almost hopelessly, but leaving conscience still alive, and aspiration still uncrushed, or the death of every remnant of what is good, the ossification of the soul, the painless extinction of the moral being, its very self?[1]

Thou knowest, Lord! Thou know'st my life's deep story,
    And all the mingled good and ill I do!
Thou see'st my shame; my few stray gleams of glory;
    Where I am false and where my soul rings true!

Like warp and woof the good and ill are blended,
    Nor do I see the pattern that I weave;
Yet in Thy love the whole is comprehended,
    And in Thy hand my future lot I leave!

Only, dear Lord! make plain the path of duty;
    Let not my shame and sorrow weigh me down,
Lest in despair I fail to see its beauty,
    And weeping vainly miss the victor's crown![2]

[1] *Life and Letters of the Rev. F. W. Robertson*, 239.   [2] H. W. Hawkes.

JUDAS ISCARIOT.

III.

THE TRAITOR.

LITERATURE.

Ainger, A., *The Gospel and Human Life* (1904), 226.

Ainsworth, P. C., *The Pilgrim Church*, 52.

Austin, A. B., *Linked Lives* (1913), 97.

Blakiston, F. M., *The Life of Christ*, ii. (1913) 276.

Bruce, A. B., *The Training of the Twelve* (1871), 371.

Burn, A. E., *The Crown of Thorns* (1911), 1.

Carpenter, W. B., *The Son of Man among the Sons of Men* (1893), 63.

Davies, D., *Talks with Men, Women and Children*, iv. (1892) 599.

Dawson, W. J., *The Man Christ Jesus* (1901), 358.

De Quincey, T., *Collected Writings*, viii. (1897) 177.

Edersheim, A., *The Life and Times of Jesus the Messiah*, ii. (1887) 471.

Fairbairn, A. M., *Studies in the Life of Christ* (1881), 258.

Holtzmann, O., *The Life of Jesus* (1904), 457.

Ingram, A. F. W., *Addresses in Holy Week* (1902), 1.

Jones, J. D., *The Glorious Company of the Apostles* (1904), 239.

Ker, J., *Sermons*, i. (1885) 282.

Killip, R., *Citizens of the Universe* (1914), 207.

Liddon, H. P., *Passiontide Sermons* (1891), 210.

Lightfoot, J. B., *Sermons Preached in St. Paul's Cathedral* (1891), 58.

Lorimer, G. C., *Jesus the World's Saviour* (1883), 210.

Maclaren, A., *The Wearied Christ* (1893), 286.

Moulton, J. H., *Visions of Sin* (1898), 93.

Neander, A., *The Life of Jesus Christ* (1880), 123, 419.

Peck, G. C., *Ringing Questions* (1902), 201.

Rattenbury, J. E., *The Twelve* (1914), 285.

Salmon, G., *Cathedral and University Sermons* (1900), 88.

Simpson, P. C., in *Men of the New Testament* : Matthew to Timothy (1905), 205.

Stalker, J., *The Trial and Death of Jesus Christ* (1894), 110.

Stephen, R., *Divine and Human Influence*, i. (1897) 187.

Stevenson, J. G., *The Judges of Jesus* (1909), 1.

Wakinshaw, W., *John's Ideal City* (1915), 122.

Whately, R., *Dangers to Christian Faith* (1857), 213.

Dictionary of Christ and the Gospels, i. (1906) 907 (J. G. Tasker).

Expositor, 3rd Ser., x. (1889) 161 (G. A. Chadwick).

Literary Churchman, xxvii. (1881) 130 (C. Marriott).

Preacher's Magazine, xxiv. (1913) 197 (E. S. Waterhouse).

THE TRAITOR.

Verily, verily, I say unto you, that one of you shall betray me.— John xiii. 21.

JUDAS is one of the standing moral problems of the gospel history. What was the character of the man? What motives induced him first to seek and then to forsake the society of Jesus? Why did he turn traitor? Why was he so little penetrated by the spirit and awed by the authority of Christ as to be able to do as he did? And why, having done it, did he so swiftly and tragically avenge on himself his deliberately planned and executed crime? These questions invest the man with a fascination now of horror and now of pity; of horror at the crime, of pity for the man. If his deed stands alone among the evil deeds of the world, so does his remorse among the acts and atonements of conscience; and the remorse is more expressive of the man than even the deed. Lavater said, "Judas acted like Satan, but like a Satan who had it in him to be an apostle." And it is this evolution of a possible apostle into an actual Satan that is at once so touching and so tragic.

¶ In the Vision of Hell the poet Dante, after traversing the circles of the universe of woe, in which each separate kind of wickedness receives its peculiar punishment, arrives at last, in the company of his guide, at the nethermost circle of all, in the very bottom of the pit, where the worst of all sinners and the basest of all sins are undergoing retribution. It is a lake not of fire but of ice, beneath whose transparent surface are visible, fixed in painful postures, the figures of those who have betrayed their benefactors; because this, in Dante's estimation, is the worst of sins. In the midst of them stands out, vast and hideous, "the emperor who sways the realm of woe"—Satan himself; for this was the crime which lost him Paradise. And the next most conspicuous figure is Judas Iscariot. He is in the mouth of Satan, being champed and torn by his teeth as in a ponderous engine.[1]

[1] J Stalker, *The Trial and Death of Jesus Christ*, 110.

I.

WAS HIS CONDUCT SATANIC?

1. This is not a belief held by modern scholars. But there are good writers who take the statement that "after the sop Satan entered into him" almost literally. " The kingdom of evil," says Dr. John Ker, "as well as that of good, has a personal head. That he should have the power of tempting is no more strange than that human spirits should possess it. He can no more compel than they, and he gains in influence only as we yield him place. The experience of many temptations points to such a power in operation. There is a halo cast round worldly objects and a glow of passionate attractiveness breathed into them, which are not in themselves, and which can scarcely come from the mind that looks on them. Crimes are committed and souls bartered for such miserable bribes that to the rational spectator it is utterly unnatural, and the man himself wonders at it when the delirium is past. Our great dramatic poet has seized this feature of sin— this strange *residuum* in temptation, which indicates an extra-human agency,—and has set it down to those unseen powers of evil which 'palter with us in a double sense.' It does not diminish any man's responsibility, but it should increase his vigilance. Not only are these powers unable to constrain the will, but they have no influence of seduction, no delusive atmosphere at command, where the heart has not prepared for it, by cherishing the sin long and deeply."

" Judas was in truth," says Dr. W. J. Dawson, " a man demented. His jealous passion had swollen into such force that he was no longer capable of sober reason. He was mad with resentment, anger, and despair : the dream of his life was shattered, and the spirit of revenge had become his only guide. This is certainly the most charitable, and it is the most probable, view of his subsequent behaviour. From the moment when he seeks the priests to the bitter last act of the appalling tragedy, we are dealing with a madman, capable of a madman's cunning, and passing through paroxysms of frantic rage to the final paroxysm of frantic grief and ineffectual remorse."

2. But terrible as the crime was which Judas committed, and however we may attribute it to Satanic influence, we must be careful not to think of him as a solitary monster. Men of his type are by no means so rare as some may imagine. History, sacred and profane, supplies numerous examples of them, playing an important part in human affairs. Balaam, who had the vision of a prophet and the soul of a miser, was such a man. Robespierre, the evil genius of the French Revolution, was another. The man who sent thousands to the guillotine had in his younger days resigned his office as a provincial judge because it was against his conscience to pronounce sentence of death on a culprit found guilty of a capital offence. A third example, more remarkable than either, may be found in the famous Greek Alcibiades, who, to unbounded ambition, unscrupulousness, and licentiousness united a warm attachment to the greatest and best of the Greeks. The man who in after years betrayed the cause of his native city, and went over to the side of her enemies, was in his youth an enthusiastic admirer and disciple of Socrates. How he felt towards the Athenian sage may be gathered from words put into his mouth by Plato in one of his dialogues—words which involuntarily suggest a parallel between the speaker and the unworthy follower of a greater than Socrates: "I experienced towards this man alone (Socrates) what no one would believe me capable of : a sense of shame. For I am conscious of an inability to contradict him, and decline to do what he bids me ; and when I go away, I feel myself overcome by the desire of popular esteem. Therefore I flee from him, and avoid him. But when I see him, I am ashamed of my admissions, and oftentimes I would be glad if he ceased to exist among the living ; and yet I know well, that were that to happen, I should be still more grieved."

¶ By the open door out of which he had thrust the dying Christ "Satan entered into Judas." Yet, even so, not permanently. It may, indeed, be doubted, whether, since God is in Christ, such can ever be the case in any human soul, at least on this side eternity. Since our world's night has been lit up by the promise from Paradise, the rosy hue of its morning has lain on the edge of the horizon, deepening into gold, brightening into day, growing into midday-strength and evening-glory. Since God's Voice wakened earth by its early Christmas-Hymn, it has never been quite night there, nor can it ever be quite night in any human soul.[1]

II.

WAS HIS CONDUCT PATRIOTIC?

1. Ours is an age of toleration, and one of its favourite occupations is the rehabilitation of evil reputations. Men and women who have stood for centuries in the pillory of history are being taken down; their cases are retried; and they are set up on pedestals of admiration. Sometimes this is done with justice, but in other cases it has been carried to absurdity. Nobody, it would appear, has ever been very bad; the criminals and scoundrels have been men whose motives have been misunderstood. Among those on whose behalf the attempt has thus been made to reverse the verdict of history is Judas Iscariot. Eighteen centuries had agreed to regard him as the meanest of mankind, but in our century he has been transmuted into a kind of hero. The theory is of German origin; but it was presented to the English public by De Quincey.

Archbishop Whately put forward a theory similar to that of De Quincey. Judas was one who, believing in our Lord's power, sought to put Him in a position in which He would be compelled to exercise it in some startling, unique, and triumphant way. It never, according to this view, occurred to Judas that our Lord would submit to arrest or death; in putting Him, by an act of betrayal, into danger, he gave Him the opportunity (which he never doubted would be used) of confounding His enemies. Such an opportunity was wanting; nay, Judas may even have believed that our Lord desired such an opportunity; the disciple read his Master's wishes and created the opportunity which he believed his Master would welcome and use.

But no theory of the kind can be maintained. The facts are against it. If, knowing the supernatural powers of Jesus, he had no fears that He could suffer evil from the hands of His enemies, and delivered Him into the power of the Jewish authorities in order that He might be forced to assert His Messianic claims, why should he bargain with them for thirty pieces of silver? He

---

[1] A. Edersheim, *The Life and Times of Jesus the Messiah,* ii. 471.

could in many ways have accomplished this end, without taking the attitude of a traitor. The statements of the Evangelists about his covenant with the chief priests, his conduct at the arrest, his return of the money, the words of Peter respecting him, and especially the words of the Lord, "Good were it for that man if he had not been born," conclusively show that he sinned, not through a mere error of judgment, while at heart hoping to advance the interests of his Master, but with deliberate perfidy, designing to compass His ruin.

¶ The deed of Judas has been attributed to far-reaching views, and the wish to hasten his Master's declaration of Himself as the Messiah. Perhaps—I will not maintain the contrary—Judas represented his wishes in this way, and felt justified in his traitorous kiss; but my belief that he deserved, metaphorically speaking, to be where Dante saw him, at the bottom of the Malebolge, would not be the less strong because he was not convinced that his action was detestable. I refuse to accept a man who has the stomach for such treachery as a hero impatient for the redemption of mankind and for the beginning of a reign when the kisses shall be those of peace and righteousness.[1]

2. Nor can it be pleaded that Judas acted merely as a disappointed enthusiast. All the disciples were disappointed enthusiasts, but only he sought revenge on Christ by betraying Him. It is sometimes said that the sin of Peter in denying his Lord was scarcely less than that of Judas in betraying Him; but the sins were totally different in quality and nature. Any man, under the extreme pressure of danger or temptation, may deny the convictions that are really dear to him; but there is a gulf as wide as the world between such denial and deliberate betrayal. The most heroic of men in some hour of utter darkness may sign his retraction of a truth as Cranmer did, and afterwards may nobly expiate his crime as Cranmer did, by thrusting his unworthy hand into the martyr flame; that is weakness of the will; it is failure of courage, but it is not deliberate betrayal. But in all the closing acts of Judas it is the deliberation of his wickedness that is so dreadful. Every step is studied; every move is calculated. He works out his plot with a steadfast eye, an unflinching hand. He will not stir till he is sure of his compact; he studies with

[1] George Eliot, *Impressions of Theophrastus Such.*

astute intelligence the hour and place of his crime; all is as planned and orderly as the strategy of some great battle. Had he broken utterly from Christ in the moment when he went over to the side of the priests, we might at least have pitied him, and, in part, respected him. We might have numbered him with those misguided patriots who, from motives which are tortuously honest, burn the idols they had once adored. But Judas does not take this course. It is an essential part of his hideous compact with the priests that he must play the part of the loyal friend of Jesus to the last. He moves upon his road toward tragic infamy without compunction, without one backward thought, without a single pang of pity or of old affection. The most vivid touch in the appalling picture is the smile with which he asks his Master, who has just declared His knowledge that He will be betrayed— "Lord, is it I?" Judas knows in that moment that Christ is perfectly aware of his conspiracy, and yet he says, "Is it I?" He is so sure of success, so confident that it is no longer in the power of the heavy-hearted Galilæan to thwart his scheme, that he can mock Him with the insult, "Is it I?" Morally cold, intellectually astute, and now filled with the deliberate madness of revenge, it is little wonder that the world has discerned in this hard, impenetrable wickedness of Judas a sin beyond forgiveness, in which no germ of renovating good can be discerned.

¶ Cæsar defended himself till the dagger of a friend pierced him; then in indignant grief he covered his head with his mantle and accepted his fate. You can forgive the open blow of a declared enemy against whom you are on your guard; but the man that lives with you on terms of the greatest intimacy for years, so that he learns your ways and habits, the state of your affairs and your past history—the man whom you so confide in and like that you communicate to him freely much that you keep hidden from others, and who, while still professing friendship, uses the information he has gained to blacken your character and ruin your peace, to injure your family or damage your business,— this man, you know, has much to repent of.[1]

[1] M. Dods, *The Gospel of St. John*, ii. 97.

III.

WHAT WERE HIS MOTIVES?

Judas is to be regarded neither as simply Satan incarnate nor as merely a disappointed patriot. There were several motives at work, all on the level of ordinary humanity.

1. The leading motive was probably *avarice*. This is, at any rate, the most obvious motive. " There is no vice," says Farrar, " at once so absorbing, so unreasonable, and so degrading as the vice of avarice, and avarice was the besetting sin in the dark soul of the traitor Judas."

Avarice is one of the most powerful of motives. In the teaching of the pulpit it may seldom be noticed, but both in Scripture and in history it occupies a prominent place. It is questionable if anything else is the cause of so many ill deeds. Avarice breaks all the commandments. Often has it put the weapon into the hand of the murderer; in most countries of the world it has in every age made the ordinary business of the market-place a warfare of falsehood; the bodies of men and the hearts of women have been sold for gold. Why is it that gigantic wrongs flourish from age to age, and practices utterly indefensible are continued with the overwhelming sanction of society? It is because there is money in them. Avarice is a passion of demonic strength; but it may help us to keep it out of our hearts if we remember that it was the sin of Judas.

¶ We do great injustice to Iscariot in thinking him wicked above all common wickedness. He was only a common money-lover, and, like all money-lovers, did not understand Christ— could not make out the worth of Him, or meaning of Him. He never thought He would be killed. He was horror-struck when he found that Christ would be killed; threw his money away instantly, and hanged himself. How many of our present money-seekers, think you, would have the grace to hang themselves, whoever was killed? But Judas was a common, selfish, muddle-headed, pilfering fellow; his hand always in the bag of the poor, not caring for them. Helpless to understand Christ, he yet believed in Him, much more than most of us do; had seen Him do miracles, thought He was quite strong enough to shift for

Himself, and he, Judas, might as well make his own little bye-perquisites out of the affair. Christ would come out of it well enough, and he have his thirty pieces. Now, that is the money-seeker's idea, all over the world. He doesn't hate Christ, but can't understand Him—doesn't care for Him—sees no good in that benevolent business; makes his own little job out of it at all events, come what will. And thus, out of every mass of men, you have a certain number of bagmen—your "fee-first" men, whose main object is to make money. And they do make it—make it in all sorts of unfair ways, chiefly by the weight and force of money itself, or what is called the power of capital; that is to say, the power which money, once obtained, has over the labour of the poor, so that the capitalist can take all its produce to himself, except the labourer's food. That is the modern Judas's way of "carrying the bag" and "bearing what is put therein."[1]

2. Judas was probably also *ambitious* and "loved the pre-eminence." Why did he care for money? Because he wished to be someone, to shine, to be noticed, to have power. Perhaps it was with this object that he joined the band at first; and, fearing he was going to miss it, he struck out for himself. It is the old mistake, constantly repeated, of supposing that power lies in something without, rather than in something within.

Contrast St. John! A fisherman's son, without the shrewd-ness, the ability, possibly the prestige, that belonged to the man of the South! Who could predict that his name would one day be known throughout the world and that his writings would absorb the attention of the greatest minds that civilization has known? He has not the mark of a Socrates or a Demosthenes, nor does he seem to be like one of the old prophets—only a plain fisherman's son. Earnest; and though religious, yet stormy and perhaps passionate; a Son of Thunder, with much that is earthly and poor. And yet he it is who not only impresses his own countrymen, but sits like a seer in Asia with crowds of disciples trying to catch every word.

¶ Writing to his mother on his forty-ninth birthday, Professor Charteris says:

"My life has been one of amazing mercy. I hope my ambitions are now understood and put away. I don't know; but I wish they were. Ambition is an unholy thing, because it

[1] Ruskin, *The Crown of Wild Olive*, § 33 (*Works*, xviii. 414).

prevents a man from *waiting* upon God. That is how it comes to be sin. From it may the Lord deliver us all." [1]

3. But deeper than either greed or ambition, as indeed the root of these vices, there possessed the soul of Judas an intense *selfishness*. " The essence of every evil," says Maclaren, " is selfishness, and when you have that, it is exactly as with cooks when they have what they call ' stock' by the fireside. They can make any kind of soup out of it with the right flavouring. We have got the mother-tincture of all wickedness in each of our hearts, and therefore do not let us be so sure that it cannot be manipulated and flavoured into any form of sin."

And what is selfishness but the visible result of a nature that is absorbed with the things of the world ? Judas was impervious to spiritual influences, else he had not lived so closely with Christ to betray Him at the last. Judas could boast of being a clear-sighted man, who saw things as they really were, and was not misled by the illusive dreams of which the heads of his brethren were full. How was it that they could see what he could not see, and had faculties capable of recognizing the greatness of a Master whom he only despised as a mistaken enthusiast ? It is this absolute deadness of spiritual perception that was the radical flaw in the character of Judas, and that makes the study of his history really profitable for our example and warning. It is a very exceptional thing that one of us should be under a tempta-tion to anything that may be called treachery ; but we may all do well to bear in mind that what made the fall of Judas possible was that he was clear-sighted with respect to material objects, and to all the things of this life, but that the spiritual world was quite invisible to him.

Judas had the same chances of better things as his brother-Apostles had. There were mixed motives, no doubt, in the hearts of all. The narrative shows us that the worldly spirit sometimes broke forth in rivalry (Mark ix. 33, 34, and x. 35–37), and in covetousness (Matt. xx. 26); the leaven of worldliness was there. But in the other Apostles devotion and fidelity to their Lord overmastered the lower impulses of their hearts. " One man," as Bishop Thirlwall says, " cannot be described as more selfish than

[1] K. D. McLaren, *Memoir of Professor Charteris*, 120.

another." What is true is that one man curbs selfishness less than his neighbour does. The comrades of Judas had weaknesses and worldly desires, even as he had; but they yielded themselves to the good influence which was so near them. They did not wholly understand Christ's teaching; but that teaching, even when not fully grasped, being followed by willing hearts, lifted their conceptions to higher levels, and helped to free them from the moral tyranny of self. But in Judas the self-interest was allowed to grow; he fostered it in thought; he nourished it by habitual embezzlement of the funds entrusted to him. Character grows from habits; and he adopted bad ones.

¶ Few things disgust his fellow-men more, or render them more unwilling to help him, than self-seeking or egotism on the part of a man who is striving to get on. A thoroughly selfish fellow may score small successes, but he will in the end find himself heavily handicapped in the effort to attain really great success. Selfishness is a vice, and a thoroughly ugly one. When he takes thought exclusively of himself, a man does not violate only the canons of religion and morality. He is untrue to the obligations of his station in society, he is neglecting his own interests, and he will inevitably and quickly be found out. I have often watched the disastrous consequences of this sin, both in private and in public life. It is an insidious sin. It leads to the production of the hard, small-minded man, and, in its milder form, of the prig. Both are ill-equipped for the final race; they may get ahead at first; but as a rule they will be found to have fallen out when the last lap is reached. It is the man who possesses the virtue of true humility, and who thinks of his neighbours, and is neither critical nor a grumbler if they have good fortune, who has his neighbours on his side, and therefore in the end gets the best chance, even in this world, assuming always that he puts his soul into his own work.[1]

4. Did Judas become utterly evil? Did his wicked treachery put him absolutely beyond all Divine mercy? Mr. J. E. Rattenbury asks these questions, and answers No. "You remember," he says, "that in His last prayer Jesus mentions Judas. He calls him 'the son of perdition,' and Martin Luther translates that term as 'a lost child.' We assume that Jesus was repudiating Judas when He called him the son of perdition. But is that true? Was He not really praying for him—speaking of him tenderly as a lost

[1] Lord Haldane, *The Conduct of Life*, 16.

child? Listen to His prayer as He prays for all His disciples:

"'While I was with them in the world, I kept them in thy name: those that thou gavest me I have kept, and none of them is lost, but the son of perdition'—the lost child.

"No, Jesus was not tearing Judas out of His heart when He made that prayer; He was lamenting over His dear friend, telling His Father about His lost child. Put yourself in the place of Jesus, and think how He would pray. He had a number of disciples and friends whom He loved, and He came to the end of His life, and prayed His Father to continue to keep His friends in His love; He was gratified that He had been able to keep those who had been true to Him; but there was one exception, and in the midst of that prayer of thanksgiving you can hear the broken heart of Christ sobbing, 'But there is a lost child. I have lost none save one.' Oh! the heart-break in it! 'There is a lost child.' It is thus that He thinks of Judas."[1]

¶ It is indeed difficult to conceive how Judas could through eternity arrive at peace, with such a memory ever present with him. We can scarcely conceive how even the fullest forgiveness of God could enable him to forgive himself, or purge his memory of its mortal agony. It is evident that the purer we become we must increasingly abhor and loathe all sin, especially in ourselves; and thus it would appear that if memory remains in the future stages of our being, the retrospect of past transgression must become ever increasingly painful to us. Yet we cannot doubt but that there must be a sufficient antidote in the Divine love even for this form of agony—a power to give perfect peace even to a Judas when he turns to God. I believe that it is our ignorance of the nature of Divine love—of its power and sweetness and blessedness—which makes it so difficult for us to conceive of such a deliverance. And as that love, though it passes the reason to conceive it, is yet in harmony with reason, we may suppose that one of its consolations to a Judas will be, not only that God has brought a blessing to the world out of his transgression, but that, through the very horror of that fearful act, his own soul has been brought into a deeper trust in God, and thus into a deeper righteousness than, it may be, he could otherwise have attained.[2]

[1] J. E. Rattenbury, *The Twelve*, 293.
[2] T. Erskine, *The Spiritual Order*, 254.

¶ The lesson which the sin of Judas brings with it is the rapidity of sin's growth and the enormous proportions it attains when the sinner is sinning against light, when he is in circumstances conducive to holiness and still sins. To discover the wickedest of men, to see the utmost of human guilt, we must look, not among the heathen, but among those who know God; not among the profligate, dissolute, abandoned classes of society, but among the Apostles. Had Judas not followed Christ he could never have attained the pinnacle of infamy on which he now for ever stands. In all probability he would have passed his days as a small trader with false weights in the little town of Kerioth, or, at the worst, might have developed into an extortionous publican, and have passed into oblivion with the thousands of unjust men who have died and been at last forced to let go the money that should long ago have belonged to others. Or had Judas followed Christ truly, then there lay before him the noblest of all lives, the most blessed of destinies. But he followed Christ and yet took his sin with him: and thence his ruin.[1]

[1] M. Dods, *The Gospel of St. John*, ii, 104.

JUDAS ISCARIOT.

IV.

THE EXAMPLE.

LITERATURE.

Abbey, C. J., *The Divine Love* (1900), 110.
Austin, A. B., *Linked Lives* (1913), 97.
Bacon, L. W., *The Simplicity that is in Christ* (1892), 309.
Blunt, J. J., *Plain Sermons*, ii. (1868) 256.
Bruce, A. B., *The Training of the Twelve* (1871), 371.
Burn, A. E., *The Crown of Thorns* (1911), 1.
Burrell, D. J., *A Quiver of Arrows* (1902), 297.
Carpenter, W. B., *The Son of Man among the Sons of Men* (1893), 63.
Fairbairn, A. M., *Studies in the Life of Christ* (1881), 258.
Davies, D., *Talks with Men, Women and Children*, iv. (1892) 599.
Dawson, W. J., *The Man Christ Jesus* (1901), 358.
Deems, C. F., *Jesus* (1880), 603.
Edersheim, A., *The Life and Times of Jesus the Messiah*, ii. (1887) 471.
Farrar, F. W., *The Life of Christ* (1894), 471.
,,   ,,   *The Life of Lives* (1900), 431.
Hough, L. H., *The Men of the Gospels* (1913), 40.
Ingram, A. F. W., *Addresses in Holy Week* (1902), 1.
Jones, J. D., *The Glorious Company of the Apostles* (1904), 239.
Ker, J., *Sermons*, i. (1885) 282.
Killip, R., *Citizens of the Universe* (1914), 207.
Liddon, H. P., *Passiontide Sermons* (1891), 210.
Lightfoot, J. B., *Sermons Preached in St. Paul's Cathedral* (1891), 58.
Little, W. J. K., *Sunlight and Shadow in the Christian Life* (1892), 270.
Lovell, R. H., *First Types of the Christian Life* (1895), 158.
Maclaren, A., *Leaves from the Tree of Life* (1899), 153.
Morrow, H. W., *Questions Asked and Answered by Our Lord*, 235.
Moulton, J. H., *Visions of Sin* (1898), 93.
Parker, J., *The Ark of God* (1877), 40.
Rattenbury, J. E., *The Twelve* (1914), 285.
Rawnsley, R. D. B., *Village Sermons*, iii. (1883) 74.
Salmon, G., *Cathedral and University Sermons* (1900), 88.
Simcox, W. H., *The Cessation of Prophecy* (1891), 269.
Stalker, J., *The Trial and Death of Jesus Christ* (1894), 110.
Wakinshaw, W., *John's Ideal City* (1915), 122.
Dictionary of Christ and the Gospels, i. (1906) 907 (J. G. Tasker).

THE EXAMPLE.

Holy Father, keep them in thy name which thou hast given me, that they may be one, even as we are. While I was with them, I kept them in thy name which thou hast given me: and I guarded them, and not one of them perished, but the son of perdition.—John xvii. 11, 12.

Is not the case of Judas so exceptional that his temptation is not our temptation, that his crime cannot be our crime, and that therefore his fall has no lesson of warning for us? Nay, his sin seems so unnatural and monstrous that we have some difficulty in even realizing it. The contrast is too violent between the Apostle and the traitor—the intimate communion with the Holy One here; the vile perfidy to the Friend and Saviour there; the unique advantages here, the unparalleled baseness there. The perfect example of the Master, the elevating society of the fellow-disciples, the words of truth, the works of power, the grace, the purity, the holiness, the love—all these forgotten, spurned, trampled under foot, to gratify one miserable, greedy passion, if not the worst, at least the meanest, that can possess the heart of man. On this moral contrast our Lord lays special emphasis. "Have not I chosen you, the twelve, chosen you out of the many thousands in Israel, in preference to the high-born and the powerful, in preference to the rabbi and the scribe and the priest, chosen you a mere handful of men to be My intimate friends, My special messengers now, to sit on twelve thrones judging the twelve tribes of Israel hereafter; and yet one among you is not faithless only, not unworthy, not sinful only, but a very impersonation of the Accuser, the Arch-fiend himself?"

Our experiences may recall some faint type of such a contrast, where the circumstances of the criminal and the baseness of the crime seem to stand in no relation to each other. We may have seen some one member of a family, brought up under conditions the most favourable to his moral and religious development, watcned over by parents whose devoted care was never at fault, growing up among brothers and sisters whose example suggested only innocence and truthfulness, breathing, in short, the very atmosphere of holiness and purity and love; and yet he has fallen—fallen we know not how, but fallen so low that even the world rejects him as an outcast. He is a traitor to the family name, he has dragged the family honour in the mire. And yet, until lately, he was, to all outward appearances, as one of the rest —sharing the same companionships, joining in the same amusements, learning the same lessons, nay, even wearing the same family features, speaking with his father's voice, or smiling with his mother's smile.

¶ How peculiarly does the warning of Judas come home to those who in our own day "do the work of a gospeller," whose life is spent in proclaiming the message Judas spoke in the villages of Galilee long ago. Surely if anyone could be safe from the seductions of worldliness, it must be the man or woman whose voice is day by day telling the glad news to old and young, pointing to eager seekers the narrow path that leads to everlasting life. Is it so? Has the preacher never felt within him the vague but horrible consciousness that the oft-repeated message is becoming for him a parrot cry, that he knows the way of salvation so well by heart that the tenderest of God's words wakes no loving echo in his soul, that faith is frozen into an "ism," and that no instrument fashioned of man has power to expel nature— nature, alas! ever prone to degrade? Have the gaols of our country never opened to men from whose lips thousands once heard the truth, while within them worldliness was having its perfect work, sapping the power which alone kept that gospel from being only the most hideous of hypocrisies? Yes; Judas is not the only fallen apostle whose name the tears of God have blotted out of the Book of Life.[1]

I.

The Lost Opportunity.

1. If the tragedy of any man's life consists in the contrast between what he is and what he might have been, between depths to which he has fallen and heights to which he might

[1] J. H. Moulton, *Visions of Sin*, 108.

have risen, there was never doom so tragic as his who, terrible contradiction! was at once the Apostle and the betrayer of his Lord. For to what had he been called? What was it that he might have been? One of the twelve precious stones on the breast-plate of the everlasting High Priest; one of the twelve foundations of the Heavenly Jerusalem, one of the twelve Apostles of the Lamb, even of them that in the regeneration, in the new heaven and the new earth, should sit on thrones judging the twelve tribes of Israel; one whom in all ages and throughout all the world the Church should have held in highest honour and most thankful remembrance, as of those who stood nearest to her Lord when He sojourned among the children of men. Such he might have been; and what is he? A name which is beneath every name, the darkest blot in the page of human story; and, when we seek to pierce into the awful darkness beyond, we know only that One who knows all destinies, and who measures all dooms, declared of him what He never in so many words declared of any other, "It had been good for that man if he had not been born."

2. Called to be an Apostle! What a magnificent opening for usefulness! But we never find the traitor, Judas, mentioned foremost in any work of love or bringing others to Jesus for healing of soul or body. When the crowds were fed he was there, and helped to distribute food as he was bidden. But though treasurer of the party, it was not Judas who offered to go and buy food. It would make too large a gap in his hoard of savings, if it were possible. The miracle itself might seem to confirm his hopes of an earthly kingdom. The crowds were very anxious to make Jesus a king. It must have been a disappointment to Judas when the Lord hurried the disciples into their boat and sent them away, evidently lest they should lose their heads with the crowd and try to force on Him assumption of temporal sovereignty.

The only time when his voice was heard was in grumbling against Mary for wasting precious ointment on her Lord. Think of all that his opportunity meant—hourly companionship and conversation with the sinless Son of Man, always so gentle, kind, forgiving, and moreover wise and firm, a leader who could command reverence as well as love. Judas's nature was too cold and calculating to have much enthusiasm roused in him. The harvest of his earthly expectations was blighted; the summer of his life was ended, and he was not saved. One hope only remained—to enrich himself amid the wreck of Christ's fortunes, and he grasped at it; and lo! the pelf for which he sold his soul burnt his fingers. As blood-money it was hateful to him. He flung it down before the chief priests who had paid it over to him, and went and hanged himself.

3. Because Judas did not profit by the fellowship of Christ, he was the worse for it. For that double effect always attends contact with Christ. It is either a blessing or a curse. Fire softens wax, but it hardens clay; air nourishes the growing plant, but it helps to corrupt and destroy the cut flower. So the influence of Jesus, which was changing the fickle Peter into the man of rock and the hot-tempered John into the Apostle of Love, was making Judas capable of the crime of history. Yes, the very purity and holiness of Jesus did but harden Judas and intensify his hatred of the good he saw but would not follow, until he was prepared in the madness of his hate to betray Jesus to a cruel death. And that same solemn lesson Judas teaches to us. Privileges unused become curses.

¶ Judas heard all Christ's sermons.[1]

¶ Why does St. John love, and why does Judas fail? No complete answer can be forthcoming. The reply lies in the inscrutable mystery of the human will. Both had the same opportunity, both were open to the same influences. But the one set out to be what God intended him to be, and let the warmth of family love, the strength of the Baptist's affection, and the indescribable power of the love of the Son of God enter in, expand, develop, and enrich the self. The other had a plan of his own. He would make his mark, satisfy his stirring ambitions; and so, being ever restless, ever craving to find some new opportunity, he only had occasional glimpses of love, never got really warmed by it, never felt its stimulating power; and at last the light went out, and darkness and his own place were all he knew. Judas sought to win his soul and lost it; St. John lost his soul for Christ's sake and found it. The one became less and less of man, the central activities that Love keeps going gradually slackening, and at last stopping altogether; the other grew day

[1] Thomas Goodwin.

by day into the perfect man, through the expansive power of that inner fire of love that was fed continuously by the love of Christ.[1]

II.

THE GRADUAL DESCENT.

1. It is an old and a true saying, that no man ever became utterly base at once. Utter baseness requires a long education; but it is carried on in secret, and so we do not notice it. The heinous, shocking crime first startles us, but it is only the end of a long series. It was so, no doubt, with Judas. He had had, as every man, whether good or bad, has in some form or other, an evil tendency in his heart. Here was his trial; here might have been his moral education. That tendency became his master, and plunged him in headlong ruin.

There was, first of all, the pleasure of fingering the coin; then there was the desire of accumulating; then there was the reluctant hand and the grudging heart in distributing alms; then there was the silent appropriation of some trifling sum, as indemnification for a real or imagined personal loss; then there was the first unmistakable act of petty fraud—and so it went on and on, until the disciple became the thief, the trusted became the traitor, the Apostle of Christ the son of perdition.

¶ Was any woman, do you suppose, ever the better for possessing diamonds? but how many have been made base, frivolous, and miserable by desiring them? Was ever man the better for having coffers full of gold? But who shall measure the guilt that is incurred to fill them? Look into the history of any civilized nations; analyse, with reference to this one cause of crime and misery, the lives and thoughts of their nobles, priests, merchants, and men of luxurious life. Every other temptation is at last concentrated into this; pride, and lust, and envy, and anger, all give up their strength to avarice. The sin of the whole world is essentially the sin of Judas. Men do not disbelieve their Christ; but they sell Him.[2]

2. There is to our minds an inexpressible meanness in the fact that it was not the prospect of any vast amount of wealth that tempted him. That would not have justified or excused him, but it

[1] G. H. S. Walpole, *Personality and Power*, 169.
[2] Ruskin, *Ethics of the Dust*, Lect. i. § 10 (*Works*, xviii. 217).

would have made his conduct more explicable. But that, for a sum less than £4, he should have sold such a Master and such a Friend indicates the depth of wickedness. And apart altogether from what Christ was in Himself, and what He came to do, which have gathered round this deed of Judas a criminality that is unequalled, there was a baseness in the whole character of his act which makes it hideous, and which has made his name synonymous with badness in its worst form.

But the magnitude of any passion in the human soul is altogether independent of the limits of its opportunity for indulgence. Tyranny is as possible in a cottage as on an Eastern throne; though it may have to content itself with more restricted gratification. Envy, pride, sensuality, maliciousness, though they may be gratified on a vast area, and with terrific results to millions, or within the narrowest limits of a very humble lot, are, as passions, in the one case what they are in the other—powers that overshadow and gradually absorb all else in the soul, and give it throughout the impress and colour of their own malignity. Just as there are bodily diseases which, at first unobtrusive and unnoticed and capable of being extirpated if taken in time, will spread and grow until first one and then another limb or organ is weakened or infected by them, so that at last the whole body is but a habitation for the disease which is hurrying it to the grave; so in the moral world one unresisted propensity to known wrong may in time acquire a tyrannical ascendancy that will make almost any crime possible in order to gratify it.

¶ The creed which makes human nature richer and larger makes men at the same time capable of profounder sins; admitted into a holier sanctuary, they are exposed to the temptation of a greater sacrilege; awakened to the sense of new obligations, they sometimes lose their simple respect for the old ones; saints that have resisted the subtlest temptations sometimes begin again, as it were, by yielding without a struggle to the coarsest; hypocrisy has become tenfold more ingenious and better supplied with disguises; in short, human nature has inevitably developed downwards as well as upwards, and if the Christian ages be compared with those of heathenism they are found worse as well as better, and it is possible to make it a question whether mankind has gained on the whole.[1]

---

[1] J. R. Seeley, *Ecce Homo*, chap. xxiv.

¶ All men who know themselves are conscious that this tendency [degeneration], deep-rooted and active, exists within their nature. Theologically it is described as a gravitation, a bias toward evil. The Bible view is that man is conceived in sin and shapen in iniquity. And experience tells him that he will shape himself into further sin and ever-deepening iniquity without the smallest effort, without in the least intending it, and in the most natural way in the world if he simply let his life run. It is on this principle that, completing the conception, the wicked are said further in the Bible to be lost. They are not really lost as yet, but they are on the sure way to it. The bias of their lives is in full action. There is no drag on anywhere. The natural tendencies are having it all their own way; and although the victims may be quite unconscious that all this is going on, it is patent to every one who considers even the natural bearings of the case that "the end of these things is Death." When we see a man fall from the top of a five-storey house, we say the man is lost. We say that before he has fallen a foot; for the same principle that made him fall the one foot will undoubtedly make him complete the descent by falling other eighty or ninety feet. So that he is a dead man, or a lost man, from the very first. The gravitation of sin in a human soul acts precisely in the same way. Gradually, with gathering momentum, it sinks a man further and further from God and righteousness, and lands him, by the sheer action of a natural law, in the hell of a neglected life.[1]

3. When Judas let the character which he had slowly formed go out into his terrible treachery, he felt as if a bridge were broken behind him. In that bewildering night in the garden, he was swept from the side of Christ, and only then did he begin to realize what he had done and what he had lost. He could no more look upon the face of the Master he had sold. The trustful, happy circle of the Twelve was broken, and he, of them all, was left utterly alone. However they might meet in secret, and fearfully, to speak of their past and their future, of the death of their love and hope, he felt that he had no more part or lot among them. There is not any distance in space or time, not any change in circumstances, which will so cut a man off from his fellow-men as one sin will do. But it will generally be found that this sin is the outcome of a secret life which stands discovered by it. It is God's way of letting us see, even now, what

[1] H. Drummond, *Natural Law in the Spiritual World*, 101.

final judgment will disclose, the revelation of an utter incompatibility, which makes a man seek no more a fellowship where he never had a true share.

> We are not worst at once. The course of evil
> Begins so slowly, and from such slight source,
> An infant's hand might stem the breach with clay.
> But let the stream grow wider, and Philosophy,
> Aye, and Religion too, may strive in vain
> To stem the headlong current.

III.

THE GIFT AND THE TEMPTATION.

1. As is often the case, one of the master temptations of Judas lay along the lines of his greatest ability. The natural superiority of a Judæan, joined with a keen, practical talent which his colleagues lacked, accounted easily for his promotion to the rank of treasurer, to keep the small store which satisfied the company's scanty needs and enabled them to practise the luxury of giving to those who were even poorer than themselves. But who is there that, in thoughtful moments, has not stood almost in a shuddering awe at the fact that the bag should have been committed to Judas, as it were to evoke and provoke his sin, that sin to which he was tempted the most, and to give him an easy opportunity of indulging it? And yet will any deny that this, too, is only one example more of that which is evermore recurring in that mysterious world in which our lives are being lived? Is it not true that men continually find themselves in conditions especially calculated to call out the master sin of their hearts?

2. Let it not be forgotten that Judas sinned and fell after repeated warnings. The general tone of our Lord's teaching respecting worldliness was one constant warning. To a man like Judas, trying to secure his own interest, and making this the prime object of his thoughts, the words, "Ye cannot serve God and mammon," would come like a trumpet-note of alarm. But, besides general language like this, there are utterances of our Lord which, in the light of Judas's character, sound like direct and special efforts to awake him from his dream of self. We may, for

example, read in the light of Judas's designs the parable of the Unjust Steward. The steward has wasted his master's goods; he has been unfaithful in his trust. Judas has been unfaithful; he has tampered with the bag. The steward is awakened by the danger he is in of losing his position. How does he act? He secures his retreat by making negotiations with the other side. Judas is alarmed by the thought that his position may be insecure. How does he act? He opens up negotiations with the enemies of Christ. It is a clever scheme. As far as worldly and unprincipled sagacity can go, it is shrewd. The actor shows a determination to secure himself at all costs. But does it answer? In this world it may. Unscrupulous smartness does sometimes succeed on earth. The faithless steward may secure for himself a refuge among those partners of his guilt whom he has placed under an obligation—yes, in the world, in earthly habitations, it may be so; but such methods will secure no welcome, when men fail, in eternal habitations. The irony of the warning is an arrow for the heart of Judas.

Or, again, the parable of the Wedding Garment had its message for the traitor. It was one thing to refuse to come to the wedding; it was another to come, and to come in the beggarly array of one's worldliness. To disregard the invitation was a fault; but to accept it without entering into the spirit of it, to be there in hollow and empty form, the mockery of its gladness, a dark shadow upon its brightness—this was to provoke a darker doom than the sin of refusal met. Did the heart and mind of Judas not feel that the picture had familiar touches, and that the message of the parable was for him as well as for others?

Still more emphatic is the warning, given at the time when our Lord had by His action refused the Kingdom, and when, consequently, doubts began to grow strong in the mind of Judas. The disciples were diminishing in numbers; the refusal of the temporal crown followed by the spiritual teaching respecting the bread of life was too much for the carnal-minded among Christ's followers; the signs of disaffection and discontent were easy to read. The heart of Judas was already a traitor's heart; worldliness and self-interest were slowly and surely vanquishing every loyal obligation. Then it is that our Lord speaks the words which reveal in one moment the schemer's heart in all its hideousness, "Did not I choose you the twelve, and one of you is a devil?" Must not the soul of Judas have whispered to itself, "It is I. To this image must I come if I allow this thing to gain the mastery over me"?

Christ's effort to save His disciple from sinking into such an abyss of baseness did not end here. As the crisis draws near, He puts forth fresh and final attempts to save him. " Ye are not all clean," He said, at the time when it was not yet too late for the traitor to cleanse his fault. Christ still stood near at hand in the garb of service, stooping to wash the earth stains from His disciples' feet. "Ye are not all clean." He had washed Judas's feet when He said it; but the cleansing of the feet was not enough for one whose heart was still foul. Yet it was not then too late. The foulest might yet be bathed in the stream of the cleansing love of Christ. But the words of Christ wake no softening thoughts in the traitor's mind.

One more effort Christ will make. At the supper-table He quotes the words, "He that eateth my bread lifted up his heel against me" (John xiii. 18). Later, still more explicitly, "One of you shall betray me" (John xiii. 21). Even then it was not too late. The last step had not been taken by Judas. But, as with a man sliding down a steep place, the impetus of temptation was too strong. He takes the food from the hand of Christ. With treason in his heart, he does not hesitate to take that pledge of affection and loyalty. There is treachery in doing so; the Nemesis of base acts is further baseness. "After the sop, then Satan entered into him" (John xiii. 27). The crisis is passed at that moment. He will not turn back now. "That thou doest, do quickly" (John xiii. 27). He "went out straightway; and it was night." An hour later, his treason was an accomplished fact.

The inward story of Judas's life is a story of help refused and warning disregarded. The tender efforts of his Lord and Master to save him are put away.

We should wonder the less perhaps if we only reflected what a blinding, hardening power, one fixed idea, one set purpose, one dominant passion in the full flush and fervour of its ascendancy exerts upon the human spirit, how it blinds to consequences that are staring us in the very face, how it deadens the remonstrances to which in other circumstances we should have at once yielded, how it carries us over obstacles that at other times would at once have stopped us; nay, more—and what perhaps is the most striking feature of the whole—how the very interferences for which otherwise we should have been grateful are resented, how the very appeals intended and fitted to arrest become as so many goads driving us the more determinedly down the path.

¶ *June 25, 1826.*—Lord Chief-Baron told us a story of the ruling passion strong in death. A Master in Chancery was on his death-bed—a very wealthy man. Some occasion of great urgency occurred in which it was necessary to make an affidavit, and the attorney, missing one or two other Masters, whom he inquired after, ventured to ask if Mr. —— would be able to receive the deposition. The proposal seemed to give him momentary strength; his clerk sent for, and the oath taken in due form, the Master was lifted up in bed, and with difficulty subscribed the paper; as he sank down again, he made a signal to his clerk,—" Wallace."—" Sir ? "—" Your ear—lower—lower. Have you got the half-crown ? " He was dead before morning.[1]

IV.

TREACHERY.

The one crime which society judges hardly, for which it holds no penalty too severe, is treachery. Of other sins the world is a lenient critic. It deals very gently with the profligate; it is full of excuses for the self-willed and violent. It has a sympathy with passion—the passion of the sensualist, or the passion of the headstrong—which softens its judgment. But the traitor receives no mercy at the bar of public opinion. The instinct of self-preservation does not leave society a choice. It could not hold together, if perfidy were overlooked. The betrayal of a friend, the betrayal of a cause, the betrayal of one's country—these are unforgiven and unforgotten crimes. Even treachery to a treacherous cause is barely tolerated. The law employs it, and disguises it with a specious title. We call it "turning King's evidence," but still it is repulsive. We avail ourselves of the treachery, but we loathe the traitor. It is an ugly name and an ugly thing, to which no social or political necessity can altogether reconcile us.

[1] *The Journal of Sir Walter Scott*, 216.

Address the next man you meet as Judas, and he will probably be angry. Address him as Peter or Thomas, and, unless coincidence is at work, the probabilities are that he will simply be amused at your mistake. Why the difference? It is because the career of Judas has indelibly stained his name with the suggestion of treachery; and all the world hates a traitor. In a large upper room in the Palace of the Doges in Venice there is a series of portraits of past rulers of the city. One of the lines of these portraits is broken by a sudden blank. It confronts you black and sinister; and naturally you ask for an explanation. "There," answers the guide, "was once a portrait of one of the doges. But he sold the city to her enemies; and so they blackened his picture out." The action of the civic authorities expressed dramatically the attitude of most of us towards a traitor.

¶ We shudder at the associations called up by the memory of Judas Iscariot, whose very name has become a byword; and whose person and character an eternal type of impiety, treachery, and ingratitude; his crime, without a name, so distances all possible human turpitude that he cannot even be held forth as a terror to evil-doers; we set him aside as one cut off; we never think of him but in reference to the sole and unequalled crime recorded of him. Not so our ancestors; one should have lived in the middle ages, to conceive the profound, the ever-present, horror with which Judas Iscariot was then regarded. The devil himself did not inspire the same passionate hatred and indignation. Being the devil, what *could* he be but devilish? His wickedness was according to his infernal nature; but the crime of Judas remains the perpetual shame and reproach of our humanity. The devil betrayed mankind, but Judas betrayed his God.[1]

For what wilt thou sell thy Lord?
"For certain pieces of silver, since wealth buys the world's
    good word."
But the world's word, how canst thou hear it, while thy
    brothers cry scorn on thy name?
And how shall thy bargain content thee, when thy brothers
    shall clothe thee with shame?

For what shall thy brother be sold?
"For the rosy garland of pleasure, and the coveted crown of
    gold."

[1] Mrs. Jameson, *The Poetry of Sacred and Legendary Art*, i. 255.

But thy soul will turn them to thorns, and to heaviness
  binding thy head,
While women are dying of shame, and children are crying for
  bread.

            For what wilt thou sell thy soul?
"For the world." And what shall it profit, when thou shalt
  have gained the whole?
What profit the things thou hast, if the thing thou art be so
  mean?
Wilt thou fill with the husks of having the void of the might-
  have-been? [1]

[1] E. Nesbit, *Ballads and Verses of the Spiritual Life*, **91**.

MARY MAGDALENE.

LITERATURE.

Adeney, W. F., *Women of the New Testament* (1899), 195.

Baker, F. A., *Sermons* (1896), 360.

Clow, W. M., *The Day of the Cross* (1909), 285.

Dixon, A. C., *Milk and Meat* (1893), 120.

Dods, M., *Footsteps in the Path of Life* (1909), 34.

Ealand, F., *The Spirit of Life* (1906), 74.

Farquhar, J., *The Schools and Schoolmasters of Christ* (1911), 130.

Gurney, T. A., *The Living Lord* (1901), 19.

Harden, R. W., *The Evangelists and the Resurrection* (1914), 98.

Holden, J. S., *Life's Flood-Tide* (1913), 89.

Ingram, A. F. W., *Addresses during Holy Week* (1902), 30.

Liddon, H. P., *Easter in St. Paul's* (1892), 12.

Macnutt, F. B., *The Inevitable Christ* (1901), 17.

Milligan, G., in *Women of the Bible* : Rebekah to Priscilla (1904), 217

Morrison, G. H., *The Wings of the Morning* (1907), 97.

Stanford, C., *From Calvary to Olivet* (1893), 33, 94.

Stone, D., *The Discipline of Faith* (1904), 93.

Whyte, A., *Bible Characters* : Joseph and Mary to James (1900), 95.

Wiseman, N., *The Messages of Christ*, 63.

Wright, D., *The Power of an Endless Life* (1897), 189.

Catholic Encyclopædia, ix. (1910) 761 (H. Pope).

Dictionary of the Bible, iii. (1900) 284 (J. B. Mayor).

Dictionary of Christ and the Gospels, ii. (1908) 139 (D. Smith).

Encyclopædia Biblica, iii. (1902), col. 2970 (P. W. Schmiedel).

MARY MAGDALENE.

They have taken away my Lord, and I know not where they have laid him.—John xx. 13.

LET us see first what we are told about Mary Magdalene, and then what her story has to teach us.

I.

WHAT WE KNOW OF MARY MAGDALENE.

1. Her name is probably derived from the town of Magdala or Magadan, now *Medjdel*, which is said to mean "a tower." It was situated at a short distance from Tiberias, and is mentioned in connexion with the miracle of the seven loaves. An ancient watch-tower still marks the site.

Almost all we know of her early life is told us in a single sentence of St. Luke's Gospel. It was the custom of devout Jewish women to accompany the Rabbi under whose teaching they had been blessed, and to minister to his wants. And so St. Luke tells us, "The twelve were with him, and certain women which had been healed of evil spirits and infirmities, Mary that was called Magdalene, from whom seven devils had gone out, and Joanna the wife of Chuza Herod's steward, and Susanna, and many others, which ministered unto them of their substance."

It must have often occurred to thoughtful readers of the Gospels to ask how Christ and His disciples were supported during those three years, seeing that they had all given up their ordinary employment. Christ declared when sending forth His missionaries that the labourer was worthy of his hire, and told them to trust to the hospitality of the people; and this they no doubt did. But practically it is not a satisfactory thing to be always thus dependent. There were times and places in which both Christ and His disciples were unpopular, and it became necessary, as well as advisable, to be independent. That they were in the habit of receiving money for this purpose is evident both from the fact that the community had a treasurer, and that we are told of the disciples, when passing through Samaria, going "into the city to buy food." Where did they get the money? The freewill offerings of people benefited may have done something in this direction, but looked at practically, thirteen men, in a country like Palestine, could hardly be wholly supported in that way. Besides, we have no hint that such freewill offerings were either asked or given. The true answer to the question of their support is that these women, who were evidently in some cases women of means, "ministered unto them of their substance." This indeed is given as the explanation of their presence among the disciples.

¶ When we come to think of it, how natural it was that Jesus Christ by His character should win the devotion of the women of the world. There is something in perfect strength, and yet perfect gentleness, which appeals to the best part of woman's nature; and it is one of those things which make it so peculiarly damnable, when a man avails himself of the best side of a woman's nature to lure her to her ruin, that it is the best side which the strength of a man or what she thinks is mingled strength and gentleness really calls out. And therefore when there is working in the world perfect strength and perfect gentleness, can we wonder that that incarnation of it won the heart of woman? [1]

2. We have seen that in the first mention of Mary Magdalene's name she is spoken of as one "from whom seven devils (or demons) had gone out" (Luke viii. 2). And without giving any mystical interpretation to the "seven," it evidently implies a possession of peculiar malignancy (cf. Luke xi. 26). This is not the place in which to enter on a detailed discussion of the meaning of demoniacal possession, but in general it pointed to a wholly abnormal state of life, in which the unhappy victims found themselves under the influence of some evil power that for the time had gained complete mastery over them. And it was clearly from some such miserable state that Mary had been

[1] A. F. W. Ingram, *Addresses during Holy Week*, 35.

delivered through the direct intervention—so we may safely infer —of Jesus Himself.

Perhaps in some street of Magdala, the city of her youth, He found her, torn with frenzy; and in upon "the wretchedness of despair, the divided consciousness, the long-continued fits of silence" which darkened her life, there broke that calm, clear voice which restored her to sane and happy womanhood and freed her from the terrors of the devil-haunted past. No wonder that she loved Him and with woman's whole-hearted devotion hung about His footsteps in Galilee and "ministered unto him," content in some poor measure thus to repay her infinite debt!

Across this simple, natural, and most winsome history, tradition has written a legend, very fascinating to morbid and prurient minds, which foully asperses the character of the Magdalene. She has been identified with the woman who was a sinner, who kissed the feet of Jesus and wiped her sudden tears with her hair. The name Magdalene, so dear to the Apostolic band, has thereby become a synonym for a woman of shame. There is not a particle of evidence for this dishonouring identification. The story of the woman who was a sinner can be read in the preceding chapter of the same Gospel, and there is not a hint that she and Mary are one. The root out of which the baseless legend grew is the suggestion that the "seven devils" may be only another expression for the "many sins" in Luke's pathetic incident. But the seven devils no more implied riotous and wanton conduct then than *dementia* would now. The simple fact that Mary was permitted to join the devout women who followed Jesus, and is found in the companionship of women of unsullied name and of social honour, is sufficient to refute the assertion.

Seven times
The letter that denotes the inward stain,
He on my forehead, with the truthful point
Of his drawn sword inscribed. And, "Look," he cried,
"When enter'd, that thou wash these scars away."

We do not know just what Mary Magdalene's seven scars were. But for our learning, Dante's own seven scars are written all over his superb autobiographical book. And Dante's identical scars are inscribed again every returning Fourth Day in Bishop Andrewes's *Private Devotions*. Solomon has the same scars also:

"These six things doth the Lord hate. Yea, seven are an abomination unto Him." And, again: "When he speaketh fair, believe him not, for there are seven abominations in his heart." And John Bunyan has the very same number at the end of his *Grace Abounding*: "I find to this day these seven abominations in my heart." And then Bunyan is bold enough, and humble-minded enough, to actually name his scars for the comfort and encouragement of his spiritual children.[1]

3. In the company of the other attendant women Mary Magdalene travels up to Jerusalem on that last dread journey, which, Jesus had told them, was to His death. She is of the group of those who stand afar off watching the crucifixion. In every list of these women given by the Synoptic Evangelists her name comes first. It would seem, therefore, that here also Mary Magdalene may have taken the lead among the women. Perhaps it was her devotion that encouraged the others to be present at the execution, though womanly instinct would naturally shrink from the appalling spectacle. A fearful fascination draws her to the fatal spot, and she brings her companions with her. There is nothing to be done. But if their presence were perceived by the Sufferer it would afford that solace of sympathy for which His soul had more than once craved in vain. We cannot quite bring the various accounts into agreement on this point. The Synoptists place the women "afar off"; St. John at the foot of the cross. His mother must have been close at hand when Jesus committed her to the charge of the beloved disciple. We shall never be able to settle some of these minor details. But of course it is quite possible that both accounts are correct: that the women were first at a distance, and then, as the darkness gathered and the agony grew more intense, crept up closer till they actually found themselves among the soldiers near the foot of the cross.

Mary remains in the dusk of the evening watching what she must have looked on as the final resting-place of the Prophet and Teacher whom she had honoured. Not to her had there been given the hope of the resurrection. The disciples to whom the words that spoke of it had been addressed had failed to understand them, and were not likely to have reported them to her. The Sabbath that followed brought an enforced rest, but no sooner

[1] A. Whyte, *Bible Characters*, 95.

is the sunset over than she, with Salome and Mary, the mother of James, "bought sweet spices, that they might come and anoint" the body, the interment of which, on the night of the crucifixion, they looked on as hasty and provisional.

4. Next day, being the first day of the week, they set out on their errand to the grave, in the dawn. Two of the Evangelists use the phrase, "very early in the morning." "Very early in the morning," St. John says, "when it was yet dark." St. Mark says, "After the sun had risen." Perhaps the first phrase points to the time when they left their lodging, the second to the time when they reached the tomb. Other solutions of the difficulty have been suggested. It might not have been too dark to distinguish objects; the fresh, faint flame of the morning might be already beginning to tinge the gloom; and both writers, each in his own way, aimed only at expressing the general idea that it was about the time of daybreak.

According to the most probable explanation of the Evangelical narratives, Mary Magdalene arrived at the sepulchre alone and first of all. St. John describes her as coming alone to the sepulchre, finding it empty, and then going to fetch St. Peter and himself; whereas the other three Evangelists speak of a group of women, of whom Mary Magdalene was one,—St. Matthew names two, St. Mark three,—as visiting the sepulchre, finding it empty, conversing with the angels who guarded it, and then going away to inform the disciples. Now the best way of accounting for this divergence is to make what in the circumstances and with the persons concerned would be a very natural assumption. We may assume, without doing violence to the text of the Gospels, that this entire company of women, of whom Mary Magdalene was one, set out together from the city before daybreak to visit the tomb of Jesus, which was outside the walls; but that Mary Magdalene, under the impulse of her strong and tender love, gradually moved away from the rest, and hastened on before them. Just as an hour or two later, on that same morning, St. Peter and St. John ran together to the sepulchre, but "the other disciple did outrun Peter, and came first to the sepulchre," so there is reason to think it had been with Mary Magdalene. Her more ardent love was impatient of the measured pace of others, who indeed loved Jesus well, but assuredly loved Him less than she.

It is not easy to determine the exact order of the events that followed; but apparently Mary, on finding the tomb empty, at once ran and summoned Peter and John, returning along with them. And then, after they had left—the other women having previously departed—she herself remained "standing without at the tomb weeping" (John xx. 11). She could not tear herself away from the spot. Not that she believed that Jesus had actually risen and would appear to her; she only longed to know whither His body had been taken.

The first answer to her longing came in a wholly unexpected manner. As she "looked"—and the word in the original points to fixed, silent contemplation—"into the tomb," she saw "two angels in white sitting, one at the head, and one at the feet, where the body of Jesus had lain." And in answer to their question why she wept, she replied in words in which all her love and anxiety found expression: "Because they have taken away my Lord, and I know not where they have laid him." It never occurred to Mary apparently to address any inquiry to the angels; but, satisfied now that the tomb was indeed empty, and, unwilling to continue a conversation which served only to revive her grief, "she turned herself back." And in the very act of doing so, she beheld "Jesus standing, and knew not that it was Jesus." Her eyes, like the eyes of the disciples afterwards on the Emmaus road, were still holden. Not yet was she prepared for the full vision of her glorified Lord.

5. We cannot tell why Mary did not at once see that it was Jesus who was speaking to her. And yet her want of perception is not so very mysterious. She was not in the mood to notice anybody through the veil of her tears. When the soul is absorbed with its own internal feeling of sorrow, the faculties of observation are not very keen. And Jesus alive was the very last person Mary expected to see when she was engaged in the search for His dead body. She took the Speaker for the gardener, the most likely person to be found in this private enclosure so early in the day. When Jesus was crucified He was stripped of His clothes, the Romans allowing no clothing to the victim of the cross except the

loin-cloth—the *subligaculum*. But this was all that labourers wore at their work in the hot climate of Palestine. If Jesus had appeared just as He would have been after leaving the burial bandages behind in the tomb, He would have looked like a man prepared for his work. But this was very different from His appearance with tunic and cloak as Mary had been accustomed to see Him in the old days. It was quite natural, therefore, that in her present distracted condition of mind Mary should take Him for the gardener, whom in outward appearance He resembled.

"Sir," she said, "if thou hast borne him hence, tell me where thou hast laid him, and I"—as if no thought of her woman's weakness could hinder the resolution—"will take him away." It is not unnatural to suppose that at this point there was a pause. "Mary," says Dr. Westcott, "received no answer, and fell back to her former attitude of mourning. Simple human love had, as it seemed, done its uttermost and done its uttermost in vain." But the moment of her greatest need was the moment also of her highest help. "Jesus saith unto her, Mary." It was but a single word, but it was enough. The personal address, the familiar tones, dispelled every doubt. And at once she turned to the Lord with the simple confession of her new-found faith: "Rabboni; which is to say, Master."

It seems as if she had reached forward to hold Him by the feet, for He said, "Touch me not." He held her back as He did not hold back the others, of whom it is said a little later, "They came and took hold of his feet and worshipped him." He held her back because to touch His feet was not the need of her soul. How else can we explain the difference between this and that which happened later to the others? He held her back that she might be deepened. He pointed her on to that spiritual communion which in the future was to be hers. "Touch me not; for I am not yet ascended"—implying the unseen communion which was to be hers when He should have ascended to the Father. And He gives her an immediate work to do for Him. "Go unto my brethren, and say to them, I ascend unto my Father and your Father, and my God and your God."

She went and told the disciples that she had seen the Lord, and with that her story ends. Now what are we to learn from this brief biography?

II.

WHAT WE MAY LEARN FROM HER.

1. *Mary Magdalene's story tells us that sorrow is often blind.*— For a moment let us think of the last scene. A sorrow, of which those can judge in part who have lost the dearest object of their heart's love, was rending the soul of Mary. "She stood without at the sepulchre weeping." She had lost, not Him only who had been to her more than any human creature can be to another in this world—not Him only, but the body; not even the poor comfort was left of embalming the body. It was a grief too deep for fear. The vision of angels alarmed some other women. But perhaps Mary saw nothing strange in those appearances through her tears; and there seems to have been no unearthly sound to her ear in the voice which asked, "Why weepest thou?" for it drew forth only the words, "Because they have taken away my Lord, and I know not where they have laid him." But now there is another Presence of which Mary becomes conscious. Some movement behind her there may have been, or some sound, for it is said she turned herself, and, being turned, there was the figure of a man. The thought of this sorrowing woman was cramped within the closest bonds of earth. It centred in a grave. It was clinging round a dead body. Where was this dead body? It was gone. The eye of Mary was upon the empty tomb, and there her very soul was fixed. "I know not where they have laid him." She could not get beyond that. It held her bound. Neither the vision nor the voice of an angel could touch the numbed sense. No wonder that Mary thought this was the gardener. "In the place where he was crucified there was a garden; and in the garden a new sepulchre wherein was never man yet laid. There laid they Jesus." There was no one so likely as the gardener to be standing near the mouth of that sepulchre—no one so likely, but yet it might, of course, be someone else. Why did Mary not know that it *was* someone else? The darkness was not the cause. It was not darkness that caused Mary to think that Man was the gardener. "She *saw* Jesus." St. John's actual word is, "She beholdeth Jesus"; it expresses the fixing of the eye upon an object as with a certain intentness. In this way Mary, when she

was turned, looked upon Jesus, but she knew not that it was
Jesus.

Sorrow is a very engrossing thing. We hear it spoken of as
a purifying discipline. And this, no doubt, is its purpose, and a
sympathizing friend will tell the suffering person that this is the
purpose. But the sympathizing friend is not the suffering person.
It is so very easy to say a true thing; but to *feel* it, and give to
this true thing the force which indeed belongs to it, and would
come forth from it if it were felt—this is very hard. Suffering
absorbs thought; it gathers round itself all the outgoings of the
mind; it tones with its own colouring all surrounding objects; it
looks off from the withered treasure, and sees only the rust and
the moth; it looks off from the wreck of property, and sees only
the misadventure of circumstance or the fraud of men; it looks
off from the desolated hearth, and sees only the place where the
dead was laid. In the garden it can see only the gardener.

¶ I have heard mourners gathered at a funeral say afterwards,
"I could not tell you who was there." All the great passions in
their full intensity have a certain blinding power about them.
But neither love nor hate nor jealousy nor anger is more effectual
in scaling up the eyes than is the pressure of overwhelming grief.[1]

> When in darkness and clouds
>   The way of God is concealed,
> We doubt the words of His promises,
>   And the glory to be revealed.
>
> We do but trust in part;
>   We grope in the dark alone;
> Lord, when shall we see Thee as Thou art,
>   And know as we are known?
>
> We say, they have taken our Lord,
>   And we know not where He lies,
> When the light of His resurrection morn
>   Is breaking out of the skies.[2]

2. *Love always wins the victory.*—For what is rightly-regulated
love but moral power of the highest order? As St. Paul puts
it, "The love of Christ constraineth us." Few men have ever
explored the heights and depths of our human nature more

[1] G. H. Morrison, *The Wings of the Morning*, 100.   [2] Phœbe Cary.

thoroughly than did St. Augustine, and St. Augustine has a saying which shows how highly he valued the invigorating and transforming power of love. "Only love," he said, "and then do what thou wilt." Love is indeed the very muscle and fibre of moral force. If the condition of mankind is bettered, this is effected by those who love their fellow-men. If goodness is embodied in life and character, this is by those who begin by seeing, however imperfectly, the beauty of goodness. They are enamoured of it before they try to make it their own. If truth is sought and found, amid and across difficulties which have seemed insuperable, this is not seldom by intellects to which truth has presented itself as an object in itself so beautiful as to win the love of their hearts. And if Mary rose in the dark night to visit the grave of her slain Master, and to pay Him such honours as her poverty could yield, this was because her soul was on fire with the moral power of a strong and pure affection, which was to be rewarded presently by the attainment of its object.

There is a kind of love that faces facts, and it is a noble and courageous love. It opens its eyes wide to dark realities, and bowing the head it says, "I must accept them." But there is an agony of love that does not act so; it hopes against hope and beats against all evidence. It is only women who can love like that, and it was a love like that which inspired Mary. No one will ever doubt John's love to Jesus. No one will ever doubt the love of Simon. "Simon, son of Jonas, lovest thou me?" "Yea, Lord, thou knowest that I love thee." But the fact remains that on that Easter morning Peter and John went to their homes again, and only a woman lingered by the grave.

The applications of a truth like this crowd upon us! To love Jesus with that absorbed intensity which makes it the supreme passion of the heart is the hidden secret of the Christian life. It is good to assimilate the ideas of Jesus, and find your mind illuminated and your purposes directed by them. It is good to spend yourself in His service, and find your energies freely and joyfully exercised in it. It is good to see, in moments of faith, the coming of His Kingdom, and to mark how all the toils and efforts and aspirations of men are hastening its consummation. But it is better to love Jesus. For then no word of His shall be dark, no call of His shall be strange, and the very desires of His

heart shall be ours. Until you have come to the hour when a
sense of Christ's personal love and leading awakes within you that
sense of need which can be satisfied only by giving, that love
which is stronger than death, you have not come to the hour for
which your soul is waiting—waiting as the trees wait for the
spring, as the poet waits for his song!

¶ *9th December, 1710.*—This night I was in bad case. I find
it is not easy for me to carry right, either with or without the
cross. While I was walking up and down my closet in heaviness,
my little daughter Jane, whom I had laid in bed, suddenly raising
up herself said, She would tell me a note; and thus delivered
herself:—Mary Magdalen went to the sepulchre.—She went back
again with them to the sepulchre; but they would not believe
that Christ was risen, till Mary Magdalen met Him; and He
said to her, "Tell My brethren, they are My brethren yet." This
she pronounced with a certain air of sweetness. It took me by
the heart: "His brethren yet" (thought I); and may I think that
Christ will own me as one of His brethren yet? It was to me
as life from the dead.[1]

> Then comes the happy moment: not a stir
> In any tree, no portent in the sky:
> The morn doth neither hasten nor defer,
> The morrow hath no name to call it by,
> But life and joy are one,—we know not why,—
> As though our very blood long breathless lain
> Had tasted of the breath of God again.
>
> And having tasted it I speak of it,
> And praise Him thinking how I trembled then
> When His touch strengthened me, as now I sit
> In wonder, reaching out beyond my ken,
> Reaching to turn the day back, and my pen
> Urging to tell a tale which told would seem
> The witless phantasy of them that dream.
>
> But O most blessèd Truth, for Truth Thou art,
> Abide Thou with me till my life shall end.
> Divinity hath surely touched my heart;
> I have possessed more joy than earth can lend:
> I may attain what time shall never spend.
> Only let not my duller days destroy
> The memory of Thy witness and my joy.[2]

[1] *Memoirs of Thomas Boston of Ettrick.*   [2] Robert Bridges.

3. *To the love that conquers is given the service of love.*—"Go unto my brethren, and say to them, I ascend unto my Father and your Father, and my God and your God." Jesus gives Mary a work to do: to tell His brethren of His resurrection and His coming ascension; reminding them that His Father is their Father, His God their God. It is ever so with us. Each Christian life ought to be a life of witness. Each Christian life ought to bear its testimony to the great facts of the Christian religion. "Go unto my brethren, and say to them"—sometimes in word, always in life. "They took knowledge of them, that they had been with Jesus." Those who see our lives ought to discern in them a power that is not of ourselves. They ought to know that God is our Father, and that we are His children. They ought to know that God is our God, and that we receive gifts from Him. They ought to know that our Lord has ascended into heaven, and that from heaven He pours into us His own risen and ascended life.

The work of bearing witness will be as different as our lives are different. It may be a witness to be borne to many, or it may be a witness to be borne to few; it may be a witness to be borne only to one other soul; but there it is—a witness to be borne by every Christian in his own day of grace. "Ye shall be witnesses unto me." "My witnesses." Often we forget the witness-bearing of life. Often we are tempted to think that in other circumstances, other conditions, we could do something worth doing for our Lord, and to forget that just where we are lies the power of our life that should be shining out to others. I live, yet Christ liveth and worketh in me; and because of that there ought to be a mark on my life which makes it a life of witness. How we should treasure the thought, how we should value the truth, that through us others may be helped and led on in the Christian life! How we should treasure the thought that, in the far-off Eternity, one other soul that should otherwise have been lost has been saved, because we bore witness without knowing, perhaps, what we were doing; not, indeed, of our own strength, but because we had received the life of Him who has ascended to the Father; for all that makes anything in us a witness for good comes from that stream of life which He Himself pours into us.

¶ Is not the trouble with most of our witnessing for God that it is inconstant and inconsistent, lacking unity as well as continuity? What is our hope but the indwelling Spirit of Christ, to bring every thought into captivity to the obedience of Christ, to inspire every word and deed by His love? Then will "broken lights" blend in steady shining, the fractional be summed up in the integral, and life, unified and beautified by the central Christ, radiate God's glory, and shine with divine effulgence.[1]

> Take all in a word; the Truth in God's breast
> Lies trace for trace upon our's impressed:
> Though He is so bright, and we are so dim,
> We are made in His image to witness Him.[2]

[1] M. D. Babcock, *Thoughts for Every-Day Living*, 9.
[2] R. Browning.

MARTHA AND MARY.

LITERATURE.

Adeney, W. F., *Women of the New Testament* (1899), 168.

Aitken, W. H. M. H., *The Highway of Holiness*, 141, 157.

Albertson, C. C., *The Gospel According to Christ* (1899), 91.

Brooke, S. A., *The Kingship of Love* (1903), 253.

Bushnell, H., *Christ and His Salvation*, 39.

Campbell, W. M., *Foot-Prints of Christ* (1889), 201.

Candlish, R. S., *Scripture Characters* (1872), 217.

Chadwick, W. E., *Christ and Everyday Life* (1910), 144.

Edersheim, A., *The Life and Times of Jesus the Messiah*, ii. (1887) 146, 312, 322, 358.

Fürst, A., *True Nobility of Character* (1884), 15.

Harris, J. R., *Aaron's Breastplate* (1908), 51.

Horne, C. S., *The Relationships of Life*, 31.

Keble, J., *Sermons for the Christian Year* : Miscellaneous (1880), 289.

Leathes, A. S., *The Kingdom Within* (1910), 76.

Lockyer, T. F., *The Inspirations of the Christian Life* (1894), 226.

Matheson, G., *Words by the Wayside* (1896), 6.

Meyer, F. B., in *The Life and Work of the Redeemer* (1901), 130.

Morris, A. J., *The Open Secret* (1869), 74.

Morrison, G., *The House of God* (1875), 159.

Moule, H. C. G., *From Sunday to Sunday* (1903), 171.

Purchase, E. J., *The Pathway of the Tempted* (1905), 172.

Rigg, J. H., *Scenes and Studies in the Ministry of Our Lord* (1901), 133, 156.

Rowlands, D., in *Women of the Bible* : Rebekah to Priscilla (1904), 153.

Russell, A., *The Light that Lighteth every Man* (1889), 225.

Stimson, H. A., *The New Things of God* (1908), 141.

Thompson, J. R., *Burden Bearing* (1905), 135.

Trumbull, H. C., *Our Misunderstood Bible* (1907), 217.

Watson, J., *The Life of the Master* (1902), 307.

MARTHA AND MARY.

Now as they went on their way, he entered into a certain village : and a certain woman named Martha received him into her house. And she had a sister called Mary, which also sat at the Lord's feet, and heard his word. But Martha was cumbered about much serving ; and she came up to him, and said, Lord, dost thou not care that my sister did leave me to serve alone ? bid her therefore that she help me. But the Lord answered and said unto her, Martha, Martha, thou art anxious and troubled about many things : but one thing is needful : for Mary hath chosen the good part, which shall not be taken away from her.—Luke x. 38-42.

THE Gospels show us our Lord in public—in the Temple of Jerusalem, in the high priest's palace, in Pilate's judgment-hall, on the green hill outside the gate, or on that other hill where He delivered His sermon, or in the meadow where He fed five thousand, or in the synagogue of Capernaum, or on the lake where the eager people crowded the shore. We see Him as a Prophet, Reformer, Teacher, Martyr, as the Messiah and Redeemer. But the same Gospels lift the veil from Jesus' private life, so that we know some of the houses where He found a home in the hard years of His ministry, and some of the friends who comforted His heart. There was one house in Cana where there would ever be a welcome for Him, because on the chief day of life He had turned the water of marriage joy into wine; another in Capernaum, because there He had changed sorrow into gladness, and given a young girl back to her father from the gates of death. He had stayed in John's modest lodging at Jerusalem, as well as used the "Upper Room" of a wealthier friend. There was a room in a publican's house in Capernaum which was sacred because Jesus had feasted there and sealed as in a sacrament the salvation of Levi; and Zacchæus, to the last day of his life, saw the Master crossing his threshold that night He slept in Jericho. The family of St. Peter could have told many things of Jesus—a fifth gospel of what He said and did at His ease. But the home of the

Gospels dearest to the Christian heart is that of Bethany, where
the Master found a refuge from labour and persecution, and
constant sympathy with Mary and Martha and their brother
Lazarus.

We meet with that most interesting of all New Testament
households, the Bethany family, on three occasions in the course
of the gospel history. Twice the sisters are brought together on
the scene; in the third case the younger alone appears. This
statement goes on the assumption that the Mary and Martha of
St. Luke are the same two sisters whom St. John brings before us
in his account of the raising of Lazarus; it also rests on that
Evangelist's identification of the woman anointing Jesus with the
costly spikenard, whose name is not given in the two Synoptic
accounts of the incident—*Matthew* and *Mark*—with Mary of
Bethany.

¶ The connexion of the three incidents with the same family
is not so absolutely certain as is commonly supposed; at least
there have been careful readers to whom it has appeared more
than doubtful. St. Luke, it may be observed, gives us only the
earlier incident,—that in which Mary sits at the feet of Jesus while
Martha is cumbered with much serving, an incident which we
meet with in his Gospel alone,—this evangelist neither mention-
ing the raising of Lazarus, which is not referred to by any of the
synoptists, nor giving the anointing in the last week at Jerusalem,
which the other two Synoptic Gospels record. In introducing
his story he does not fix the locality at Bethany; he simply says
that "as they went on their way" Jesus "entered into a certain
village," not naming the place, apparently for the reason that he
does not know where it is. But since he inserts the incident in
the course of his account of a tour in Galilee, the impression left
on the mind of an unprejudiced reader would naturally be that
the unknown village was situated somewhere in that district.
Hence harmonists have suggested that the family had been living
at the earlier period in Galilee, and had subsequently moved to
the neighbourhood of Jerusalem, while, on the other hand, there
have not been wanting critics who have pounced on the seeming
discrepancy as an evidence of the untrustworthiness of the Fourth
Gospel, the author of which, they have suggested, has arbitrarily
transported Mary and Martha from the north country to Bethany.
But surely it is enough to suppose that St. Luke inserts his
incident where it occurs in his Gospel, with its vague indication
of locality, because there was nothing in the source from which he

derived it to determine where it occurred. It may be remarked that immediately before this he gives the parable of the Good Samaritan, the scene of which is laid in the neighbourhood of Jerusalem, and which therefore would be most appropriately spoken by our Lord in that locality. May it be that both of these paragraphs come from some fragmentary notes of one of Christ's visits to Jerusalem which failed to state the locality to which they belonged?

There is not only the fact of the names being the same, and Martha is by no means so common a name as Mary. The distinctive traits of character which come out with startling vividness in the Third Gospel are repeatedly suggested by more delicate hints in the Fourth, raising the probability practically to a certainty that we have the same pair of sisters introduced to us in each case.[1]

I.

BETHANY.

Bethany is mentioned neither in the Canonical books nor in the Apocrypha of the Old Testament; it makes its appearance for the first time in the New Testament, and is not named in Josephus. Its situation is relatively easy to determine. We know that it was on the road from Jericho to Jerusalem, at a distance of fifteen furlongs from the latter, lying thus on the east, or rather south-east side of the Mount of Olives. Origen asserts that in his time the position of Bethany was known. In the fourth century, the Bordeaux Pilgrim mentions a place where the "crypta" of Lazarus was to be seen. Eusebius records that "the place of Lazarus" was shown, and Jerome adds that it was two miles from Jerusalem.

The village still exists. As the traveller leaves Jerusalem upon the Jericho road, he arrives, after about half an hour's walk from the Damascus gate, which takes him into the Kedron valley, and then upward around the southern shoulder of Olivet, at the houses, grey, dilapidated, and not beautiful, of Bethany. Or he may take another line, and ascend Olivet to its summit, past the obtrusive structure of the huge Russian convent at the top of the road, and then find his way over fence and field to the minor hills

---

[1] W. F. Adeney.

of the eastward side of the mountain, where it looks down upoɼ Bethany.

There is a charm about the surroundings, certainly when seen in spring, as there always is a charm over the rural landscape of that land of many-hued soil and of thronging flowers. But the villages of Palestine are seldom if ever in themselves pleasant to the eye, and certainly Bethany is not; actual or impending decay seems written upon its dwellings. Yes, but still it is Bethany. The immortal memories dignify and beautify it all. For, indeed, there is that wonderful peculiarity about the memories of Palestine, that they are memories and so much more. In Rome, and in Athens, our thoughts are with "the great departed" in "the silent land." At Jerusalem they are with Him who was dead, but behold He is alive for evermore; His very name is life and hope; He is Lord of the future even more than of the past; He is, above all things, Lord of the present, "with us, all the days."

¶ There are particular times when the name has a particularly soothing music in its sound for the Christian. Whisper to him of Bethany, when he sits in his desolate home, and, wandering back through the past, thinks of a face that is vanished, a voice that is mute, and a sacred mound in the churchyard,—whisper to him then of Bethany, and his grief is assuaged, as he thinks that Jesus wept there, and his face brightens, as he gets a motto from the Lord's own lips which faith can inscribe on the tombstone, "I am the resurrection and the life: he that believeth in me, though he were dead, yet shall he live." Whisper to him of Bethany in those moments of half-unbelief, when doubts and fears about the grounds of his religious opinions, and the reality of things unseen assert themselves—when suspicions which he thought had been shorn of their strength, rise again Samson-like, and, laying their hands on the pillars that support his hopes, threaten to shake the whole fabric into ruins; speak to him of Bethany then, and his faith again triumphs, as he sees Him who had been crucified rising up through the parting clouds into heaven to be alive for evermore, as His people's friend and guardian. Whisper to him of Bethany when he is wearied with his daily toils; when the wrinkles of anxiety come out on his brow; when losses, and crosses, and failures have made him peevish and morose; and he can enter the house of Martha and Mary, and sitting down at the feet of Jesus, have all his vexations dissipated, as he hears about the "good part that shall never be taken away."[1]

[1] G. Morrison, *The House of God*, 159.

II.

The Home in Bethany.

1. One of the most pathetic utterances which Christ ever made about Himself is the single reference to His homelessness. "The foxes have holes, and the birds of the air have nests; but the Son of man hath not where to lay his head." Christ never had a home of His own. From the time when He left His father's home in Nazareth where He was brought up, He was a wanderer. To all the comfort which the word suggests, to all the sacred joy associated with the name, He was a complete stranger. That His nature craved for fellowship is evidenced by the references He made to His loneliness, and by His frequent communion with the Father. That He needed the quietness and peace which others find within the privacy of their own homes is proved by His frequent retirements to the solitude of the desert or of the mountain. The home at Bethany appears to have been to Christ a haven of quiet and rest, where He sought refuge from the storms and tumult to which His Judæan ministry exposed Him. It was a land-locked harbour protected from the wild gusts of fierce passion and bitter malice which confronted Him as He steered His course amidst the angry billows and sunken rocks of the neighbouring Jerusalem. In Bethany there was always a home which offered a loving welcome, and there were hearts which responded with a sincere affection.

It was, as the whole history shows, a wealthy home. It consisted of two sisters—the elder, Martha (a not uncommon Jewish name, being the feminine of *Mar*, and equivalent to our word "mistress"); the younger, Mary; and their brother Lazarus, or, *Laazar*.

It was a beautiful friendship that united the Lord with this family. Their home was very evidently one of His favourite resorts. He turned to it for its friendly peace. Perhaps He found in this little circle a love that was not tainted with interested ambition. Perhaps He found a friendship that sought no gift and coveted no place. Perhaps He found a full-orbed sympathy, unbroken by suspicion or reserve. Perhaps He found a confidence which was independent of the multitude, and which

remained quietly steadfast whether He moved in public favour or
in public contempt. At any rate, Jesus was at home "in the
house of Martha and Mary," and here all unnecessary reticence
was changed into free and sunny communion. He loved to turn
from the heated, feverish atmosphere of fickle crowds to the cool
and restful constancy of these devoted friends. When the eyes of
His enemies had been following Him with malicious purpose, it
was spiritually recreating to look into eyes that were just quiet
"homes of silent prayer." After the contentions of the Twelve,
and their frequent disputes as to who should be greatest, it was
good to be in this retired home where friends found love's reward
in love's sacrifices, and the joy of loving in the increased capacity
to love. It is therefore no wonder to read that Jesus went out to
Bethany.

He was not there simply to eat, drink, sleep, and be let alone.
He could not be hidden in that way. The overflowing soul must
find expression. And among friendly hearts and kindred minds it
would be a veritable "saints' rest," a "heart's ease," a garden of
delights, refreshing to the soul as the work of Eden, to hold
converse concerning the things of the Kingdom. Such work and
fellowship, so like to those of heaven, would also be allied thereto
in the rest involved.

> The fellowship of kindred minds
> Is like to that above.

2. The Gospels give us three scenes in the family life of the
two sisters and their brother, in each of which Jesus is the
central figure.

(1) The first is a picture of quiet life, and shows us that the
Master was not always working at the highest pressure, but had
His hours of rest. Weary with the discussions of Jerusalem,
which He had been visiting at a Feast, Jesus, who had no love for
cities, escaped to Bethany for rest. Whereupon we see the kindly
Martha showing her affection in much serving, impatient with
her sister because she thought she neglected the offices of a genial
hospitality. We see there, too, the pensive and spiritual Mary
sitting at Jesus' feet, earnestly drinking in the words that fell
from His lips. We seem to hear the gentle but serious rebuke
addressed to the one, and the language almost of benediction in

which He commended the other who, He said, "hath chosen the good part, which shall not be taken away from her."

(2) The second visit of Jesus to Bethany is associated with one of those swift and unexpected family calamities which affect the imagination by their poignant contrast, and invest life with a profound seriousness.

Lazarus lay dead; the light of his sisters' domestic life seemed extinguished for ever, and the whole world seemed desolate and blighted; their hearts sank within them under the cruel weight of a great sorrow. And in that hour of anguish and distress to whom did their thoughts turn? To the Man whom Martha had received. But the long hours creep slowly away, and still Jesus does not appear. "Oh, if He were here our brother would not die!" And then when the funeral is over, and the first intensity of the anguish has passed away, a rumour reaches them of His approach. Martha hears it. The Master is coming, and Martha, with her natural impulsiveness, rushes out to meet Him, and salutes Him with the words which had been rising in her heart over and over again all the time—"Lord, if thou hadst been here my brother had not died." And there He stands gazing at her—oh, how tenderly—and she hears Him groaning in His troubled spirit. Mary has joined them now, and tears are flowing fast all round, and His eyes are dry no longer. What a moment it must have been for Mary and Martha when they knew that He who loved them so truly was weeping as with their tears, and sharing their sorrow! "*Jesus wept*"; and the friends around said, as well they might, "Behold, how he loved him!" Another moment and Jesus was standing by the closed tomb, lifting up His heart in that wonderful prayer, "Father, I thank thee that thou hast heard me." They stood looking on, wondering what was to come next. Then was heard the voice of power, "Lazarus, come forth," and he that was dead came forth. The king of terrors yields his prey and gives back his victim to the glories of a new, a resurrection life. There he stands before them, the very Lazarus that they had lost, their own dearly loved brother still. What a moment it was when the man whom they had mourned as dead clasped his sisters to his bosom! One can imagine the joy too deep for words that filled their hearts and welled up in their brimming eyes, while He who was the Resurrection and the Life looked on, smiling on all the ecstasy which He had caused.

¶ Those who believe in Jesus may weep for their dead, for Jesus wept. But they may not doubt His love in suffering them to die; they may not doubt that for them the transition is blest. Still may we treasure that of them which is dear.

> We make them a hidden, quiet room
> Far in the depth of our spirit's gloom:
> Thither, O thither, wrung with woe,
> In yearning love we often go:
> There, O there, do the loved abide,
> Shadowy, silent, sanctified!

But they in their true life are with the Lord.

> It is they who lament for us who are
> From the eternal life so far.

And therefore we will take up the language of faith and hope, and say—

> If this be so, we shall look no more
> At the night of the former gloom:
> We shall not stay and make sad delay
> At the dark and awful tomb,
> But rather take to our mourning hearts
> The balm and blessing this trust imparts—
> What the Scripture saith in the ear of Faith
> Of the excellent joys that crown the head
> Of every one of the faithful dead.[1]

(3) Once more we see Jesus with His friends, and now the circumstances are less harrowing, and still more beautiful. As Jesus has arrived for the Passover—His last feast before all things should be fulfilled—He goes to stay with them during Passion Week, so that, whatever may be the controversy and dispeace of the day in Jerusalem, He may cross the Mount of Olives, and rest in Bethany. To celebrate His coming, and as a sacrifice of thanksgiving for a great deliverance, the family give a feast, and each member thereof fills a natural place. Lazarus, the modest head of the household, now surrounded with a mysterious awe, sits with Jesus at the table; Martha, as was her

---

[1] A. Russell, *The Light that Lighteth every Man*, 230.

wont, was superintending the feast with an access of zeal; and Mary was inspired of the spirit of grace, and did a thing so lovely and so spiritual that it will be told unto all time, and will remain the picture of ideal devotion. With a wealthy family it was customary to have in store a treasure of fragrant ointment for the honouring of the dead; but there came into Mary's mind a more pious use for it. Why pay the homage to a dead body, and render it when the person can receive no satisfaction? Far better that in their lifetime our friends should know that they are loved, and should be braced for suffering by the devotion of loyal hearts. Before His enemies have crowned Him with thorns, Mary will pour the spikenard on His head, and before they have pierced His feet with nails she will anoint them with her love, so that the fragrance of the precious ointment may be still on His hair when He hangs upon the cross.

The odour of ointment filled the room, and two persons passed judgment. One understood and condemned—Judas, who was arranging the betrayal of Jesus, and had lost an increase for his bag. One understood and approved, and that was the Master, who, with the shadow of the cross falling on His soul, was comforted by a woman's insight and a woman's love. Her own heart taught her the secret of sacrifice; her heart anticipated the longing for sympathy; and so beautiful in its grace and spiritual delicacy was her act that Jesus declared it would be told to her praise wherever the Gospels were read.

¶ The Onyx is the type of all stones arranged in bands of different colours; it means primarily, nail-stone — showing a separation like the white half-crescent at the root of the finger-nail; not without some idea of its subjection to laws of life. . . . Banded or belted stones include the whole range of marble, and especially alabaster, giving the name to the alabastra, or vases used especially for the containing of precious unguents, themselves more precious; so that this stone, as best representative of all others, is chosen to be the last gift of men to Christ, as gold is their first; incense with both: at His birth, gold and frank-incense; at His death, alabaster and spikenard. . . . These vases for precious perfume were tall, and shaped like the bud of the rose. So that the rosebud itself, being a vase filled with perfume, is called also "alabastron"; and Pliny uses that word for it in describing the growth of the rose.[1]

[1] Ruskin, *Deucalion*, vol. i. chap. vii. § 15 (*Works*, xxvi. 172).

¶ The vulgar irritation of the apostles at the " waste " involved in this beautiful and significant act of the anointing of the Messiah—those very apostles from whom had come Peter's confession and who had seen the Transfiguration ecstasy—gives us the measure of the disharmony, the utter want of comprehension, the creeping conviction of failure, now existing amongst them. Romantic enthusiasm has been transformed into prudence and "common sense": perhaps the worst form of degeneration with which any leader of men has to contend. Through their unworthy and unloving criticisms strikes the solemn and tragic comment of Jesus on this, probably the greatest spontaneous acknowledgment of Messiahship which He received—"She hath done what she could. She is come aforehand to anoint my body to the burying." They are the loneliest words in literature. Removing their speaker by a vast distance from the common prudent life of men, from all human ideals and hopes, they bear within themselves the whole mystery of the Cross, the "King reigning from the Tree."[1]

III.

The Sisters.

The three scenes in the house at Bethany are not all related in the same Gospel, yet the sisters are true to their character throughout.

Now, if we were to read even a small part of the literature that has been written on Martha and Mary, we should be astonished and perhaps bewildered by the variety of ways in which their characters are contrasted.

1. "Martha," says an American author, "is the ritualistic Episcopalian, proper, orderly, devout, reading her prayers from a book, and worshipping in silence her acknowledged Lord. But Mary is inclined to be an unconventional Methodist, zealous, impulsive, careless of precedent, praying the prayer that springs to her lips from an overflowing heart, and expressing her gratitude in most unexpected ways." To complete the picture, Lazarus is offered as "the Presbyterian of the family, solid, sound, silent, philosophical."

[1] Evelyn Underhill, *The Mystic Way*, 131.

2. By mystical writers Martha has been taken to represent the active and Mary the contemplative life. If, for instance, you were to turn to Madame Guyon's Commentaries upon the interior sense of the Scriptures, you would find her discoursing something like this:

"Martha receives Jesus into her house; that is as much as the active life can attain to. But Mary, who signifies the contemplative life, was seated. That 'being seated' expresses the repose of her contemplation; in that sacred rest she does nothing but listen to the voice of her dear Master, who teaches, nourishes, and quickens her with His own word. Oh! Mary, happy Mary, to hear that word! It made itself heard because you put yourself in a state to hear it: you listened for it, and you rested in that silence and that peace without which it is not possible to hear that word which is heard only in heart-silence!"

St. Teresa, however, whom Dr. Rendel Harris calls "the most practical and level-headed of the ascetical school of mystics," shows an inclination towards Martha and away from Mary, as commonly interpreted; and we can perhaps read between the lines and conclude that she had been a little overdone with those in her convent who practised too exclusively the cult of the younger sister. "Martha," she says, "was a true saint though she did not achieve Contemplation. What more could one wish than like her to have Christ often in one's house, and to serve Him and to sit at His very table? Had Martha been rapt like Mary, who would have given the Lord to eat? Those of the Active life are the soldiers who fight in the battles; those of the Contemplative are the standard-bearers who carry aloft the banner of humanity, across which lies the Cross. And remember, if the standard-bearer drops the standard, the battle has to be lost."

> Oh, when those mystic barriers
>   Our Maries pass, we dream
> That in some fair Elysian
>   Their thirst has found the Stream;
>
> But the Marthas are our cottagers
>   Who make our fireside bliss.
> The Beatific Vision—
>   She never talked of this.

A sudden mist our seeing blurs,
Such sacramental grace
Hath poured its revelation
Into that patient face;

And neighbour-hand toward neighbour stirs,
Her sainthood to confess
By love's own consecration,
Memorial kindliness.

3. A more modern conception, but somewhat akin to the last, is the contrast that is seen in the two sisters between the busy, practical person and the quiet, thoughtful, or sentimental. Martha is clear-headed, practical, serving in many things, never resting so much as when serving. She would work, and keep others working, and nothing pained her so much as dust and grime. Mary, her sister, was quiet, thoughtful, and studious. She was good as gold, and she also could work. She had been busy all the morning helping her sister; but when Jesus came, she would throw up all work and sit and listen to Him, and Martha had to prepare food and serve it.

Martha supplies the business-like prose, Mary the poetry, of religion, which—though some may ask, as did Sir Isaac Newton, when *Paradise Lost* was read to him, " Very good; but what does it prove? " and others, " What does it do? "—soars into a region too high for evidences, and performs service too refined and subtle for ordinary tests. Martha rears the needful things of life in the garden of the Lord; Mary cultivates its flowers. Martha " serves " the meals of " the household of faith "; Mary brings the costly spikenard. In the Divine ceremonial, Martha gives the sacrifices, Mary the sweet incense; and as " the house was filled with the odour of her ointment," so the spiritual temple of God is fragrant with her perfumes.

Yea, Lord!—Yet some must serve.
Not all with tranquil heart,
Even at Thy dear feet,
Wrapped in devotion sweet,
May sit apart!

Yea, Lord!—Yet some must bear
  The burden of the day,
  Its labour and its heat,
  While others at Thy feet
  May muse and pray!

Yea, Lord!—Yet some must do
  Life's daily task-work; some
Who fain would sing must toil
Amid earth's dust and moil,
  While lips are dumb!

Yea, Lord!—Yet man must earn,
  And woman bake the bread!
And some must watch and wake
Early, for others' sake,
  Who pray instead!

Yea, Lord!—Yet even Thou
  Hast need of earthly care,
I bring the bread and wine
To Thee, O Guest Divine!
  Be this my prayer![1]

4. But it must not be forgotten that the difference which our
Lord Himself points out is between one who has many things on
her mind and one who has few. The words in which He rebuked
Martha are, according to the margin of the Revised Version,
which probably represents the best manuscripts: "Martha,
Martha, thou art anxious and troubled about many things, but
few things are needful, or one." The "few" things would be in
contrast with the "many" things with which, as St. Luke tells
us, Martha was troubled. Jesus thinks that Martha is preparing
a needlessly sumptuous meal, one much more elaborate than is
necessary, especially considering the cost of it to the hostess in
trouble and temper. Then the few things would be a few dishes.
Jesus really does not care to see a great display of viands got
together in honour of Himself. Much less would suffice; nay,
a single dish would be enough. That was all He had been
accustomed to at the frugal table in the carpenter's cottage at
Nazareth. He has no inclination to be the object of lavish

[1] Julia C. R. Dorr.

hospitality. Had He not said on another occasion, "My meat is to do the will of him that sent me, and to accomplish his work"? and had He not warned His disciples not to toil for the meat that perisheth? It was another thing when the labour was lovingly bestowed by generous hands for the sake of honouring Him. Still this was not the sort of honour He cared for, and He certainly could not accept it at the cost of a spoilt temper and a family quarrel. Wordsworth's ideal of "plain living and high thinking" is much nearer to the mind of Jesus.

It is true that many resent the emphasis which is in this way put upon simplicity of life and occupation. They dislike the new reading, "a few things, Martha, or one." They dislike the abandonment of an old interpretation, which has certainly had gracious results attaching to it. "You have spoiled my best sermon," said one of the Revisers when the change was agreed on. And certainly it does sound much higher to say that the one thing needful was to choose Christ and attach oneself to Him; and it looks like a bathos to make Christ peep into the kitchen and say to Martha not merely that three courses are as good as ten, but that one course is as good as three! Why should our Lord trouble to simplify life and our ideas of what life consists in? The answer is that both our happiness and our usefulness depend upon the simplifications which we introduce into life, or which He introduces for us. And the limitation works out in this way: it relieves us from distraction, and it finds us the leisure which is necessary for the cultivation of the spiritual life.

But, whether the "many" and the "one" refer to dishes at the table or not, Martha was wrong in being anxiously worried over many things that might be done, instead of attending faithfully to her single duty of the hour. This Jesus recognized, and therefore He reproved her. Mary was right in doing the one thing that was to be done, when her Divine Master and Guest wanted just that duty done, and for this Jesus commended her.

(1) One danger of giving attention to many things is to neglect the distinction between things that are important and things that are unimportant. The secret of the highest and purest success in life lies in the ability first to choose and then to make effort after those things which are of really greatest worth. Of course, together with this choice, there must be a

ceasing to strive after things of no intrinsic or permanent value. This is what Jesus meant when He said, "Seek ye first the kingdom of God and his righteousness."

¶ Much time, and thought, and means are expended on the merest framework of life; on house and dress; on excursions and evening gatherings; on useless accomplishments, and the acquirement of artificial manners and movements; while what should gladly be our great subjects of thought, if we are honest in claiming to be immortals, are too often relegated to a narrow corner of the week.[1]

(2) Another danger is restlessness, fuss, and discontent. How clearly, how vividly we see Martha, the good-hearted, bustling, over-anxious mistress and very-much-manager of the household! She is so very busy about so very many things; and all the time she is firmly convinced in her own mind that all she does and all she would provide is absolutely necessary. Not one of all this multitude of things must be wanting. Custom, and her own reputation in her own eyes and among her neighbours, demand them all. The amount of mental and physical energy which she consumed in providing and preparing and arranging the "many things" which she deemed necessary, she probably never computed, nor did she stay for a moment to consider whether she had forgotten one or two things which in intrinsic worth might be of far greater value than the sum total of all the other things about which she was busying herself. Her mind was too divided to think clearly: part of it was running on this thing and part on that, and yet another part on something else; and her bodily movements were a reflection of her mental ones. As we say, she was all the time in a bustle, running here and there, anxious, distracted, worried; and because she was so she was much inclined to blame others, even the Lord Jesus, who were really guiltless of the cause of her unhappiness.

Each to his own: yet surely I have read
    How of two sisters (each to Him was dear),
One listened but to what the Saviour said,—
        Thought to be near
The Lord Himself were best:—the other ran
Laid plates, clashed dishes, filled and set the can;

[1] G. Morrison, *The House of God*, 169,

And all to serve Him. Yet the Lord preferred
  A quiet face, and that turned up to read
The reason of His silence or His word;
  And said indeed
Somewhat, I fancy, of a better part
Near to His Feet, but nearer to His Heart.

Choose thou, then, Martha, if thou wilt; perchance
  The joy of serving is enough for thee.
Let me choose Mary; yea, love's arrogance
  Is all for me:
Nay, more than Mary—let me seek His side
And sit by Him in penitential pride.[1]

5. Is it not possible to combine them? May there not be a
Martha and a Mary in one person? At least may we not desire
to have both in the happy home? It is a grateful thought, says
Dr. John Watson, that Jesus, who was homeless and a wanderer,
who was often hungry and thirsty, who was soon to be shamefully
used and tortured, had Bethany with its two hostesses. One of
them cared for His body, and this is woman's work, so that Martha
is the patron saint of all good housewives and careful mothers
and skilful nurses; and the other entered into His thoughts and
plans, so that Mary is the chief type of the women who see
visions and understand deep things, and show us the example of
saintship. Within this haunt of Jesus were found the two people
who make the complement of religion—Martha, the type of
action; and Mary, of meditation. They stand together in the
great affairs of the Church: St. Peter and St. John, St. Francis
and St. Dominic, Erasmus and Luther; they are in our homes:
the eager, strenuous, industrious people on whom the work falls,
and the gentle, gracious, thoughtful souls, who are the consolation
and quietness of life. Between the two kinds no comparison
must be made, upon neither must any judgment be passed; both
are the friends of Jesus, and the helpers of the world.

¶ Do not let us forget amidst the sweet perfume of the
unguent that the Lord Jesus Christ *sat at meat.* I am right glad
that Mary brought the alabaster box to anoint her Lord. But I
am glad, too, that busy Martha had taken the trouble, as I am
sure she would, to get for Him just that which she thought He

[1] R. H. Benson, *Poems,* 67.

would relish most. That He should sit at meat was quite as important as the anointing, and even more necessary.[1]

> I cannot choose; I should have liked so much
> To sit at Jesus' feet,—to feel the touch
> Of His kind, gentle hand upon my head
> While drinking in the gracious words He said.
>
> And yet to serve Him!—Oh, divine employ,—
> To minister and give the Master joy,
> To bathe in coolest springs His weary feet,
> And wait upon Him while He sat at meat!
>
> Worship or service,—which? Ah, that is best
> To which He calls us, be it toil or rest,—
> To labour for Him in life's busy stir,
> Or seek His feet, a silent worshipper.[2]

[1] M. G. Pearse, *In the Banqueting House*, 111.
[2] Caroline Atherton Mason.

MARTHA.

LITERATURE.

Adeney, W. F., *Women of the New Testament* (1899), 168.

Atwool, H. C., *At His Feet* (1906), 71.

Brooke, S. A., *The Kingship of Love* (1903), 253.

Campbell, W. M., *Foot-Prints of Christ* (1889), 201.

Candlish, R. S., *Scripture Characters* (1872), 217.

Chadwick, W. E., *Christ and Everyday Life* (1910), 144.

Edersheim, A., *The Life and Times of Jesus the Messiah*, ii. (1887) 146, 312, 322, 358.

Fürst, A., *True Nobility of Character* (1884), 15.

Greenhough, J. G., in *The Call of God* (1901), 147.

Jowett, J. H., *Things that Matter Most* (1913), 200.

Leathes, A. S., *The Kingdom Within* (1910), 76.

Lockyer, T. F., *The Inspirations of the Christian Life* (1894), 226.

Mackay, W. M., *Bible Types of Modern Women* (1912), 199.

Meyer, F. B., in *The Life and Work of the Redeemer* (1901), 130.

Morris, A. J., *The Open Secret* (1869), 74.

Morrison, G., *The House of God* (1875), 159.

Murray, A., *Why do You not Believe ?* (1894), 34.

Pearse, M. G., *In the Banqueting House* (1896), 107.

Rigg, J. H., *Scenes and Studies in the Ministry of Our Lord* (1901), 133, 156.

Russell, A., *The Light that Lighteth every Man* (1889), 225.

Rutherford, R., *That Good Part* (1891), 1.

Stimson, H. A., *The New Things of God* (1908), 141.

Thomas, E., *Jesus the Home Friend*, 43.

Thompson, J. R., *Burden Bearing* (1905), 135.

Trumbull, H. C., *Our Misunderstood Bible* (1907), 217.

MARTHA.

Martha, Martha, thou art anxious and troubled about many things.—
Luke x. 41.

WE have already seen that the contrast between Martha and
Mary of Bethany may be taken in more ways than one, and that
it is possible to look at the sisters as complementary, what is
strong in the one character balancing what is weak in the other,
and so giving us a woman that is according to the full stature of
womanhood in Christ. Let us now dismiss from our minds the
idea of comparison. Let us take Martha by herself and Mary by
herself. Enough is told us in the Gospels to make each of them
a profitable study.

Taking Martha first, we notice that of the three occasions on
which we see the sisters in their home in Bethany, Martha is
prominent on the first two occasions, but is merely mentioned as
present—and characteristically *serving*—on the third occasion.
We may therefore leave that incident to Mary in which she has
the leading place. We shall thus look first at Martha's Faults
and then at Martha's Faith.

I.

MARTHA'S FAULTS.

1. Martha makes a strong appeal to the present generation,
especially to comfort-loving men and energetic women. We
respond with approval to the words which George Eliot puts into
the mouth of one of her characters in *Scenes of Clerical Life*:
" I've nothing to say again' her piety, my dear ; but I know very
well I shouldn't like her to cook my victual. When a man comes
in hungry an' tired, piety won't feed him, I reckon. Hard carrots
ull lie heavy on his stomach, piety or no piety. I called in one

day when she was dishin' up Mr. Tryan's dinner, an' I could see the potatoes was as watery as watery. It's right enough to be speritial—I'm no enemy to that; but I like my potatoes mealy. I don't see as anybody 'ull go to heaven the sooner for not digestin' their dinner—providin' they don't die sooner, as mayhap Mr. Tryan will, poor dear man."

¶ But even the comfort-loving husband or bachelor is compelled sometimes to wish for a little neglect. Dr. Rendel Harris asks: Did you ever have your papers put in order, or your books dusted? Was not the person who undertook that arduous task of the opposite sex and of the sisterhood of St. Martha? Is not the sorting of papers and the rehabilitation of the outsides of books as much a matter of feminine diaconate as the peeling of potatoes or the beating of eggs? But I need not labour the point: it has been done for me by Dr. John Watson in his story of Rabbi Saunderson. Rabbi Saunderson had a housekeeper whose name was Mrs. Pitillo (Martha Pitillo was her long name, for certain), and he tells us of her gifts in the following strain:—

"She had the episcopal faculty in quite a conspicuous degree, and was, I have often thought, a woman of sound judgment.

"We were not able at all times to see eye to eye, as she had an unfortunate tendency to meddle with my books and papers, and to arrange them after an artificial fashion. This she called tidying and, in its most extreme form, cleaning. With all her excellences, there was also in her what I have noticed in most women, a flavour of guile, and on one occasion, when I was making a brief journey through Holland and France in search of comely editions of the Fathers, she had the books carried out into the garden and dusted. It was the space of two years before I regained mastery of my library again, and unto this day I cannot lay my hands on the Service-book of King Henry VIII., which I had in the second edition, to say nothing of an original edition of Rutherford's *Lex Rex*. It does not become me, however, to reflect on the efforts of that worthy woman, and, if any one could be saved by good works, her place is assured. I was with her before she died, and her last words to me were, 'Tell Jean tae dust yir bukes ance in sax months, and for ony sake keep ae chair for sittin' on.' It was not perhaps the testimony one would have desired in the circumstances, but yet, Mr. Carmichael, I have often thought that there was a spirit of—of unselfishness, in fact, that showed the working of grace." [1]

2. It is easy for us all to sympathize with Martha in her

---

[1] J. Rendel Harris, *Aaron's Breastplate*, 67.

desire to entertain Jesus worthily. It must have seemed to her
as if she could not do enough in showing Him all hospitality.
And, indeed, this festive season was a busy time for the mistress
of a wealthy household, especially in the near neighbourhood of
Jerusalem, whence her brother might, after the first two festive
days, bring with him honoured guests from the city.

But it is evident that Martha got some harm as well as some
good out of Jesus' visit; for she seems to have been sadly flustered
and flurried, and even somewhat peevish and irritable. She seems
indeed to have been out of temper with the Master as well as with
her sister, and to have implied some little reproach on Him as
well as on Mary. But why all this disturbance and irritation?
Surely it all came of this, that she was thinking more of serving
Christ than of pleasing Him. If she had paused to reflect, she
must have seen that a sharp, half-reproachful word, and the
obvious loss of composure and temper, would cause the Master a
good deal more pain than the best-served meal in the world could
give Him pleasure. She was busy about Christ, but she failed to
enter into sympathy with Christ. She waited upon Him outwardly, but she did not understand how to minister to His
inmost Spirit; and so, even while inviting and welcoming Christ
into her household, she forfeited that peace and calm which it is
Christ's joy to bring to His own.

We need not question Martha's love to Christ. What we
must question, however, is whether she made her service the fruit
of her love. In all the New Testament works are approved and
appreciated, but they follow faith and are the outcome of love.
Think, for example, of some of the homely truths insisted on by
St. Paul. They are the plain, simple duties such as ordinary men
and women are called upon to perform in the home and in society,
but he puts them on a footing quite different from ordinary
standards and ideas. If we read, for example, his Epistle to the
Romans we shall see, first of all, the great principles of the faith
laid down. The great facts of God's relation to and dealing with
man are first of all enumerated; then, as a consequence of this,
on no lower ground, duty—plain, simple, everyday duty inspired
by God. It is just the same when we read his Epistles to the
Ephesians and to the Colossians: the plan and purpose join duty
to the highest and greatest of all sources. It is Mary first of all

at the feet of Jesus, choosing the better part that shall not be taken away, and presently doing, in the inspiration of it, little acts of duty, which become new things with a new power under its influence, new adornments to her character, new tokens of her love. The love of Christ which constraineth us must be precisely such a power as that—always directing us, always with us, so vast in its greatness that no crisis can come to our lives in which it cannot help us, so fine and penetrating in its power that the simplest little acts rest just as truly upon it as the greatest deeds to which our Master shall ever call us. The glory of a true womanhood is in that tenderness and care which sees that nothing is too small to be performed faithfully, for the consecrating power of love can produce from these little things a rich spiritual harvest.

¶ Unutterably precious to me is the woman, the native of the hills, almost my own age, or a little younger, whose spirit is set upon the finest springs, and her sympathies have an almost masculine depth, and a length of reflection that wins your confidence, and stays your sinking heart. The lady can't do it. This class, of what I suppose you would call peasant women (I won't have the word), seems made for the purpose of rectifying everything, and redressing the balance, inspiring us with that awe which the immediate presence of absolute womanhood creates in us. The plain, practical woman, with the outspoken throat and the eternal eyes. Oh, mince me, madam, mince me your pretty mincings! Deliberate your dainty reticences! Balbutient loveliness, avaunt! Here is a woman that talks like a bugle, and, in everything, sees God.[1]

3. The dangers of giving the first place to the work itself are many. We may notice these five: Absorption, Fussiness, Worry, Temper, and Fault-finding.

(1) *Absorption.*—We know that Christian work in itself is intensely interesting; indeed, there is nothing more likely to become engrossing. We all know how absorbed men may become in their own special pursuits. For instance, we have read about Sir Isaac Newton, who used to be so absorbed in his mathematical and astronomical researches that he was scarcely able to give a thought to the common duties and circumstances of life, and used frequently to make the most ridiculous blunders about common-

[1] *Letters of T. E. Brown.*

place things, because he took so profound an interest in, and was so fully occupied with, his own great discoveries. And so it is with other branches of knowledge. When men devote their attention to a particular branch of knowledge or science, it becomes a sort of passion, and they no longer find it necessary to stimulate themselves to exertion in that particular; rather they have to check or curb themselves, in order to prevent their minds from becoming too deeply absorbed in their favourite studies. And it sometimes happens that when the mind is given over to some special pursuit, interest in their work becomes so keen that men seem to lose all power of checking themselves, and their brains go on working, as it were, automatically, when they do not intend them to be working at all.

¶ I well remember some years ago hearing a touching story of a late Cambridge professor, who was one of the greatest Greek scholars of our time. For some few months before he died he was advised by his friends to shut up his books, give up his studies, and go as much as possible into social life, in order that he might be drawn away from those subjects in which his mind had become so absorbed that his constitution was impaired; indeed, he was threatened with softening of the brain. On one occasion he was in a drawing-room surrounded by cheerful company, when a half-sad smile passed over his countenance as he observed to a friend, "What is the use of you shutting up my books and not allowing me to work? While I have been here I have traced the derivations of three distinct Greek words, and detected their connection with certain Sanscrit roots." Such was the force of his ruling passion.[1]

¶ When I was immersed in some foolish cogitations, my father, who was a good angler, would come into my study on a fine breezy day, and ask me to go with him to the banks of the Don or the Deveron, to indulge in a few days' fishing. A reasonable young man and a good son would have jumped at this, but I obeyed with indifference, because that particular excursion did not suit my humour, or rather had not been shaped out in my plans; and instead of being good company to my father, jogged on behind, humming a tune to myself! . . . Such is the evil growth and the unkindly fruit of every sort of self-absorption, however pious, or poetical, or philosophical. The worst kind of selfishness, no doubt, is that kind of aggressive greed which is never satisfied with its own, and feeds upon appropriating what

[1] W. H. M. H. Aitken, *The Highway of Holiness*, 159.

belongs to others. But it is selfishness also, and of a most unhuman kind, when a man systematically denies himself to his fellows, and does not readily yield himself to the claims which one man, in a thousand shapes, is entitled to make on another.[1]

(2) *Fussiness.*—Martha is not so much active as fussy; there is no sense of beauty or peace in her work, save that of getting ready for the Master's meal; none of that element of self-forgetfulness which is of so deep a necessity for the religious life of mankind.

Now to correct this noisy fussiness we need to learn to imitate Mary and to sit at Jesus' feet, and in silence and stillness of soul to hear His words. No amount of service will make up for the loss of this inward and secret fellowship of the soul with Christ—this hidden life of love, in which Christ and the consecrated heart are bound together in a certain holy intimacy and familiarity. This it is that sanctifies even the most commonplace toil, and the loss of this robs even the holiest things of their sanctity. At Jesus' feet—that is our place of privilege and of blessing, and here it is that we are to be educated and fitted for the practical duties of life. Here we are to renew our strength while we wait on Him, and to learn how to mount on wings as eagles; and here we are to become possessed of that true knowledge which is power. Here we are to learn how real work is to be done, and to be armed with the true motive-power to do it. Here we are to find solace amidst both the trials of work—and they are not few—and the trials of life in general; and here we are to anticipate something of the blessedness of heaven amidst the days of earth; for to sit at His feet is indeed to be in heavenly places, and to gaze upon His glory is to do what we shall never tire of doing yonder.

¶ In the vocabularies of the early Christians there is a word which is difficult to translate. It is the word σχολάζω—the Christian takes time, or has leisure. It occurs in the First Epistle to the Corinthians (1 Cor. vii. 5)—"that ye may have leisure for prayer." So in Polycarp: "The Christian takes time for prayer" (σχολάζει). And the corresponding Latin word *vacat* is everywhere in some classes of writers: shall we translate it, "The Christian is free for Christ, is free for prayer"? Well, it is only by the culture and habits of the spiritual life that this

---

[1] J. S. Blackie, *Notes of a Life*, 36.

blessed leisure and beautiful vacancy and long-expected holiday is obtained. And if we insist on going into all the pleasures, knowing all the people, having everything handsome about us, and the like, we shall never know either the life of the turtle-dove or the perfume and beauty of the lily. And we may say nearly the same thing over people that insist on going to meetings every night in the week, and are too tired to talk to the Lord either when they lie down or when they rise up. As St. Bernard says, they are a very dusty people; and if they had known better, they might have been covered with another kind of dust, of which the Psalmist speaks when he talks of "wings of a dove covered with silver, and her feathers with yellow gold." [1]

¶ Nothing annoyed Dr. Temple more—though in this he was not singular among bishops—than the fussing of officials, lay or clerical, at Confirmations. The vicar or curate who made himself over-active or prominent in his efforts to marshal the candidates was pretty certain to be beckoned and curtly reprimanded in two words—"Don't fidget!" [2]

> One lesson, Nature, let me learn of thee,
> One lesson which in every wind is blown,
> One lesson of two duties kept at one
> Though the loud world proclaim their enmity—
>
> Of toil unsever'd from tranquillity;
> Of labour, that in lasting fruit outgrows
> Far noisier schemes, accomplish'd in repose,
> Too great for haste, too high for rivalry.
>
> Yes, while on earth a thousand discords ring,
> Man's fitful uproar mingling with his toil,
> Still do thy sleepless ministers move on,
>
> Their glorious tasks in silence perfecting;
> Still working, blaming still our vain turmoil,
> Labourers that shall not fail, when man is gone. [3]

(3) *Worry.*—Martha was worried. If she had not been worried she would not have burst into Christ's presence with her complaint of Mary. Now worry is never a help in any proper occupation of man or woman. It is a hindrance in any and every

---

[1] J. R. Harris, *Aaron's Breastplate*, 75.
[2] *Memoirs of Archbishop Temple*, ii. 179.
[3] Matthew Arnold.

line of practical service. Particularly is it true that in house-keeping, where woman is at her best, and where her power is greatest for good to all those who are within the sacred circle of home influence as permanent members or occasional visitors, worry and fretting and trouble of mind are only disturbing elements, tending to the lessening of the matron's power, and to the discomfort of all who are in any way dependent on her for comfort or supply. On the contrary, quietness of mind, restful-ness of spirit, and composure of manner, are elements of power in a housekeeper, and of good to all who are affected by her efforts or labours.

To be "cumbered," as Jesus said Martha was, is, as the Greek word means, to be "distracted," to be drawn this way and that, instead of being intent on the one thing to be done. Even in getting a dinner, or in doing anything else, Martha, in the exercise of this trait, could not give her whole attention to the one thing she had to do. In this Martha lacked the main essential of a good housekeeper—the ability to give her undivided attention to the one thing she had to do for the time being. This is clearly implied or included in the rebuke of Jesus. Again, to be "anxious," as the Revision reads, or to be "careful," as the old version gave it, and "troubled" about many things, is to be per-plexed and in a tumult as to pressing duty. That, surely, was not right in Martha, and Jesus plainly pointed out her error. We are distinctly told not to be anxious or to be troubled at any time, and the housekeeper or the business man who fails at this point fails in a vital matter.

The specific faults of worrying and being drawn away from the one duty of the hour, and of being over-anxious, that Jesus pointed out in Martha, are as clearly reprehended and warned against in the Sermon on the Mount and elsewhere as are theft and murder; yet, strange to say, Martha is often commended by professing Christians, not in spite of her faults, but as if those very faults were admirable. Comfort-loving husbands sometimes think of Mary as a pious do-nothing, who might be fitted for a high place in the future life, but who was not fitted for this life. Martha, on the other hand, is considered by them as the sort of practical housekeeper who would have the dinner ready on time, and the rooms swept, and the beds made. In their opinion, she is the kind of housekeeper for the average home. Some active and efficient wives and housekeepers are even willing to speak of themselves frankly as "busy Marthas," when they would never want to be called "lively Sapphiras." This they do, not by way of admitting their unworthiness and incompetence, but in the thought that they are claiming a share of real merit.

¶ At the time of the Boxer Rising in China, when foreigners were being massacred and their property destroyed, the Viceroy wrote in his diary on June 15, 1900:

"My wife declares that I shall become insane over these national troubles. She is wrong, just as she often is. I should go insane if I had nothing to bother me. My normal mental state for half a century has been that of perturbation. Perhaps it is well that the Patriotic Peace Fists are giving me something to worry over, thus keeping my mind in its normal state."[1]

¶ I have often occasion to converse with poor people about their little worries, their cares and trials; and from the ingenious way in which they put them, so as to make them look their very worst, it is sometimes easy to see that the poor man or woman has been brooding for long hours over the painful thing, turning it in all different ways, till the thing has been got into that precise point of view in which it looks its very ugliest. It is like one of those gutta-percha heads, squeezed into its most hideous grin. And I have thought, how long this poor soul must have persisted in looking at nothing but this dreary prospect before finding out so accurately the spot whence it looks most dreary.[2]

(4) *Temper.*—It seems clear that poor Martha had lost her temper. Instead of quietly calling Mary to her assistance she complained to her Guest of her sister's conduct, actually seeking His interference to secure the aid that was not forthcoming voluntarily. Will anyone say that this act of Martha's was courteous or considerate toward her Guest? Would it be polite or kindly or proper toward a guest in your house, whom you were entertaining, or preparing to entertain, to burst in upon him when he was talking with another member of the family, and to suggest to him bluntly that he ought to know better than to keep away from her proper work in the household a needed member of the family with whom he was conversing? Can a woman be called

---

[1] *Memoirs of the Viceroy Li Hung Chang,* 242.
[2] A. K. H. Boyd, *Recreations of a Country Parson,* ii. 129.

a good housekeeper who would conduct herself in this way as a hostess?

Martha is quite indignant, and does not care to conceal it. And there are people of her class who, while they are very useful in a church, and do a great deal of work, are very frequently indeed, like Martha, somewhat short-tempered. They have a great deal of energy, and a great deal of enthusiasm; but when things do not go exactly as they wish, the hasty word soon slips out, and the unpleasant thought is harboured, and that soon takes all the joy and all the blessing out of Christian work. How often is the work of the Church marred by this hasty spirit, and the Master grieved in our very attempts to honour Him!

¶ I heard somewhere an old legend which spake of Martha, who was preparing to entertain the Lord Christ at the evening meal. The room was ready, and the table was spread. All was peaceful and comfortable within. Outside a storm was raging, the wind was howling, and the rain beating. Suddenly Martha heard a knock at the door, and hastened to open it, expecting to see Jesus. But there stood instead a weary, ragged, desolate beggar, who murmured, "I am hungry. Give me bread. Give me bread." "No," cried Martha, "I have no time for beggars. I am going to entertain the Lord Christ." And she slammed the door in the beggar's face. Shortly after, there came another knock, and again Martha opened the door. This time there stood a half-famished, white-faced little child, who moaned, "Give me bread. Give me bread." "No," cried Martha, "I have no time for children. I am going to entertain the Lord Christ." And as the angry woman was about to slam the door, the child vanished, and there stood the sublime figure of Jesus, who said, "Inasmuch as ye did it not unto one of these, my brethren, even these least, ye did it not unto me."[1]

(5) *Fault-finding.*—Jesus was pleased with the activity of Martha so far as it was driven by affection. The loving care in it allured Him and won His regard. No reproof could well be kinder than His. What jarred Him was the blame she gave to Mary, and the claim she made to have her work and anxiety extolled; for, indeed, that piece of selfish claim lies hid beneath her words.

¶ It seems at first sight that finding fault with others is rather a noble and conscientious thing to do; if you are quite sure that

[1] C. E. Walters, *The Deserted Christ*, 133.

MARTHA

you are right, and have a strong belief in the virtuous and high quality of your own principles, you begin to practise what is called dealing faithfully with other people, pulling them up, checking them, drenching them with good advice, improving the tone. Such people often say that of course they do not like doing it, but that they must bear witness to what they believe to be right. Of course, it is sometimes necessary in this world to protest; but the worst of the censorious habit of mind is this, that it begins with principles and then extends to preferences. . . . One of the things which it is absolutely necessary to do in life is to distinguish between principles and preferences; and even if one holds principles very strongly, it is generally better to act up to them, and to trust to the effect of example, than to bump other people, as Dickens said, into paths of peace.[1]

¶ There are a good many Marthas in our Universities, and they belong to both sexes. How common it is to hear grudging praise given, and the student complaining of the better luck which has given undue advantage to his neighbour. Now, there may be undue advantage in circumstances, and there often is. But according to my experience it makes far less difference in the long run than is popularly supposed. What does make the difference is tenacity of purpose. A man succeeds in four cases out of five, because of what is in him, by unflagging adhesion to his plan of life, and not by reason of outside help or luck. It is rarely that he need be afraid of shouldering an extra burden to help either himself or a neighbour. The strain it imposes on him is compensated by the strength that effort and self-discipline bring. And therefore the complaints of our Marthas are mainly beside the point. They arise from the old failing of self-centredness—the failing which has many forms, ranging from a mild selfishness up to ego-mania. And in whatever form the failing may clothe itself it produces weakness.[2]

II.

MARTHA'S FAITH.

In that most pathetic story of the raising of Lazarus from the dead which is related in the Fourth Gospel, Martha has a prominent place. Her sorrow is great, but in that she does not

[1] A. C. Benson, *Along the Road*, 92.
[2] Lord Haldane, *The Conduct of Life*, 17.

notably differ from her sister. What is peculiar to Martha is the test that is made of her faith.

It is Martha who receives the great words from Jesus about the resurrection. She takes with dreary acquiescence His promise that Lazarus shall rise again, supposing it to be a conventional consolation referring to the orthodox Jewish doctrine of a general resurrection at the end of the world. There is little comfort for her in that. It is true enough. She knows it already. Has she not been taught it from her childhood? But that mysterious event is very remote. If only Jesus had been in time she would have had her brother restored to her in this life, a very different thing. Then Jesus proceeds to His own profound teaching about the resurrection.

"If Thou hadst come, our brother had not died."
    Thus one who loved, to One who came so late;
    Yet not too late, had she but known the fate
Which soon should fill the mourners' hearts with tide
Of holy joy. Now she would almost chide
    Her awful Guest, as though His brief delay
    Had quenched her love and driven faith away.
"If Thou hadst come," oh could we only hide
    Our heart's impatience and with meekness stay
To hear the Voice of Wisdom ere we speak.
We mourn the past, the tomb, the buried dead,
    And think of many a bitter thing to say,
While all the time True Love stands by so meek,
    Waiting to lift anew the drooping head.[1]

Martha's faith had broken down before that awful sepulchre. Up to the time when her brother died she had believed, as most religious Jews believed, the traditional theory about the dead and their resurrection. She had believed they would sleep in the dust with no conscious existence at all until some far-off last day, and then "the just, at least, would be raised from the dust and begin life again." She had believed it, as we all believe the things that we have been told, because she never had cause to doubt it. But then the testing came. The grim fact of death confronted her. For the first time in her life, perhaps, she saw it in its naked, terrible reality. It had seized and laid low and turned to

[1] George Matheson.

corruption the one being whom she probably loved best on earth. And when she saw the body carried to the grave and hidden out of sight there, her heart sank like a lump of lead, her hope of resurrection faded out like a torchlight quickly quenched. And when the Lord said, "Thy brother shall rise again," she answered in words that were purely mechanical, words repeated from memory, with no faith in them: "I know that he shall rise again at the last day." There was no comfort at all in that. He was dead to her for ever. And then Jesus, knowing the blank cold faithlessness which had crept over her, repeated the gracious promise and assurance of immortality: "He that believeth on me, though he die, yet shall he live: and whosoever liveth and believeth on me shall never die," and finished with the question, "Believest thou this?" And this word and Martha's answer suggest certain thoughts.

The words of Jesus are too great and wonderful to be fully taken in at once, and it may not be easy to accept on its own account what is perceived in them. But Martha has full faith in Christ, and on that ground she does not hesitate to assent to what He says. She believes that Jesus is no other than the Christ, the Son of God, the Great One expected by her people. Such a clear confession as this, uttered in circumstances of the greatest depression, at once places the speaker in the very front rank of the disciples of Jesus. It may be set side by side with St. Peter's historic confession at Cæsarea Philippi. The wonder of it is that this glorious outburst of faith was possible at the very time when the inexplicable conduct of Jesus was the occasion of the keenest disappointment. That is what marks Martha's faith as sublime. It would not have been at all surprising if a faith which under ordinary circumstances was serene and settled should have been disturbed and overclouded at such a moment as this. Had it been so we could have pardoned the distressed sister, setting down to her love for her brother and the intense grief at a loss which she thought Jesus might have prevented, some temporary lack of confidence in the Master who had tried her so severely. There is nothing of the kind. The earthly scene is gloomy as the grave; but not a shadow passes over her heavens. Faith rises triumphant, and in spite of an amazing disappointment perceives with clear vision and declares with unfaltering voice the supreme truth that He who was the very occasion of the dis-appointment was the Christ of God.

¶ Nowhere is the majesty of our Lord more impressively expressed than in His dealings with death. Mythology records how Hercules successfully wrestled with Death, and brought back to the upper world the body of Alcestis. But how pale is the classic fable by the side of the resurrections of the New Testament! Here a mightier Hercules smote the King of Terrors. "He brought to naught him that hath the power of death." Let this fact comfort me in the prospect of death, in the article of death. Christ is everything to me to-day, and He will not be less on my last day. No; then He will be specially precious.[1]

¶ In course of a letter to a lady sympathizing with her on the death of her father, Maurice wrote, "The Apostle said that 'if the Spirit of Christ dwells in us he shall also quicken our mortal bodies.' Why not believe that those words are spoken simply and sincerely; that they represent facts which have been accomplished, which are accomplishing themselves every hour? You are weary of words which you have heard from me and others about some final deliverance of the human spirit from its sin and woe. You cannot be too weary of them if they interfere in the least degree with the message, 'I am the resurrection and the life,' which was spoken once to a woman sorrowing for her brother, which is spoken now by the same voice to every woman sorrowing for brother, father, husband, child; an ever-present warrant for all hope of a future resurrection, of a future life. Not a future but an eternal life, the life of God, the life of love, is what Christ tells us of."[2]

> Alas for him who never sees
> The stars shine through his cypress-trees!
> Who, hopeless, lays his dead away,
> Nor looks to see the breaking day
> Across the mournful marbles play!
> Who hath not learned, in hours of faith,
>   The truth to flesh and sense unknown,
> That Life is ever lord of Death,
>   And Love can never lose its own![3]

[1] W. L. Watkinson, *The Gates of Dawn*, 233.
[2] *The Life of Frederick Denison Maurice*, ii. 623.
[3] J. G. Whittier, *Snow-Bound*.

MARY.

LITERATURE.

Adeney, W. F., *Women of the New Testament* (1899), 168.
Aitken, W. H. M. H., *The Highway of Holiness*, 141, 157.
Alexander, A., *The Glory in the Grey* (1915), 22.
Allon, H., *The Vision of God* (1877), 117.
Bain, J. A., *Questions Answered by Christ* (1908), 81.
Binney, T., *Sermons*, ii. (1875) 188.
Bushnell, H., *Christ and His Salvation*, 89.
Caird, J., *Essays for Sunday Reading* (1906), 59.
Campbell, R. J., *The Song of Ages* (1905), 109.
Dawson, W. J., *The Reproach of Christ* (1903), 97.
Denney, J., *The Way Everlasting* (1911), 282.
Edersheim, A., *The Life and Times of Jesus the Messiah*, ii. (1887) 146, 312, 322, 358.
Forbes, J. T., *God's Measure* (1898), 21.
Hall, W. A. N., *The Radiant Life* (1914), 36.
Hart, H. G., *Sermons Preached in Sedbergh School Chapel* (1901), 146.
Lewis, A., *Sermons Preached in England* (1906), 89.
Liddon, H. P., *Passiontide Sermons* (1891), 227.
Macaulay, A. B., *The Word of the Cross* (1914), 172.
McFadyen, J. E., *The City with Foundations* (1909), 63.
Matheson, G., *Thoughts for Life's Journey* (1907), 54.
Morrison, G. H., *Flood-Tide* (1901), 92.
Neff, F., in *Drew Sermons for 1910* (1909), 259.
Peabody, F. G., *Mornings in the College Chapel*, ii. (1908) 182.
Pearse, M. G., *In the Banqueting House* (1896), 107.
Purves, P. C., *The Divine Cure for Heart Trouble* (1905), 163.
Rigg, J. H., *Scenes and Studies in the Ministry of Our Lord* (1901), 133, 156.
Ritchie, D. L., *Peace the Umpire*, 79.
Skrine, J. H., *Saints and Worthies* (1901), 128.
Tuckwell, W., *Nuggets from the Bible Mine* (1913), 179.
Walters, C. E., *The Deserted Christ* (1910), 125.
Watson, J., *The Inspiration of Our Faith* (1905), 1.

MARY.

Mary hath chosen the good part, which shall not be taken away from her.—Luke x. 42.

THE company of good women was to Jesus, as to many other delicate and spiritual natures, a relief and refreshment, because He found Himself in an atmosphere of emotion and sympathy. The sisters of Bethany were of different types, although one in kindness and loyalty, and their separate individualities stand out in relief from the story. Martha was chiefly concerned that their Guest should be served, and her desire was to compass Him with every observance of hospitality. She was full of plans for His comfort and rest, so that for once He should have no care or burden. Her energy and ingenuity, all inspired by love, were unceasing, and showed the traces of that religious spirit which knows no quietness, and expends itself in the works of charity It was inevitable that Martha should be impatient at times with Mary, to whom this bustle of goodness was altogether foreign. The joy of Mary was to sit at the Master's feet and drink in every word which fell from His lips, for here was that religion which hides truth within the heart as great treasure. Martha was concerned with what is external, Mary with what is spiritual; and if the Master gently chided Martha, He was not indifferent to her solicitude for Him; and if He praised Mary, it was not for inaction, but for inwardness.

There are three occasions recorded on which Jesus was with the Bethany family, and on each occasion Mary's character is clearly revealed. On the first occasion she was a Learner, on the next a Mourner, and on the third a Worshipper.

I.

THE LEARNER.

1. Mary "sat at the Lord's feet, and heard his word." Several thoughts suggest themselves to our minds as we see her sitting there. Let us dwell upon them for a few moments.

(1) First, sitting at His feet she is taking the place of the lowly; and only those who wish to be such can learn of Jesus. The proud and self-confident, whether they be intellectually proud, or morally proud, or spiritually proud, will ever have to go empty away; but "such as are gentle, them shall He learn His way."

¶ My time fails me—my thoughts how much more—in trying to imagine what this sweet world will be when the meek inherit it indeed, and the lowliness of *every* faithful handmaiden has been regarded of her Lord. For the day *will* come, the expectation of the poor shall not perish for ever. Not by might, nor by power, but by His Spirit—the meek shall He guide in judgment, and the meek shall He teach His way.[1]

(2) Next, it is the place of true honour and dignity; for it is better to be a junior scholar in the school of Christ than to be a distinguished philosopher untaught by Him. It used to be the boast of the ancient Christian apologists that the merest babe in Christ was familiar with the true solution of problems that had vainly exercised the greatest thinkers of the heathen world. We may still affirm that there is an inward and practical knowledge of God and of His relations with us which can never be acquired by any acquaintance with the mere theory of religion, or by any educational process save that which takes place when, in all humility of soul and self-distrust, we sit at Jesus' feet.

¶ Let all our employment be to know God; the more one knows Him, the more one desires to know Him. And as knowledge is commonly the measure of love, the deeper and more extensive our knowledge shall be, the greater our love; and if our love of God were great, we should love Him equally in pains and pleasures.[2]

[1] Ruskin, *Fors Clavigera*, Letter xciii. (*Works*, xxix. 476).
[2] Brother Lawrence.

'Tis joy enough, my All in All,
At Thy dear feet to lie;
Thou wilt not let me lower fall,
And none can higher fly.[1]

(3) While she was sitting there she was in a position, not only to learn by Him, but to learn of Him. It was not merely that she heard the truth from Him; it was rather that she found the truth in Him. He was Himself to her the Truth. She found in Him the "Word of God." Everything about Him spoke—that tender earnestness, that womanlike sympathy, that manly indignation against all that was false and mean and hypocritical. His winsome manner, His benevolent expression, the eloquent glance of those eyes, now sorrowful or plaintive, now kindling into vehement flame, His look, His features, even the very tones of His voice—all seemed to her a revelation, and such a revelation as rendered her heart spellbound, as by the charm of some great Enchanter, while she drank in the wondrous lessons and felt the new, strange joy of such discoveries in her heart.

¶ The pure in heart shall see the truth means that—given equal data and the same intellectual advantage—the morally better man will strike the truth more nearly, will be more happy in his guesses and ventures, since he is more in harmony with reality, more subtly responsive to its hints. Not only the mind but the whole soul is the organ of truth. . . . Christ is not merely a truth to be believed, but a way to be trodden, a life to be lived. We get to know Christ as fellow-travellers, fellow-workers, fellow-soldiers get to know one another—by mingling their lives together.[2]

2. What is the result of sitting at Christ's feet? One good result we see in the case of Mary. When her sister bursts upon them with the complaint, "Lord, dost thou not care that my sister did leave me to serve alone?" she makes no retort. Keble observed this with satisfaction: "She goes on quietly sitting at our Lord's feet; perhaps she does not even hear her sister's complaint, so entirely is she taken up with listening to His sacred and gracious word. Or if she thinks at all of what Martha is saying, her thought is just this, that she will leave it to Jesus to reply for her. She says to herself what the Psalmist said when

---

[1] Cowper.   [2] George Tyrrell, *Oil and Wine*.

he heard men speaking mischievous things against him: 'I, as a deaf man, heard not; and I was as a dumb man that openeth not his mouth.' The Psalmist then said, and Mary seems to say with him, in silence, 'In thee, O Lord, do I hope: thou wilt hear, O Lord my God.'"

"O sister! leave you thus undone
    The bidding of the Lord;
Or call you this a welcome? Run
    And deck with me the board."
Thus Martha spake: but spake to one
    Who answered not a word:
        For she kept ever singing,
        "There is no joy so sweet,
    As musing upon one we love
        And sitting at His feet!"

"O sister! must my hands alone
    His board and bath prepare?
His eyes are on you! raise your own:
    He'll find a welcome there!"
Thus spake again, in loftier tone,
    That Hebrew woman fair.
        But Mary still kept singing,
        "There is no joy so sweet,
    As musing upon Him we love
        And resting at His feet."[1]

II.

THE MOURNER.

When Mary is next introduced to our notice she is again at Jesus' feet, and this time she is at His feet as a mourner. "Then when Mary was come where Jesus was, and saw him, she fell down at his feet, saying unto him, Lord, if thou hadst been here, my brother had not died" (John xi. 32). And she did not say any more. She had placed the matter in Christ's hands, and there she lay at His feet in her sorrow. Blessed are those mourners whom sorrow gently leads to Jesus' feet!

[1] Aubrey de Vere.

The scene is described by Edersheim: It seems that the Master "called" for Mary. This message Martha now hasted to deliver, although "secretly." Mary was probably sitting in the chamber of mourning, with its upset chairs and couches and other melancholy tokens of mourning, as was the custom; surrounded by many who had come to comfort them; herself, we can scarcely doubt, silent, her thoughts far away in that world to and of which the Master was to her "the Way, the Truth, and the Life." As she heard of His coming and call, she rose "quickly," and the Jews followed her, under the impression that she was again going to visit and to weep at the tomb of her brother. For it was the practice to visit the grave, especially during the first three days. When she came to Jesus, where He still stood, outside Bethany, she was forgetful of all around. It was as if sight of Him melted what had frozen the tide of her feelings. She could only fall at His feet and repeat the poor words with which she and her sister had these four weary days tried to cover the nakedness of their sorrow.

Not a word more is said of Mary at this time. She is left at the feet of Jesus, comforted.

¶ There is a point beyond which neither the experience of others nor even the utterances of the inspired Word can instruct or comfort the heart; it must have rejoicing in itself and not in any other; it must learn of its Lord as none save Himself can teach. Its prayer is, "Make me to hear thy voice." It knows much about Jesus, *but it desires to know Him*; it can no longer rest in opinions, in ordinances, in Christianity received as a system, in anything save in Christ, and in actual communion with Him.[1]

III.

THE WORSHIPPER.

1. Jesus had arrived at Bethany six days before the Passover— that is, on a Friday. The day after was the Sabbath, and "they made him a supper." It was the special festive meal of the Sabbath. The words of St. John seem to indicate that the meal was a public one, as if the people of Bethany had combined to do

[1] Dora Greenwell, *The Patience of Hope*, 103.

Him this honour, and so share the privilege of attending the feast. In point of fact, we know from St. Matthew and St. Mark that it took place "in the house of Simon the leper"—not, of course, an actual leper, but one who had been such. Perhaps his guest-chamber was the largest in Bethany; perhaps the house was nearest to the synagogue; or there may have been other reasons for it, unknown to us—least likely is the suggestion that Simon was the husband of Martha, or else her father. But all is in character.

Again Martha is serving, but she no longer complains of her more impassioned sister; again Mary is worshipping, in a characteristic way pouring forth the great passionate love of her heart: both are rapt and adoring worshippers now. Memories of the past are crowding upon them. The solemn scenes of the Passover are just at hand, and their hearts are full of indefinable premonitions. Another Sabbath, and their Lord will have endured His Passion, and Mary will be weeping at the sepulchre.

Under some great impulse of love, Mary produces her precious box of ointment, and pours it upon the head and feet of her Lord.

> Her eyes are homes of silent prayer,
>   Nor other thought her mind admits
>   But, he was dead, and there he sits,
> And He that brought him back is there.
>
> Then one deep love doth supersede
>   All other, when her ardent gaze
>   Roves from the living brother's face,
> And rests upon the Life indeed.
>
> All subtle thought, all curious fears,
>   Borne down by gladness so complete,
>   She bows, she bathes the Saviour's feet
> With costly spikenard and with tears.
>
> Thrice blest whose lives are faithful prayers,
>   Whose loves in higher love endure;
>   What souls possess themselves so pure,
> Or is there blessedness like theirs? [1]

This was no ordinary anointing. It was distinguished by the costliness of the perfume, and by the lavish generosity with

[1] Tennyson, *In Memoriam.*

which it was poured out. Not a word was said; the act itself
said all that was necessary to those who were worthy to understand it. An ancient Greek poet describes his poems as " having
a voice for the intelligent," and this woman's act has the character
of a poem. It has the "loveliness of perfect deeds, more strong
than all poetic thought." In some way it must have come from a
sense of debt to Jesus. Mary owed to the Lord what she could
never repay. She had sat at His feet and heard His word. She
had received her brother again from the dead; she had herself
received the life eternal. She had a finer sense than others that
Jesus could not be with them long, and she must do something to
give expression to her feelings. The ointment was nothing; she
was pouring out her heart at Jesus' feet.

2. If no more were said, then the incident would remain
lovely and beautiful, and we should turn to it with that delight
which we feel in any narrative that kindles fine emotion. But
the true interest of the incident lies in Christ's interpretation of
it. There is nothing that happens in human conduct that has
not some relation to eternal truths and principles, and Christ at
once puts the whole episode into relation with these truths and
principles. Let us observe, therefore, precisely what it is that
He says and does.

(1) The first thing that He does is to receive the gift without
embarrassment. We do not always remember that it requires a
certain magnanimity of nature to accept a gift as well as to
bestow one. There is a stubborn sourness of nature in many of
us which masquerades as independence of character, and which
makes us uncomfortable under benefaction. The chief reason
why men reject the grace of God is because they cannot endure
the thought of a gift. Could they earn eternal life, could they
add virtue to virtue till they had built up their claim to the
heritage of God, this they would do; for this they would struggle,
sacrifice, and aspire; for this they would macerate the body and
crush the heart in a ligature of iron rules and regulations; and
men have done it in every age. If a new crusade were proclaimed
to-morrow, and men could be brought to believe that its rewards
were real, and that by enduring its sacrifices they might win a
place in Paradise, millions would flock to its standard, as millions

are still ready to obey the call of Muhammad. But human nature has not magnanimity enough to accept God's free gift; and thus the great hindrance in the salvation of men is not the crimes and sins of men, but the diabolical force and persistency of human pride. Christ sets us an example of how to receive as well as of how to give. He might have resented an honour so sudden and public; He might have felt in it a certain embarrassing indelicacy, and have shrunk from its seeming ostentation and from the position in which it placed Him in regard to the spectators. He does nothing of the kind. He receives the gift with perfect simplicity, grace, and courtesy, and raises the whole episode into a light unutterably solemn and affecting when He says: "She hath done what she could: she is come aforehand to anoint my body to the burying."

Our actions always perform a ministry beyond our immediate intentions. "It is impossible," says Mark Rutherford, "to limit the effect which even an insignificant life may have." You speak a kindly word, for example, to someone, and, if you think at all about what you have done, you attach little importance to the episode. But the person whom you have treated in that manner has an inner history of his own, and you have affected him in relation to experiences that you know nothing about. The things that wear a different appearance for him in consequence, the temptations you have helped him to overcome, the difficulties you have encouraged him to face, are recorded in a book which is sealed to your eyes. And not only is such a person's own life influenced to a degree and in a variety of ways that you never anticipated, but also the lives of others with whom he comes in contact participate indirectly in the beneficent effects of what was to you a simple, and soon became a forgotten, incident. "Never was a sincere word utterly lost," says Emerson, "never a magnanimity fell to the ground, but there is some heart to greet and accept it unexpectedly." There is a promise and a potency in deeds and words, in looks and hand-grasps and thoughts of kindness and love, far exceeding our poor imaginations.

"She is come aforehand to anoint my body to the burying." Not many of us are beforehand with our love; most of us are behindhand. Joseph and Nicodemus were behindhand; they loved Jesus, but they were men, wise men, strong men, unsentimental men, and so they saved their spices for the dead body of Christ. They did not bring any love to Him before He died, but as soon as He was dead Joseph became bold, and went in and craved His body, and wrapped it in fine linen, and they brought myrrh and aloes, a hundred pounds' weight, for its anointing. How much better the woman's alabaster box of costly oil, the fragrance of which the living Christ scented! Does not our love need to learn to be beforehand? The most of us have some love, but we take care that it blossoms too late, and its fragrant exhalations often perfume only the grave of the beloved.

¶ It was from Seoul, in Korea, that Mrs. Bishop sent out the New Year's card on which she quotes the ancient Persian proverb of "Three things that never return":
> The Spent Arrow,
> The Spoken Word,
> The Lost Opportunity.[1]

¶ In the summer of 1901 Tolstoy had a serious illness. After he had somewhat recovered, the doctor recommended his removal to a warmer and more genial climate. Accordingly he and his family left Yasnaya Polyana for the Crimea. From Sevastopol the party drove to Yálta by road. At the first station, where they stopped to change horses, Tolstoy walked on ahead, and met a young fellow (apparently a shop-assistant or small tradesman), of whom he inquired the name of some place on the shore below. The stranger answered the poorly and strangely clad old man contemptuously; and, when the Countess drove up, was amazed to see him get into the carriage and drive off. Turning to P. A. Boulanger (Tolstoy's friend), who was waiting for a second carriage, the fellow asked who that old man was.
"Count Tolstoy," was the answer.
"What? Count Tolstoy, the writer? . . . Oh, my God, my God!" exclaimed the other in despair, flinging his cap into the dirty road. "I would have given all I possess to see him; and how I spoke to him!"[2]

> Early they came, yet they were come too late;
> The tomb was empty; in the misty dawn
> Angels sat watching, but the Lord was gone.

[1] A. M. Stoddart, *The Life of Isabella Bird (Mrs. Bishop)*, 330.
[2] Aylmer Maude, *The Life of Tolstoy: Later Years*, 591.

Beyond earth's clouded day-break far was He,
Beyond the need of their sad ministry;
Regretful stood the three, with doubtful breast,
Their gifts unneeded and in vain their quest.

The spices—were they wasted? Legend saith
That, flung abroad on April's gentle breath,
They course the earth, and evermore again
In Spring's sweet odours they come back to men.
The tender thought! Be sure He held it dear;
He came to them with words of highest cheer,
And mighty joy expelled their hearts' brief fear.

Yet happier that morning—happier yet—
I count that other woman in her home,
Whose feet impatient all too soon had come
Who ventured chill disfavour at the feast,
'Mid critics' murmur sought that lowliest Guest,
Broke her rare vase, its fragrant wealth outpoured.
And gave her gift aforehand to her Lord.[1]

(2) Christ receives the gift, rightly interpreting its spirit, but
He does more: He proceeds to defend it from the charge of
extravagance. "Why this waste?" said the jealous bystanders
—for you will observe that this was not the saying of Judas
only, it was the comment of "some that had indignation among
themselves."

Probably there is no subject on which we have such unjust
and muddled notions as what constitutes extravagance. We do
not call a man extravagant who spends a thousand pounds on
horses and wine, provided his income justifies him; but if the
same man were to spend one hundred pounds on books he would
be called extravagant, because we grudge any expenditure on the
things of the mind, but none whatever on the pleasures of the
body. We do not call a man extravagant who spends a large
sum on the building of a mansion for himself, but if the same man
spent a tithe of the sum on building or beautifying a house for
God, his children would feel that he had robbed them. Or to
come to lesser matters, there are those who would not accuse
themselves of extravagance if they spent a considerable sum on
seats at the theatre, the opera, or the concert hall, but would

[1] Sophie W. Weitzel, *From Time to Time.*

never dream of giving any such sum for a seat in a church, and would think long before they devoted such a sum to any purpose of charity.

Calmly, and with majesty, Christ rules that love's prodigality is blameless; that there are times when the practically useful must be set lower than the morally beautiful. And this act He praised for its beauty. It was beautiful even as a work of art is beautiful, namely, as the clear and apt and forcible outward expression of a noble inward feeling.

Nor in this does Christ judge alone. The judgment of human nature has pronounced in the same sense before and since. When David pours out unto the Lord the water, of which he would not drink, from the well of Bethlehem—for "is not this the blood of the men that went in jeopardy of their lives?"—might we not exclaim, "What waste of the hard-won luxury!" But we love him the more for his magnificent chivalry. What waste of treasure, time, and labour it was that chased the sculptured masses of masonry on the cathedral fronts! Yet, who grudges? For in a great critic's words, those ancient builders "have taken with them to the grave their powers, their honours, and their errors; but they have left us their adoration." When some poor worthless creature is plucked from the clutch of fire or water by some strong and gallant fellow who gets his own death-hurt in doing it, we murmur, perhaps, for a moment (who can help it?) to think that gold should be thrown away to redeem dross, the hero to save the weakling; yet we feel the loss had been sadder if the brave man had paused to weigh values and saved himself for better uses.

And precisely here, not elsewhere, is the great contribution Christ has made to morality, or the department of duty. He inaugurates, in fact, a new Christian morality, quite superior to the natural ethics of the world. Not a new morality as respects the body of rules, or code of perceptive obligations,—though even here He instituted laws of conduct so important as to create a new era of advancement,—but new in the sense that He raised His followers to a new point of insight, where the solutions of duty are easy, and the otherwise perplexing questions of casuistry are for ever suspended; even as this woman friend of Jesus saw more through her love, and struck into a finer coincidence with

His sublime future, than all the male disciples around her had been able to do by the computations of reflective reason. Nay, if Judas, who, according to John, was the more forward critic, had been writing just then a treatise on the economics of duty, her little treatise of unction was better.

As well might they have looked on the summer fields and asked to what purpose this waste in the growth of lily and rose? Might not all this fertility of nature, instead of running to waste on useless flowers, have gone to grow provender for cattle or food for man?

¶ Alexander the Great, when a child, was checked by his governor Leonidas for being overprofuse in spending perfumes: because on a day, being to sacrifice to the gods, he took both his hands full of frankincense, and cast it into the fire: but afterwards, being a man, he conquered the country of Judæa (the fountain whence such spices did flow), he sent Leonidas a present of five hundred talents' weight of frankincense, to show him how his former prodigality made him thrive the better in success, and to advise him to be no more niggardly in divine service. Thus they that sow plentifully shall reap plentifully. I see there is no such way to have a large heart as to have a large heart. The free giving of the branches of our present estate to God, is the readiest means to have the root increased for the future.[1]

¶ Lying in the field this July day I take up a tall grass stem in flower. Its delicacy, grace, the poise of its head, are lovely beyond speech. But the whole field, ten acres of it, is covered with tall stems equally delicate, graceful, and with the same perfect poise. For whom does this beauty exist?[2]

(3) The third point in the defence is contained in the words, "She hath done what she could." Unfortunately this expression is capable of being misunderstood, and has indeed been widely understood in a sense exactly the opposite of that which it was intended to bear. In our modern idiom, "She hath done what she could " is almost as much apologetic as eulogistic. The undertone is, "It was not much, of course, but what more could one expect? There is no room for reproach or censure." This is precisely the reverse of what the words mean. The disciples did not reproach the woman for doing so little, but for doing so much ; and Jesus justified her, not by reducing her act to smaller propor-

[1] Thomas Fuller.
[2] Mark Rutherford, *Last Pages from a Journal* (1915), 293.

tions, but by revealing it in all its depth and height, and showing that it was greater than she herself knew.

She did what she could because she did it in faith. The guests at the feast of Bethany, most of them, notwithstanding the recent miracle which had summoned Lazarus from his grave to a seat at that very table, were living as most men live: they were living in the present, without a thought of the future; they were living in the visible, without a thought of the unseen. Mary looked higher than the world of sense, deeper into the future than the passing hour. She knew what Jesus had said about His personal claims to be before Abraham, to be One with the Father; and she took Him at His word. She knew that He had foretold His death and burial and resurrection; and she took Him at His word. As He sat at that board, eating and talking like everyone else, it was not every soul that could set aside what met the eye of sense and discern the reality; not everyone who could see that there was that beneath the form of the Prophet of Nazareth which is worthy of the most passionate homage of the soul; not everyone who would reflect that, ere many days had passed, that very Form would be exposed upon a cross to the gaze of a brutal multitude, while life ebbed slowly away amid overwhelming agony and shame. Mary did see this. "In that she hath poured this ointment on my body, she did it for my burial."

¶ We are more apt to see the comfort in the words, "She hath done what she could," than the solemnity of them. They are a tender recognition, but a tremendous challenge. "What she could" means all she could. The Master compares us, not with others, but with ourselves. There is the mercy. But with our best selves, with our possible selves, there is the rub.—What I did, subtracted from what I might have done, gives the bad remainder, the immoral debit, the moral discredit. "There's a kindness in His justice that is more than liberty." Thank God for it, but let us not misunderstand the truth and think we are at liberty to do what we happen to feel like. Did the Lord say of Sapphira, "She hath done what she could"?[1]

It was her best, and yet how poor
    That cruise of spikenard sweet and rare!
She entered in at Simon's door
    With trembling, though familiar there.

[1] M. D. Babcock, *Thoughts for Every-Day Living*, 43.

What could she give to Him whose call
Had brought her brother back from death?
It was her best, yet poor and small
For Him, the Lord of pulse and breath!

He took the fragrant gift: a wreath
Of praise He twined about her name.
It lit for Him the cave of Death:
"Against my burial she came!"[1]

(4) The great words in which Jesus justified the breaking of the alabaster box on His own behalf embody a principle which should run through all wise life. The words were these: "The poor ye have always with you; but me ye have not always." The principle is this—that opportunities differ in value and importance, and that wisdom consists in reading their value aright and in selecting the one which will not be always with us. Certain things may be done at any time; certain other things must be done now or never. Certain privileges may be enjoyed at any time; certain others now or never. Every life is confronted at many points with this strange contrast—between the ordinary opportunities which come with every day, and some great opportunity which, if not grasped at once, may vanish for ever. The poor and Jesus! There is the living contrast which is symbolical of so much in our life. The presence of the poor we can depend on; the pathetic commonplace is ever about us; but unique opportunities are not always with us. They are rare. Sometimes they come to us but once; and though we should wait for a century, they would never come again.

For no man knows what the gods may send,
Or the day when the word will come
That shall change the ways of his life, or lend
A voice to a soul born dumb.
And never man shall plumb
The depths of a sleeping past.[2]

¶ Marcus Aurelius says: "To the better of two things, if thou findest that, turn with thy whole heart: eat and drink ever of the best before thee."[3]

---

[1] George T. Coster.   [2] D. H. S. Nicholson, *Poems*, 2.
[3] Walter Pater, *Marius the Epicurean*, ii. 37.

NICODEMUS.

LITERATURE.

Ainger, A., *Sermons in the Temple Church* (1870), 180.

Baldwin, G. C., *Representative Men of the New Testament* (1859), 161.

Banks, L. A., *Christ and His Friends* (1895), 116.

   ,,   ,,   *The Great Saints of the Bible* (1902), 276.

Beecher, H. W., *Henry Ward Beecher in England, 1886*, pt. iii. 49.

Bell, C. D., *Night Scenes of the Bible*, ii. (1886) 95.

Bernard, J. H., *From Faith to Faith* (1895), 33.

Carpenter, W. B., *The Son of Man among the Sons of Men* (1893), 185.

Chapin, E. H., in *The World's Great Sermons*, vi. (1909) 29.

Clow, W. M., *The Day of the Cross* (1909), 353.

Davidson, A. B., *The Called of God* (1902), 247.

Drummond, H., *The Ideal Life* (1897), 185.

Durell, J. C. V., *The Self-Revelation of Our Lord* (1910), 84.

English, E., *Sermons and Homilies* (1913), 155.

Gray, W. A., *Laws and Landmarks of the Spiritual Life* (1895), 151.

Greenhough, J. G., in *Men of the New Testament* : Matthew to Timothy (1905), 129.

Hough, L. H., *The Men of the Gospels* (1913), 55.

Jones, J. D., *The Hope of the Gospel* (1911), 126.

Lucas, B., *Conversations with Christ* (1905), 12.

Matheson, G., *The Representative Men of the New Testament* (1905), 115.

Reid, J., *Jesus and Nicodemus* (1906).

Rendall, G. H., *Charterhouse Sermons* (1911), 85.

Sanday, W., *The Authorship and Historical Character of the Fourth Gospel* (1872), 69.

Skrine, J. H., *Saints and Worthies* (1901), 121.

Whyte, A., *Bible Characters* : Joseph and Mary to James (1900), 36.

Dictionary of the Bible, iii. (1900) 543 (J. H. Bernard).

Dictionary of Christ and the Gospels, ii. (1908) 244 (E. H. Titchmarsh).

Encyclopædia Biblica, iii. (1902), col. 3406 (E. A. Abbott).

NICODEMUS.

There was a man of the Pharisees, named Nicodemus, a ruler of the Jews.—John iii. 1.

NEVER is the mysterious difference between Jesus and other men more apparent than in the supremely instructive and impressive account of the quiet interview which He gave in the silence of night to Nicodemus, a ruler of the Jews. The one theme which occupies the strained attention of the two men, the one point on which they speak with intense earnestness and latent passion, is the condition of entrance into the Kingdom of God, the state of mind and heart which fits a man for the Divine régime which they both expect to begin without delay. And we are smitten with awe as we observe that one of the two Teachers who together discuss this absolutely vital problem offers a solution which is intended for other men, but has no reference to Himself. He who lays down the law, "Except a man be born anew, he cannot see the kingdom of God," speaks as one who has never been, because He has never needed to be, born again. Here is an amazing assumption, which will be found to underlie all His teaching from the beginning to the end. He can say, as no other man has ever been able to say, "Which of you convinceth me of sin?" "The prince of this world cometh, and hath nothing in me." "I do always the things which are well pleasing in my Father's sight." He who knows what is in man makes no mistake about Himself, and His consciousness is the consciousness of sinless perfection— the consciousness of a man who never needs to repent and ask forgiveness, never requires to be born again. Let this supreme miracle be once accepted and appreciated, and every other miracle falls into its proper place. That the conqueror of sin should also be the conqueror of disease and sorrow and death seems nothing strange. The moment we grant the sinlessness of Jesus, we enter a region in which the supernatural becomes the natural.

¶ Renan claimed for himself the absolute coldness which proposed as its only object to take note of the most delicate and the most severe shades of truth. Yet when he wrote his Life of Christ for the people, he expunged the frank passages in his famous book, passages such as that in which he argued that Christ countenanced a fictitious resurrection of Lazarus arranged by the sisters. He omitted also what he had said about Christ's devouring fanaticism. These were fit for his scientific readers; but he was willing to make concession to the preference of the vulgar for a popular hero. So, without in the least changing his real opinion, he indulged the general appetite for a stainless figure, and erased all the traces of fanaticism and finesse. To do that was to forget that, after all, truth is sacredness, and sacredness is truth, and that deception in any and every form can in the end work nothing but evil. Yet we will not bear too hardly on Renan. What we are convinced lay at the back of his reticence was the feeling that if Christ were once proved to be frail and stained like the rest of us, the glory of the world would be quenched.[1]

I.

COMING TO CHRIST.

It is related that Nicodemus came to Jesus by night, and in two later chapters of the same Gospel he is referred to as " he that came to Jesus by night," " he who at the first came to him by night" (John vii. 50, xix. 39 ; in the former text the R.V. has " before " instead of " by night "). This detail seems to have become a fixed element in the tradition, and there would no doubt be much speculation as to the motive and meaning of the nocturnal visit. Why did the ruler of the Jews seek communion with Jesus by night rather than by day ? He has often been stigmatized as a coward, who did under the cover of darkness what he would have been ashamed to be seen doing by daylight. But there is not a word to indicate that his visit was resented either as an untimely intrusion or as an act of cowardice. If he came to Jesus by night, at any rate he did come ; and since he evidently came with a sincere desire to know Jesus better, he was welcome. Jesus had frequent occasion to condemn Pharisaism as a system, but it would be a great mistake to imagine that He regarded every

[1] W. R. Nicoll, *The Church's One Foundation*, 112.

Pharisee as a hypocrite. There were high-minded men like Hillel and Gamaliel among the Jewish Rabbis ; and to an earnest Pharisee no less than to a contrite publican Jesus was ready to say, " No man can come to me, except the Father which sent me draw him " ; "and him that cometh to me I will in no wise cast out." What Christian who recalls his first timid approaches to Christ can truthfully say that he was actuated only by the highest and purest motives ? And who would care to have his first tentative inquiries about the way of salvation immediately discussed by critical and derisive comrades ? Christ is too generous to confound any anxious inquirer with awkward questions as to his motives. Well pleased to receive him on any terms, He goes straight to the point, leading him without any hesitation into the deep things of personal and experimental religion.

¶ Nicodemus was a scholar. He was the teacher of Israel. And so, when I see him seeking Jesus, I seem to behold scholarship at the feet of Christ. It would be a real difficulty in the way of accepting Christianity, says Dr. Gwatkin, if it did not attract the best men of every time. But it does ! It had a Paul and an Origen and an Athanasius and an Augustine in the early days ; it has had a Newton and a Kepler and a Faraday and a Clerk-Maxwell and a Tait and a Kelvin in these days of ours. The mightiest minds find in Christ their Master. And at the head of the procession of the gifted and the learned who own Christ as Lord is this great teacher of Israel who came to Jesus by night.[1]

¶ Now and again we have proofs of the fact, from quarters and in forms the least likely, that there are hidden Christians— secret allies of Christianity. One instance of secret discipleship may be cited, remarkable chiefly for the unexpected reason assigned—I refer to the case of an eminent man of science. Although an avowed believer in a personal God, he was understood to have rejected the doctrine of a supernatural Christ ; yet after his death there was found a paper in his desk in which he expresses his attitude to Christ in these words : " I believe in my heart that God raised Him from the dead, and I have not confessed Him with the mouth, because in my time such confession is the only way to get up in the world." A disciple secretly through fear of misunderstanding ![2]

[1] J. D. Jones, *The Hope of the Gospel*, 137.
[2] W. A. Gray, *Laws and Landmarks of the Spiritual Life*, 158.

II.

SEEKING LIGHT.

Nicodemus soon reveals the fact that he has come to Jesus, not as a solitary individual, but rather as the representative of a party, the adherent of a school. He speaks almost as if he had been deputed to state the case of many others, who had together been taking the mysterious person and mighty deeds of Jesus into careful consideration, and whose preliminary verdict he repeats in the well-weighed words, "We know that thou art a teacher come from God: for no man can do these signs that thou doest, except God be with him." They had felt that they could not rest there. Having gone so far, they must go farther. Was it not advisable that one of their number should approach Jesus, and sound Him as to His doctrine? But that there might be no talk about it, let him go by night.

Nicodemus therefore comes to Jesus half in a receptive and half in a critical frame of mind. He craves more light. His judgment is suspended. He feels that he cannot make up his mind until he has a fuller knowledge of the facts. And so far he was quite reasonable. He was doing only what millions have done since. Christianity makes a mighty appeal to intellect as well as to feeling. It is to be accepted by men who are fully persuaded in their own minds. Christ is the Light of the world, and desires us to become Christians with open eyes, loving the highest only when we see that it is the highest. So far from seeking to hide anything, Christianity welcomes the fullest and most searching inquiry into its nature and credentials. It is not an esoteric religion, whose jealously guarded secrets are revealed only to a few initiates. Christ as the living Truth imparts Himself to all who have ears to hear and hearts to understand. While it is a Catholic dictum that mystery is the mother of devotion, it is a Protestant principle that knowledge is the mother of devotion. And both are true. The more we know of Christ and His religion, the more does our sense of wonder grow; the more we know of His Divine love, the more do we feel that it passeth knowledge.

¶ Religion is not a mere system of thought upon which the mind can exercise its logic, while the soul is untouched and irresponsive. It is a life produced by the touch of the Divine Spirit, and apart from that contact, even the perception of spiritual verities is impossible. The reason may convince us of the existence of God, it may satisfy us of the reality of the relation between God and man, but it can never enable us to perceive the beauty of that life of communion with God which is the very heart of true religion. Reason is the activity of the human mind working on the materials presented to it, and though it may infer a Mind above the human, it can no more attain to communion with that Mind than the man can lift himself to the starry world his eyes behold. Religion is the activity of the spirit responding to the influence of the Divine Spirit; a life of feeling, not a process of thought; a Divine conception within the soul, not a human perception. In the deepest sense it is not the stretching out of lame hands to find a God, it is the grasping of the outstretched hand of God.[1]

> Through that pure Virgin-shrine,
> That sacred vail drawn o'er thy glorious noon,
> That men might look and live, as glo-worms shine,
>   And face the moon,
> Wise Nicodemus saw such light
> As made him know his God by night.
>
> Most blest believer he!
> Who in that land of darkness and blinde eyes
> Thy long expected healing wings could see,
>   When Thou didst rise;
> And, what can never more be done,
> Did at mid-night speak with the Sun![2]

III.

THE DIVINE TEACHER.

Jesus made no complaint that Nicodemus, and those for whom he might be speaking, regarded Him as a Teacher. He who spent more time in training twelve disciples than in any other task was not likely to demur when any man came to Him for

---

[1] Bernard Lucas, *Conversations with Christ*, 16.
[2] Henry Vaughan.

instruction. He is the greatest Teacher who has ever come from God, and His invitation to all men is, " Come and learn of me, and ye shall find rest unto your souls." It is His purpose to impart to men an education such as cannot be received in any school or college or university of secular knowledge—to make them wise unto salvation. To His chosen disciples He said at the end of their three years' curriculum, " All things that I have heard of my Father I have made known unto you "; and He promised that after He was gone, the Spirit of truth—His own Spirit—would come to guide them into all truth. Verily a Teacher come from God! But also more than a Teacher. For the risen Christ who allowed Mary Magdalene to address Him as " Rabboni," " my Teacher," welcomed also the adoring words of the doubting but at last believing disciple, " My Lord and my God."

¶ " We know that thou art a teacher come from God." Perhaps this confession expresses not amiss the feeling both of the world and of the Church toward Christ still. He is a teacher come from God. Those who profess to believe in Him have scarcely got further; for at what problem are all earnest minds so hard at work as at this problem of Christ? And what is called the world no longer cares to dispute the truth of these words in one sense or another. He is a teacher come from God. There is a feeling now among men, the majority of men, that Christ is the Highest Being the world can ever see; and that His teaching is from God, in some higher sense than that of any other. This is the feeling even among men whom we do not call believing. I do not stop to speculate whether there may not be some genuine faith under this apparently rather negative confession; or whether this position, which men of thought are now taking up with regard to Christ, be really a gain or a loss to religion. On the one hand, it may seem a gain that they concede so much, even though their concessions do not amount to faith in Him. On the other hand, half a truth is sometimes more dangerous than a whole lie. That which is plainly false will deceive no one; that which is false at heart, but glittering with a gilding of truth, may draw and seduce many.[1]

¶ The mode of Christ's teaching is not the ratiocinative but the intuitional—not philosophical but spiritual—in this having more affinity to the woman's side of human nature than the man's. But so also does the Jewish, as distinct from the Greek, form of

[1] A. B. Davidson, *The Called of God*, 251.

thought appeal to the deep, inmost nature, not to the reasoning power. Therefore may we look on the Jewish mode of presenting truth in Psalms and Prophets as formed beforehand to be pre-paratory for Christ's own mode of teaching. It was the fore-casting shadow of what He chose as best; best, as suiting the great mass of mankind, simple as well as learned, young as well as old; best, as being adapted to the great principle of salvation by faith, by trust, which mere human reason spurns, and suited also to His descent as the woman's seed, keeping predominant that side of the nature which fell first, and is to be first in recovery.[1]

IV.

THE HEART OF CHRISTIANITY.

1. Jesus honours Nicodemus most by taking him by the straightest path and at the swiftest pace to the very centre of the Christian faith and life. It might have been pleasanter for Nicodemus if He had kept him viewing for a while the outposts of Christianity, instead of leading him at once to the citadel; if they had lingered together on the threshold of the temple of truth, instead of immediately penetrating the inner shrine. But time was precious, and that night had to be made the most memorable in Nicodemus' life. So, without any prelude, Jesus at once utters the mighty truth, "Except a man be born anew, he cannot see the kingdom of God."

In emphatically proclaiming that truth Christ does what John the Baptist had done not long before—He lays the axe at the root of Pharisaic pride. He knew, as everybody else knew, that the Pharisees had not accepted the baptism of John. In the great revival, when multitudes of all classes had come to the austere prophet for baptism in the Jordan, the Pharisees had stood aloof. They "rejected for themselves the counsel of God, being not baptized of him." They were in the habit of saying of any Gentile who embraced Judaism, "He is born again"; but that a Jew, and above all such a Hebrew of Hebrews as every Pharisee counted himself, should need to be born again before he could enter into the Kingdom of God—this was monstrous, incredible! When the Kingdom of the Messiah came, every

[1] John Ker, *Thoughts for Heart and Life*, 213.

conscientious and law-abiding Jew would naturally have a place in it, and the Jewish nation would, equally as a matter of course, have precedence of all the Gentiles.

That was the creed of the time. But Jesus fairly staggered Nicodemus, and shook the foundations of Jewish piety, by proclaiming, "Except a man be born from above, he cannot see the kingdom of God." Not "except a publican or sinner," not "except a Greek or Roman," not "except a barbarian of wild Scythia or heathen of dark Ethiopia," but "except a man." And Nicodemus knew that Jesus was not wasting time upon abstract propositions, but was speaking to the point, plainly meaning that Nicodemus and all those in whose name he was speaking needed to prepare themselves for the Kingdom of God by humbling themselves under God's mighty hand, coming to a deep sense of their sin, and receiving a new heart and a right spirit.

The Pharisee, like every common man, needed to be born of water and of the Spirit. He had refused the water of repentance which John had offered, and he may now refuse the life-giving Spirit which Jesus offers. But the refusal cannot alter the fact: "Verily, verily, I say unto thee, Except a man be born of water and of the Spirit, he cannot enter into the kingdom of God." Thus Jesus effects a simultaneous process of levelling down and levelling up—levelling down the Jews, even the best of them, and levelling up the Gentiles, even the worst of them. Thus He makes them all one before God, one in need and one in privilege: every man *must* be born anew, and every man *may* be born anew. Thus He obliterates all distinctions. That obliteration was, in the eyes of the Jews, His unpardonable sin, but it is now, in the eyes of all mankind, His unique and inalienable merit.

¶ The doctrine of the new birth is still a source of perplexity and amazement to many. It is said of an Archbishop of York [Dr. Drummond] that he once rebuked one of his clergy in words that sound strangely from the lips of a Christian preacher, saying, "He would be better employed in preaching the morality of Socrates than in canting about the new birth." There are many who dismiss the truth as the cant of evangelicalism; who see nothing but absurdity or impossibility in it. It is easy to misunderstand or misrepresent a truth which is instinct with the grace and hope of the gospel. Yet where there is any glimmer of spiritual intelligence, the idea of the new birth quickly commends itself. The Old Testament promise, "A new heart also will I give you," misleads no one, and the new birth is equally intelligible. For it must never be forgotten that the expression "born from above" is only a figure—one illustration among the many which are employed to describe the beginning of salvation in the soul of man. It is a passing "from darkness to light," "from the power of Satan unto God," a "conversion," turning to God from idols. It is a "redemption" from slavery, a "rising from the dead into newness of life." It is a "justification" as in a court of law. There is no end to the symbolism of salvation. All the great experiences of the life of man which involve a radical or effectual change are susceptible of spiritual significance. The figure of birth differs from all others only in the pregnancy of its meaning, and in its suggestiveness of mystery and human helplessness. The life of the Kingdom of God is something different from the natural life of man. The experience with which it begins is so thorough in its effects and so hidden in its method that it is likened to a birth. In no clearer way could the distinctively spiritual character of that life be described.[1]

2. If Nicodemus reeled under the blow which the quiet words of Jesus inflicted on his pride, he quickly recovered himself. There was something, not only in the authoritative manner of Jesus, but also in Nicodemus' own conscience, which made it impossible for him to question even for a moment the truth announced by the Teacher come from God. At home among his books, over which he had burned so much midnight oil, he might have questioned, and repudiated, the humiliating doctrine. In the Sanhedrin among his peers he would have heard it not only questioned but even ridiculed on every side. But in the presence of Jesus, whose pure eyes searched the depths of his soul, he inwardly acknowledged the truth that even a law-abiding Pharisee needed to undergo as radical a change of heart as a profane publican or a godless pagan.

But, granting that a man—even a superman, such as every Pharisee imagined himself to be—must be born again before he can enter the Kingdom of God, there arises an extremely difficult problem as to the way in which this is to be done. To the wit of man it is not only a difficult but an absolutely baffling problem. How can an old man, bound by all the habits of a lifetime, free

[1] John Reid, *Jesus and Nicodemus*, 66.

himself from his past, and begin a new life? It may be necessary, and who will deny that it is desirable? Who has not sometimes said in tones of infinite regret:

> Oh, to go back across the years long vanished,
> To have the words unsaid, the deeds undone,
> The errors cancelled, the dark shadows banished,
> In the glad sense of a new world begun;
> To be a little child, whose page of story
> Is yet undimmed, unblotted by a stain,
> And in the sunrise of primeval glory
> To know that life has had its start again!

Yet what seems so desirable, and what Jesus declares to be indispensable, may after all be impossible. That is the feeling of Nicodemus and of all thoughtful men in every age. They have come to an impasse. Ah! if it were but possible to be little children over again—to begin to live life again, to undo all the evils of our life, to be living and yet without the evils that have gathered about our life, to have no memory of sin, to feel nc blots on our soul, to have made no mistakes in life, to have done no wrong, nothing that calls up the blush on our cheek, to have nothing against which we fret and dash ourselves in vain, like poor captive creatures against the iron cage that holds them, torturing ourselves over an irrevocable unworthiness; to have the joy and the unclouded hopefulness, the fresh and unstained powers of the child—to be born again when one is old! Can it be?

¶ A man who is converted in the New Testament sense is one who has surrendered to forces immeasurably greater than anything he has of himself; one who has awakened to the overwhelming consciousness of a spiritual world brought to a focus before him in the Person of Christ; one who finds the little bay of his individual life, with all its little pebbles and little shells and little weeds, flooded by the tide of a great deep, over which the very Spirit of God broods.[1]

¶ There is a touching little poem by Dora Greenwell (*A Good Confession*), suggested by the inscription on a tombstone in a country churchyard in Wales, which tells how he who lies below passed away at the age of eighty, and yet—referring to the date

[1] H. Wheeler Robinson, *The Christian Doctrine of Man*, 322.

of his conversion to Christ—was only "four years old when he
died"—

"If you ask me how long I have been in the world, I'm old
   —I'm very old;
If you ask me how many years I've lived, it'll very soon be
   told—
Past eighty years of age, yet only four years old!"[1]

V.

THE SPIRIT OF GOD.

Jesus' answer to Nicodemus' pathetic and almost despairing
question—the question which rises from the troubled heart of
humanity itself—is sublimely simple. He indicates that man's
extremity is God's opportunity, and that the thing which seems to
us impossible becomes easy when we have all Omnipotence to aid
us. The new life which is the true life is the gift of God. The
Spirit breathes where He lists, in the souls of the young or the
old, the virtuous or the vicious, the Jew or the Gentile, the Pharisee
or the publican; and everywhere His breath is life-giving. The
life which He imparts, like every other form of life, is an ultimate
reality which man can neither create nor define. But of its truth
there can be no reasonable question. Every man who sincerely
repents of his sin and accepts Divine forgiveness passes out of
death into life. He is "born, not of blood, nor of the will of the
flesh, nor of the will of man, but of God." And being so born, he
can see the Kingdom of God. And this new life is mediated to
him by the Son of man, lifted up that whosoever believeth in
Him may have life eternal.

The Spirit does His work by glorifying Christ, imparts life by
revealing Christ: "He shall take of mine, and declare it unto
you." Regeneration is the beginning of a supernatural life, in
which man realizes himself by living in, with, for, and like Christ.

¶ The act of being born again is as mysterious as God. All
the complaints which have been showered upon this doctrine have
referred to the act—the act with which we have really nothing to
do, which is a process of God, the agency of the unseen wind

[1] G. Jackson, *First Things First*, 247.

of the Spirit, and which Jesus Himself has expressly warned us not to expect to understand. "Thou canst not tell," He said, "whence it cometh or whither it goeth."

But there is nothing to frighten search in this. For precisely the same kind of mystery hangs over every process of nature and life. We do not understand the influence of sunshine on the leaves of a flower at this spring-time, any more than we do the mysterious budding of spiritual life within the soul; but botany is a science for all that.

We do not give up the study of chemistry as hopeless because we fail to comprehend the unseen laws which guide the delicate actions and reactions of matter. Nor do we disbelieve in the influence of food on the vital frame because no man has found the point exactly at which it passes from dead nourishment into life. We do not avoid the subject of electricity because electricity is a mystery, or heat because we cannot see heat, or meteorology because we cannot see the wind. Marvel not then, from the analogy of physical nature, if, concerning this Spirit of Regeneration, we cannot tell whence it cometh and whither it goeth. It is not on that account unintelligible that a man should be born again.[1]

VI.

NOT ASHAMED OF CHRIST.

1. The Evangelist does not tell us at what time of the night or in what frame of mind Nicodemus left the presence of Jesus. But he gives us two later glimpses of the man, both of which are in the highest degree suggestive. The time came when the chief priests and Pharisees tried to arrest Jesus. They failed, however, because their own servants refused to obey orders, choosing to incur the displeasure of their masters sooner than lay hands on Him who, as they declared, spake as never man spake. Angry as the masters were at such insubordination, they did their best to conceal their feelings. After all, what did they care for the opinion of the vulgar crowd—the mob who did not know the law? What really mattered was the opinion of the learned and influential class. Had any of the rulers or of the Pharisees believed in the Nazarene? Nicodemus was present and heard the question, which sounded like a challenge. And he took a bold

[1] Henry Drummond, The Ideal Life, 190.

step. His conscience said that silence would be treason and cowardice. He knew that he would despise himself for ever if he failed to speak out. And rising to his feet, he calmly, plainly, and rightly told all the victims of passion and prejudice that they were doing what their own law forbade them to do—judging a man to whom they had never given a hearing.

Our chief interest in the dramatic scene lies in the last speaker. Nicodemus *has* given Jesus a hearing—has spent a never-to-be-forgotten night in intimate fellowship with Him—and this is the result. He is making rapid progress. If he does not yet say, "I, a ruler and a Pharisee, believe in Him," he at least fervently wishes that all his fellow-rulers could see what he has seen and hear what he has heard. He would not fear the issue. Lack of faith is often but another name for imperfect knowledge. There is much less invincible ignorance in the world than one might think. Let Christ have a chance. Let Christianity be heard, and it will speak to the heart of mankind with self-evidencing power. The Word of life needs only to be seen, looked upon, handled. The Truth is great and will prevail.

¶ In the supreme court which resolves to lay hands on Jesus, there is one dissenting voice—the voice of Nicodemus. It is the last voice we should have expected. We are disposed to say, " Is this the man who a little while ago was eager to sink himself in the spirit of the age!" He now stands forth opposed to the age —stands out as a solitary individual breasting the waves of a crowd, and cries with fearless love of justice, " Does our law judge any man before it hears him ! " We marvel at the spectacle. It is not that we see a growing stature—we expect time to bring that. It is that we witness a transformation. Nicodemus has changed his weakness into a strength. He has become strong in the very point in which he was defective. On the night in which he stood before Jesus he was unwilling to be alone ; on the day in which he stands before the Sanhedrin he is unwilling to be in company. He asserts the right of his own individual soul. He is a fine example of the difference between what is called nature and what is called grace. Nature can improve a man ; grace transforms him.[1]

2. Nicodemus reappears a second time in the gospel story, at the end of the greatest of all dramas. Things have reached a

[1] G. Matheson, *The Representative Men of the New Testament*, 127.

head with the Teacher come from God ; His life-blood has been shed on the cross, and the dishonoured body hangs disowned upon the tree. Will no man be bold enough to own it ? Will not the force of love break through even the terrible array of the unanimous verdict of the world ? It will. And of the two men who at that moment were strong enough to brave opinion, Nicodemus, the modest, shrinking, timid ruler, was one. "And Joseph of Arimathæa . . . besought Pilate that he might take away the body of Jesus : and Pilate gave him leave. And there came also Nicodemus, which at the first came to Jesus by night, bringing a mixture of myrrh and aloes, about an hundred pound weight. Then took they the body of Jesus, and wound it in linen clothes with the spices, as the manner of the Jews is to bury."

¶ As the two good men [Nicodemus and Joseph] stood by the cross, what would pass through the mind of Nicodemus ? Would it not be this : "As Moses lifted up the serpent in the wilderness, even so must the Son of man be lifted up." How reverently and lovingly they two handle that body ! What a funeral ! only two mourners, but many spectators, for all the angels in heaven were looking on. It was the burial of the King of kings. Dr. Mason of New York was once at the funeral of a young man, and he thought the pall-bearers were going a little too fast. He went forward, and, touching them softly, he said, "Walk softly ; you are carrying a temple of the Holy Ghost." If that could be said of a follower of Christ, what of the blessed Master Himself ? Nicodemus is hazarding his life as well as his reputation. He is lavishing his wealth on Christ. Christ's dying love has filled his heart. He counts it an honour to roll the stone to the sepulchre-door, as the angel did to roll it back. Learn like Nicodemus to confess a Christ that died. Men preach the imitation of Christ, but it is the death of Christ that brings life to the soul.[1]

[1] *Reminiscences of Andrew A. Bonar*, 326.

CAIAPHAS.

LITERATURE.

Broade, G. E., *The Sixfold Trial of Our Lord* (1899), 9.

Brodrick, M., *The Trial and Crucifixion of Jesus Christ of Nazareth* (1908), 61.

Burn, A. E., *The Crown of Thorns* (1911), 13.

Cameron, A. B., *From the Garden to the Cross* (1896), 83.

Clow, W. M., *The Day of the Cross* (1909), 13.

English, E., *Sermons and Homilies* (1913), 109.

Farrar, F. W., *The Life of Lives* (1900), 482.

Gifford, E. H., *Voices of the Prophets* (1874), 75.

Hough, L. H., *The Men of the Gospels* (1913), 63.

Inge, W. R., *All Saints' Sermons* (1907), 30.

Innes, A. T., *The Trial of Jesus Christ* (1899), 10.

Lightfoot, J. B., *Sermons Preached in St. Paul's Cathedral* (1891), 75.

Little, W. J. K., *Sunlight and Shadow* (1892), 229.

Luckock, H. M., *Footprints of the Son of Man as traced by St. Mark*, ii. (1886) 252.

Maclaren, A., *Christ in the Heart* (1886), 257.

„   „   *Expositions* : St. Matthew xviii.–xxviii. (1906), 286, 290.

„   „   „   St. John ix.–xiv. (1907), 107.

Morrison, G. H., *The Footsteps of the Flock* (1904), 265.

Mortimer, A. G., *Meditations on the Passion of Our Most Holy Redeemer*, i. (1903) 111.

Moulton, J. H., *Visions of Sin* (1898), 117.

Rosadi, G., *The Trial of Jesus* (1905), 155.

Simcox, W. H., *The Cessation of Prophecy* (1891), 278.

Smith, J., *Short Studies* (1901), 191.

Stalker, J., *The Trial and Death of Jesus Christ* (1894), 14.

Stevenson, J. G., *The Judges of Jesus* (1909), 83.

Watson, J., *The Life of the Master* (1902), 363.

Churchman's Pulpit : Lenten Season, v. 130 (G. T. Shettle).

Dictionary of the Bible, i. (1910) 338 (J. A. M'Clymont).

Dictionary of Christ and the Gospels, i. (1906) 251 (C. A. Scott).

Expositor, 6th Ser., i. (1900) 407 (W. M. Macgregor).

Expository Times, x. (1899) 185 (E. Nestle).

CAIAPHAS.

Now Caiaphas was he which gave counsel to the Jews, that it was expedient that one man should die for the people.—John xviii. 14.

Of all the men mentioned in the crucifixion records, Caiaphas is surely the most despicable. He was that not uncommon phenomenon, a man of low character in a high place. In religion he found, not a conviction, but a career; and so there fell upon him the Nemesis of those who traffic in high things, without making to them adequate spiritual response.

1. Who was this Caiaphas, and what were his antecedents? The real ruling spirit in the Sanhedrin was the aged Annas, who had been high priest twenty years before, till Valerius Gratus, Pilate's predecessor, deposed him for exceeding his powers. Annas had five sons, who were high priests one after the other, and his daughter's husband was Joseph Caiaphas, a man of more supple and adroit character than Annas and his family, as is shown by the fact that he remained high priest for eleven years. Annas was still regarded by the Jews as high priest *de jure*, and there can be little doubt that the family played into each other's hands, and divided among themselves the most important and lucrative posts at the Temple.

2. Thus Caiaphas belonged to the sect of the Sadducees. Now Christ's great opponents throughout His ministry had been the Pharisees. They met Him at every turn, and strove to refute Him. But many of them were well affected to Him. One of them became a disciple; another laid His crucified body in his own tomb. Some of them may have thought it possible to win the brilliant young Rabbi of Nazareth to their ranks. The Pharisees alone would not have put Jesus to death. But the Sadducees, except in one instance, did not controvert with Jesus.

They were the priestly party, and were to be found chiefly in Jerusalem. Their lives and interests centred in the Temple. When Christ crossed their path, when His growing influence threatened theirs, when His leadership became a peril to their predominance, and His popularity a danger to their safety, they did not parley with Him. They acted. " They took counsel to put him to death," and rested neither day nor night until He hung upon the cross. It was the Sadducees who crucified Christ. And the leader of the Sadducees was Caiaphas.

I.

HIS CONDUCT

We have only a few glimpses of Caiaphas in the Gospels· He appears and speaks a few words and then passes from view. But his words are always very influential, and the glimpses we have of him allow us to look right into his life and see what manner of man he was.

1. From an early day, probably, his spies kept him informed concerning Christ; and it is quite certain that on the day after Jesus cleansed the Temple, every priest in Jerusalem knew everything there was to know about Him. From that time onward our Lord must have been classified by Caiaphas as a dangerous person; and the high priest no doubt made up his mind that He must be either silenced or slain. This resolve did not, however, mean that Caiaphas gave way to panic. He simply reckoned up our Lord from his own standpoint, he made up his mind as to his own policy, and he was content to wait until events justified both the declaration of that policy and the carrying out of it.

What Caiaphas must have anticipated at last came to pass. Jesus raised Lazarus from the dead. Full of alarm, the Pharisees joined their old enemies the Sadducee " chief priests " in a council deliberation. They expressed their agitation in words which admitted the reality of the Wonder-worker's " signs," while they dexterously brought out the one point of danger which they knew was sure to rouse the Sadducees. If the authorities of the Jewish

Church continued to leave alone the man who ignored their right to license or to suppress Him, the whole people would flock to His standard. And then the dreaded Romans, so relentless to crush every kind of association among their subjects, lest haply its object might be political, would put out the iron hand of empire and destroy with one easy stroke their "place and nation." Their holy and beautiful "place," where their fathers worshipped God, and from which the Sadducees derived so comfortable an income —their "nation," the chosen people of God, which formed so appreciative an audience for the display of Pharisee holiness—all would be swept away, and what were they to do?

But however they might agitate or hesitate, there was one man who knew his own mind—Caiaphas, the high priest. He had no doubt as to what was the right thing to do. He had the advantage of a perfectly clear and single purpose, and no sort of restraint of conscience or delicacy kept him from speaking it out. He was impatient at their vacillation, and he brushed it all aside with the brusque and contemptuous speech: "Ye know nothing at all! The one point of view for us to have is our own interests. Let us have that clearly understood: when we once ask what is 'expedient for us,' there will be no doubt about the answer. This man must die! Never mind about His miracles, or His teaching, or the beauty of His character. His life is a perpetual danger to our prerogatives. I vote for death!"

John regards this selfish, cruel advice as a prophecy. Caiaphas spoke wiser things than he knew. The Divine Spirit breathed in strange fashion through even such lips as his, and moulded his savage utterance into such a form that it became a fit expression for the very deepest thought about the nature and the power of Christ's death. He did indeed die for that people—thinks the Evangelist—even though they have rejected Him, and the dreaded Romans *have* come and taken away our place and nation; but His death had a wider purpose, and was not for that nation only, but also that "He should gather together in one the children of God that are scattered abroad."

¶ "It is expedient that one man should die." We all acknowledge the truth of this prophecy, as the Evangelist acknowledged it. But what would Caiaphas himself have said if he had foreseen the result? I turn over the pages of history, and I find that a

few years after these words were uttered, Caiaphas was deposed
from the high priesthood by these very Romans whom he was so
very eager to conciliate.   I look further, and I read that some
thirty years later still, while many present at this council of
priests and Pharisees were yet living, the Romans did come and
take away both their place and nation ; and this, because in place
of believing on the true Christ, whose Kingdom was not of this
world, who commanded to give tribute to Cæsar, they chose as
their leaders false Messiahs, political adventurers, whose schemes
of earthly dominion were dangerous to the power and the majesty
of Rome.[1]

2. Once resolved on the removal of the dangerous Teacher, the
high priests endeavoured to secure it as quickly and as quietly as
possible.   The Galilæan multitude must be avoided, for the arrest
of "the Prophet Jesus, from Nazareth of Galilee," would rouse all
the smouldering antagonism between Galilæan and Judæan, and
provoke a riot which would bring down the rough hand of Rome
on both alike.   But after the feast Jesus would presumably have
retired to the north again.   Their only chance, therefore, was to
make Him somehow a Roman prisoner before His friends could
effect a rescue.   But that proved a difficult task.   Surrounded
throughout the week by loyal and admiring crowds, or attended
constantly by the bodyguard of devoted disciples, He could not be
taken without speedy alarm being given.   The treachery of Judas
at last helped them out of their difficulty ; and when the opportunity came, though on the very day they most wished to avoid,
they took a force large enough to overpower all opposition likely
to be met at such an hour, and arrested Jesus in Gethsemane.

At last Jesus and Caiaphas were face to face ; and the time
for which the high priest had plotted had really commenced.
Imagine the scene in that awful room in the high priest's house.
Since the meeting was illegal, it will probably have been also
more or less informal ; but something like the ordinary procedure
of the Sanhedrin must have been followed.   At the central
point of the inner circumference of a semicircle sat Caiaphas,
the president of the court ; and to the right and left of him were
seated his colleagues.   At each end was a clerk, the one to record
votes for acquittal, the other those for condemnation.

[1] J. B. Lightfoot, *Sermons Preached in St. Paul's Cathedral*, 78.

The proceedings of the court were scandalous. Caiaphas had cynically avowed his intention of destroying the prisoner on political grounds, and stuck at nothing to carry out his purpose. In the first place, the trial was begun and finished in one night. This was illegal. The proper course was to put the prisoner in ward till the next day, as was done with Peter and John. Next, the private official interrogatories addressed by the magistrate to the prisoner, before hearing witnesses, were quite illegal by Jewish law, though they are permitted in France. When Jesus replied to them, "Why askest thou me? ask them that have heard me," He was claiming His legal rights. Thirdly, the demand for confession, at the end of the questioning, was expressly forbidden by the Jewish doctors. Fourthly, the contradictory evidence of the "two false witnesses" was accepted as a charge of blasphemy, and the rest of the trial, which up till now had been quite vague, was a trial for blasphemy. But as even that court could not *convict* on such evidence, another attempt was made to cross-examine the Prisoner, again illegally. Jesus again asserted His legal rights and refused to answer. The concluding scene was held probably in the great hall called Gazith, and the court now consisted of the whole Sanhedrin, seventy-one in number, who sat in a semicircle with the presiding judge in the middle of the arc. The forms of a law-court were now forgotten in a wild scene of excitement. "Art thou the Christ? Tell us!" cried the judges. "If I tell you, ye will not believe," said the Prisoner, breaking silence at last. Then the high priest saw his opportunity and rose. "I adjure thee by the living God, that thou tell us whether thou be the Christ, the Son of God." The answer came: "I am." At once Caiaphas rent his robe from the top to the bottom, as the law was when one heard the name of God blasphemed, and cried: "He hath spoken blasphemy: what need of witnesses? Ye heard him. What think ye?" They all answered, "He is *Ish Maveth*—a man of death."

¶ Caiaphas little thought that he was sealing the doom, not of his prisoner, but of himself, his office, and his nation. In the sight of God, and in the eye of history too, it was not Jesus, but the high priest and the high priesthood who were tried, found guilty, and condemned on that day.[1]

[1] W. R. Inge, *All Saints' Sermons*, 33.

¶ The great importance of the trial for our purpose lies in the fact that the issue raised was Christ's claim to be the Son of God, the Messiah of Israel, and a King. He was tried unfairly and judged unjustly, but the true issue was raised. He died, then, because before the Jews He claimed to be the Son of God and the Messiah, and before Pilate to be Christ and King.

All generations since have felt that the judged was the Judge. The men were really standing before the bar of Christ, and all appear in terrible distinctness, revealed by the Light of the world.

Caiaphas, seeing his occasion in the terror of the nation that the Romans might efface them, and urging that this victim would appease the suspicion of their conquerors, and preserve the nation —a consideration so important as to make it of no consequence whether He was innocent or not—is a type of one who misinterprets the Divine covenant which he represented.

And Jesus, what shall we say of Him ? The great characteristic of the history is missed in reading it, for the events pass quickly in the terse narrative. It is the almost utter silence before all the judges, and the complete passiveness in the hands of those who insulted—all this, accompanied, as has been truly imagined, by a look, not of fortitude and tension, but rather of recollection, as if there was nothing in all these insults and questions to which any answer or expostulation was appropriate, but rather a current of inevitable passions which must be, but the moving spring of which is beyond the reach of words. No morbid dejection, no personal resentment, but a complete detachment from all earthly passion, and at the same time a conscious drawing out of deep springs of strength and consolation, which no human malice could reach to choke—infinitely above them all, their Judge while they judged Him.[1]

II.

HIS CHARACTER.

Did Caiaphas know that he was killing an inspired Prophet ? No, of course he did not. "Brethren, I wot that through ignorance ye did it, as did also your rulers," is the Apostolic verdict. The high priest condemned the Messiah to death in ignorance ; and are we sure that the prayer, " Father, forgive them, for they know not what they do," was meant to apply only to the Roman soldiers ? But ignorance is not always an excuse. Ignorance is a consequence

[1] W. R. Nicoll, *The Incarnate Saviour*, 249.

as well as a cause. If the high priest, when confronted with the Son of God, saw in Him only a mischievous agitator, to be suppressed in the interests of the Church, we must ask, Why was this judicial blindness sent upon him?

Self-interest mixed with religious formalism was the cause of Caiaphas' fall. It was accelerated by his unscrupulousness. Take these three strands separately.

1. *Self-interest.*—Our Lord had exposed the selfishness and hypocrisy of the ruling class with merciless severity. Only a few days before He had overturned the money-changers' tables in the Temple court as a protest against a highly ingenious and lucrative form of extortion, out of which the high officials enriched themselves. The sacrificial animals could be bought only on the spot, at a price fixed by the priests; and, as Roman money was not taken, those who brought it must exchange it for shekels—and the rate of exchange was fixed by the priests. This arrangement had been denounced and attacked; and therefore the rulers thought, " It is expedient (not for us, of course, but for the people) that he should die." Do we ever give our parliamentary and other votes for ourselves or our class, and then find some patriotic reason for our choice?

This selfish consideration of our own interests will make us as blind as bats to the most radiant beauty of truth; ay, and to Christ Himself, if the recognition of Him and of His message seems to threaten any of these. They tell us that fishes which live in the water of caverns lose their eyesight; and men that are always living in the dark holes of their own selfish, absorbed natures also lose their spiritual sight; and the fairest, loftiest, truest, and most radiant visions (which are realities) pass before their eyes, and they see them not. When you put on regard for yourselves, as they used to do blinkers upon horses, you have no longer the power of wide, comprehensive vision, but only see straight forward upon the narrow line which you fancy is marked out by your own interests. If ever there comes into the selfish man's mind a truth, or an aspect of Christ's mission, which may seem to cut against some of his practices or interests, how blind he is to it! When Lord Nelson was at Copenhagen, and they hoisted the signal of recall, he put his telescope to his blind eye and said, "I do not see it"! And that is exactly what this self-absorbed regard to one's own interests does with hundreds of men who do not in the least degree know it. It blinds them to the plain will of the commander-in-chief flying there at the masthead. "There are none so blind as those who will not see"; and there are none who so certainly will not see as those who have an uneasy suspicion that if they do see they will have to change their tack.

Look at the contrast. Against the overbearing insolence of Caiaphas, "Ye know nothing at all," set the perfect resignation of Christ, "Not my will, but thine be done." Against the selfish and cruel policy of Caiaphas, "It is expedient for us—for you and for me—that one man should die," set the absolute renunciation of Christ, "I lay down my life for my sheep." "It is expedient for you that I go away."

¶ Interest in the common good is at present so weak a motive in the generality, not because it can never be otherwise, but because the mind is not accustomed to dwell on it as it dwells from morning till night on things which tend only to personal advantage. When called into activity, as only self-interest now is, by the daily course of life, and spurred from behind by the love of distinction and the fear of shame, it is capable of producing, even in common men, the most strenuous exertions as well as the most heroic sacrifices. The deep-rooted selfishness which forms the general character of the existing state of society is so deeply rooted only because the whole course of existing institutions tends to foster it; and modern institutions in some respects more than ancient, since the occasions on which the individual is called on to do anything for the public without receiving its pay are far less frequent in modern life than in the smaller commonwealths of antiquity.[1]

2. *Religiosity.*—One of the awful warnings to be derived from this most terrible event in the history of mankind is the blindness, the vanity, the capability of unutterable wickedness which may co-exist with the pretentious scrupulosities of an external religionism. The priests and Pharisees had sunk into hypocrisy so deep and habitual that it had become half-unconscious, because it had narcotized and all but paralyzed the moral sense. They were infinitely particular about peddling littlenesses, but, with a hideous

[1] J. S. Mill, *Autobiography* (ed. 1908), 133.

cruelty and a hateful indifference to all their highest duties to God and man, they murdered, on false charges, the Lord of Glory. A vile self-interest—the determination at all costs to maintain their own prerogatives, and to prevent all questioning of their own traditional system—had swallowed up every other consideration in the minds of men whose very religion had become a thing of rites and ceremonies, and had lost all power to touch the heart or to inspire the moral sense. "The religion of Israel," it has been said, "falsified by priests, perverted from the service of the Living God into a sensuous worship—where the symbol superseded the reality, the Temple overshadowed the God, and the hierarchy supplanted His law—could find no love in its heart, no reverence in its will, for the holiest Person of its race; met Him not as the fruition of its hopes, and the end of its being, but as the last calamity of its life, a Being who must perish that it might live."

For Caiaphas something may be said. All that he knew of religion was bound up with the Temple service. This was not, in his view, a vulgar conflict about the material advantages of the priesthood; he was a custodier of a great tradition, which was seriously threatened by the Galilæan ministry. By clearing the Temple courts, Jesus had called attention to an abuse which the priests had suffered to grow up; and on the same occasion He had declared that, though the sanctity of the Temple were altogether destroyed, He could of Himself rear up a new order of right worship. He set His own decision against that of Moses, and affirmed or limited parts of the Law as one who had authority. And in all this He won the assent of many. The man healed of blindness was bold, in face of the council, to declare, "He is a prophet." Officers sent to report His words returned with a new sense of awe, for "never man spake like this man." Men of rank within the council—Nicodemus and Joseph—were wavering; for this obscure man, of whom the worst was credible, was somehow able to break the weapons which were used by Caiaphas against Him, and held on His dangerous way, unfixing men's regard for the ancient order of religion. So disdain changed to irritation, and that deepened into hatred against One who threatened what was sacred in the high priest's eyes. And throughout that process, Caiaphas never once was able to see

Christ justly; he saw a distorted imagination of Him through the mist of his own ignorance and his threatened interests. And when, at length, Jesus stood before him, Caiaphas was unable to see Him from the constraint of habit. He sought not for the truth about his Prisoner, but for a better persuasion that he already knew the truth.

¶ Carlyle quotes out of the Koran a story of the dwellers by the Dead Sea, to whom Moses was sent. They sniffed and sneered at Moses; saw no comeliness in Moses; and so he withdrew. But Nature and her rigorous veracities did not withdraw. When next we find the dwellers by the Dead Sea, they, according to the Koran, are all changed into apes. "By not using their souls, they lost them." "And now," continues Carlyle, "their only employment is to sit there and look out into the smokiest, dreariest, most undecipherable sort of universe. Only once in seven days they do remember that they once had souls. Hast thou never, O traveller! fallen in with parties of this tribe? Methinks they have grown somewhat numerous in our day." The old Greek proverb was that the avenging deities are shod with wool; but the wool grows on the eyelids that refuse the light. "Whom the gods would destroy, they first make mad"; but the insanity arises from judicial blindness.[1]

> But when we in our viciousness grow hard,—
> O misery on't!—the wise gods seel our eyes;
> In our own filth drop our clear judgments; make us
> Adore our errors; laugh at's while we strut
> To our confusion.[2]

¶ And now we have reached the Eighth Circle [of the Inferno] —the circle in which Dante keeps us so long. He calls it Malebolge: Evil Ditches. It slopes all round downwards and is divided into ten ditches. Around each ditch there runs a mole or embankment, and bridges of stone at intervals make causeways, by which to pass across the ditches. The shape of Malebolge is that of a basin, with a central hollow, and the embankments, of course, drop in level, from first to last, so that the bridges and embankments are always higher in each upper ditch than in the lower ditches, on the side nearest to the outer wall. . . . The Sixth Ditch—of the Hypocrites—is, to me, the most arresting. It is the only place, besides the descent to the Seventh Circle, where the ravages of the Crucifixion earthquake are in evidence.

[1] Joseph Cook, *Boston Monday Lectures*, i. 35.
[2] Shakespeare, *Antony and Cleopatra*, III. xi. 111.

Weary and weeping, these sinners tramp their round, weighed down with monks' hoods, gilded externally but fashioned of lead. At one point in each circuit of their external course they march over a recumbent naked figure, with arms outstretched, impaled upon the ground with three stakes, reminding us of the three nails of the Cross. It is Caiaphas, the arch-hypocrite, whose sin we all know. Annas, his father-in-law, and all the Sanhedrim of his time are near him. He has to feel through all eternity the weight of all the hypocrisy that has not been repented. Vergil starts at sight of Caiaphas. Is it because he realizes here a deeper meaning than he had when in his *Æneid* he prophesied " Unum pro multis dabitur caput " (*Æneid*, v. 815)? [1]

3. *Unscrupulousness.*—Lastly, Caiaphas was lost because of his unscrupulousness. We are told sometimes that the wise can always find employment in remedying the mistakes made by the good. But the worst mistakes are made not by the good, but by the unscrupulous—by those who, to quote a homely phrase, are "too clever by half." The unscrupulous man is a disastrous partner in any enterprise; in the direction of national or religious policy he is simply ruinous. History shows us many venerable institutions, many promising movements, undone by falling into the hands of a clever and ambitious knave. Of those who do evil that good may come, the Bible says shortly, " Their condemnation is just."

The one thing you can say in seeming favour of Caiaphas is that he was clever. Note the precise force of that word. It is set forth that Caiaphas was clever and not that he was wise. In this we hit upon a valuable distinction the world needs to master. Men and women are meant by God to be spiritual ; and since the spiritual is the line of our destiny, therefore goodness is the only true wisdom ; and crafty villainy is only the worse for its cleverness. Do we believe this ? Which would trouble us more, to be called a sinner, or to be spoken of as a fool ? There is many a man who is rather complimented when an acquaintance calls him a sinner, but who flames with anger when alluded to as a fool. Think what that means. If you have any doubt as to whether goodness is the truest wisdom, consider what follows, and at least learn how clever villainy reveals its true quality by simply appearing.

[1] H. B. Garrod, *Dante, Goethe's Faust, and other Lectures*, 109.

No one can accuse Caiaphas of weakness. He was a strong and alert man of inflexible purpose, able to command men and secure results. If he had fought on the right side, what a warrior he would have made! If his dominant personality had been surrendered to Jesus, what a Christian leader he would have become! As it is, he stands forth typical of what strength and selfishness will make of a man. He failed to understand the meaning of events. He failed to understand the real significance of Jesus. He beat his strength in vain against the walls of God's purpose. Pride and selfishness and a secular mind had blinded his eyes and hardened his heart. When he died the new religion was girding itself to conquer the world.

¶ Cleverness is something very petty. It is the quick perception of single points; it does not imply any great grasp; rather it excludes it. You may speak of a clever boy, because, having his faculties still undeveloped, he sees single things quickly and clearly. To speak of a clever man or woman would be a disparaging term. It would imply want of grasp or compass. But this cleverness is a great temptation to vanity. The single remarks strike persons, and they admire them. Some smile shows it; and the person goes his way and is self-satisfied and his vanity is nourished. And these petty tributes may be the more numerous, because they are petty.

Now just watch yourself for the little occasions in which you think yourself cleverer than another. Perhaps you won't call it clever, but something more solid; a true perception of things. Set yourself against any supposed superiority to any one. One grain of love is better than a hundredweight of intellect. And after all, that blasted spirit, Satan, has more intellect than the whole human race.[1]

¶ The Church needs leaders. She needs men of wise counsel and prompt energy and determining speech. She needs men who will patiently and untiringly serve her tables. But the office they fill is full of giddy and dazing temptations. No class of men need more the continual reconsecration of aim and the fresh baptism of the Spirit. But these are gained only as men keep themselves in the faith and love of Jesus. The man to whom Christ is a name, or only an instrument of service, is a danger to the Church. But the man to whom He is Lord, in whose heart a deep devotion maintains its unquenched fire, may make mistakes, may seem to endanger sacred interests, but his blunder-

[1] *Spiritual Letters of Edward Bouverie Pusey*, 104.

ing will be wiser than the cold prudence of the ecclesiastic. The great names in the Church of God, from Moses and Samuel to Wesley and Chalmers, have been men who lived in such adoring love to Christ that they dared to break with the old order and lead men in new departures owned and blessed of God. Ah, had Caiaphas only known his Lord, what a wonderful page of grace would have been written in this gospel: " And they that laid hands on Jesus led him away to Caiaphas. And when Caiaphas looked upon Him, and saw Him meek and lowly, he was deeply moved. And Jesus turned and looked upon Caiaphas, and in that hour his heart smote him, and his eyes were cleansed, and he saw the Son of God. And he came down from his high priest's seat, and took off the ephod he wore, and put it upon Jesus, and, being high priest that same year, he prophesied: 'Behold the Lamb of God which taketh away the sins of the world. Behold the King of Israel.' And he kneeled down before Him and said: 'Thou art an High Priest for ever, after the order of Melchizedek!'" Alas, there is no such scripture. Christ was only the stone of stumbling, and the rock of offence to him, on which he fell to be broken for ever.[1]

[1] W. M. Clow, *The Day of the Cross*, 23.

PILATE.

LITERATURE.

Broade, G. E., *The Sixfold Trial of Our Lord* (1899), 21, 33.
Brodrick, M., *The Trial and Crucifixion of Jesus Christ of Nazareth* (1908), 102.
Brooke, S. A., *Sermons,* ii. (1875) 294.
Burn, A. E., *The Crown of Thorns* (1911), 27.
Bush, J., *Modern Thoughts on Ancient Stories,* 156.
Buss, S., *Roman Law and History in the New Testament* (1901), 174.
Cameron, A. B., *From the Garden to the Cross* (1896), 132, 181.
Candlish, R. S., *Scripture Characters* (1872), 297, 320, 339.
Carpenter, W. B., *The Son of Man among the Sons of Men* (1893), 35.
Clow, W. M., *The Day of the Cross* (1909), 27.
Doney, C. G., *The Throne-Room of the Soul* (1907), 83.
English, E., *Sermons and Homilies* (1913), 95.
Farrar, F. W., *The Life of Lives* (1900), 494.
Hough, L. H., *The Men of the Gospels* (1913), 71.
Innes, A. T., *The Trial of Jesus Christ* (1899), 61.
Lightfoot, J. B., *Sermons Preached in St. Paul's Cathedral* (1891), 91.
Little, W. J. K., *Sunlight and Shadow* (1892), 242.
Lucas, B., *Conversations with Christ* (1905), 246.
Moulton, J. H., *Visions of Sin* (1891), 187.
Mursell, A., *Hush and Hurry* (1902), 18, 29.
Peabody, F. G., *Mornings in the College Chapel,* ii. (1908) 185.
    ,,   ,, *Sunday Evenings in the College Chapel* (1911), 197.
Robertson, F. W., *Sermons,* i. (1875) 292.
Rosadi, G., *The Trial of Jesus* (1905), 219.
Sewell, W., *The Character of Pilate* (1850).
Simcox, W. H., *The Cessation of Prophecy* (1891), 287.
Smith, H. A., in *A Book of Lay Sermons* (1905), 3.
Stalker, J., *The Trial and Death of Jesus Christ* (1894), 43.
Stevenson, J. G., *The Judges of Jesus* (1909), 153.
Trench, R. C., *Sermons New and Old* (1886), 134.
Vaughan, B., *Society, Sin and the Saviour* (1908), 89.
Watson, J., *The Life of the Master* (1902), 373.
Whyte, A., *Bible Characters* : Joseph and Mary to James (1900), 121
Dictionary of the Bible, iii. (1909) 875 (G. T. Purves).
Dictionary of Christ and the Gospels, ii. (1908) 363 (A. Souter).
Preacher's Magazine, xxiv. (1913) 295 (E. S. Waterhouse).

PILATE.

What I have written, I have written.—John xix. 22.

1. WE do not commonly remember, it costs us an effort to re-member, how very largely we are indebted to the Fourth Gospel for our conceptions of the chief personages who bear a part in the Evangelical history, when these conceptions are most distinct. If we analyze the source of our information, we find again and again that, while something is told us about a particular person in the other Gospels, yet it is St. John who gives those touches to the portrait which make him stand out with his own individuality as a real, living, speaking man. The other Evangelists will record a name or perhaps an incident. St. John will add one or two sayings, and the whole person is instinct with life. The character flashes out in half a dozen words. Out of the abundance of the heart the mouth speaketh. So it is with Thomas, with Philip, with Martha and Mary, with several others who might be named.

Pilate furnishes a remarkable illustration of this feature in the Fourth Gospel. Pilate is the chief agent in the crowning scene in the Evangelical history. He is necessarily a prominent figure in all the four narratives of this crisis. In the first three Gospels we learn much about him; we find him there, as we find him in St. John, at cross purposes with the Jews; he is represented there, not less than by St. John, as giving an unwilling consent to the judicial murder of Jesus. His Roman sense of justice is too strong to allow him to yield without an effort; his personal courage is too weak to persevere in the struggle when the con-sequences threaten to become inconvenient. He is timid, politic, time-serving, as represented by all alike; he has just enough conscience to wish to shake off the responsibility, but far too little conscience to shrink from committing a sin.

But in St. John's narrative we pierce far below the surface. Here Pilate is revealed to us as the sarcastic, cynical worldling, who doubts everything, distrusts everything, despises everything. He has an intense scorn for the Jews, and yet he has a craven dread of them. He has a certain professional regard for justice, and yet he has no real belief in truth or honour. Throughout he manifests a malicious irony in his conduct at this crisis. There is a lofty scorn in his answer, when he repudiates any sympathy with the accusers, "Am I a Jew?" There is a sarcastic pity in the question which he addresses to the Prisoner before him: "Art *thou* the King of the Jews?" "Art *thou* then a King, thou poor, weak, helpless fanatic, whom with a single word I could doom to death?" He is half-bewildered, half-diverted, with the incongruity of this claim. And yet there is a certain propriety that a wild enthusiast should assert his sovereignty over a nation of bigots. So he sarcastically adopts the title: "Will ye that I release unto you the King of the Jews?" Even when at length he is obliged to yield to the pópular clamour, he will at least have his revenge by a studied contempt. "Behold your King." "Shall I crucify your King?" And to the very last moment he indulges his cynical scorn. The title on the cross was indeed unconsciously a proclamation of a Divine truth, but in its immediate purpose and intent it was the mere gratification of Pilate's sarcastic humour. "Jesus of Nazareth (could any good thing come out of Nazareth?), Jesus of Nazareth, the King of the Jews!" He has sacrificed his honour to them; but he will not sacrifice his contempt: "What I have written, I have written."

¶ Like all who yield what they know they should not give up, Pilate tried to cover his weakness by obstinacy. If he had asserted himself a little sooner, he would have escaped his bad preeminence. He did not know what he had written, in imperishable characters, in the record of his deeds; and, while he thought himself announcing with fitting dignity his determination, he was declaring that the black lines he had traced would last for ever. Strange that the awful truth of the ineffaceableness of our deeds should come from his lips! Blessed we if we have learned that He whom Pilate slew will blot out our sins from His book.[1]

2. We know nothing of Pilate apart from his administration of Judæa. His family name Pontius leaves open the possibility that he was descended from the brave Samnite general Gaius

[1] A. Maclaren.

Pontius, the hero of the Caudine Forks. Philo quotes from Agrippa I. a comprehensive account of the man: "Inflexibly obstinate by nature, he was as reckless as he was implacable." The same witness describes "his openness to bribes, his acts of insolence, his robberies, his outrages, his tyrannies, his unbroken series of murders without form of trial, his insatiable and devastating savagery."

His acts abundantly bear out this description. Incapable himself of understanding why any one should care "what is truth," he set himself from the first to trample upon the religious prejudices which he so heartily despised. When he entered on his province, he sent his men into Jerusalem by night with flags showing the figure of the Emperor. For six days the Jews fruitlessly protested and entreated, and Pilate answered by preparing a general massacre at Cæsarea, whither the eager people had hastened; he yielded only when he had satisfied his insolence by securing the people's submission. He impounded the Temple treasures to build an aqueduct, and overawed the people by scattering among them plain-clothes men secretly armed with clubs. St. Luke tells us of Galilæan pilgrims, otherwise unknown, whose blood Pilate mingled with the sacrifices they came to offer.

¶ It will, perhaps, help us to realize the position of Pilate if we compare it with that of a French general despatched from the idle and fashionable life of the boulevards to administer the government of Algiers. There would be a like contemptuous estimate of the race to be kept in subjection by military force; a lofty sense of superiority which would lead its possessor to regard the exercise of cruelty towards them as something quite different in its nature from cruelty towards his fellow-countrymen. This would be readily called forth under the irritation of *émeutes* or petty revolts, seen to be foolishly weak, yet quite sufficient to cause annoyance. Just as St. Arnaud, the scandalous and favourite marshal of Napoleon the little, exasperated the Kabyles of the Atlas by atrocious cruelties, which were rewarded with disgraceful decorations, so Pilate inaugurated his administration by first outraging the religious sensibilities of those under his authority, and then treacherously murdering those who protested against his insults.[1]

¶ In his volume of essays entitled *Liberty, Equality, Fraternity*, Fitzjames [who held that, in regard to religions, the

[1] W. E. Skinner, *A Book of Lay Sermons*, 4.

State cannot be an impartial bystander, and who disputed John
Stuart Mill's view on the subject] discusses at some length the
case of Pontius Pilate, to which I may notice he had often applied
parallels from Ram Singh and other Indian experiences. Pontius
Pilate was in a position analogous to that of the governor of a
British province. He decides that if Pilate had acted upon Mill's
principles he would have risked "setting the whole province in a
blaze." He condemns the Roman persecutors as "clumsy and
brutal"; but thinks that they might have succeeded "in the same
miserable sense in which the Spanish Inquisition succeeded," had
they been more systematic, and then would at least not have been
self-stultified. Had the Roman Government seen the importance
of the question, the strife, if inevitable, might have been noble.
It would have been a case of "generous opponents each working
his way to the truth from opposite sides," not the case of a
"touching though slightly hysterical victim, mauled from time to
time by a sleepy tyrant in his intervals of fury."[1]

3. This man, then, was the governor, that is, procurator, of
Judæa to whom the Jewish council delivered Jesus. He had
already been condemned to death, and gladly would the Jewish
authorities have carried it out in the Jewish fashion—by stoning.
But it was not in their power: their Roman masters, while
conceding to the native courts the power of trying and punishing
minor offences, reserved to themselves the prerogative of life and
death; and a case in which a capital sentence had been passed in
a Jewish court had to go before the representative of Rome in the
country, who tried it over again, and might either confirm or
reverse the sentence.

What a spectacle was that! The heads of the Jewish nation
leading their own Messiah in chains to deliver Him up to a
Gentile governor, with the petition that He should be put to
death! Shades of the heroes and the prophets who loved this
nation and boasted of it and foretold its glorious fate, the hour of
destiny has come, and this is the result!

¶ Luther, strange to say, was inclined almost to apologize for
Pilate, whom he describes in his *Table Talk* as "a kindly man
of the world," that "scourged Christ from compassion, that he
might thereby quiet the insatiable rage and fury of the Jews."
"Pilate," he adds, "is a better man than any of the princes of the
empire (at present) who are not Evangelical. He kept firmly to

[1] Leslie Stephen, *The Life of Sir James Fitzjames Stephen*, 326.

the Roman rights and laws, affirming that he could not suffer an innocent man to be put to death, his cause unheard, convicted of no one evil deed. Therefore he tried all honourable methods to set Christ free. But when they spoke to him of the displeasure of Cæsar, he was carried away, and let the Roman laws and rights go. For he thought, 'It is only one man, poor, and, moreover, despised. No one will take the case up. What harm can his death do me? It is better that one should die than that the whole nation should be set against me.'

"When Pilate asked Christ, 'Art thou the King of the Jews?' 'Yes,' He said, 'I am; but not such a king as Cæsar, else would My servants and soldiers fight for Me to set Me free. But I am a King sent to preach the Glad Tidings, that I might bear witness to the Truth.' 'Oh,' said Pilate, 'if thou art a king of that kind, and hast such a kingdom as that, consisting of the Word and the Truth, thou wilt do no harm to my kingdom.' And Pilate doubtless thought, 'Jesus is a good, simple, harmless man, who is talking about a kingdom no one knows anything about. Probably he comes out of some forest, or out-of-the-way region, and is a simple creature who knows nothing of the world or its government.'"[1]

4. It is not our purpose to follow the trial of Jesus by Pilate through all its tortuous and humiliating scenes. Our purpose is to inquire into Pilate's character. It is from these scenes that we learn what manner of man he was, but they are familiar to us, and we shall proceed at once to gather from them the features of this man's character which led him to play his great part so ignobly. We shall find that his failure was due to unbelief, worldliness, and weakness.

I.

UNBELIEF.

Pilate first hears what the people have to say—then asks the opinion of the priests—then comes back to Jesus—goes again to the priests and people—lends his ear—listens to the ferocity on the one hand, and feels the beauty on the other, balancing between them; and then he becomes bewildered, as a man of the world is apt to do who has had no groundwork of religious

[1] Luther, *Table Talk*, iv. 172, 398.

education, and hears superficial discussions on religious matters, and superficial charges, and superficial slanders, till he knows not what to think. What *could* come out of such procedure? Nothing but that cheerlessness of soul to which certainty respecting anything and everything here on earth seems unattainable. This is the exact mental state which we call scepticism.

Out of that mood, when he heard the enthusiast before him speak of a Kingdom of the Truth, there broke a sad, bitter, sarcastic sigh, "What is truth?" Who knows anything about it? Another discoverer of the undiscoverable! "*Jesting* Pilate!" says Bacon; with Pilate the matter was beyond a jest. It was not a question put for the sake of information. It was not put for the sake of ridicule, for he went out to say, "I find no fault in him." Sarcasm there was perhaps, but it was that mournful bitter sarcasm which hides inward unrest in sneering words, that sad irony whose very laugh rings of inward wretchedness.

Long ago he had shared in the speculation of the time; no educated man could escape it. Sect after sect had claimed to tell the truth, and men had found nothing to satisfy them, no ground on which to rest, till at last, in weary carelessness, Pilate, like hundreds, had hushed the cry of his heart for truth and turned to worldly life, hearing only, with a smile of scorn, of the efforts still made by enthusiasts to find the undiscoverable. When, behold, storming in upon his soul from the lips of a wretched Jew over whom he had the power of life and death, in a common room, came the old haunting question of his youth—truth, truth, what is it? For a moment the outward world faded into its real unreality; for a moment the sleeping thirst was stirred; for a moment he looked back and recalled the vain efforts of years, the hopes worn out by length of time, the surrender of the wearisome pursuit—and "What is truth?" broke from his lips. It came on him with a shock of strange surprise. "What is this," he might have said, "that wakes within me the long-forgotten thrill, this breath of youthful aspiration — truth, truth, and its deceiving beauty—why eat my heart again over a vain quest; why go back to kindle an exhausted flame?" And, as Bacon says, and this time truly, he did not wait for a reply.

So unchanged is human nature that we seem to be reading the history of many lives in our own day. Our youth has been rife with speculation; the great spiritual questions of Immortality, Necessity, Free Will, Evil and its origin, our relation to a God, or a Fate, or a Chance, have tossed us to and fro for years. At school, at home, at college, on entering manhood and womanhood, the great questioning has moved our soul. And at first we took our pleasure therein. We loved the lonely hours in the mist in which we saw strange shapes of good, mysterious folding and unfolding of light and gloom which seemed to tell truths as wonderful as beautiful. But as each question seemed to receive its answer another question started up, and what seemed to answer it threw doubt upon the previous answer; till at last the mist sank down, and our weary eyes saw no more changes, no more visions there. It was hard to breathe in that atmosphere, and we were chilled to the bone with disappointment. So we passed out of it into what we called practical life, saying to all these questions with the poet, "I know not; let me do my duty. The past has been failure; let me use the present." We turned to professional, literary, or mercantile life, shut up that misty chamber, drowned the key, deeper than ever plummet sounded, and said to ourselves, "There may be an answer to these matters, but I can never find it. I will agree to postpone them; let others take them and judge them according to their law, I whistle them down the wind."

¶ Jesting Pilate had not the smallest chance to ascertain what was Truth. He could not have known it, had a god shown it to him. Thick serene opacity, thicker than amaurosis, veiled those smiling eyes of his to Truth; the inner *retina* of them was gone paralytic, dead. He looked at Truth; and discerned her not, there where she stood.[1]

II.

WORLDLINESS.

Pilate had been a public man. He knew life; he had mixed much with the world's business and the world's politics: had come across a multiplicity of opinions, and gained a smattering of them all. He knew how many philosophies and religions pretended to an exclusive possession of Truth; and how the

[1] Carlyle, *Past and Present*, bk. i. chap. ii.

pretensions of each were overthrown by another. And his in-credulity was but a specimen of the scepticism fashionable in his day—the scepticism of a polished educated Roman, a sagacious man of the world, too much behind the scenes of public life to trust professions of goodness or disinterestedness, or to believe in enthusiasm and a sublime life. And his merciful language, and his desire to save Jesus, was precisely the liberalism current in our day as in his—an utter disbelief in the truths of a world unseen, but at the same time an easy, careless toleration, a half-benevolent, half-indolent unwillingness to molest the poor dreamers who chose to believe in such superstitions.

¶ And such is Pilate in our modern life—the superior person, restrained and worldly-wise, emancipated from vulgar enthusiasms, not entangled in other people's troubles, unaffected by the majesty of truth even when it stands straight before his face. And over against this jaunty neutrality stands, to-day, as it stood in this Passion Week in Jerusalem, the spirit of Jesus Christ, the erect and self-respecting faith of man in communion with the Eternal. Over against the trimmer in political life stands the loyal worker for political reform; over against the literary critic with his fine contempt stands the creative scholar with his unstained ideals and aims. Before the self-indulgent woman of the conventional world, smiling at the folly of serious views, stands the woman who has found a great new joy in the service of less favoured lives.

I see these types of the Christian life coming up one by one to-day before Pilate's judgment-seat. I see the patient student stand before the scoffing critic; I see the persistent reformer smiled at by the stay-at-home; I see the self-forgetting servant of the common good fail, and the self-indulgent time-server succeed; I see the life that tries to be faithful bearing heavy burdens, and the life that is content to be worldly gain its end. It is all as if Jesus Christ passed once more from Pilate's judgment-hall to the agony of Gethsemane, while Pilate withdrew once more behind his curtains to the composure of his self-satisfied life; as if the Christian life had still to defend itself, and the neutral had but to judge and go; as if right were for ever on the scaffold and wrong for ever on the throne. I see the intellectual dilettantism of the present day, and its moral levity, and its religious indifferentism, sitting on the scorner's judgment-seat, and I hear their light-hearted fling of, "What is Truth?" as they go their way of self-satisfied success. And then I wait; and I see these Pilates of the present time, like him who thought he sat in judgment on the Christ, have their little day of imaginary importance, and then simply shrivel up into specks in the world's history; remembered only because they happened one day to stand near the life which they jauntily condemned. And I see the faithful servants of the truth, as they go their way with their crosses upon their shoulders, finishing the work that is given them to do; and they have the confident step of those whose passion is a victory, whose cross is a crown, and whose place is not among the Cæsars but among the saviours, not with the courtiers of Pilate but with the disciples of Christ.[1]

¶ To an old pupil at Oxford, Dr. Arnold wrote from Rugby in the spring of 1835, lamenting the spread of a spirit of indifference and dilettantism. "I suppose," he said, "that Pococuranteism (excuse the word) is much the order of the day amongst young men. I observe symptoms of it here, and am always dreading its ascendancy, though we have some who struggle nobly against it. I believe that 'Nil admirari' in this sense is the Devil's favourite text; and he could not choose a better to introduce his pupils into the more esoteric parts of his doctrine. And therefore I have always looked upon a man infected with this disorder as on one who has lost the finest part of his nature, and his best protection against every thing low and foolish."[2]

¶ Dilettantism he abhorred. He earnestly warned the students attending the local schools of art against it, exhorting them to painstaking work and faithful, persistent endeavours after excellence. "There is not the slightest hope," he told them, "for the dabbler or the dilettante. Of all the contemptible creatures to be found in this earth it contains none more contemptible than a dabbler or dilettante in art, science, or social philosophy." He pointed to Michael Angelo, with his beetle brows, large, square, prominent cheekbones, straight-cut, hard-pressed mouth, and bruised nose, all proclaiming, "There is no dilettantism here."[3]

III.

WEAKNESS.

1. Compelled to take the leading part in a transaction where high moral qualities were supremely demanded, Pilate proved

---

[1] F. G. Peabody, *Sunday Evenings in the College Chapel*, 213.
[2] A. P. Stanley, *Life and Correspondence of Thomas Arnold*, i. 419.
[3] A. B. Bruce, *The Life of William Denny*, 265.

himself to be without them, and made a great crime possible by his feebleness of character. This is quite consistent with his bravado and recklessness on other occasions.

He seems to have been a man with some refinement, reflective, almost philosophical, possessing the literary habit, and with it, as so often happens, an impatience of the vulgar matters which excite the crowd, with a certain indolence which nevertheless did not kill his ambition or dull his interest in philosophical questions, with more love of speculation than desire for decision; weak morally, timid politically, and yet driven by weakness into acts which looked like relentless cruelty; for the worst cruelties of the world are the product of weakness and fear. He was one of those men whom we wonder at and pity, for they are weak men placed in circumstances which need vigour and calmness. Such are the men who, if placed in quiet and peaceful times, might ripen into philosophical mildness and dilettante amiability, tinged with a pleasant and not very serious cynicism; but who, in stormy and troublous days, being thrust into positions of high trust and imperative responsibility, hesitate, evade, vacillate, resolve and un-resolve, and end by being the perpetrators of horrors which revolt the world, and which would have been impossible to sterner and stronger natures.

¶ I don't quite understand you about Pilate. Surely *his* strength, at any rate, was not "to sit still." He sat still and washed his hands, and it was all wrong. If he had "put a decisive act between himself and temptation," he would have seized his chance. What he did was the weakest thing he could do, not the strongest. It is only when sitting still is the hardest, most difficult, course that there is strength in it. Again I sympathize. I have so often made my own temptations much harder in the end, because I did not pluck up courage enough to do the decisive act, when I knew it ought to be done. We are not taught that we should let the temptation get as bad as possible before we try to do anything; else why should we pray, "Lead us not into temptation"?[1]

¶ One of the greatest of English novelists has drawn for us, in a manner wonderfully true to human nature, the character of one who reached the depths of depravity simply through the habit of always yielding to selfish interest in little things. Such is Tito Melema in George Eliot's *Romola*. In describing one of

[1] *Gathered Leaves from the Prose of Mary E. Coleridge*, 275.

Melema's base actions, the writer sets down a sentence which every young man and woman would do well to lay to heart. "Tito," she says, "now experienced that inexorable law of human souls, that we prepare ourselves for sudden deeds by the reiterated choice of good or evil which gradually determines character." Pilate in real life points the same moral as Tito Melema in fiction, and it is one that is terribly serious because of the subtlety and frequency of the temptation. The habit of wrongdoing in little things is the certain preparation for a fatal fall in a great time of testing. The fearless doing of right in defiance of self-interest or peril is the training of a hero and a saint.[1]

¶ There was one peculiarity in Goethe's nature, namely, a singular hesitation in adopting any decisive course of action— singular, in a man so resolute and imperious when once his decision had been made. This is the weakness of imaginative men. However strong the volition, when once it is set going, there is in men of active intellects, and especially in men of imaginative apprehensive intellects, a fluctuation of motives keeping the volition in abeyance, which practically amounts to weakness; and is only distinguished from weakness by the strength of the volition when let loose. Goethe, who was aware of this peculiarity, used to attribute it to his never having been placed in circumstances which required prompt resolutions, and to his not having educated his will; but I believe the cause lay much deeper, lying in the nature of psychological actions, not in the accidents of education.[2]

2. We may pity the weak who fail, but can we blame them? It is not for us to judge; but we can learn. One lesson is clear. Weakness often fails, because it does not make use of the strength which is at hand. No man is beaten without remembering in the hour of his defeat the lost opportunities which might have been turned into means of victory. Pilate failed, and Pilate's name is covered with the memory of his shameful weakness; but Pilate did not fall unwarned, or fail for want of helpful and stimulating influences.

(1) He was a Roman, and the national and traditional characteristics of his race might have been summoned to his aid. Roman firmness and vigorous Roman administration, however much enervating vice may have become fashionable, were not

---

[1] W. E. Skinner, *A Book of Lay Sermons*, 15.
[2] G. H. Lewes, *The Life of Goethe*, 492.

wholly dead. They must still have appealed as ideals to men who had any knowledge and any patriotic love of the history of Rome. If weakness was a vice in Roman eyes, was not the consciousness of this a witness against feebleness and unjust irresolution in any Roman governor?

¶ Bad execution of your designs does less harm than irresolution in forming them. Streams do less harm flowing than when dammed up. There are some men so infirm of purpose that they always require direction from others, and this not on account of any perplexity, for they judge clearly, but from sheer incapacity for action. It needs some skill to find out difficulties, but more to find a way out of them. There are others who are never in straits : their clear judgment and determined character fit them for the highest callings; their intelligence tells them where to insert the thin end of the wedge, their resolution how to drive it home. They soon get through anything : as soon as they have done with one sphere of action, they are ready for another. Affianced to Fortune, they make themselves sure of success.[1]

(2) He had a home, and the partner of his home joys was a woman who at least was no dullard, but whose thought and sagacity went forth with sympathy to her husband in his work. Her voice spoke to him in the moment of his temptation, and was lifted up against the fatal policy of evasion and feebleness. The dream of Pilate's wife, and the message to which it gave rise, must not be flung aside as a mere picturesque addition to the story. People do not dream of matters of which they know nothing. The occurrence of the incident suggests to us that there must have been previous thought and previous knowledge. "That just man" whose memory haunted the woman in her dreams was one who must have been more than a casual prisoner brought before the ruler. Can it have been that His fame had reached Pilate's household beforehand? Can it have been that some of His strange utterances and wonderful works had been told in the hearing of Pilate or his wife? Whatever the earlier history may have been, this woman, whose thoughtful disposition made her a helpmeet to Pilate, was evidently impressed in some way with the moral beauty and spiritual dignity of the Prophet of Nazareth, and her influence was exerted to stay the feet of her husband on the fatal downward path of irresolution and injustice.

[1] Balthasar Gracian, *The Art of Worldly Wisdom*, 42.

¶ In Luther's day a distinction was drawn between different kinds of dreams. One class was sent, as men of that age believed, directly by the devil. To this class they thought the dream of Pilate's wife belonged. Some one asked Luther what was the purpose of the evil one, in seeking thus, through a dream, to hinder the crucifixion of Christ. The doctor answered that perhaps he thought, " I have murdered many prophets, and yet things have got worse and worse. They are too faithful, and this Man also has no fear. I prefer that He should remain alive. Perhaps I might be able to kill or mislead Him through some temptation. In this way I might accomplish more ! "

So you went and you told him my word, as he sat on the ivory throne;
He was troubled and pale as he heard, but he gave you an answer? None!
He is dazed and daunted, the Roman, by Jews, and the venomous gleam
Of their eyes—can he list to a woman or hearken the tale of a dream?

Can he argue of mercy or ruth, while they cry for the cross and the rods?
He smiles, and he asks "What is truth?" when they show him the signs of the gods;
By the washing and wiping of hands he is cleansed from the blood of the just;
As the water is dried upon sands, so a life flieth back to the dust.

For the murderous multitude foam, and the palace is pale with alarm,
He looks, and the pitiless dome of the heavens is empty and calm,
He heard not the hurrying sound as of ghosts that arose from the deep;
He saw not the gathering round me of terrors that torture sleep.

But they clouded the glass of my brain, the Powers of the Air, while I slept,
Infinite ominous train, out of void into void as they swept.
Are the myriad Manes warning that evil shall come as a flood?
Or the kindly divinities mourning for the sorrow of innocent blood?

For above came a crowd and a sighing; as late in the last
watch of night,
When in cities besieged is a crying of people run wild with
affright;
When the streets are all thronged in the gloom, for with day
comes slaughter and storm,
So my ear rang with voices of doom, and mine eye saw a
vanishing Form.

Who is He for whom spectres are risen to threaten, and
spirits to weep?
Who is this whom ye bear from your prison, the face which
I saw in my sleep?
The hours seem to hover and wait—is a Nemesis loading their
wings?
I am stirred by forebodings of fate, and the sense of unspeak-
able things.[1]

(3) There was yet another restraining hand which the providence of the hour brought to Pilate's aid. This was the hand of
the Prisoner at the judgment-seat. The narrative shows us the
singular spectacle of the weak and the accused man giving moral
aid to the strong one who was His judge. Christ's replies to
Pilate are not so much replies on the case as replies on the moral
responsibility of Pilate at the moment. He is more anxious to
save Pilate from moral ruin than Himself from death. He turns
Pilate's thoughts upon himself. "Sayest thou this thing of thyself?" He speaks to him of the sublime and spiritual kingdom
of the truth, higher and more enduring than any splendour of
imperial Rome. He lifts His judge into the serene atmosphere of
heaven. "Every one that is of the truth heareth my voice." He
reminds Pilate of that Divine source of all judgment and power
to whom every judge and mighty one of the world is finally
responsible. He tells that power is not a thing of pride, but a
responsibility and a trust. It is given from on high. In all these
the hand of help is reached forth to Pilate. Pilate sees it; his
conscience makes him uneasy; he is aware that he is thrusting
away from him some truly spiritual and real aid. But the weakness and ambition of his nature are too much. He struggles, but
he struggles in vain, and he is swept away, a worthless and unre-
sisting piece of wreckage, on the wave of popular tumult.

[1] Sir A. C. Lyall, *The Dream of Pilate's Wife.*

¶ It is interesting to think what Pilate might have become had he, like one of his officers, confessed the Crucified to be the Son of God. What an Easter Day the resurrection morning would have been to him and his wife! What a tribute of gratitude men of succeeding ages would have paid him: churches in his honour, children named after him, books written about him! It was a great opportunity, but he missed it, missed it because it awakened no need. And Pilate passes away as a disappointed, broken life. The old legend, that he still haunts one of the Swiss lakes, is only typical of the feeling his memory awakes: a restless shadow ever seeking, but in vain, the opportunity he flung away.[1]

¶ There is a well-known short story by Anatole France where Pontius Pilate is represented in retirement near the end of his life talking over old times with a pleasure-loving friend who had known him in Judæa. During supper the talk falls upon the qualities of the Jewish women, and the friend speaks of Mary of Magdala whom he had known during her unrepentant days in Jerusalem. He recounts the manner of his parting from Mary, who left him to join the band of a young miracle-worker from Galilee. "His name was Jesus; He came from Nazareth, and was crucified at last for some crime or other. Pontius, do you remember the man?" The old procurator frowned and raised a hand to his forehead as one who searches through his memory. Then, after some moments of silence, "Jesus," he muttered, "Jesus of Nazareth? No, I don't remember Him."[2]

[1] G. H. S. Walpole, *Personality and Power*, 135.
[2] H. Sturt, *The Idea of a Free Church*, 224.

HEROD ANTIPAS.

LITERATURE.

Broade, G. E., *The Sixfold Trial of Our Lord* (1899).
Brodrick, M., *The Trial and Crucifixion of Jesus Christ of Nazareth* (1908).
Buss, S., *Roman Law and History in the New Testament* (1901), 112.
Cameron, A. B., *From the Garden to the Cross* (1896), 157.
Candlish, R. S., *Scripture Characters* (1872), 166.
Carpenter, W. B., *The Son of Man among the Sons of Men* (1893), 11.
Clow, W. M., *The Day of the Cross* (1909), 43.
English, E., *Sermons and Homilies* (1913), 127.
Farrar, F. W., *The Herods* (1898), 166.
Hough, L. H., *The Men of the Gospels* (1913), 79.
Innes, A. T., *The Trial of Jesus Christ* (1899).
Luckock, H. M., *Footprints of the Son of Man as traced by St. Mark*, ii.
    (1886) 262.
Maclaren, A., *Christ in the Heart* (1886), 317.
Moulton, J. H., *Visions of Sin* (1898), 153.
Robertson, F. W., *Sermons*, iii. (1876) 270.
Rosadi, G., *The Trial of Jesus* (1905).
Stalker, J., *The Trial and Death of Jesus Christ* (1894), 58.
    „   „   *The Two St. Johns* (1895), 271.
Tipple, S. A., *Days of Old* (1911), 157.
Whyte, A., *Bible Characters* : Joseph and Mary to James (1900), 142.
Dictionary of the Bible, ii. (1899) 358 (A. C. Headlam).
    „   „   „   (Single-volume, 1909), 344 (H. S. Nash).
Dictionary of Christ and the Gospels, i. (1906) 721 (W. P. Armstrong).
Encyclopædia Biblica, ii. (1901), col. 2030 (W. J. Woodhouse).

HEROD ANTIPAS.

Now when Herod saw Jesus, he was exceeding glad : for he was of a long time desirous to see him, because he had heard concerning him ; and he hoped to see some miracle done by him. And he questioned him in many words ; but he answered him nothing.—Luke xxiii. 8, 9.

OF all the Herods known to history the one with whom the reader of the New Testament is best acquainted is Herod Antipas. He was one of the sons of Herod the Great. On the death of his father he became ruler of Galilee and Peræa, his title being tetrarch, although by courtesy he was sometimes called king. It is this Herod's spiritual history that we are now to follow. It is comprehended under two titles: (1) Herod and John; (2) Herod and Jesus.

I.

HEROD AND JOHN.

1. In spite of the meanness and misery of his life, we are bound to confess that Herod was a religious man. In a sense all the Herods were religious. If it had not been so, they would not have been tolerated by the Jews, to whom it was ever a sore thought that they belonged to the hated offspring of Edom. Their religion was primitive enough, we might safely say savage enough, and therefore mixed with elements of treachery, blood-thirstiness, and lust. Yet it was religion of a sort. The feeling after God was there, and as evidence of its existence there was always a conscience that could be wrought to a pitch of bitter remorse.

¶ As the eye is correlated with light, so is every specific organ correlated with some external arrangement, without which it would not have existed. Now apply this doctrine to that moral or spiritual faculty which in the majority of men acknowledges

the presence of a spiritual observer and judge of absolutely secret
thoughts and motives. Can we suppose that this sense of shame
without the presence of any bodily observer, this sense of peace
and even joy which streams in from outside just as it would do,
though in larger measure, from the sympathy of a friend, is a mere
imaginative overflow from the conception of ourselves as we
should feel if our mind were transparent to the eye of those
we wished to please? Surely the quiver of the whole nature to
observation *from within* bespeaks as distinct an organ of our minds
as the sensitiveness of the eye to light bespeaks an organ of our
bodies. If the structure of the eye implies light, if the structure
of the ear implies sound, then the structure of our conscience as
certainly implies a spiritual presence and judgment, the access of
some being to our inward thoughts and motives.[1]

2. It is therefore no surprise to be told that, when Herod
learned of the proximity of John the Baptist to his palace at
Machærus, he sent for him, gave him what we might call a chapel
to preach in, went often himself to hear him, heard him gladly,
and did many things which John bade him do. It was because
this man had his burdened conscience that the religious revival
which was beating in so many young hearts in Galilee became a
thing of deep interest to him. It was because he had his uneasy
spirit that he sought the companionship of so unlikely a court
preacher as John. It was because he had his wounded spirit that
he observed him, and did many things gladly, that he might get
an anodyne for his pain.

¶ George Fox's *Journal* for 1657 contains a record of his visit
to Scotland, and of his being summoned, when in Edinburgh,
before the Council as an unauthorized preacher.

"They asked me," he says, "what was the occasion of my
coming into that nation? I told them, I came to visit the seed
of God, and the intent of my coming was, that all in the nation
that professed the Scriptures might come to the light, Spirit, and
power, which they were in, who gave them forth. They asked
me whether I had any outward business there? I said, 'nay.'
Then they bid me withdraw, and the door-keeper took me by the
hand, and led me forth. In a little time they sent for me again,
and told me, I must depart the nation of Scotland by that day
seventh night. I asked them, 'why, what had I done? What
was my transgression, that they passed such a sentence upon me

[1] R. H. Hutton, *Aspects of Religious and Scientific Thought*, 133.

to depart out of the nation?' They told me, they would not dispute with me. Then I desired them to hear what I had to say to them; but they said, they would not hear me. I told them, Pharaoh heard Moses and Aaron, and yet he was a heathen and no Christian, and Herod heard John the Baptist; and they should not be worse than these. But they cried, 'withdraw, withdraw.' Whereupon the door-keeper took me again by the hand, and led me out."[1]

3. There was one thing, however, which Herod would not do. Go back a little into his history. He had married the daughter of Aretas, king of the Nabatæans, and all was well with him. The marriage secured peace between his country and the neighbouring country of Arabia; it pleased the Emperor at Rome; and by all we know it gave Herod a happy home. But in an evil day he visited Rome, where his brother Philip was living. Philip's wife Herodias and he entered into an adulterous intrigue, and when he left she left with him. The daughter of Aretas fled to her father's house, and Herod and Herodias were now living together at Machærus. John the Baptist disapproved of the connexion and was not afraid to say so. He said plainly to Herod, "It is not lawful for thee to have her." Herod was displeased. Herodias was still more deeply offended. And John was cast into one of the dungeons which were a notorious feature of that fortress-palace.

¶ There are some men whom God has gifted with a rare simplicity of heart, which makes them utterly incapable of pursuing the subtle excuses which can be made for evil. There is in John no morbid sympathy for the offender: "It is not lawful." He does not say, "It is best to do otherwise; it is unprofitable for your own happiness to live in this way." He says plainly, "It is wrong for you to do this evil." Earnest men in this world have no time for subtleties and casuistry. Sin is detestable, horrible, in God's sight, and when once it has been made clear that it is not lawful, a Christian has nothing to do with toleration of it. If we dare not tell our patron of his sin we must give up his patronage.[2]

4. Then, "when a convenient day was come," as St. Mark puts it—it was his birthday—Herod "made a supper to his lords, and

[1] *The Journal of George Fox* (ed. 1901), i. 401.
[2] F. W. Robertson, *Sermons*, iii. 276.

the high captains, and the chief men of Galilee." It was an occasion after Herod's own heart. He loved the display of it, the sense of importance it gave him, and the opportunity of self-indulgence. He was altogether in his element, when unexpectedly the door opened, and Salome, the daughter of Herodias by her husband Philip, came in and danced before them all. Herod must have been taken aback. But the lords were delighted and he joined in the applause. The more shamelessly she danced the more delighted they were. Herod sprang to his feet and, by way of showing his appreciation, offered the girl anything that she would ask—even if it were the half of his kingdom. Salome consulted her mother. Herodias seized the opportunity to exact the vengeance she had been waiting for. "Ask the head of John the Baptist," she said. And in a short time John's bleeding head was brought in upon a dish and given to the girl, who gave it to her mother.

¶ So did the spectre of Death invade the gay assembly on Herod's birthday. But on whom did the grisly shadow fall? Not on the prisoner, who, ere the fiendlike woman seized her prey, was singing the song of the redeemed around the Throne, in the new-found ecstasies of heaven. They truly died who lived to bear on their seared consciences the guilt of prompting, of executing, of approving that foul murder. Assuredly there was death in the cup that stupefied the revellers' sense of right, and made them stifle God's last warning. How truly might all such sots as they who tarry now as Herod's court tarried then around the poisoned liquor salute their god with the echo of the gladiators' cry, "*Evoe, Liber! Morituri te salutamus!*"[1]

5. Herod was sorry. He had lost his religion. He lost his religion that day he intrigued with his brother's wife; but he did not know it. He still had delight in hearing sermons. He still did many things which the preacher bade him do. And that is the best test we have of sincerity in hearing sermons. But now the preacher whom he had heard so gladly, and whom he had obeyed, perhaps at some little cost to his convenience, was dead. He himself was his murderer. However his conscience will torment him in the future, he can no longer keep up the pretence of being a religious man. He had done many things which John

[1] J. H. Moulton, *Visions of Sin*, 176.

bade him do, but there was that one thing which he would not do, and now it had slain his religious life. It was an ugly sin. But it does not need an ugly sin to slay a man's religious life. A very proper sin, and even a very little sin, will do it, if he refuses to give it up.

¶ Herod's crime haunted him. His guilty soul was shaken by superstitious dread; and, Sadducee though he was, denying the doctrine of the Resurrection, the idea took possession of him that the murdered Baptist had risen from the dead, endowed, as befitted a visitant from the unseen world, with mysterious and miraculous powers. It came to pass with Antipas as with many an unbeliever:

> Just when we are safest, there's a sunset-touch,
> A fancy from a flower-bell, some one's death,
> A chorus-ending from Euripides,—
> And that's enough for fifty hopes and fears
> As old and new at once as nature's self,
> To rap and knock and enter in our soul,
> Take hands and dance there, a fantastic ring,
> Round the ancient idol, on his base again,—
> The grand Perhaps! We look on helplessly.
> There the old misgivings, crooked questions are.[1]

II.

HEROD AND JESUS.

1. Herod could no longer look upon himself as a religious man. Yet he went up to Jerusalem as usual to the Passover. Why not? The murder of John the Baptist weighed more heavily upon his conscience than the abduction of his brother's wife. But it was nothing to the world. Who cared what became of the Baptist? Only those few disciples who came by night and carried away his headless body for burial. If he could go to the Passover while living with Herodias there was nothing to prevent his going after the death of John. Herod went up to Jerusalem to keep the feast.

2. Now it happened that Jesus also had gone up to Jerusalem

[1] Browning, *Bishop Blougram's Apology.*

to that Passover. And while He was there He had been betrayed by one of His disciples into the hands of the Jewish authorities, and had been brought before the Sanhedrin, who had promptly condemned Him to death. Not having the power to put Him to death themselves, they sent Him to Pilate, the Roman governor, to have their sentence ratified and to have Him executed. But Pilate made some difficulty about it. It was beneath the dignity of a Roman procurator to put any man to death at the bidding of another court. The accused must be tried according to the laws of Rome. So Pilate examined Him, and announced to the Jews that he found no fault in Him. This, of course, did not satisfy the priests. They had condemned Him to death and they were determined that Pilate should put Him to death, whatever he thought of His guilt. Pilate was not a little perplexed. Fortunately he discovered that Jesus belonged to Galilee, which was part of the country over which Herod ruled. And Herod was at that very time in Jerusalem. Pilate sent Him to Herod.

3. When Herod was told that Jesus was coming he was "exceeding glad." It was not the first time that he had heard of Him. When they first told him about the new Prophet who had appeared, Herod had said an extraordinary thing, "It is not a new prophet," he had said, "it is John whom I beheaded: he is risen from the dead." Herod had repented that rash speech many a day since then, and had wondered how he ever could have been betrayed into the folly of it. But when a man outrages his conscience, it frequently finds some way of making a fool of him. Some time after he had made inquiries about Jesus, not perhaps with any evil intention, more probably to satisfy a certain craving for rest of conscience that still remained with him. The Pharisees, however, advised Jesus to keep out of his way, and for once Jesus took their advice. Herod might think he had good motives, but what were they worth? "Go and say to that fox," said Jesus. It was a word as plain as John had ever uttered.

¶ Why "fox"? Why not panther or wolf?—either of which epithets, on the supposition that Herod meditated slaughter, would have been more appropriate. Yet, notwithstanding the wolfish profession, the reality may have been vulpine and no more. For a fierce, blustering tongue does not always betoken a ferocious spirit, is sometimes due to the craft of cowardice. A savage threat, instead of expressing an equally savage intention, may have been only a mask, behind which timid anxiety hides itself, hoping therewith to scare.[1]

¶ It is a large part of our daily lesson and discipline and duty in this life to be able to give the proper characters, and to apply the proper epithets, to men and to things; and to do that at the right time and in the right temper. It is a large and an important part of every preacher's office especially to apply to all men and to all their actions their absolutely and fearlessly right and true names. To track out the wolf, and the serpent, and the toad, and the fox in the men in whom these bestialities dwell, and to warn all men how and where all that will end; no minister may shrink from that. All the vices and all the crimes of the tetrarch's miserable life, and all the weakness and duplicity of his contemptible character, are summed up and sealed down on Herod Antipas in that one Divine word that day: "That fox."[2]

4. So Herod had never seen Jesus till now. When he saw Him he was exceeding glad, "for," says St. Luke, "he was of a long time desirous to see him, because he had heard concerning him; and he hoped to see some miracle done by him." What miracle could he hope to see? Herod may not have named it to himself, but there was one miracle which he wished Jesus would work above all other miracles in the world. He wished that He would do some miracle by which he might recover his old religious life and the thrill with which he once heard John the Baptist—although he kept his sin. And when Jesus came he questioned Him in many words, "*but he answered him nothing.*" And in the bitterness of his disappointment, poor Herod with his soldiers set Jesus at nought and mocked Him, and, arraying Him in gorgeous apparel, sent Him back again to Pilate.

5. Is it the end of Jesus? No; but it is the end of Herod. Secular history tells us certain things that happened to him in later life, all following from that evil choice of his early manhood. But that is the end for him and for us. "Jesus answered him nothing."

¶ You know what reprobation is? This is reprobation— "Herod questioned Jesus with many words, but he answered him nothing." That is reprobation. It is our reprobation begun when

[1] S. A. Tipple, *Days of Old*, 161.   [2] A. Whyte.

God answers us nothing. When, with all our praying, and with all our reading, and with all our inquiring, He still answers us nothing. Herod's day of grace had lasted long, but it is now at an end. Herod had had many opportunities, and at one time he was almost persuaded. At one time he was not very far from the Kingdom of Heaven. But all that is long past. Herod had smothered and silenced his conscience long ago, and now he is to be for ever let alone.[1]

¶ A few words will suffice to tell how Nemesis overtook Herod, even in this life. " By what things a man sinneth, by these he is punished," and Herod was ultimately brought to ruin by the woman he had married, for whose sake he had murdered John.

Caligula, immediately after his accession, gave to Agrippa, the brother of Herodias, the tetrarchies of Lysanias and of Philip, who had, three years before, left Salome a temporary widow. The title of king was bestowed on the fortunate adventurer, who had once by his extravagance run into such difficulties that he was glad to accept the charity of Antipas, and an appointment as superintendent of the market at Tiberias. Herodias's envy and ambition were roused by her brother's advancement, and she gave her husband no peace until he took her to Rome to sue for the same title. Herod was intensely reluctant. Caligula had been closely attached to Herod's rival from the first, and in the meantime there had been added the raving madness which turned Rome into a shambles during the last two or three years of the young emperor's short reign. But the stronger will of Herodias once more prevailed, and the pair went up to Rome to sue for favours from the wild beast on the throne. The interview took place at Baiae, the favourite Roman watering-place, in the summer of 39 A.D. An envoy of Agrippa brought some dangerous charges of treason against Antipas, which the old fox, for all his cunning, was unable to confute. Caligula promptly banished him to Lyons in Gaul, and a few months later gave his tetrarchy to the accuser Agrippa. Herodias, as Agrippa's sister, was expressly excepted from the sentence, but she proudly declined to abandon the husband her ambition had ruined. They went together into Gaul, where, according to one authority, Caligula caused Herod to be put to death. Thus did God avenge His chosen.[2]

[1] A. Whyte.   [2] J. H. Moulton, *Visions of Sin*, 130.

SIMON OF CYRENE.

LITERATURE.

Barrow, E. P., *The Way not a Sect* (1911), 98.

Benson, R. M., *The Final Passover*, iii. pt. II. (1893) 187.

Cameron, A. B., *From the Garden to the Cross* (1896), 302.

Carter, T. T., *Meditations on the Suffering Life and the Glorified Life of Our Lord* (1875), 104.

Clow, W. M., *The Day of the Cross* (1909), 157.

Critchley, G., *When the Angels have gone Away* (1899), 101.

Cunningham, R. T., *Memorials* (ed. D. Miller, 1890), 162.

Davies, D., *Talks with Men, Women and Children*, ii. (1890) 59.

Huntington, F. D., *Christian Believing and Living* (1885), 246.

Mackintosh, H. R., *Life on God's Plan* (1909), 242.

Maclaren, A., *A Year's Ministry*, ii. (1888) 45.

Macmillan, H., *The Mystery of Grace* (1893), 48.

Peabody, F. G., *Mornings in the College Chapel*, i. (1896) 168.

Speirs, E. B., *A Present Advent* (1900), 192.

Stalker, J., *The Trial and Death of Jesus Christ* (1894), 133.

Vaughan, J., *Sermons* (Brighton Pulpit), xv. (1877), No. 1048.

Christian Age, xliii. (1893) 194 (F. D. Huntington).

Christian World Pulpit, lxxvii. (1910) 140 (J. H. Renshaw).

Churchman's Pulpit : Holy Week, vi. 363 (G. T. Shettle).

SIMON OF CYRENE.

And they compel one passing by, Simon of Cyrene, coming from the country, the father of Alexander and Rufus, to go with them, that he might bear his cross.—Mark xv. 21.

And as they came out, they found a man of Cyrene, Simon by name: him they compelled to go with them, that he might bear his cross.—Matt. xxvii. 32.

And when they led him away, they laid hold upon one Simon of Cyrene, coming from the country, and laid on him the cross, to bear it after Jesus.—Luke xxiii. 26.

1. SOME men are born to distinction. They inherit an honoured name, a name which has been associated for generations past with dignity and power; they step at once into a position prepared for them, where they are set on an eminence and are observed by all. Whatever their characters may be, their position renders them conspicuous. Other men win distinction. There is nothing remarkable about them to begin with; they are merely units in the multitude of men and women. But by and by they show that they have qualities of an uncommon stamp; by their character or genius they *force* the attention of their fellow-beings, and at last rise to distinction and fame.

There is another class still, considerably smaller perhaps than either of these two, but still a class that does exist. It is composed of people who have honours thrust upon them, without any effort or even desire upon their part. They are often unwilling to accept them, and feel them a burden rather than a pleasure. Occasionally, for instance, we meet with people who have suddenly come into possession of great wealth, and have been lifted out of a humble station into a life of ease that is strange to them. Especially if they are old people, they often feel in their inmost hearts a regret for the old, accustomed, obscure life which they have lost. This perhaps is a rare phenomenon, but it is not entirely unknown. Simon the Cyrenian belonged to the last class. He was forced to become a distinguished man in spite of himself. He little thought, as he walked into Jerusalem that morning, that he was to carry a cross before the day was over. Had Simon suspected anything of the kind, he would probably have stayed at home. Cross-bearing was a path to distinction which he had no ambition to tread. And yet Simon became a famous man that day.

¶ Out of strange quarries delved by angel-hand, rough-hewn from ruins of primeval sin, topstone of nature still God's master-piece, wondrous material for self-sacrifice: designed by perfect love for perfect life, guided along his way, sometimes in sanctuary, sometimes on sea: moulded by marvel of God's providence, in passionate devotion holding fast to Earth's Redeemer, the Atoning Christ: circled by Sacramental grace, at the inspiring meeting-point of human and Divine coincidence: ushered in by destiny, and breathless with expectancy, cometh the man. Who, think you, would of his free will have gone to Libyan Cyrene to find God's man to bear the Cross for Christ when nature failed?[1]

2. A brief verse from each of the Synoptists is all we have regarding Simon. Yet each is not just the echo of the others. Each puts the incident in his own way; and so we find, as might be expected, a touch supplied by one which is not given by the others. Thus we are helped to a complete picture in our own minds. We see the melancholy procession on its way from the Prætorium to Calvary. Jesus is in its midst. Accompanying Him are the two thieves, bound for the same tragic end. The soldiers are there in strong force, with their centurion at their head, charged with the safeguarding of the prisoners and the carrying out of the sentence of crucifixion. And the mixed multitude are there, priests, rulers, people of all classes and conditions, enlivening the way with their brutal pleasantries. Onward the procession moves through street after street, bringing people forth from their houses to inquire what it all means, and to add to Jesus' reviling foes or to His few silent friends, according as the sight happens to touch them. At length it reaches the gate of the city, and makes for the hill in the open country beyond the walls, where ceremonial defilement from malefactors dying was supposed no longer to be feared.

[1] A. Daintree, *Studies in Hope*, 91.

The malefactor who was to be crucified had to carry the cross from the hall of judgment to the place of execution. Jesus had begun to carry the cross according to this custom, but He now gave way beneath its weight. The terrible physical suffering which He had endured had worn all His strength away, so that now He sinks to the ground exhausted, and nigh fainting, the cross pressing Him to the earth—"a man of sorrows, and acquainted with grief." The soldiers are in a dilemma. It is evident that Jesus must get assistance, He can go on no longer. The crowd presses round Him, gazing at Him with, on the whole, little if any more pity than a crowd bestows on a horse that has fallen on the street. What is to be done? The soldiers will certainly not lower themselves by helping a criminal to carry His cross. The Jews will do nothing to assist; they would flout the idea of touching that accursed piece of wood, the symbol of the Roman despotism which they hate. The soldiers look around for someone who will serve their purpose, but they see no one. The Jews about them have friends in Jerusalem : it would be dangerous to rouse a Jewish mob by forcing anyone there to undertake the hateful task. Too much blood has been shed of late in these very streets, collisions between the soldiers and the people, which they are careful to avoid. They are almost at their wits' end. But just at this moment they catch sight of Simon.

He is on his way into the city, rejoicing as he comes near the gate at the prospect of ending a long journey, and of being in time to join in the Passover celebrations. He is on pilgrimage to the Holy City, and a crowd of high and sacred feelings are filling him. He is coming up to observe the most sacred of Jewish feasts. And here is the Divine Paschal Lamb coming forth to meet him, on His way to be slain on Calvary. Could he ever have hoped to see such a sight? Could it be supposed that one looking as he was for the consolation of Israel would see at once in that most melancholy sight the fulfilment of his grandest hopes? Jesus bending and ready to fall under His heavy cross, and going to die upon it—could this be the consolation and the glory of Israel? Could He be the long-looked-for Messiah? Or was it true that the Paschal Lamb, associated with the great deliverance from Egypt's bondage, slain, roasted, eaten, was after all but the type of the true Messiah, and that Simon, coming to observe the type, was to find in that cross-bearing Jesus on His way to Calvary the veritable antitype? It was even so, as Simon, we have reason to believe, soon came to know.

¶ The Cross gives us Ormuzd and Ahriman, not in cloudy epic, but in actual history; goodness fighting evil, not with earthly weapons, but spiritual; fighting, by suffering, by giving, by loving, by dying. And you, in your turn, get the heart of this by trying it, by living it. You find what loving is by loving, what forgiveness is by forgiving, what the Cross of Calvary is by the cross in your own soul. You become an initiate of Christianity by the Christian experience, and by that alone.

> Though Christ in Joseph's town
> A thousand times were born,
> Till He is born in thee
> Thy soul is still forlorn.
> The Cross on Golgotha
> Can never save thy soul;
> The cross in thine own heart
> Alone can make thee whole.

It is here, in the cross of holy, sacrificing love in God, in the cross of holy sacrificing love in your own soul, that you reach the world's deepest secret, that you find the heart of things.[1]

> God draws a cloud over each gleaming morn.
> Wouldst thou ask, why?
> It is because all noblest things are born
> In agony.
>
> Only upon some Cross of pain or woe
> God's Son may lie.
> Each soul redeemed from self and sin must know
> Its Calvary.[2]

Let us look first at Simon's opportunity, how it came and how he received it, and then at his great gain.

I.

SIMON'S UNEXPECTED OPPORTUNITY.

1. The whole story sounds like a bit of romance. We might almost say that it was a chance conversion. What moved Simon

[1] J. Brierley, *Faith's Certainties*, 59.   [2] Frances Power Cobbe.

to take that particular turning which brought him to Christ and
His cross, and just at the very moment he was needed? For
if he had delayed a minute or two, he would have been too late.
We cannot say. He is like the man mentioned in our Saviour's
parable, who was walking home one evening across the fields,
when suddenly he noticed a place where the rains had washed
the earth away, and there unexpectedly found a treasure. Simon,
too, found that day something he had never expected to find,
something he had never once thought of; but ever after it was
the treasure of his life.

2. Doubtless to Simon this encounter seemed at the moment
the most unfortunate incident that could have befallen him—an
interruption, an annoyance and a humiliation; yet it turned out
to be the gateway of life. Thus do blessings sometimes come in
disguise, and out of an apparition, at the sight of which we cry
out for fear, may suddenly issue the form of the Son of Man.

Whatever form of cross-bearing is laid upon us, we feel at
first that it is a pressed service, a compulsion which is trying and
oppressive. We feel the pain of having to give up our way
and to have our liberty restricted. At first we are filled with
resentment against the gospel of Christ for spoiling our plans
and pleasures. But by and by, as God's grace works in us and
makes us willing, the service that we most hated we shall learn
most to love. The cross that crushed us to the earth will support
us and lift us to heaven. The things that seemed against us we
shall find working together for our good. The compulsion of
painful circumstances that brought us to Christ will issue in
richer life and grander liberty; and the constrained service will
be changed into a lifelong fidelity.

¶ In a letter written to her intimate friend, Miss Lily
Schlumberger, Adèle Kamm thus refers to that critical time when
she presented to God as a "willing sacrifice" the ruin of her
earthly hopes:

"My last great spiritual conflict took place at Cannes, when,
after a trying journey, I realized that I must remain in bed
altogether, that the longed-for recovery was not to be, and when,
to crown everything, two vertebræ began to swell, and were so
painful that I had to lie on my back entirely. . . . For a month I
was just about as rebellious as any one could be, and I used to

cry my heart out every night, till one day our clergyman sang me a beautiful hymn [by Karre] called 'The Cross' ['It is at the Cross that the way begins']. These beautiful words touched me. I grew calmer as I meditated on the sufferings of Jesus Christ, which were so much greater than my own, and were borne willingly out of love to us, and especially as I thought of His sublime, glorious love on the Cross. Oh! *how* I prayed that God would help me to accept my cross, and begin a new life of pure love to God and man. And God did answer me. I am not a bit good, not in the least what I ought to be, but these dreadful conflicts are over, and for a whole year now I have not had any of those dark times which nearly drove me to despair, when a cloud seemed to come between my soul and God."[1]

3. Simon's experience might have had the opposite effect from what it did have, and he might have cursed in his heart not only the soldiers and the mob, but Christ Himself, the innocent cause of his misfortune, and sullenly refused to think of Him unless as having given occasion for his public disgrace. And it is, alas! true that cross-bearing does not always bring blessing with it, or lead those who have to suffer nearer to Christ, but rather tends to harden their hearts against God's pleadings with them, and to make them sullen and defiant. And yet it is clearly one of God's ways—it may seem to us a very roundabout way—of arresting us when we are going on our own paths; and we should pray to be able to see His hand in it, and to get out of it what of good and blessing He intends to bring to us by it. Simon came to see that, though he thought that day he was bearing the cross for Christ, Christ had really been bearing it for him. And so what he had shrunk from as a disgrace and a pain he welcomed as an honour and a joy, and by becoming a Christian bore his Master's cross all his life, and walked by His side not only for a few minutes on the way to Calvary, but every day in the streets of Cyrene.

¶ *15th April 1870.—Crucifixion!* That is the word we have to meditate to-day. Is it not Good Friday? To curse grief is easier than to bless it, but to do so is to fall back into the point of view of the earthly, the carnal, the natural man. By what has Christianity subdued the world if not by the apotheosis of grief, by its marvellous transmutation of suffering into triumph, of the

[1] *A Living Witness: The Life of Adèle Kamm*, 55.

crown of thorns into the crown of glory, and of a gibbet into a symbol of salvation? What does the apotheosis of the Cross mean, if not the death of death, the defeat of sin, the beatification of martyrdom, the raising to the skies of voluntary sacrifice, the defiance of pain?—" O Death, where is thy sting? O Grave, where is thy victory?"[1]

¶ Why fearest thou to take up the Cross which leadeth to a kingdom? In the Cross is salvation, in the Cross is life, in the Cross is protection against our enemies, in the Cross is heavenly sweetness, in the Cross is strength of mind, in the Cross joy of spirit, in the Cross the height of virtue, in the Cross the perfection of holiness. There is no salvation of the soul, nor hope of everlasting life, save in the Cross. Take up therefore thy Cross and follow Jesus, and thou shalt go into life everlasting. He went before, bearing His Cross, and died for thee on the Cross, that thou mayest also bear thy Cross and desire to die on the Cross with Him. For if thou be dead with Him, thou shalt also live with Him. And if thou be a partaker of His sufferings thou shalt be a partaker also of His glory. Behold! everything dependeth upon the Cross, and all lieth in our dying thereon; for there is no other way unto life, and to true inward peace, but the way of the Holy Cross, and of daily mortification.[2]

> Looking back along life's trodden way,
>   Gleams and greenness linger on the track;
> Distance melts and mellows all to-day,
>   Looking back.
>
> Rose and purple and a silvery grey,
>   Is that the cloud we called so black?
> Evening harmonizes all to-day,
>   Looking back.
>
> Foolish feet so prone to halt or stray,
>   Foolish heart so restive on the rack!
> Yesterday we sighed, but not to-day,
>   Looking back.

4. What do we mean by cross-bearing now? Surely he bears the cross of Christ who honestly and willingly suffers pain or loss in order to further in the world that for which Christ died. And if He died that the weary and heavy-laden should be raised and

---

[1] *Amiel's Journal* (trans. by Mrs. Humphry Ward), 167.
[2] Thomas à Kempis, *The Imitation of Christ*, chap. xii.

cheered, then you would suppose that every stooping form would be touched by us as His form, and every burden lightened as if it were part of the weight which pressed Him down. "Daughters of Jerusalem, weep not for me." Thus He checked the tears of idle emotion—but only that He might draw out a deeper depth of action. "Inasmuch as ye have done it," He said, "unto one of the least of these my brethren, ye have done it unto me."

You might suppose that in nineteen centuries Christians would have learned this simple lesson by heart, and have made the lifting of human sorrow the first test of Christian love. But what do we find? We find that in that long past which lies behind us the tragedy of the Saviour's cross has been made too much a spectacle, a moving drama, complete and apart, and too little a plan, a process, continued and perfected in us. "It is finished," He cried. But the work of the cross will never be finished until sorrow and sighing have fled wholly away. His own part was finished; He would have done more if they had suffered Him to do it; the wooden beams were unfastened, laid aside, and the very site of the cross is now unknown; but the true cross, of which that other was but an emblem, still remains, and is loaded, or lightened, for Him and for humanity, as we do our part well or ill.

¶ Thomas à Kempis ever preaches the *Cross* as life's great secret and underlying fact. Christ is to him the perfect example of self-abandonment and oneness with God, and His Cross is the universal Cross. His victory is the triumph of all disciples who live in Him. While the mystic generally thinks solely or mainly of the Incarnation, Thomas à Kempis never forgets the Cross, and thereby at once he safeguards personality as well as preserves his religion from ecstatic excesses. Dying to self and living to God —renouncing self and regaining self in the holy Jesus' love, are the keynotes of his message. The following of Jesus is to him cross-bearing, as the road to inner consolation and peace.[1]

¶ That was a great word which Luther spoke when he told the maidens and housewives of Germany that in scrubbing floors and going about their household duties they were accomplishing just as great a work in the sight of heaven as the monks and priests with their penances and holy offices. Indeed it had been said before Luther, and by a woman. Margery Baxter, the

[1] D. Butler, *Thomas à Kempis*, 133.

Lollardist of the fifteenth century, had the pith of the matter. "If," she said to her sisters, "ye desire to see the true Cross of Christ, I will show it to you at home in your own house." Stretching out her arms she said: "This is the true Cross of Christ, thou mightest and mayest behold and worship in thine own house; and therefore it is but vain to run to the church to worship dead Crosses." In a word, holiness is in our daily service, and the holy places are where it is faithfully done.[1]

> When men of malice wrought the crown for Thee,
>   Didst Thou complain?
> Nay; in each thorn God's finger Thou didst see,
>   His love thro' pain.

> His finger did but press the ripened Vine,
>   Thy fruit to prove,
> That henceforth all the world might drink the wine
>   Of Thy great love.

> So when the darkness rose about Thy feet
>   Thy lips met His,
> Amid the upper light, in Death's long sweet
>   Releasing kiss.

> And shall I cry aloud in anger when
>   Men make for me
> A Cross less harsh? Nay, I'll remember then
>   Thy constancy.

> And if the darkness hide me from Thy sight
>   At God's command,
> I'll talk with Thee all thro' the prayerful night,
>   And touch Thy hand;

> Greatly content, if I whose life has been
>   So long unwise,
> May, wounded, on Thy wounded bosom lean
>   In Paradise.

II.

SIMON'S IMMEASURABLE GAIN.

1. Surely it was an immeasurable gain to Simon. For in the first place this *rencontre* issued in his salvation and in the salva-

[1] J. Brierley, *Religion and To-Day*, 194.

tion of his house. The Evangelist calls him familiarly "the father of Alexander and Rufus." Evidently the two sons were well known to those for whom St. Mark was writing; that is, they were members of the Christian circle. And there can be little doubt that the connexion of his family with the Church was the result of this incident in the father's life. St. Mark wrote his Gospel for the Christians of Rome; and in the Epistle to the Romans one Rufus is mentioned as resident there along with his mother. This may be one of the sons of Simon. And in Acts xiii. 1, one Simeon—the same name as Simon—is mentioned along with a Lucius of Cyrene as a conspicuous Christian at Antioch: he is called Niger, or Black, a name not surprising for one who had been tanned by the hot sun of Africa. Altogether, we have sufficiently clear indications that in consequence of this incident Simon became a Christian. It would have been contrary both to nature and to grace that any man should come so near Jesus, and should do so much for Him, and not be called into His Kingdom.

¶ Canon Carus tells how the verse in St. Luke's Gospel referring to Simon of Cyrene proved a finger of light once to Simeon of Cambridge. "At an early period of his ministry, and when he was suffering severe opposition, he was in much doubt whether it was his duty to remain in Cambridge. . . . He opened his little Greek Testament, as he thought and intended in the Epistles, and, finding the book upside down, he discovered he was in the Gospels, and his finger on Luke xxiii. 26, 'They laid hold on one Simon (Simeon), and on him they laid the cross,' etc. 'Then,' said Mr. Simeon, 'lay it on me, Lord, and I will bear it for Thy sake to the end of my life; and henceforth I bound persecution as a wreath of glory round my brow.'"[1]

> I saw a Cross of burning gold
> And jewels glorious to behold:
>
> Over it a golden crown,
> All the people falling down.
>
> I saw an ugly Cross of wood,
> On it there were stains of blood:
>
> Over it a crown of thorn,
> Plaited for the people's scorn.

[1] J. Moffatt, *The Gospel of St. Luke*, 154.

Cross of gold, no fruit was thine,
Nothing but the empty shrine.

Cross of wood, thou living tree,
The true Vine clung fast to thee.[1]

2. But St. Mark tells us at the same time that Simon's reward was greater than the saving of his own soul. It was the answer of his most instant and constant and urgent prayers. Away in Cyrene this pilgrim to the Holy City had left two little sons, and as he looked upon them, exiles from the land of Israel, as he taught them the fear of the God of Jacob, the very passion of his heart was distilled into prayer, that they might grow in the faith and obedience of God. Christ read the heart of His cross-bearer as he walked by His side. He saw the names Rufus and Alexander graven on Simon's heart. And the great reward was given to Simon of seeing both his sons known and loved and honoured in the Church of Christ.

¶ It is not given to every man of God to have his sons follow in his steps. So many influences may bear in upon the impressionable heart of youth, that a father's counsel may remain unheeded, and a father's example be scorned. But no man shall ever bear the cross of Christ without reaping a reward in his children. In the brave Disruption days in Scotland, of which I may speak without heat or passion (for whatever be your judgment on the cause, there is no man who does not honour the deed), there were men who bore the cross after Jesus. Not only, and not chiefly, by those in the ranks of the ministry, who found fame shining on the path of sacrifice, but by many in obscure homes the stern cross was accepted. By costly sacrifice, by long years of patient self-denial, by the enduring of scorn and the suffering of loss, these men and women followed Christ. They left behind them the house of prayer round which their dead were lying; they stood on the moors in the bitter winter blasts of 1844, and by the sea-shore, where their psalms were mingled with the hoarse chant of the waves; they refused emolument and advantage for conscience' sake; they poured with unstinting hand the gifts of their poverty into the common cause; they turned their faces from friendships it broke their hearts to lose—they bore the cross of Christ. And mark their reward. Their children to-day stand strong in the faith and devotion of Christ, their sons' names are

[1] Mary E. Coleridge.

loved and honoured in the Church; they are loyal to every cause which promotes the righteousness of the people. When you question them they will tell you that their faith was kindled by their father's sacrifice. He bore a cross for Jesus.[1]

3. Before we leave this interesting story, there is one lesson which we must try to learn. The cross which Simon helped to carry was Christ's cross, not his own. Can we do the same? Christ's cross-bearing is not over yet; after nineteen hundred years He is still carrying it; and somehow we cannot but think of Him as continually tired and needing help. We think of Christ as crucified, and we push Him far back from us, and speak as if the pain of the cross were gone from Him for ever and He were now peaceful and happy evermore. But as long as there are sin and misery in the world, how can Christ be happy? Every day there are things going on which make Him miserable. That is a strong word to use, but knowing Christ as we do, can we use any other? We can help Him to bear His cross. We can do something to relieve the sin and the wretchedness beside which we live; and in relieving it we are making Christ's cross easier for Him to bear.

¶ Intimacy with Christ must begin, for the sinner, by being a fellowship with His sufferings. And, indeed, there is no other way. As no man can come to the Father but by Christ, so no man can come to Christ but by the path of those sufferings by which He put Himself on the level of sinners. The Cross is the doorway through which he must pass.[2]

¶ To his sister Maria, Mr. Denny wrote from Buenos Ayres a few weeks before his tragic death:
"The Cross of Christ is no longer to you the symbol of a bargain between a vindictive Deity and a self-sacrificing Deity, between the individual and selected soul and the Trinity, but the expression of the great truth of life that self-renunciation, the way of the Cross, is the only pathway in spiritual life, and that not as a duty or a trial, but as the only means of freedom, hope, and joy. People will tell you Buddha taught this, and that all the ascetics have taught the same; but their teaching was not like Christ's. They wanted to kill self, an impossible feat. He meant the self to be lost in love for others, and devotion to them;

[1] W. M. Clow, *The Day of the Cross*, 165.
[2] A. Chandler, *The Cult of the Passing Moment*, 92.

that by the miracle of spiritual life the lost self should return on
the great spiral of progress to its old point in the plane, but to
such elevation in height that it shines clothed with immortality,
and light, and love as with the garments of God's kingdom. This
was the joy that was set before Him. This is the unhoped,
unexpected joy set before our dim eyes." [1]

> Now with wan ray that other sun of Song
>   Sets in the bleakening waters of my soul:
> One step, and lo! the Cross stands gaunt and long
>   'Twixt me and yet bright skies, a presaged dole.
>
> Even so, O Cross! thine is the victory.
>   Thy roots are fast within our fairest fields;
> Brightness may emanate in Heaven from thee,
>   Here thy dread symbol only shadow yields.
>
> Of reapèd joys thou art the heavy sheaf
>   Which must be lifted, though the reaper groan;
> Yea, we may cry till Heaven's great ear be deaf,
>   But we must bear thee, and must bear alone.
>
> Vain were a Simon; of the Antipodes
>   Our night not borrows the superfluous day.
> Yet woe to him that from his burden flees,
>   Crushed in the fall of what he cast away.[2]

[1] A. B. Bruce, *Life of William Denny*, 430.
[2] Francis Thompson, *Ode to the Setting Sun*.